DERVISH DUST

DERVISH DUST

THE LIFE AND WORDS OF

JAMES COBURN

Robyn L. Coburn

FOREWORD BY JAMES H. COBURN IV

Potomac Books

AN IMPRINT OF THE UNIVERSITY OF NEBRASKA PRESS

Library of Congress Cataloging-in-Publication Data
Names: Coburn, Robyn L., author. | Coburn,
James H. IV, writer of foreword.
Title: Dervish dust: the life and words of James Coburn /
Robyn L. Coburn; foreword by James H. Coburn IV.
Description: [Lincoln]: Potomac Books, an imprint
of the University of Nebraska Press, [2021] |
Includes bibliographical references and index.
Identifiers: LCCN 2021021843
ISBN 9781640124059 (hardback)
ISBN 9781640125001 (epub)
ISBN 9781640125018 (pdf)
Subjects: LCSH: Coburn, James. | Actors—United
States—Biography. | BISAC: BIOGRAPHY &
AUTOBIOGRAPHY / Entertainment & Performing Arts
Classification: LCC PN2287.C553 C63 2021 |
DDC 791.4302/8092 [B]—dc23
LC record available at https://lccn.loc.gov/2021021843

Set in Garamond Premier by Laura Buis.
Designed by N. Putens.

For Jayn Holly Coburn, that she
might know her grandfather

CONTENTS

ILLUSTRATIONS

RATIONALE FOR THE TITLE

James Coburn wanted to call his memoir *Dervish Dust*. In an interview with Nancy Mehagian in 2002, he explained his choice:

"A dervish is a special name for a wandering mendicant, or someone who just goes off and wanders around the world, taking in and giving off impressions. The word *dervish* means 'doorway'—a door to another dimension.

"The whirling dervishes came out of the Rumi school. They do their thing—there's a main guy in the middle, and the others whirl around him like the solar system. Their left hands are lowered and their right hands are raised, to symbolize the connection between heaven and earth. It's a meditation in motion. Ecstasy was what they went for and what they got—whirling in ecstasy.

"A dust dervish, or dust devil, is like a little cyclone. They spin in the desert. The dervish dust is what is left behind after the dervish finishes spinning.

"My life would be the spinning of the dervish, and the dust would be my memoirs."

FOREWORD

James H. Coburn IV

"What is it like to be James Coburn's son?"

I don't really remember how old I was when I first heard that question. It's happened thousands of times, and it has never stopped. As recently as this week, somebody worked out who I was and asked me that very question.

My basic answer is that it's hard for me to know what it was like compared to someone else's experience growing up. It was all normal for me, going to movie sets, hanging out, and having a father who was the center of attention when we walked into a room, so I didn't really have a different perspective.

My earliest memory of Dad comes from when I look at the picture of him dressing me, while holding his cigarette in a long cigarette holder. I have fleeting memories of our time in Paris when I was a baby, images of being in the park in Paris: trees, walkway, maybe snow, freezing temperatures. I remember arriving at Tower Road. I'm not sure Dad was around that day. Maybe he was. I remember the first night there. I was initially given a room next to my parents' room. It was uncomfortably hot.

Later I moved from my room to what had been Lisa's room. And eventually I moved from that room to the house behind the garage. I had Don DeLew's *Freeway* painting hanging in that house. My friends and I would often trip our asses off. It was a good life. But it was just normal life back then. We ran wild. We ran around the streets like we owned them. We did what we did, which wasn't much, with reckless abandon.

I will never forget the sound of Dad driving his California Ferrari home, up Tower Road, how he would roar up the street. It was unmistakable. You could hear it echoing through the canyon. "There's Mom and Dad," or "There's Dad coming home." And I would do the appropriate thing, like rush around to turn off the TV because I wasn't supposed to be up so late. I'd have to have the TV off before they got to the driveway or they'd see the light and they'd bust me.

One way my childhood was different from others' was when I was going to El Rodeo Elementary School. Most kids got dropped off by their parents or rode their bikes from nearby houses. Neither of my parents had a job to go to every day, so they were not interested in waking up at the ass crack of dawn to drive me to school. My mother had a very, very serious rule that you did not call or communicate or come to the house before ten o'clock in the morning. If you called before ten, it had better be fucking important, or my mother would rip you a new asshole. Seriously.

My mother and father were not interested in driving their kids to school. That was an outrageous idea. Either you're going to get yourself to school on your bicycle—which was perfectly valid, but a long way, and I did that for a long time—or if the weather's really bad, Andreas (the gardener) is going to take you down there, if he's not too hungover.

But my best memories of Dad were those carefree days of driving around with him—not the long drives to Desert Hot Springs to visit his parents, but times like going to Dolores and having double-decker Jumbo Jims in the car. Dolores was a drive-in place down at La Cienega and Wilshire. We would pull up in his California Ferrari, which had no top, and we'd have malts and burgers and fries in the car.

I always enjoyed traveling with Dad when it was just us. I suppose it was because he was forced to pay attention to me, which was something he didn't do very much of in our daily life at home. It was great when it was just the two of us. One time we drove from Albuquerque through the Painted Desert, the Petrified Forest, and the Grand Canyon on to Las Vegas. We stopped at everything that looked cool, just because we felt like it, like the Ice Caves in New Mexico. We bought interesting little souvenirs. I wish I had that shit today. When we got to the Grand Canyon, Dad hired an airplane, and we flew around inside the Grand Canyon for an hour or so. It was great fun.

We never explored philosophy or anything. We talked about stuff, and I would time the miles on my tachometer. After the Grand Canyon, we hauled ass to Vegas, over a hundred miles per hour, and pulled into Caesars Palace in Dad's gold 308 GTS Ferrari. Don Rickles was playing, like always. We went to the show. Rickles pointed Dad out, of course, gave him a little shit, his typical shtick. I think I was about twelve, thirteen years old. It was a very adult program, but I stayed the whole time.

Dad gave me shit for walking into the casino and putting a dollar into a slot machine. It was the biggest slot machine I had ever seen. I put in a dollar, and I immediately won twenty bucks. Dad got mad at me because we were going to get in trouble—he'd get in trouble—and I shouldn't be gambling. "That's not a smart thing to do with your money." Meanwhile he was a closet poker player and used to take all the money from his army mates.

During the shoot of *Pat Garrett and Billy the Kid*, he and I had some time together around Christmas in Mexico, just the two of us. That was fun. We flew to Mazatlán and stayed at this very nice hotel. We walked to the market and bought fireworks. I guess you could buy them anywhere in Mexico at that time. We were shooting fireworks off the balcony right into the ocean below and could see them exploding underwater. Our hotel room was just above the rocks. Then I went down on the beach and was shooting off fireworks from there when I burned down a cabana—it was made from palm fronds and caught fire. Nobody was the wiser.

One time when I was at boarding school in Chester, New Jersey, Dad was traveling through New York. I took the train to Grand Central, then a cab to some fantastic hotel, where we hung out. We went out to eat that first night and had steak frites. We rode around in limousines. We went shopping. "You need a coat, kid. Let's go to Bergdorf Goodman." He knew how to shop. It was a very nice break for me.

In 1993 Dad and Paula had their wedding in Paris. The day before, Frank Messa and I walked around, including climbing to the top of Notre Dame and lighting a candle. We had very little cash, so wandering was just about all we could do. At the wedding, despite the minders, when we opened the door to exit, we found the stairs full of paparazzi. There was a sea of them, so it was difficult to get out of there. We pushed our way through.

On the wedding night, the whole group went to a joint where they spent the night knocking the tops off champagne bottles with swords, including Dad and Paula. It was a great show with amazing food and a huge family celebration, including the owners and other patrons. It felt like we took over the whole place.

One of the last trips I went on with Dad was to Canada during the shoot for *Snow Dogs*. Paula had to be in LA, so I volunteered to go hang out with Dad on the set. I don't know if I was there for a week or ten days. Every couple of nights, we would go out to dinner. One night we would have Italian; the next night, Japanese. No matter where we went, they would not let him pay. People were very kind. They seemed thrilled just having him in their restaurant.

He really wasn't very healthy during that shoot, and I had to take him to the hospital while I was there; and I had to protect him too. It was a big responsibility, but that's what I was there to do. And I enjoyed being of service to Dad.

While reading the manuscript for this book, what fascinated me most were the army stories and the progression from the Compton days to being a movie star. I didn't realize that he had been such a prolific actor in the theater. And in fact I don't think I knew how much he was working in general. I'm talking about the sixties and seventies when I was a little kid. He worked a lot. That's a new insight. I never really had an appreciation for how much he worked. I didn't grasp it. He worked his ass off.

I have also gained perspective about his true self-centered nature. His focus in life was doing work. That's what he loved to do, and that's what he did. Not so unusual really. Most people who love what they do, work hard at it because they love it. Dad knew the value of his work because it made everything possible. I don't think that was ever lost on him. He loved the Tower Road house as much as I did, but I got so much more benefit from it because I was there more, while he was away so much.

When we were at home together, we would play snooker. Dad played pool too, but between us, it was all about the snooker. We would smoke a little pot and play snooker. We played a game called golf on the snooker table. Dad would burn through a Montecristo Cuban cigar over the course of a game or two, or three. Sometimes we would play into the wee hours of the morning. People would come and go, join our game, or I would come and join theirs.

There are many people who are part of his story. Dad had these friendships. There were quite a few of them, all over the world. His relationships featured strongly in his life—Herb Kreztmer, Hilly Elkins, and John Paul DeJoria. They were great friends. They spent a lot of time together, traveling. I remember watching Dad and his buddy Bruce Lee working out in the backyard. That was perfectly normal too. Murray Korngold was his friend, way back when. I think that his relationship with Frank Messa was a highlight. Frank was a big part of his life for a long, long time. I think Frank was Dad's best friend.

This book captures Dad's essence. It is a very good picture of the cool persona of my dad. When I was young, I didn't get that Dad was considered cool. He was just Dad. Once in a while, as a family, we would go down to Beverly Hills to eat at Hamburger Hamlet or to pick up Chinese takeout from Ah Fong's or pizza from Jacopo's. Dad loved to eat.

That was when I first realized that he had fans. Dad always said yes to people wanting autographs. He was always generous in that way. Having people come up to my dad and want to speak to him or express their appreciation to him—that was just normal life too. Sometimes they'd ask me for my autograph. I don't know why they'd want mine. I'd look up at Dad and he'd say, "Just sign your name, kid." It was all normal for me.

PROLOGUE

Tonight was going to be special.

It had started as a typical quiet day. James Coburn, who preferred to be called Jim, got up in the morning and had his usual light breakfast of coffee and toast, perused the newspaper as he did every day, and most likely listened to some of his favorite music. He'd been filming in Santa Barbara, so it was nice to be home for the weekend to relax.

Later, when the time came, it took him only a few minutes to get dressed. His tuxedo hung ready. His biggest challenge was to push his arthritis-misshapen toes into his polished shoes. He stuffed his trademark polka-dot kerchief into his breast pocket and felt satisfied. For him elegance was effortless. Then he sat down to wait for his wife to be ready.

Ever since the nominations had been announced, Coburn's team had campaigned to encourage the Academy voters to watch a screening of Paul Schrader's *Affliction* and had ensured that Jim himself was seen all around town. The film received numerous nominations when screened at all the major festivals. But an Oscar nom was the big one. And Coburn was arguably the front-runner in his category.

Paul Schrader himself had attended a soiree at the Coburn house a few weeks earlier. He described the attendees as including "every Academy member over the age of fifty" and noticed Coburn spoke to each and every one of them.[1] But that was hardly unusual behavior for Jim Coburn. He had always been charming and gregarious, known to his colleagues for his professionalism and courtesy. He followed the Sufi philosophy that friendship is a garden to be nurtured. As Schrader remarked, "He was very beloved around the town. They really liked him."

James Coburn had been to the Oscars three times before, as a presenter. The first time was in 1966. Along with Virna Lisi and wearing full white-tie-and-tails regalia, he presented the two Best Music Score awards, as they were then, which was fitting given his lifelong love of music. That January his bona fide hit film had opened, whose eponymous character, Derek Flint, would forever be identified with him. *Our Man Flint* established him as a major leading man and cemented his credentials as the coolest cat around.

The next time was in 1973, when he joked with Diana Ross and presented Joel Grey with his Best Actor in a Supporting Role award for *Cabaret*. The ceremony was somewhat overshadowed by Marlon Brando's refusal by proxy of his Best Actor award, but that year Coburn was riding high. Three of his movies—some of his best starring performances—were about to be released, *Pat Garrett and Billy the Kid*, *The Last of Sheila*, and *Harry in Your Pocket*. He was planning a project with his good friend Bruce Lee. He was still content with his first wife and children's mother, Beverly, and he still lived in the beautiful Moorish-style villa at the tip-top of Beverly Hills, filled with Asian and Middle Eastern art, that he called his monastery.

Much had changed by his third visit to the Oscars in April 1979, when he and Kim Novak presented the Best Cinematography award to Nestor Almendros for *Days of Heaven*. He was in the middle of his acrimonious divorce from Beverly and found his current love affair canvassed in the gossip columns. In addition his rheumatoid arthritis was starting to give him serious pain.

Perhaps most surprising of all, at that point in his life, was that most of the work he had lined up for the year would be shot locally, with the only exception being the action flick *Firepower*, a Caribbean junket he inherited from friend Charles Bronson. He had not starred in a movie shot primarily in California since 1967's *Waterhole #3*, instead jetting to various parts of Europe,

Mexico, the Caribbean, Canada, and other parts of the United States. In between films he roamed India, the Middle East, Europe, and North Africa as well as Central America and Japan. He considered his home a base from which to travel. Travel, he loved. Feeling trapped at home, not so much.

Regardless of his personal troubles, he was not one to dwell on his difficulties when there was work to be done. That night in 1979, he gave the audience his famous megawatt smile and soldiered through the banter with Novak.

Now twenty years later, this coming ceremony, the evening of March 21, 1999, was going to be very special. Coburn had acted in movies nominated for various Academy Awards before, and he would do so again, but this was *his* first nomination, and most importantly, he was finally going to get to take his wife, Paula, to the Oscars.

When they were ready to leave, Jim would have said, "You look beautiful, baby." They would have traveled down in the two-person elevator that was an essential in this huge house and walked out past the Chinese gong hanging in their foyer before getting into the waiting limo, where his manager Hilly Elkins and Elkins's wife Sandi were to join them on the trip to the ceremony in downtown Los Angeles.

Hilly recalled the conversation they had on the way to the Dorothy Chandler Pavilion, "I said to Jim, 'You're gonna win this.' And he said—well, I can't quote what he said, but it was negative on the idea. He said, 'We didn't win anything. You're full of crap. We're not going to win this.'"[2] Perhaps his denial was a defense mechanism.

When they arrived to walk the crush on the red carpet, Paula was radiant in the late afternoon sun—"golden hour," as filmmakers call it—a fitting companion for one of the last grand old men of Hollywood. They stopped for the usual interviews, Coburn giving due credit and kudos to costar and nominee Nick Nolte and director Paul Schrader. In the end, they had to hurry through the colonnade entranceway and under the crystal chandeliers soaring over the foyer to make it to their seats in the front row, slightly to the side, barely in time for host Whoopi Goldberg's hilarious entrance as "The African Queen."

They were hardly settled when the first award, Best Actor in a Supporting Role, was announced by Kim Basinger. "The Oscar goes to . . . James Coburn for *Affliction*."

His speech encapsulated his whole career: "My, my, my . . . I've been doing this over half my life. I finally got one right, I guess. Y'see, some you do for money. Some you do for love. This is a love child."[3]

DERVISH DUST

I

The Days of Fun and Frolic

From my father, I learned more what not to do than what to do, and that came in the form of fear of the Depression. When we left Nebraska, we had nothing. Everything was taken away. And before we left, we had money and we had position in the town. We had to get out. So we came to California. After the big move and the downfall of the Coburn dynasty, my mother was like the guide—the mover and the maker of certain decisions. My father was just crushed by the whole thing. He just didn't have a clue how to come out of this. It was just awful. He was supposed to be the leader of the gang. It turns out my mother really was the leader of the gang. He would follow.

—JAMES COBURN, 2002

It was March 1935, and the vast Dust Bowl of the Great Plains was forcing thousands to flee their useless farms and move west to California. They'd heard there was still work in California, in the great orange groves, in the cities by the sea, or in the oil fields. Harrison Coburn; his wife, Mylet; and his son, Jimmie; accompanied by Mylet's youngest sister, May Belle Johnson, had driven south from the farming country of northeast Nebraska to join the exodus along Route 66. "What a great trip that was. I had such a ball. One of those great transitions."[1]

Jim Coburn, six years old, was excited to see something new and different from his relatively pampered life in the small town of Laurel, Nebraska. "I knew it was something about the Depression. That we 'had to leave because of the Depression,' but I didn't know what the fuck it meant."

For his father, Harrison, this forced journey felt like failure. Harrison had grown up in Laurel, part of one of Cedar County's esteemed leading families. Their social doings, from church work and bridge parties to out-of-town vacations, often appeared in the local paper.[2] The town's park was even named Coburn Park.

The family had first come to Laurel in 1894, when it was booming thanks to the new railway junction. Harrison's grandfather, J. H. Coburn, and father, Daniel Dutton Coburn (always called D.D.), were astute businessmen, buying into the town's general store. By 1910 the family owned several buildings in the town and land nearby. Then D.D. saw the potential in the new techno-logical marvel—automobiles—and started a car dealership in 1911. Within ten years, the town streets were lined with Coburn Fords.

Harrison was just fourteen years old when his mother, Altha, passed away from thyroid disease in 1916. She was a refined, gentle lady with long, thick hair worn in a Gibson Girl–style bun on the top of her head. As a hobby, she decorated fine china, hand painting apple blossoms and rosebuds. When she died, her only daughter, Irma, was just twelve years old. The eldest son, Darrell, was a young adult of eighteen, while the youngest son, Paul, was only four.[3]

In hindsight it seems James Coburn had a lot of his grandfather in him. Like Jim, D.D. had a charismatic personality. There were family stories whis-pered about his eye for the ladies and his wanderlust, something else Jim seemed to inherit. In 1916, at the age of forty-eight, D.D. began traveling regularly to the spa city Excelsior Springs, Missouri, where the mineral spring waters were reputed to be a cure-all, suggesting that he suffered from the family affliction—rheumatoid arthritis. D.D. had gone as far as Chicago, the glamorous big city, in his travels.

"[Grandfather] was a bit of rounder—a playboy, hustler, hanging out in bars, making deals. My grandmother died, and he was off to Chicago in no time at all and brought home a hussy named Elsie. Everyone called her 'the hussy.' Whatever he had after the Depression, she took it all. Going to Chicago was a big deal at the time. I didn't even know what Chicago was."[4]

Folks were wrong when they called the widow Mrs. Elsie Steere "the hussy from Chicago."[5] In fact she was a local girl from the neighboring town who had lived as a newlywed in Chicago and had moved back home with her young son when her husband was killed in World War I. But she was only twenty-five when she married fifty-two-year-old D.D. in January 1921. The disapproving gossip continued relentlessly for years, becoming part of the family folklore.

D.D.'s son Harrison left high school in his senior year in 1921 to attend special mechanic's training at Ford. He didn't seem to have any choice in the matter but at twenty was expected to take his place as a manager in the family's wildly successful auto business, the Coburn Motor Company. His brother Darrell had returned from the war an invalid, most likely from being gassed, but was already running the dealership in the neighboring county. They not only sold Model A Fords and Fordson tractors but also serviced all the vehicles in the towns and farms in the county. They were riding high on the booming economy.

It was the perfect time for Harrison to get married and start a family of his own, and he began courting a pretty, dark-haired schoolteacher working in nearby Dixon. Miss Mylet Signe Alvina Johnson was one of eleven children whose family, like Harrison's mother's, were farmers of Swedish descent.[6] "Grandfather had a farm on an Indian reservation. That's where my mother grew up and became a schoolteacher. I imagine she was a good teacher. She spoke Swedish. All the siblings spoke Swedish. And of course there were dozens of cousins. And they all mingled together. So there was always a familial kind of thing. Mother didn't go to college, but she taught school on the Indian reservation, just outside of Laurel. Tip Top, a little red schoolhouse sitting on top of a hill, halfway between the towns for the farm kids.

"My mother loved teaching the Indian kids, but even she had this kind of bigoted attitude about them. 'We're the white people.' She was teaching them a new culture but did not bother to learn anything about their own. A big family like she had, God, you'd think they would learn something. But I never heard her talk about anything, nor any of her family. Strange to have contact and not take advantage of it."[7]

Harrison and Mylet were married in August 1925. Harrison's sister, Irma, by now one of the operators at the local telephone exchange, moved in with them.

August 31, 1928, was hot—the hottest day anyone could recall. It was so hot that even seventy-five years later Aunt Irma remembered running home from work through the dusty heat, hurrying to help her sister-in-law the afternoon when future movie star James Harrison Coburn III was born into the comfortable family.

The stock market crash of October 1929 had little immediate effect on the social doings of Laurel, or on little Jimmie's life. No one knew the drought of 1930 would stretch into four more long years. Car sales began to dwindle, but it all seemed temporary.

Mylet sheltered Jimmie from bad news and troubles in the world. In 1932 she made sure that he attended the new experimental nursery school, run by girls from the local high school's advanced home economics class as a lab project. He played at the sand table, with wheelbarrows and blocks, with forty-one other children.

He started kindergarten with the 1933 school year, having just had his tonsils out. There was plenty to do, including practicing for the Thanksgiving pageant. He was given the special job of hall-and-basement inspector. His first teacher remembers him as a happy little boy.[8]

His friend Marian Beebee also remembers him fondly. "Jim was kind of like my brother. If you see the school pictures, [my brother] Allan and Jim always had their little bow ties on."[9]

When people say "the good old days," they are envisioning times like Jim's Capraesque early life in a small country town—running in and out of each other's homes, seeing relatives all around, and playing sandlot softball with Marian and her brother Allan, "even though we weren't big enough to be really good at it," Marian says. "At that time, we played every day, you know." Summers felt longer in those days when school didn't start until after the harvest.

Sometimes Jimmie did get up to mischief. "The only friends I had were in kindergarten when I was living in Laurel. Johnny Maloney, I'll never forget him as long as I live. I almost killed him. He threw a red-handled popgun at me. It hit me—I still have a scar across my nose. I reached in the garage and got this rake. As big as this rake was, I could barely lift the thing. Whoomp! I hit him right down his back. It ripped off his jacket and dug into his skin. He went running home, and I don't blame him, because I missed his head by an inch. We never fought much after that, thank God. I was taller than him, but he was stronger. He was Irish, and his father was a pharmacist. Really strict. Johnny became one of the executives at Wrigley's. I've met up with him a couple of times—once was in Chicago. He evidently heard that I was in Chicago, doing some publicity, so he came to see me. I had seen him a few times when I was twelve or fourteen and went back to Laurel to see my aunt."[10]

Slowly but surely the Depression took hold in Laurel. The drought continued. D.D. sold some of his buildings, and he and Elsie separated. She sold most of the furniture from their house before leaving town. Folks bartered and shopped at the flea market—making do instead of buying new, especially new cars. The Coburn Motor Company could not make the payments of forty-eight dollars per month, and the building and loan association foreclosed their mortgage.

Finally the company closed its doors forever in mid-January of 1935. Irma rented rooms in the back of the Bell Telephone office, where she was now chief operator, and brought D.D. to live with her. Harrison and Mylet decided to move to California. They invited Mylet's sister, May Belle Johnson, to come along.

The idea of going somewhere new was exciting to Jimmie. "They told me we were going to California. 'Is that where they had the war?' 'No, that is where they had an earthquake.' 'Oh, what's an earthquake?' 'Well, that's where the earth shakes and quakes, and buildings fall down.' So then, I knew what an earthquake was."

This description was completely accurate since the 1933 Long Beach earthquake had caused buildings to fall, including the town hall in Compton, their destination, chosen because Mylet's brother lived there. They packed up their trailer, said farewell to their friends, and set off, with Marian Beebee "waving and waving at them when they drove up Main Street."[11]

Coburn recalled, "It was a 1931 silver-topped Model A Ford pulling a two-wheeled trailer. Our first stop was Wichita, Kansas. There was a dust storm blowing at the time, with all the topsoil blowing away. We were stopping in Wichita, but we couldn't find Wichita because there was this dense red fog and you couldn't see twenty-five yards ahead. It was everywhere. Inside the car, on our faces. And I was thrilled—'Wow, look at this! What's happening?'—a new impression. I didn't have any idea what it was."[12]

In their relatively new car, the Coburns got along faster than the people trundling along in battered old trucks or trudging on foot by the side of the highway. "We were passing people on the road who didn't have anything. Some of them were walking. Most of them had a horse, buggy, or a buckboard, but cars usually—old cars that could barely make it." Jimmie was fascinated as his dad dismantled the dust-choked carburetor from the engine to clean it at each gas station. "He knew how to do that, and he did it fast. It was really, really dusty."

After a while the worst dust storms were left behind. Everything seemed exotic. "We stopped at this Texas place to get some food with a big, long mahogany bar, and guys with cowboy hats and spurs sitting around. I thought it was all great. My dad was a pickle lover. He reached into a barrel to get a pickle and didn't realize they had some badass chili peppers in them, and it was really funny, him dancing around with his throat on fire trying to find some water. There was no chili in Nebraska. No, only a little horseradish—made by this old lady who made it really tasty. We ate these huge steaks, that cost a quarter or something. [My aunt] May Belle was a hot-looking lady, so these guys were all looking at us."[13]

As they continued their journey, the air became clear and they could see the distant mountains in New Mexico.

"My dad was always the first one to say, 'No, that's not a mountain. That's a cloud.' And we kept looking and saying, 'Look, it's not a cloud. It's stuck to the ground.' He hated to be wrong about anything. He made these declarations, putting his foot in his mouth, and would not back down. You'd point out that it was bullshit."

Evidently, they were not in any hurry, and much of Route 66 at that time was unpaved. It would have been a bumpy drive, and unfortunately Mylet was still recovering from having had major surgery the month before. They took a slight detour and paused in Alamogordo while Jimmie played at White Sands National Park. The gypsum made his eyes sting. "It absorbs all the moisture around it, and when you are working around it, you have to drink water all the time." But they were just passing through. Coburn would not see those sands again until he made a film there forty years later, *Bite the Bullet* (1975), portraying one of his trademark cowboys. After about two weeks, they finally arrived in California.

Life in Compton was quite a change for Jim. He and his parents, as well as his aunt, initially crowded in with Mylet's brother Emanuel Johnson and his large family. Emanuel was also an auto mechanic, working at an oil refinery, who moved his family to wherever there was work.

The house they lived in was a 1928 Spanish-style home in a new development in the city of Compton, about ten miles south of downtown Los Angeles. It was very different from what Jim was used to. Instead of elegant verandas, there were small, tiled porches. The homes looked blocky and strange with their flat roofs, tiled with terra-cotta curved tiles he had never seen before.

The whole crowd of cousins surrounding him spoke Swedish. "My mother's brother Emanuel had all these kids. My cousins, two or three years older, showed me around, took me to school." Jim started school in grade 1A at Compton Elementary to finish off the school year.

The next few years were challenging. At some point the Johnson cousins moved to Fresno to live on land that was part of the oil fields. Harrison, Mylet, Aunt May Belle, and Jim stayed in the little house on E. San Luis

Street. "My mother just took everything in stride. We had to make the best of it, and she certainly did. She just kept her chin up and kept saying, 'Go get a job.'" Harrison eventually secured work as a mechanic, working long hours in a garage. After May Belle left to be married in 1938, another uncle, Morris Johnson, came from Nebraska to live with them and work with Harrison in the garage.

Jim's school years were interrupted by trips to Laurel to see his aunt and to Thurston, Nebraska, to visit his Johnson relatives. When Uncle Darrell died so very young in 1937, nine-year-old Jim accompanied his father to Laurel for the burial and spent some time reconnecting with his old friends. It was another summer playing softball in the same vacant lot on his old street. He returned again in 1940, this time for the funeral of his grandfather Frank Johnson. Other summers when he visited, he stayed in Laurel or with friends living on farms nearby. He visited with more distant Coburn kin, descendants of D.D.'s brothers, on "an Appaloosa ranch—they had a lot of cattle, a lot of stuff, around O'Neill, Nebraska," where he learned to ride and shoot.

He was always the same easygoing, fun-loving fellow that his friends, like Marian, remember from kindergarten: "He was a great guy when he used to come back, you know. He came back the last time when he was like fourteen. And Ole and Allan my brother, and him, and Cherry Ann and myself, we all would get together in the evenings and just have a ball. He was a character. At that time he was just the same old Jim as he had always been. We had so much fun. Every evening. We were that age. We just got an old car that was so beat up that you could hardly make it go from block to block. And we just had such a ball. He was just so much fun, a real comedian, and much like he was as a child."[14]

Back in Compton, Jim continued walking to school, sometimes wading through knee-deep water. In those days, the Army Corps of Engineers was still working on the decades-long drainage project that would prevent frequent floods in Compton.[15] This cold, damp environment undoubtedly contributed to Jim's yearly bouts of bronchitis. His mother coddled him when he felt poorly, but he remembers that she "wasn't a very good cook," usually making somewhat bland Midwestern fare, but also that she made an outstanding cranberry sauce and "liked festivities."[16] Money was tight, so Mylet worked as a saleslady in a dress shop.

Throughout his youth, Jim never received affection from his father. He was just a weary, distant presence. "My father didn't have any idea how to raise a child. He was too busy trying to stick things together during the Depression. His education was not one of any great shakes. He read a lot of pulp magazines. My dad was such a frugal son of a bitch. He was tight with everything. There was a good reason for it because we didn't have any money. But even when we got money, he would spend it in weird ways. He had a kind of competition with me, for some reason, as far as I can remember. He was really competitive. I didn't realize it then. I didn't know what it was. I just thought he was being an asshole. He was never one to play ball or play catch or do any of that.

"My father was the foolish disciplinarian. He would make up rules that were stupid. Just dumb. I'd say, 'Why do you want me to do that?' and he would say, 'Just do it.' 'Well, that's silly.' And it would really piss him off. If I did something that was really out of line, something at school, I got silly or something like that, Mom would tell my dad, which made him uneasy to have to do something. His discipline was either over the top or stupid. He would come up with 'You have to stay in your room for twenty days.' 'Well, can't I go to school, Dad?' 'Well, that's at night, you have to stay in your goddamned room.' And then my mother would say, 'Harrison, I think that's a little too much. He wasn't that bad, what he did.' My mother would whittle it away, and whittle it away, down to a couple of days. It would be enough. She was a good arbitrator, and she was sweet. Pretty, a little portly, round, small, about 5'3" or 5'4". My father was 5'10"."

Later, when Coburn started acting, he would feel even more distant from his father. "He was unhappy with whatever I chose. He didn't give a shit, just as long as I got out of the house and didn't cause him any problems. That was his trip. He thought it was all right once I started making enough money to pay for his bills. He thought that was great. He never complimented me on anything. I felt sorry for him once I understood it was his fear of failing again. I realized he had to always keep this false kind of ego up in front. I don't think he ever hugged me at all, ever. I hugged him a couple of times. He got a little embarrassed."

Coburn grew up with little direction from either of his parents. Looking back, he shrugged this off as a benign neglect. "They just let me grow. They didn't guide me in any way. They *didn't*. The thing they did was just let me be. They never picked me up from school; they never took me to school. I either walked to school or rode my bicycle all the time. They never did that shitty stuff. It wasn't necessary. I could walk pretty fast. Then I got a car. I raised myself, finding my own things to be part of." Instead he turned to his friends for validation. "I had my own gang of kids that I hung out with, and they were all good guys. No one was a cheat, or a liar, or an asshole. They were all pretty good people."

His health had an ongoing influence on him at school. It barred him from athletic competition, but he was involved as a team manager and assistant under Coach Rex Dixon for the track and basketball teams at school. Bronchitis also left his voice deeper than might be expected. "Every year my voice would come back a little lower."

By the seventh grade, he had a bass singing voice. Mrs. Nell J. Spiller taught music at Roosevelt Junior High School. When she heard Jim singing, she immediately placed him in the senior choir, "because there was no junior choir," Jim says.

Mrs. Spiller ignited his love of music, and that would engage him his whole life. "Mrs. Spiller kind of looked like an owl, but a very benevolent owl. She was English with a British accent. She had a beaky nose. Not a beauty, about sixty when I met her. She taught choir and music appreciation, all in one fell swoop. We'd get in there, and we would sing our asses off for her because she always had this wonderful slanty-eyed smile on her face. She would just conduct, and we would follow her joyfully since she was a good conductor. She could conduct everything from 'Dem Bones' to Handel's 'Hallelujah Chorus' to popular songs."

During those "four wonderful years" Jim learned about singing and breathing, conducting, symphonic music, and the difference between the Russian and French composers, the Italians, and the English. Mrs. Spiller would have the class listen to different orchestras playing the same piece, from John Cage to Béla Bartók, Stravinsky, and perennial favorite, Ravel. His only disappointment was that he dearly wanted to play drums, but hearing loss in one ear (another legacy of bronchitis) bothered him enough that he had to be satisfied with playing timpani for the marching band.

It was in Mrs. Spiller's class that Jim first seriously considered acting as a pastime. Every Friday was called Audition Day. "Everyone would bring something in, a record or a piece of music, or perform a skit, say a poem, get up and do whatever they wanted to do. No end to anything, doing something. She liked when we brought in jazz. She knew about the music, the players, and through this understanding she had about things, musical, sensational, she would have an understanding about her students. And she had a great eye for talent. She would give specific assignments to certain people. Every year in this school, they would have a night. It wasn't a prom night so much as a 'senior something or other' or 'junior something or other.' You'd have a little dance and you'd have dinner at school, with a play.

"I was always doing most of the plays because she picked me to do them. I got pretty good at improvisation because all the other kids didn't know how to act at all. They didn't know anything about anything. They were always forgetting their lines, so I would act for both of them. I'd pick up here where they left off and get them back on cue. It was fun for the audience because they kinda dug what was happening.

"I was in the orchestra, the choir, and the marching band. I got to do all that stuff. It was fun. Most of my time in school, junior college, and college was doing something like that. I was either acting, playing a musical instrument, singing. We sang at all the Christmastime assemblies. As we got older and older, we went to bigger and bigger things, and it got more and more exciting all the time. Holiday things, New Year's Eve things, Thanksgiving. We'd all dress up like turkeys. She'd guide us through. What a wonderful lady."

Most importantly he thrived under her encouragement and praise. Jim felt safe because, unlike his father, Mrs. Spiller never criticized when she saw people sincerely trying. "Those were enjoyable times because I was learning how to do it, without criticism or acclaim, without any kind of fidgeting—she never, ever got on anybody's ass who really did it. I can hardly give her enough praise. Mrs. Spiller opened our hearts, our minds, and our heads through music. Her class was overcrowded, and everyone kept coming back year after year. I was accumulating knowledge about what the greatness of music really was. I still love Ravel, and Stravinsky's *The Rite of Spring*."

At the same time, Jim wanted a job, perhaps to afford more records as well as to save for his first car. His cousin Darlene, who was the same age, left school after seventh grade and at thirteen was working forty-eight hours a week as an oil worker helping to support her family while her two elder brothers continued their high school education.[17] In Jim's case, leaving school would certainly not be permitted by Mylet, even if Jim wanted to—which he did not.

However, he did find a part-time job that he loved. "I had a job working in the Tower Theatre on Long Beach Boulevard near the old mausoleum that looked like the Taj Mahal. I used to hang out and watch the funerals because I was really attracted to the architecture, which was just gorgeous. I worked in the theater, made about five dollars a week, changing the marquee and stuff like that. I made a few bucks there and got my friends and family in the theater for free.

"I was the head stooge. The stooges were the guys who ran around the sandboxes—cleaned the cigarette butts from big ceramic bowls filled with sand, filled with cigarette butts, my God. The lobby was a big puff of smoke, always. I cleaned up, kept the toilets clean. The theater was open all night long, round the clock. We only closed to clean up. There were three shifts. There was always something for the workers to do that was fun, changing the marquee at midnight. I was in showbiz, and I didn't resent any of the work. I liked it."[18]

What Jim liked most was that, as a stooge, he got to watch the movies over and over again. "I used to see the films at least six times. We'd sit in the last row, and there was one seat there that was always yours. We sat there and watched the movies. All the good ones were really great. Errol Flynn—very macho. All the Judy Garland–Mickey Rooney films. He was too much. He was a great actor as a kid. All that energy. What a personality. So much fun. When I saw Mickey Rooney, he looked like he was having such a good time, dancing and singing and playing drums and all that! Because of Mickey Rooney, I really wanted to become an actor. I told him that years later [when we met on a talk show]."

Jim worked weekends during school and took on more hours over his summer breaks. "It seemed like the summers were long. The days of fun and frolic. You're away from duties of having to work on something you didn't know or care about [at school]." Jim was at work the Sunday that Pearl Harbor was bombed. The projectionist put up a slide announcing the shocking event.

"I was there when they bombed Pearl Harbor, and we got the flash over the screen. I thought, *How dare they destroy our navy?* It was pretty hard to deny that they had done some damage. The call to arms was great. The following day everyone who was old enough was enlisting and buying a ticket for Uncle Sam. The war was on. So we changed from a regular theater showing a double feature and a cartoon to the news, *The March of Time*—'time marches on.' It was great—all the latest newsreels. We got to boo Hirohito and Hitler. Everybody booed, and then when they saw President Roosevelt, ''Ray! Hooray!' No holding back."

Jim's mother did her part by quitting the dress shop and going to work at Douglas Aircraft in Long Beach, helping to build the thirty-one thousand aircraft that the company supplied to the Allies' war effort. Jim was too young to enlist, but he wanted to help too. One summer of the war, instead of working at the Tower Theatre, he tried a different job. "I foolishly quit during the war and went to work in a foundry that made little metal wheels on swivels. It was the hottest, most unpleasant place you can imagine. I knew what hell was like after surviving two weeks in that job. I was working the graveyard shift in a place called Hawthorne."

Meanwhile his father took part in the general prosperity caused by mobilization and bought a gas station in Long Beach. "He made some bread during the war and opened a couple of gas stations. His partner fucked him out of it, and he had to go back to being a mechanic in a garage. He was very brought down by all of that."

Having saved enough money, Jim bought a car, a Winfield Roadster. "When I took my first car apart, I didn't know how to set the valves. All the rest, I could do. I think I paid $125 for it, bought from a lady whose son was in the army. I was trying to put it together, and [my dad] never helped me. I knew how to do the valves but not the tuning. I couldn't get him to do fuck all. 'You took it apart. You put it together again. That's *your* job.' 'Won't you help me with this one little bit?' 'Nah, nah, I do that all day long.' Of course, he did do that all day long. I would just find someone else to do it.

"I drove it a lot. It was like having a really hot car. We'd have these races. It was a Model A with a '29 body, a roadster body. It was like a Full Race Winfield. It had two downdraft carburetors and a V8 distributor, so it was fast. With all that stuff going, it had so much power. The babbitt goes with the inside of the rods. If you go fast, they would chew up the babbitt. I was always tearing it. It was a drag. I've always been a kind of sports car guy. I've always liked sporty cars."

Shortly after the end of the war, the family moved to a new California ranch–style house on E. Elm in Compton. This was roomier, and it more comfortably housed their frequent family visitors from Nebraska. Jim enrolled at Compton Junior College, where his mother later became an officer on the board of trustees. "She was a member of the school board and became president of the board in Compton, and she was a member of the Los Angeles District school board too. She traveled all over, as far as England. She was honored by Compton Junior College for her tenure as a board member. She always attended meetings, always voiced her opinion, right or wrong, and couldn't be convinced otherwise. My mother was a Scorpio."

Jim Coburn had grown into a tall, lanky young man—"I have long legs and short torso. That's what makes me look weird." He had mid-brown hair and piercing eyes, but his most notable feature even then was his big smile. He threw himself into college life with gusto, joining the men's glee club and the Kappa Epsilon social fraternity. As one of the new pledges, who were known as "dog meat," he survived being forced to wear goofy-looking striped overalls during pledge week. He also acted in drama club productions, where he met some of the cool cats that would remain his lifelong friends.

Evidently, he found someone to help him with his jalopy, and he no longer had to leg it to school. Soon he gathered about him both gals and guys who'd hang out together. "I was an only child, but I always had lots of friends. My buddies in Compton were all my brothers and sisters. My nostalgia about Compton is really around my friends, my group, my gang, about ten or twelve of us. We all smoked grass, really funny and good people. We all had a ball."

They would spend their summers visiting the famed Balboa Island. The Rendezvous Ballroom of the 1940s was renowned for the top jazz and big swing bands that played there. Woody Herman, Dizzy Gillespie, and Benny Goodman thrilled Coburn and his friends. "My gang from Compton and I used to go down there at least twice a week, anytime we had the bread and some chick to dance with. It was in the Rendezvous Ballroom, a big dance hall with a great big bandstand. We'd load the car up. Everyone would want to go—Sissy, Tracy, Donna, Wayne Dunstan. Wayne was my buddy. He played alto sax and eventually played in Stan Kenton's band. That's when Kenton was really hot.

"We'd leave early in the day, get a hot dog or burger along the way, go walking around Balboa, checking out the chicks, though we always had the best-looking chicks with us. [We'd pay] about $2.50 to get in, get a stamp on our hand so we could go outside and smoke a joint, come back in, and dance some more, and just hang there all night. We'd just dance our asses off, listening to these great charts and these great musicians play. It was such a joy!"

These were the wonderful, carefree days of youth, friendship, fun, and music. But things were about to change. Shortly after he graduated from Compton Junior College with an associate of arts degree, in the spring of 1950, he received an unwelcome piece of mail, greetings from the United States Government.

2

Oh, This Army

I didn't know what the fuck I was going to do. I was a little stoned and
dazed, thinking about going into the goddamned army. I didn't know
if I was going to die, not knowing if I was going to Korea.

—JAMES COBURN, 2002

James Coburn was afraid. The shadow lingered over every outing, lurked in
every conversation, kept him from sleep. It was not just the unknown that
was terrifying. It was the very real danger of death or injury. He had to face
facts. It was September of 1950. He had just been drafted and could very
well be sent to Korea to die in combat.

The Korean War began when North Korean troops overran the 38th
parallel, bringing the threat of a Communist takeover to South Korea. The
United States entered the war in support of South Korea, in the first major
test of the still-new United Nations. It was called a "police action," with the
goal of preventing the expansion of the other Communist and Socialist
superpowers. It was the first war to be played out fully, with such immediacy,
in the public arena. Unlike that day back in 1941 when the entire populace
had united in outrage, now there were conflicting opinions, arguments on
the mass media about the war. Like everyone else, Coburn listened to terrifying radio bulletins of strategic losses, confusion, and remarkably high
casualty counts.

He spent one of his last evenings as a civilian at a gloomy farewell dinner party organized by his Compton Junior College gang. In hindsight the night was notable because it was when he met his lifelong friend Pete Kameron. "I met Petey the last day I was a free man, before I went into the army, with all my girls—Sissy and Tracy and Tommie Muggleston, and Joanne Linville. All of them had this little apartment on Vine Street, on Rossmore. It was a little house that they all shared. It was great. We had all gone out to dinner, and they were saying goodbye to me and a friend of mine, Paul Phillips.

"Petey and his sidekick were song pluggers, working for some music company. They'd go around to all the DJs to get their songs on the radio. He was going back to New York, and we just kind of struck it off. I don't know what we talked about. He was in his black suit and dark tie. He was chic and kind of New York elegant. I didn't see him again until I went to New York after I got out of the army."[1]

The next day Coburn reported to Fort Ord in Monterey, California. It was one of two major staging areas in the West for troops heading for Korea. All the local draftees took their fitness tests there. He noted wryly that soldiers had to be "perfect in order to go out and be ready to die." Coburn passed every physical exam—until his hearing test.

It is one of the great ironies of Coburn's life that the very disaster that destroyed his ambition to be a professional musician, probably saved his life. The hearing loss in his bronchitis-damaged right ear, while not severe enough to let him wash out altogether, categorized him as unfit for combat. Instead of being routed to Fort Lewis and the battlefields of Korea, he was sent to Fort Hood in the dry and dusty plains of Killeen, Texas.

Here his group from California, each man with "a little something wrong" with him, were put into the Quartermaster Corps. For the time being, he was placed in the service battery, the unit responsible for supply. His unit picked up all the goods, including food, guns, and ammunition, and then distributed them. But first he had to go through basic training, with the Fourteenth Armored Field Artillery Battalion.

Considering what might have been, training with the Fourteenth was pretty cushy. "The guys training us were artillery guys. We were supposed to get infantry training, but these guys didn't know shit about training anybody. We'd get up daily at six a.m. Then we'd go have some breakfast, a really good breakfast with eggs, bacon, ham, pancakes. Because it was a service company, we had everything. We could have had roasted boar if we wanted to. Everybody was getting fat and sassy, but we weren't learning anything. There was nothing to learn. All the artillery guys did was tell stories about artillery."

However, Coburn did have to participate in drills and training exercises. He no longer had his family around, particularly his mother, to make his life easier. This new level of supervision over his life was certainly not what he had been used to. Nor could he manipulate the officers as he had his mother. He could laugh about it in later years. "Being in the army was a good/bad thing. It broke the chain—the silver cord—and got me away from my mother, who I'd always depended on if I wanted something. I couldn't whine in the army. The officers would just say, 'I ain't your mama. Goddamnit, just get your ass out there.' You could be sick as a dog. 'But I'm sick. I've got bronchitis.' 'That doesn't matter here. You can cough your ass off, and we don't care.' Really compassionate guys."

When the time came to learn to shoot, Coburn thought he would do well since he'd learned to handle a gun during his visits to some of his Nebraska farming relatives as a teenager. However, it turned out a little differently than expected. "For our training, we had the worst fucking guns. I had a carbine that shot crooked. The bullets would go off in all directions. I had always been a pretty good shot. When we were doing target practice, the target was so big, one could hardly miss it, but I couldn't even hit it. *Bang*—nothing. *Bang*—nothing. The sergeant would be saying, 'Squeeze . . . squeeze . . .'

"I finally said, 'Listen, you take this gun and you shoot. Let me see you hit the target with it.' He said, 'Listen, don't tell me what to do!' I said, 'Well, listen, man. That gun just doesn't shoot straight. Just try it and see.' So he took the gun, and after firing several shots and hitting absolutely nothing, the bullets going all over the place—we didn't know where the hell they were going except when they kicked up dirt—he handed me his own gun, saying, 'Well, okay. Let me see what you can do with this one.'

"And so I took his gun. *Bang*—bull's-eye. *Bang*—bull's-eye. Every time I shot, it was a bull's-eye. It was the antithesis of what had happened before. I was actually a sharpshooter. I have a medal for sharpshooting somewhere, but that took a new rifle. I thanked the sergeant for helping me out."

At graduation, after six weeks of basic training with guns, ammunition, bivouacs, and bazookas, "a little bit of this, a little bit of that," Coburn still knew so little about infantry that the only option for him was to stay in the service battery.

The service battery always had the best of everything. Coburn got to know the master sergeant in charge, who was also the chef of the camp. "He had these dog robbers, guys would go out there and get whatever was needed, and it was a big scam. Whoever is the big guy in the service battery gets to deal with all the other sergeants who were running the mess halls. He would see who deserved what. He was top shit, a big, fat guy. He was nicknamed Soapy for some reason."

The biggest challenge of life on the base was the relentless boredom of having nothing to do and nowhere in particular to go. With his associate of arts degree, he had more formal education than most of the guys in his battery. Plus, he had a certain status as a city sophisticate.

Most of the others were from small, rural towns. "One of my bunk mates at Fort Hood was from Kansas, a real country guy. Where most of the guys had pictures of women pinups on the wall, this guy had a framed picture of a cow. It was the cow he had raised, and his mother or father had sent him this framed picture of this cow. He loved that cow so much—it was amazing how much he loved that cow. He was a farmer kid. I, on the other hand, was the city guy, from California, which gave me a little cachet. I had been around a little bit. I didn't have anything hanging on my wall."

Other than occasional training films about syphilis, using condoms, and avoiding reefer, the only entertainment consisted of base radio broadcasts of motivational propaganda twice a week. Coburn was invited to read these, no doubt because of his voice, and he agreed and was transferred to the radio department.

Surprisingly, he was terrible at live reading. "I was really awful. I couldn't do it at all. I'd freeze and cough with bronchitis." But he did make a good friend in another radio-department colleague, Falla Valedez, who was also into jazz music. "A good bass player, he taught me to play the claves [the wooden stick percussion instrument of Cuba], and I played bells and conga drum. We had this big room, and we'd sit around and spend hours playing when we didn't have anything to do, which was most of the time. We had one radio that worked, and our sergeant was a red-headed guy who knew all the scams, so anytime we wanted to do anything, we'd come in a jeep saying we had to take the jeeps out and test them, and we would drive from one end of the camp to the other and try the radios and see if they worked. They never worked. We could never do it. So we'd have to make a report. 'There was a lot of static, so we may have to do this again tomorrow.' We spent our time fucking around like that or going to town and buying batteries. Silly things. We didn't have anything to do."

Every now and then, Coburn's friends in Los Angeles would risk mailing him a few joints in an envelope. "In Texas, it was really illegal. Falla and I would go in one of the jeeps and get stoned and talk about jazz—Latin jazz. I learned a lot." When Valedez was transferred to the First Army Corps in San Antonio to be in the army band, Coburn says, "I'd go down and see him in San Antonio."

Since he couldn't read for the radio, Coburn was pulled back into the Second Army Division. The whole battalion was slowly packing up, preparing to travel to Germany, to continue the post–World War II occupation of that country by the victors. They went by train to New Orleans, to embark on a slow boat to Europe.

They left on July 4, 1951. The uniformed soldiers paraded down the middle of Canal Street through New Orleans. After the dry plains of Killeen, the city was green, "so green and beautiful, like diamonds."

Coburn marched in the humid heat onto the *General William Mitchell* troop transport ship and immediately passed out on the deck. By the time he woke up about two hours later, the boat was moving out of the harbor, down the Mississippi Delta. He could hear the distant music of New Orleans, jazz and blues. "It was really wonderful. I wanted to get off the boat and play with them."

The trip was seventeen dreary days across the Atlantic. It was crowded and boring. To pass the time, for the first and apparently last time, he kept a handwritten journal filled with detailed observations of his associates, their shared misery, and his own feelings of loneliness and isolation, often expressed in language that revealed his poet's soul.

"The ship is over-crowded. Nearly 3000 troops, accommodations for 500 to 1000. Everyone is hot, miserable, and pissed off. Very dragged. The holds are unbearable. The stink of human, sweating bodies is overwhelming, men are sleeping on the deck at night, some with cots, some without. It's a mass of bodies trying to drain a little rest out of very poorly wrought conditions.

"The chow lines are hopelessly long and hot. Many are going without food. Waters of the gulf are calm. . . . Sun is in and out behind soft, cotton tuffed humid clouds. Sea has a purple cast. The sky, very blue overhead, warm and sticky."[2]

He certainly missed his privacy. Even in Fort Hood, the barracks had semiprivate cubicles for each man. The overcrowding, the physical discomfort, sleeping or trying to, and seasickness continue as a major theme in his diary. But he also wrote sardonic criticism of military philosophy and practices, ideas that would later appear crystallized in his satirical war movies, including *The Americanization of Emily* (1964) and *What Did You Do in the War, Daddy?* (1966).

"The men are anticipating Europe. Two reasons prevail: to get as drunk as possible and to rape all women they can. But not to do the job they've been sent there to do. This evolves from the effortless indoctrination by our planners, the officers. The instruction has all been in the negative. You will not get drunk, you will not shack up, you will not think, you will not live. No instruction is given in the communication with foreign speaking people, or courteous conduct toward them, or what to expect. What will our acceptance be? All these questions could be answered. The brain cannot, they are not capable. They seem afraid to ask suppliers where to obtain the vital info, so it therefore goes unheeded, the fear of command.

"The men are becoming restless, with so little to do and no recreation other than gambling (another thing that has been outlawed by the O.D. Gods, but is serviceably overlooked on this voyage). Reading, gambling, sleeping, writing, and standing in lines. All of the former takes place when not participating in the latter. Time drips by, bead after bead of sweat."

The powers that be instituted the regulation order of classes, PT (physical training), and KP (kitchen police), even inspections. "The ship is vibrating with the sounds of troops counting calisthenics in unison. A strained sound." Every few evenings, there was a movie screening on deck, with recent movies like *The Enforcer* (1951) with Humphrey Bogart, *Mr. Music* (1950) with Bing Crosby, and *For Heaven's Sake* (1950) with Clifton Webb playing an angel. These were short-term distractions from the unpleasant sleeping arrangements.

"The hold was a hideous, stinking sweat swallowing mess of G.I. forms, grotesquely trying to gain a position of comfort or at least some air in the airless compartment. I sweated myself to sleep."

After three days, they progressed from the calm seas of the Gulf of Mexico, around the tip of the Florida Keys, and then northeast into the Atlantic proper. The seas became rougher. The long midsummer days were still hot, but the humid weather also brought the relief of rain.

"The sea, a bit heavy. Sea sickness, a now common occurrence, is inflicting itself on numerable G.I.s. Rain came down all night and most of the morning. Finished my tour of KP at 10 hundred. I was semi-ill myself. The weather is still humid, clouds are all dark. One looks and thinks only of rain. . . . Rain all night. The day opened bright as a star, sun brilliantly shining. Some clouds floating in the atmosphere. Sea medium heavy. Men are still restless weary, blue and sea sick."

His boredom-fueled writings show the genesis of his spiritual searching, after hours spent gazing at the sea, the moon, the immensity of the stars—"just something to take the emptiness out of the time." When he could, he read, including *Pal Joey* by John O'Hara and the short story collection *Ironies* by Richard Connell—both available as armed services editions, left over from

World War II. But the truth was, he felt lonely. He had been accustomed to being surrounded by the cool cats and swinging gals of his clique, who all shared the same interests. He missed their camaraderie, especially around the arts and music. Aboard ship he felt increasingly isolated by the lack of sympathetic companions to be found among the "impotent mindless bodies." Even his conversations with "the Squares" were laced with an ironic awareness of his own difference.

"Talked with an intellectual soulmate about the difference between the huge state of Texas and the great state of Calif. Calif. was tested, tried and proved and won on all points, but one. That being size. We conceded Texas to be longer. Typical conversation. I too am becoming conscious of greater superiority of my state. My mind is groping for topics to talk, thoughts to think, no action.

"Nothing is happening with me, my energy is being wasted by expressing uncontrolled unemotional emotions. I'm beginning to hate, not because I want to. But there is nothing to love, without love, hate comes easily. Sunday ended as drearily as it started.

"The men are growing tired with one another. They irritated me from the start. I've not yet met one person interesting enough to spend any serious time with. The soldiers are becoming more and more like the asses they are supposed to be. The Army is accomplishing what they evidently set out to do. What that is exactly, I hope I never know.

"I am trying to move my emotions or adjust them to a point where anything can happen and I'll be able to accept without regret. But it's a hard, unbearable thing to try to accomplish alone. I'm still the loneliest guy in the world. I'm not even a good friend with myself."

During the long days and nights at sea, Coburn discovered a new and amazing skill at poker. He embarked with something less than $80 but finished with $250, which he unfortunately had to turn in to be issued with "script" or military payment certificates. He continued to parlay his poker-playing abilities into cash throughout his time in Europe, becoming something of a loan shark. "That was the best. Didn't cost anybody anything. Everybody paid me back one way or another. I could work out deals when the guys wanted money."[3]

"Card games were 'knocked off' on deck because of the sacred services being held in the passengers' lounge. The Blasphemy within me sounded off in salvos of laughter. But smile I did not. . . . Am winning steadily in poker, doing very little reading. . . . My luck is amazing me. . . . Poker is now the mistress of the ship. The officers condemn it. Their warnings go unheeded."[4]

His companions were uncongenial, "nauseating, egotistical Army loving bastards." The "imbecilic" sergeants annoyed him—"the usual irritating sergeants were their usual aggravating selves." The officers were uninspiring.

"An unprepared Captain 'instructed' for a half hour. He, the leader of men, stammered, rubbed his face, picked his nose, scratched his groin, and read something about the New Code of Laws the armed forces have adopted under the not so brilliant teachings. . . . No questions were asked, because they knew the answers would be just as stupid as the questions. Silly, isn't it?"

However, he still found beauty.

"The Day died a beautiful Death. The sun has been a most willing creator of colorful horizons at dusk. The clouds have been most courteous, and have used their cottoned forms meticulously, in molding a finis to the time between darknesses."

Often, after "sleeping more than is necessary" during the dull days, the motion of the ship at night kept him awake—"the ship rolled and tossed and so did I"—and when he did sleep, it was uncomfortable: "I spent a miserable night trying to sleep. I always wake up tired." But being awake when many others slept meant the chance to look out and appreciate the beauty of the night.

"The light seared and Darkness came upon us, but not until 10.00. When the moon revealed itself, it was ¾ phase. A moon of passionate orange. The sky was black velvet scattered with chipped diamonds. The water dark with but a Glistening Golden flaked walkway into the horizon. The beauty of a mid-summers night on the North Atlantic filled me with compelling emotions."

A little mawkish perhaps, but he was young.

What a relief to sight land from the English Channel. "The soldiers, especially the Texans, are flipping with joy, the assholes." And soon he was gazing with awe at the White Cliffs of Dover.

"There standing in their weathered Brilliance, the famed White Cliffs of Dover. The typical monumental buildings, the castles, rising out from atop the green hills surround Dover the walled harbor. The villages laying close to the sea, like Maidens to the lover. The type English. The land in all its Medieval splendor. Then in the green waters of the Channel, the masts of dead ships lying peacefully beneath the sea. An ironic note added as the ships, as if buried, have their own crosses on their masts, as a sign of a noble death. We picked up a pilot and sailed toward Germany."

Finally debarkation day arrived, as Coburn awoke "to the whistles of demented sergeants." He notes that it "seems strange to see soldiers smiling again."

Coburn observed the port of Bremerhaven with an admiring eye.

"Watching the strange little German men in the odd costumes unload the ship—the hardest workers I believe I've ever seen. Surrounding countryside is quite picturesque in that across the Weser River there are groups of low, red roofed houses. A steeple penetrates the sky through the trees, very green and very low. One can see for miles. A Dutch windmill sets in the field directly opposite the ship, very peaceful. In the distance factory chimney extending skyward, ejecting the smoke of industry, the only thing seen moving across the River. Fishing ships, with their nets hung, have been in and out all day, some with sails, some with motors, some with both, all busy in a quiet sort of way. The trains are odd looking contrivances, small hump-backed boxcars, and such a little engine to pull so many cars. The passenger cars are low and long and are very uncomfortable.

"The train ride from Bremerhaven was filled with new exciting things. The war devastated ruins, the beautiful scenic German countryside, the deep forests, the strange little gardens (everyone has one. They have to raise their own vegetables, in plots about 10′ × 10′ each . . . all together in a certain section of the village.) The ground that is not wooded is used fully for growing food, every inch is planted. The houses are all large in villages or towns. They walk or peddle their cycles to their land to work it. The people all carry a *handtasche*—a briefcase. You are nobody unless you have one, the coal miner to the clergyman."

This casts a new light on his character in *The Great Escape* (1963), Sedgwick "the Manufacturer," who insisted on carrying his case.

After a few days in Bremerhaven—"No electricity, no Nothing but disgusting sad exasperating G.I. Assholes, mulling around"—for the next several months, he was assigned to the "humiliating form of billet," a tent city on the U.S. base outside Mainz. There were insufficient blankets for the biting-cold nights, rain three days out of five, and notably poor food.

"Amid the swimming mosquitoes and sweat bugs, in a city of tents. We live near the once stately city of Mainz. Now the bombed ruins stand as crumbling reminders of the viciousness of men. The dark narrow streets wind, as worms crawl, lighted by a strange gas lamp. The main streets are electrically lighted. But most are dark and but moonlit. Its shadows cast of edifice, broken and vanished smiles."

The shower facilities were limited, and the latrines were "dug by me and my crew—we call ourselves the Association of Shit House Diggers USA, experienced." He then worked in the radio section, mounting and installing radios, but "without the equipment required for efficient operation." By now he had become cynical about military procedures, writing, "Another disorganized plan, we'll wait and see, then be shown, then to do, then it will be canceled, oh this Army."

This period of Coburn's life marked the beginning of his disappointment in the establishment. He was not the same starry-eyed kid who'd worked at the Tower Theatre at the start of World War II. Beginning with his father, the authority figures in his life were always unhelpful. His superiors displayed a demonstrable disconnection from the men they commanded. He once got his "ass chewed" by the captain of another battery for having his jacket off, despite the sweltering heat on deck during midsummer, and he sometimes witnessed physical brutality, officers punching enlisted men who were powerless to defend themselves.

"The morale is improving, but slowly. The way I tell this is I actually have seen some in one person. A guard (MP). He had just hit some poor misguided soldier."

The soldiers had been told that their mission was "to keep the Russians out of Western Europe." But after he lived in Germany for a while, Coburn came to a different conclusion. "I didn't see any kind of activity at all over there saying the Russians were desirous of Western Europe. The Russians weren't a real threat. They were on their ass. But no one was supposed to know that. The whole Cold War thing was invented by the Americans and the Russians to keep people on the edge, and it was all bullshit. Look how quickly it crumbled. The Russians couldn't afford to do anything. They didn't have any bread. They're on the verge of bankruptcy. Everybody else in the world knew that. But we had to keep up the work of the Cold War, stockpiling weapons so no one would fuck with us."[5]

Whenever he could, he escaped. Thanks to his poker skills and good luck, he was one of the few men to have enough money, "loot the other fools foolishly lost," to make passes off base worthwhile. He even appropriated extra passes from those issued to his section, sometimes taking one every other day. He notes that "if you happen to be a shitty soldier, they'd put you on pass during inspections so the whole barracks would not fail. Some guys were really slick, and some were really sloppy. But we have to pay our dues somewhere down the line." He still had to stand guard sometimes, and had KP duties, but also had plenty of downtime to read. His reading material included esoteric texts like Friedrich Nietzsche's *Thus Spake Zarathustra*.

Coburn's life off base was one of rich enjoyment. He discovered that he loved foreign travel, at least when it was comfortable. He was delighted with the varieties of food, cocktails, and wine. He visited Mannheim and Wiesbaden, "the city of gaiety and love. Happiness existed everywhere, even I was smiling. It is a living example of the Germany that once enjoyed life to its utmost."[6] He was also pleased with the bargain prices in Mainz, "a steak, two casks of the Rhine's wine-ish nectar. The price: but a few pennies."

But his daily army life was full of mindless-seeming busywork and regimented squalor. He cast about for some spiritual guidance, writing one of his last journal entries in a kind of desperation, asking the question that has haunted philosophers across eras:

"I sit with my mind screaming for an answer, to a question of what to people of Averageness seems unanswerable. The question is 'Why are we?' In my relative brain, I see, I hear, I touch and smell. All these are for my own use, no-one else's. They all have similar senses. Yet I know the eyes I have see within a color, hear not but a tone or overtone but hear a painting of tinted pastels in music. I smell not but the blossoms, even the earth bathed roots help beautify the Arid Atmosphere. Even to our own body, perhaps the most magnificent of all creations, and of the minds we all but do away with.

"Why are we? To live, with the fullest of life's experiences? To devote with the spiritual guidance of the unknown? Or martyr, giving of ourselves for another greater need? I've thought, All perhaps. If all need be done, then with fervor and aggressiveness should they be done.

"Why are we? To guide our minds and bodies through this life preparing for the next. Not only will the strong survive, but also the willed ones."

Luckily things were about to improve. He moved out of the latrine-digging business to become a mail clerk. "They sent me to mail school to learn how to sort mail. In the army they're always trying to teach you something."[7] Then he was ordered to learn to play soccer.

He was sent to the soccer school in Bad Kreuznach, a town famous for its therapeutic mineral springs. Coburn's duties seemed easy—play soccer for a few hours every day. He spent the rest of his time, over two weeks, enjoying the therapeutic waters. On his return to Mainz, drawing on his high school experiences as an assistant to the coach for several team sports, he set up a schedule for the three service batteries, A, B, and C, and the HQ battery, to learn soccer as part of their leisure time. At that time, soccer was not very well known in the United States. "I'm teaching, and I can't play very well. We went out to this parade ground, and we had a kickoff [with A and B]. And I say, 'Whenever I blow the whistle, everybody stop.'

"There was no stopping these guys. It turned into a total disaster. They were just kicking the ball, each other, fights broke out. When I kept blowing the fucking whistle, no one paid any attention to me at all. So I went over to the bleachers and sat down and watched them beat each other up. Finally I said, 'Well, you guys are all really shitty. Fuck you, I'm out of here. I'm going to take the C battery and the headquarters battery next.' Boom—same thing. It wasn't like they were playing a game. They were just getting it off, beating each other up. It was the dumbest thing.

"Finally, the major called me in and said, 'I thought you were supposed to be teaching them soccer.' And I said, 'Yes, sir, I gave them the outline of what soccer was like, pointed out all the positions, told them how the game was played, and then I had them kick the ball off, and all they wanted to do was kill each other. I blew the whistle. No one paid any attention to me. I'll be glad to continue doing this thing, but it seems to be absolutely ridiculous. These guys want to play [American] football. They want to tackle. They want to throw the ball. They don't want to kick the ball.' And he said, 'Well, all right, we'll do it for three more weeks. Then we'll find something else to do.' That's all I did for three more weeks. Blow the whistle, go and sit down, and watch them beat each other up. I'd have a good glass of German beer watching all this shit go down.

"Then I was told I had to find eleven guys who could play football because we were going to have the young German team come in and play. The town of Mainz against the Fourteenth Armored Field Artillery Battalion. I asked if we should have a uniform and was told we would wear the greens. The greens and army boots, and the German guys showed up in their shorts and soccer cleats and T-shirts, and they could really play. The score was a massacre of twenty to nothing.

"The major called me in and said, 'I want to thank you for your help, but it seems to me that this whole episode, we are going to have to close down. I think we should just give them a football and let them throw it around once in a while. Nah, let's just let them go out and get drunk.'"

Then Coburn was promoted to private first class and troop information and education officer (TINE), a position that suited him perfectly. Now he had the thrill of traveling around Germany by air. His main task was to operate the projector showing educational films to the troops. The topics generally addressed avoiding STDs or were about European history and Germany itself.

Part of the job involved going to other bases to collect and return the film canisters. "The artillery always has an observer plane, like a Piper, operated by a warrant officer. I'd give him a ring on the telephone and say, 'Okay, get ready. We're going off to Baden-Baden to pick up the film, then going off to Nuremberg to pick up another film, and I have to deliver another film to Stuttgart. However you want to do it.' Then we'd go flying off to all these places. It was just wonderful. We had a great time. We saw Germany from a low level, and it had been destroyed. It was so sad, but they were starting to rebuild."

He'd make flying visits to all these cities, borrow a jeep and drive to town for lunch. The local people were businesslike, always pleased to see Americans with money to spend. He enjoyed the "good wine and beer, and the sausages were out of sight."

One perk was the chance to hear live music at service clubs. Close to home base, across the river in Wiesbaden, was the home of the 686 Air Force Band, an eighteen-piece swinging jazz band with a "good drummer, good brass section, shitty piano player, lots of reeds, and a good bass player."

They played at the Eagle Club, inside the Kurhaus Hotel, Wiesbaden, a former casino that had been appropriated by the occupying Americans. The Red Cross managed it. There was something going on every night, along with great food and good company. Local German musicians and bands touring under the banner of the United Service Organizations (USO) appeared regularly. "On certain occasions, they'd break the band off into groups, and they would send them out with an act from London, usually, sometimes an American. I started hanging out with those guys. Groovy guys, swingers. There was a guesthouse that we would go to afterward because it was near the village where they stayed. Five marks a night. We were all issued cigarettes with our rations, three or four cartons a week. A pack of Camels would be worth a whole night in the village. Big, fluffy down pillows. It would be as cold as hell outside. We'd go there for beer and sandwiches—ham and cheese on brown bread with butter."

There were women too, to dance with and more, but Coburn was not much interested in the local German girls, fresh off the farm and lacking sophistication. Plus, "it was hard to keep up a conversation." Instead he started noticing a young Scottish singer and her trio making the rounds of all the soldiers' clubs throughout that part of Germany. Helen Mack had been a teen star on the music circuit in Britain, during World War II, singing classical jazz on the radio and touring with a big band–style orchestra.

It took awhile before she noticed him. "I had eyes for Helen, and she had eyes for the drummer, and the drummer had eyes for every girl. It was like a *ménage* without an *à trois*." Eventually he and Helen got it together.

Helen Mack was Coburn's first real love affair. "She was small, diminutive, with a Scottish kind of freckled face. She was cute with reddish brown hair, but she moved really well, and she could swing. It was a wonderful romance. Helen was a good singer. She sang jazz. She sang good jazz. And she sang to me, which was nice."

Coburn would travel all over Germany, wherever she was playing, and she in turn would send him postcards from cities like Rome, too far away to visit. Once he took the train to Heidelberg to meet up with Helen on a three-day pass. During that trip he came down with an infection in his prostate. "My left testicle had swollen up to the size of a grapefruit, and was it ever painful."

He ended up in Bad Kissingen, at the American hospital. It was several weeks before the swelling began to subside and he could move around again. "I became the champion Ping-Pong player of the entire ward because I was there longer than anybody else. I got to play all the time." He was ordered not to drink any beer and to wear a jockstrap ("most uncomfortable") for six months. "That was the end of my fun. There was no romance, no beer, no fun for six months. My God! Of course, I didn't wait quite that long."

Some months later he had a two-week leave. He flew to London to catch up with Helen. After the quaintness of the semirural towns in Germany, where horse-drawn carts filled with produce pulled to the side of cobbled streets to let military trucks pass, London was bustling, noisy, and modern. They took in the tourist sights, visiting the Strand and Tower Bridge and taking photos of the changing of the guard at Buckingham Palace. They also visited the coastal town of Brighton.

On the last night, before flying back to Wiesbaden, Helen was performing at an air force base near Gloucester. Wearing civilian clothes, Coburn hitched a ride along by posing as the manager of the troupe.

Before the show, early the same evening, he was propositioned by a male lieutenant at the base. "He put me in such a really strange position. He was almost pleading. And I had to say to him, 'Look, that's not my style, so sorry, buddy, but I don't go that way.'" It was very awkward at the time, but Coburn thought no more about it as he spent a wonderful night in an old place near Gloucester "sleeping on mattresses stuffed with straw, and Helen and I made love all night long."

The next morning, he had to don his uniform to fly. Unfortunately, he ran into the rebuffed lieutenant at the airport. "And of course he says, 'You're not the manager. What's going on?'" A smart-alecky reply, "Well, last night I was," didn't get him out of trouble. The lieutenant filed trumped-up charges against Helen to prevent her and her band from doing any more service shows, which was the way most of these variety artists made their money. "The whole group was stymied and stopped from working in Europe for about six weeks, until I finally had to say something. 'Sure, she was my girlfriend. I was stuck in London with no place to go. I had run out of money,' which I really had, blah, blah, blah. And so they were reinstated."

It was almost the end of his tour of duty, which had extended from twelve to eighteen and then finally to twenty-four months, although it seemed longer. "I began to grow a mustache right at the end of my tour of duty, a really long sort of mustache. The colonel, who had this tiny little mustache, really terrible looking, stopped in front of me. He says, 'Well, son, I don't mind mustaches. I wear one myself. But I don't want any of my men looking like Fu Manchu.' And I said, 'Yes, sir.' And I had to trim it. Near the end of your tour, they give you all the guard duties, KP, etc. They would come around, and everyone would have to talk to the recruiting sergeant. They never called me over. They didn't want me back again. I really had a ball, a really good time. The only shitty time was KP duty, washing pots and pans, which was only one day a month. And standing guard duty, which was only two days a month."

The last time he saw Helen was when he took her back to her hotel in Wiesbaden, in an old Mercedes cab. "She wanted me to marry her, and I said, 'Sure, sure, we'll get married.' And then she changed her mind. 'I don't think we can,' and I said, 'I don't think we can either. But anyway, I love you, baby. Whatever happens, good luck.' It was just one of those things. She said, 'Yeah.' She cried a little bit. I kissed her, and then I went back over to Mainz to my casern."

Within a few days, Coburn was traveling back to Los Angeles, free of entanglements and with a wide-open future. There was just one problem. What the heck was he going to do to earn a living?

3

A Beautiful Trip

I was ready to act. I just needed to learn how to do it.

—JAMES COBURN, 2002

Jim Coburn blew back into Los Angeles at the end of his army tour in September 1952. He immediately slotted back into his old life, almost as if he had never left. With the GI Bill available to him, he reenrolled at Compton Junior College, rejoined his old social fraternity, moved into his old room, and started once again appearing in plays at the college.

His mom didn't mind what he did with his life, provided he was happy and put his all into it. She expected excellence, an attitude that never left her. In later days her very public pride in her son sometimes embarrassed him. His stint in the military didn't make much difference to his father, who suffered increasingly with rheumatoid arthritis and still worked as a mechanic. Harrison was still distant and uncomfortable with affection, still frugal. However, his parents did always attend his productions.

Sometime during this period, the idea that he could perhaps make a living as an actor had solidified in his mind. He and his buddy Tony Carbone made a plan. They would both attend Los Angeles City College (LACC) to earn sufficient credits to transfer into the acting program at the University of Southern California (USC). Coburn found an apartment close to the college on Fountain Avenue in Hollywood, and left Compton behind forever.[1]

At LACC he and Carbone met another young actor with the same educational plan. New York transplant Robert Vaughn would eventually play a large role in Coburn's professional future and become another lifelong friend.

Vaughn appreciated the quality of the productions at LACC. Their "stunning, very, very well done" presentation of the new play *Stalag 17* by Donald Bevan and Edmund Trzcinski sealed the deal.[2] Vaughn recalls their conversation after the show: "If this is what they have to offer at this school, I don't think we can bother to go [elsewhere]." Coburn agreed he'd found his niche. "I found out very quickly that City College was where I was supposed to be and that is where I was going to learn all the things I needed to know."[3]

The drama department at City College was run by Jerry Blunt, who "fought for the department like nobody's business." The department produced at least four plays every semester, including everything from classics to recent Broadway hits to new plays written and directed by students, and many plays that were adapted as films, sooner or later. There were three performance spaces available to the students: the big proscenium Administration Auditorium from the old UCLA days; the Little Theater, an end-stage space; and the Bungalow, converted from wartime use into a three-quarter or in-the-round space. These offered the students maximum flexibility in performing for various-sized audiences.

Students performed every kind of role—"one time you'd hold a spear, in one be the minor character, then the lead"—and worked backstage learning all aspects of the theater. Coburn's first theater credit at LACC was in the technical crew for a production of Thornton Wilder's *The Skin of Our Teeth* early in the 1953 fall semester.[4]

Coburn's buddy Carbone not only acted in many of the same productions but also directed, including such plays as *Mister Roberts* in 1953 in which Coburn portrayed Dowdy, a senior officer of the crew.[5]

Innovation was encouraged, such as the presentation of a series of staged readings of three plays by George Bernard Shaw, John Dryden, and Shakespeare about the life of Cleopatra, performed in repertory over six nights. Once more Coburn stood out with excellent notices from the reviewers in the LACC newspaper, who in general tended to be tough critics:

"James Coburn . . . as Dollabella, a relatively minor part, was outstanding—a rich, deep voice and apparent understanding of his part served both him and the audience well. . . . [He is] completely at ease in the meter of the 16th century tongue. . . . As the faithful Enobarbus, [Coburn] delights with his interpretation. He is in command of his character at all times and, happily, never falls into the common trap of delivering his lines in jerked phrases rather than as a whole. . . . Looking slightly naked without his mustache, [he] was dignified and proud as Pothinus."[6]

His versatility and reliable performances in that series were responsible for that year's unanimous award of Outstanding Newcomer given by the same critics' circle. He "had a rather clear claim to the selection, with or without mustache. . . . He has the voice and the virility."[7]

LACC was a place to take creative risks, such as when Coburn was cast in the original student-written musical *Heads I Win*, portraying, of all people, Henry VIII. "God, what a trip that was. I was so miscast, but I did it anyway. It was a great learning experience. I couldn't sing at all, but I was singing sixteen songs, for Christ's sake, and changing tights four times. Tights are the hardest things in the fucking world to get in and out of. I was awful."[8]

This time he was on the receiving end of a critical remark about his singing, although he was by no means the only recipient of brickbats. Ironically the only aspect of the production given any praise at all was the wardrobe.

During this show Coburn was in a car wreck. He wasn't hurt, and it turned out to be a fortunate situation for him. It was late. He was on his way home from opening night at the LACC auditorium theater. "This old guy in his Cadillac turned right in front, drunk out of his mind, and smashed the whole front end of my '41 Chrysler and ripped it off. I got out of the car and looked at the front end. That was the end of that car. I picked up the bumper and threw it, and it just stuck in a telephone pole. I thought, *What a great shot that was.* That took all the venom out of me. 'You're fucking drunk, man, and you've just destroyed my life.'"

The driver gave Coburn his business card and drove off, inviting him to get a lawyer. The old car "didn't have any value, except to me. When I finally got the settlement, maybe two hundred dollars, I just took the money, went to Beverly Hills and bought one coat—it was dark green—black trousers and tan trousers, two ties—one blue and one black—and the shirts. They had three buttons, kinda like the ones around now. These clothes would get me through anything. They turned out to be very hip in New York." This was the start of his lifelong reputation for fashionable elegance.

Being surrounded by like-minded colleagues at school gave Coburn exactly the kind of intelligent, enjoyable camaraderie that most appealed to him. He and Carbone would have great arguments. "Tony was full of fire and brimstone. He'd put up one side, and I'd put up another, not even caring who was right or wrong—we just argued in order to find out."

Immersing himself in the busy theater program filled him with a sense of optimism. The college itself offered a wide-ranging program of cultural enrichment in all the arts, including inviting musicians to give concerts and hosting performances by international arts groups like kabuki dancers. It was a vibrant, creative atmosphere. Coburn was still a great reader and was always interested in alternative ideas, including about acting. He felt City College had "a very conventional way of teaching drama," and it bothered him that he and his friends "were all pretty conventional people," at least as far as acting went.

So when he heard that character actor Jeff Corey was holding informal classes on improvisation, he and four or five of his friends, including Carbone, who was elected to drive, decided to go see him. "It was $2.50 a night, something ridiculous. The class was at his house, in his garage. He had a little stage set up. Jeff Corey showed us how to play actions. Now actions are what you want—what you want to get out of it, what you want to do. Sometimes the improvs would get very heated. You get really strung, you know, because you were making it up and being the biggest, baddest person you could be, and the other person was playing a ninny. All of these things to overcome in relating, how to do that. That's where your talent comes in. That's where your imagination works."

Since Jeff Corey had been blacklisted in 1951, no studio would hire him as an actor. However, once word of his improv classes got out, those same studios sent their stars to attend his classes. The classes became something of a West Coast actors' melting pot.

Corey was an insightful teacher. "Jeff Corey always chose the actions, and they were for the specific talent of the specific actor. What he needed to know, what he needed to learn, what he needed to find out about himself as well as how he needed to relate to someone else onstage. That's what the real improvisations are all about—how to learn to relate to all that stuff, work that dynamic.

"I needed to break loose of my intellectuality. I would try to intellectualize everything, so Jeff would give me improvs where I had to physicalize or emotionalize, where I had to actually do something rather than talk about it. He broke me through. We had class twice a week, Tuesday and Thursday."

These classes more than anything gave Coburn the foundation for his acting skills and exposed him to other young working actors. The biggest standout in his memory was the night a new guy, fresh from New York, showed up. "Jimmy Dean was in town doing *East of Eden*. Dean would just blow your mind. We were all very jealous of him. One of the best choices that was ever made, that I saw in this class, was by Jimmy Dean. Here was the story [for the scene]: His best friend was a big fucking drunk. An alcoholic who could not stop drinking. Jimmy's action was to try to get him to stop drinking. The other guy's action was that he wanted to go out and get a drink, to buy some booze, and he needed some money. He needed to borrow some money from Dean.

"As [the scene] started, Dean shows up to the friend's door and knocks, and he is absolutely blithered, and he makes the biggest ass out of himself. Drunk, being drunk. And it shows the other guy just what drunk really looks like, and it was brilliant. He was absolutely brilliant. We were all just charmed by his choice and gave him a big applause at the end of it. What a great choice.

"See, he played the action. The action was to make [his friend] not want to drink, so Dean chose an action that would allow him to be drunk—to come in, to tell him what it was really like, to show him what it was really like, what kind of an asshole he was—then this was it. And how good he was doing that. Boy, he was great. It was wonderful to watch."

Coburn progressed and worked hard. Over summer break of 1954, he made his unofficial film debut, costarring as the villain in an obscure musical comedy titled *The Beverly Hills Woman*, which also starred Jeff Corey. Hopes for the project continued into the following year, but it was never completed. Back at school, he made a splash in *Street Scene* by Elmer Rice— "most satisfying of all the character actors"—and rose to the challenge of acting with an English dialect in Emlyn Williams's *Night Must Fall*.[9]

His greatest triumph from that period was when he was cast as one of the leads in the school's production of *The Country Girl* by Clifford Odets, playing the alcoholic actor Frank Elgin (the Bing Crosby role in the recent movie). He had a good time and got his most superlative reviews: "Odets must have had in mind someone like Jim Coburn to play his drunken actor character when he sired 'The Country Girl.' Coburn's acting was dynamic."[10]

At the end of April, he and two others had the opportunity to test at Universal International Studios, re-creating one scene for the casting directors.[11] Nothing came of that then, but the casting director for La Jolla Playhouse saw him in that production and gave him a minor role in the 1955 West Coast premiere of the acclaimed New York play *Billy Budd* by Louis O. Coxe and Robert Chapman, directed by Norman Lloyd. It starred Vincent Price and Charles Nolte, reprising his Broadway turn in the title role.[12]

Coburn's part was so small that star Charles Nolte didn't remember him from the group of young men dressed in sailor costumes. The men from the lower echelons were not invited when the stars went to see the bullfights just over the border in Tijuana, Mexico. But for a new, young actor, it was wonderful to be in a real production, and it gave Coburn that most precious commodity, his Actors' Equity card.

Being cast in this play slightly delayed a plan that he and a couple of his intrepid friends had devised toward the end of their last semester. They had decided it was time to try their luck in the big time and announced that they were going to go to New York. Coburn had told the *Los Angeles Collegian* in early June that once there, he specifically intended to study acting with "drama coach Stella Adler."[13]

Carbone owned a beat-up, vintage Essex. It wasn't comfortable but would carry the four guys—Coburn, Carbone, and two young writers named George Hoover and Jim Butler, erstwhile Collegian critic—across the country.

It was now the middle of August 1955. "We started out having breakfast at a place that served pancakes, all we could afford, near the City College. It was a famous place for actors, where we'd go late at night, walking distance from the campus. We loaded up the car with a full tank of gas. I had about thirty dollars in my pocket since I had been earning close to fifty dollars a week at the La Jolla Playhouse. We pooled our money and decided our first stop would be Las Vegas. Through the beauty of the high desert, waved goodbye to Palm Springs, talking and jiving all the way.

"As all foolish folks do, we were going to make some money, so we could live in style along the way. When we got to Vegas, naturally most of our money went down the tubes. We had enough to get to Kansas City if we stayed in little places along the way like the YMCA. We started eating very sparsely."[14]

They paused in Winslow, Arizona, because the car was making increasingly loud knocking sounds, probably a bad rod or piston. They didn't have enough money to get it fixed but thought they could at least have a look at it themselves. After all, Coburn had rebuilt his own car when he was seventeen. "We pulled into a gas station and asked the night manager if it would be all right to put the car up onto the rack so we could see what the matter was. 'It's all right if you're out of here by six in the morning, because that's when the boss comes in and he is an evil motherfucker. He runs this place like a real badass.'

"So we get it up on the rack and find that we need a new rod. We can fix it, but we have to wait until the morning when the parts shop opens, come back, and put it together. Well, sure enough at six a.m. the owner comes, and he starts ranting and raving, is really pissed off. 'Get that fucking car off my rack.' 'Well, we can't move it.' We got testy, and he got testier. 'I'm going to call the police if you don't get your car out of here in the next twenty minutes.' 'Well, that's not cool.'

"We found a place across the street from this asshole where the road went up. We pushed the car there. Tony and I got the part and, with only crescent wrenches, finally got the car running by late in the afternoon. Then we needed to put oil in it. But he wouldn't even sell us oil. 'Get the fuck out of here.' We sent George to buy six quarts of 30-weight oil since it would last longer. We had enough gas to get to the next station. The car still had the knock, but it was quieter."

The guys made their way stop by stop. In Oklahoma City, they slept at the YMCA for almost two days. But their favorite was in Kansas City. "The showers were hot, and the beds were small, but they were comfortable. They charged about $1.50 a night. You get a towel, pillow, and bed and all the amenities in the showers. Just cleaning up felt good. After Winslow we didn't want anything to do with anybody."

Eventually they made it into Manhattan "with smoke coming out of the car." The guys dropped Coburn off at his friend Joanne Linville's apartment on the Upper East Side. She wasn't expecting him, but nevertheless she gave him a warm welcome and a place to sleep for nearly two years.

It was just like the heady, halcyon days of Compton Junior College—the same group of bright young people, the same opportunities to listen to music in dark, smoky jazz clubs, have great debates, and dive into acting. He had no responsibilities, no one to take care of except himself, and nothing but the expectation of a bright future.

He divided his time between auditioning; spending his evenings at Birdland, 52nd Street Jazz, and other nightclubs; and hanging out at Linville's, smoking quite a lot of grass and playing bongos in her little garden, talking acting and music with his increasing circle of new and old friends. "A lot of weird and wonderful things happened in that little garden apartment."

The first person he met there was Sidney (sometimes spelled Sydney) Shaw, the jazz songwriter and arranger. Shaw wrote for Billie Holiday, Johnny Mathis, and Louis Armstrong, among others. Coburn took his motto, Go Bravely On, from the title of a song Shaw wrote.[15] He often spent time at Shaw's apartment. "It was a walk up on 53rd. He had two cats. He called

[one] Emma, and Lord Nelson only had one eye. The place always smelled of cat pee in the worst way.

"Sid Shaw introduced me to the Shaw Society. Joanne, Sid, and I became members, and we went down there every Tuesday night. I became familiar with George Bernard Shaw when I was a kid, watching him on the *Movietone News*. We used to do scenes from his plays, have lectures. It was great, one of the most fun societies—in fact, the only society I have ever belonged to.

"Sid was a raconteur, funny, with the loudest finger pop in the world. He knew all the musicians in town. Walked into Birdland like he owned the place. Nobody fought with him, friends with everybody. Sid was kind of like the court jester. He made any table feel like they were princes and princesses. He called Miles Davis the 'Dark Prince of Jazz.'"[16]

Coburn had arrived in New York at exactly the right moment. Count Basie was playing at Birdland every night for a month leading up to New Year's Eve. Sid got them in for free by arguing with notorious emcee Pee Wee Marquette, who would usually let them have a booth. "We'd get a booth, never pay for it. Birdland was a great club, a low-ceiling basement. The best sound of any club. The acoustics, because it was a cellar club, it was very dense, no echo. Everything was really damp. They had lights, tables, booths all around the outside, a little raised platform. It was a big swinging place with a lot of people there every night, and I wish it was right now, because I'd be living across the street from Birdland. What a trip. What a beautiful trip.

"Sid turned me on to Count Basie, the mainstay at Birdland. Count Basie hit home, man. I spent more time in Birdland than I did in the theater. I became a jazz actor because of that.

"What about music is the same as acting? It's about dynamics. And I learned about dynamics from Count Basie. I became a jazz actor rather than a studio actor. Because I loved fucking around with dynamics. I still do. I still find places in whatever I'm doing to jive it up a bit with dynamics rather than just saying the words in a fashionable way.

"Most actors today get linked to words. Some of them are good at doing that. It leaves a lot to be desired when it comes to the imagination. That's where improv is like jazz. It's like jamming. It's jazz acting—but you can't do it unless you have a text. When you are improvising, you improvise around the text. Sometimes you get stuck in a particular scene that just doesn't seem to work, or it doesn't have a key that you can unlock to make it work, so you improvise. You take a part of it, and you improvise. And it's like blowing, like a couple of tenor players having a cutting contest. And you just blow around this thing, and it's wonderful how things come out. Things that you never thought were there."

He'd only been in New York for a few weeks when he met songwriter Marvin Fisher, who was seeing Tracy from Coburn's Compton days. Fisher's family had a place on Fire Island, which they shared with a commercial agent. Various members of the gang would party over weekends out there. Coburn met the agent on his first Fire Island weekend, and she immediately sent him on an audition. Depending on the telling, there were anywhere from 50 to 150 guys there.

"She sent me on a cattle call in New York for U.S. Golf Balls. U.S. Rubber made golf balls, and it was an industrial thing. All I had to do was swing this club like I was a golfer. Anyway, I walked in this place, and it was packed. They said, 'Take your jacket off and swing this club.' And I could swing a club better than them because I had taken golf class in college. I wasn't a very good golfer, but I had a good swing. I looked good. That was all that was necessary for this thing."

An industrial is a film produced for internal use by a company, such as for staff training or conventions, rather than for public distribution. It still counts as professional work. Thus, to the astonishment of his colleagues and friends, after only three months in New York, Coburn had his Screen Actors Guild (SAG) card and was a working actor.

His next big break, in early December, was for Remington electric shavers. "I got to grow my beard and would shave it off every four days or so. The time came for me to shave it off for real, in front of the camera. There were all these guys, a line of them standing there with their shavers, and the cameras roll and everyone starts shaving, zoom, zoom, zoom, zoom. There were two cameras. . . . You were supposed to be looking in a mirror, but you can't see anything, [just the lens in the cameras]. I finish shaving, and I hear this cheer go up over on the other side. It was during the World Series, and I thought someone had just scored a home run.

"Then everyone comes running up to congratulate me. And I say, 'What?' And they tell me that 'you just shaved your beard off in under a minute, 55.2 seconds, and that's never happened before.' They were ecstatic. I couldn't believe that. I got to keep the shaver. That was the thing I was happiest about."

He also got the job, and kept busy for a whole year growing and shaving his Van Dyke–style beard. In those days, most TV was live to air, including the commercials. Once he bantered with the host of the quiz show *What's My Line* as a "Van Dyke grower."

As well as living expenses, Coburn said that the fees from these gigs paid for a semester—"about four months"—of tuition at Stella Adler's studio. Linville was attending classes there and at other places, and as she said, was "bringing it all back to him," but as far as she knows he never enrolled in the school, at least not in his early time in New York.[17] Most likely he attended classes after he had moved out to his own place. He was certainly hanging around the fringes of the theater schools, socializing with those actors, including Luther Adler. After *The Great Escape* in late 1963, Coburn started mentioning "studying with Stella Adler" to the press often, crediting her with teaching him about "style." She was always an important influence.

Stella did not single Coburn out from the crowd of students, but he described her teaching method in vivid detail. The classes were packed, between seventy-five and one hundred people. "She had a studio on 84th, I think, between Madison and 5th Avenue. An upstairs studio. We would all be waiting around smoking cigarettes and jiving. And she'd come in a limo or taxi, always a little late for our, I guess it was a two or three o'clock class, and out would come Salt and Pepper, her two little dogs, and then she'd come out, after having lunch at the Russian Tea Room, saying, 'Oh, my darlings, come. Let's go to work.'

"We'd follow her up the stairs, like [she was] the Pied Piper, and as she would go, things would be coming off, her jackets, a scarf, the gloves, etc. People would be picking them up as we'd be going, and by the time she had reached about three-quarters of the stairs to the left-hand side of the stage, she'd have her blouse unbuttoned, and she would be scratching her breast and pulling up her dress and she would say, 'First,' and then whoever was first on the list would jump onstage and everybody would quiet down.

"Her penetration, her attention was the thing that drove everything because everyone's eyes were on her, and everyone would get right into the scene that somebody was doing up there, whoever it was. Because the class was large, it was really hard to get a scene. You have to wait maybe two or three weeks, so every time you got a chance to be onstage when Stella was there, it was really something special. I saw some of the best acting I've ever seen in that class."[18]

Her way of teaching was to demonstrate. "Stella was a teacher who displayed, showed us how to do it. She didn't tell you how to do it. She said, 'I assume you're all actors so we don't have to talk about technique or any of that bullshit.' She would watch the scene, and she'd get inside the scene until the tears would roll down her eyes, and she'd clap at the end. 'Oh, it's marvelous! How do you do it? How do you do it? There's one place in there, I think . . .' Then she would get up on the stage, and she would find one line, or maybe even just a pause that would need to be filled out in a particular way. And she would take one of the characters—she played both characters—with such complete understanding of the character, and she would let it fill right in. She would take one or two lines, and there'd be a phrase, then she would do it, and you would see how it would just put everything together to make it effervescent. It would just sparkle when she did it. It was a simple, simple thing. Texture. And she would do it with such flair. And she showed us what style was.

"Style wasn't fashion. Stella taught us that fashion is bullshit. Style became something that I was very conscious of. Without style, without personality, you're just a stick out there. Maybe you've got a pretty face, maybe you've got long hair, dimples in your nose. What difference does that make? What we were looking for was a way for American actors to play kings and queens. To be able to play Shakespeare in an American way, without sounding like you were from Alabama—to do it with style, with swagger, like a king—to be able to stand. Stella went on a lot about style, how people carried themselves. You've got to have some dignity.

"We had a lot of would-be actresses who were actually models who would walk onstage and walk across the stage, and Stella would say, 'Off! Off my stage! You can't walk on the stage like that and be an actress. Get off the stage!' And shooed them off the stage. They would have paid something, whatever it was, and they would cry, and she would say, 'Don't cry. Don't cry. Learn to walk. Learn to act. You're not in fashion school here. We're not teaching you how to sell a dress, or you, or your ass. You can do that on the street, but you can't do that on my stage.'

"So she kept most of these people away. It was a bit intimidating, because she was really hard on women. She loved the men, you know. She would treat them like they were gods. But women, she was very, very hard on. She praised them to the highest heaven when they were good, when they made it. It makes me cry just to think about how she used to deal with them.

"She had that range of perception that allowed her to read people's personality, love them all, and yet be able to tell them the truth. Most of these people who call themselves acting coaches don't have the slightest idea what the truth is. Jeff Corey told the truth. If you find someone to tell you the truth, you better listen."

Having something of a regular gig allowed him to pay back his IOUs to Marvin Fisher, attend classes, and live in a constant whirl of social activity. His crowd included Petey Kameron, now back in New York and living in the same building as Sid Shaw.

"We developed a relationship built around music, esoteric activity, psychoanalytic activity, plays. And that relationship has lasted all these years. We just get together and rap about those things, and every time I find out something new about him. He and Monte Kay—nice guy, loved Monte, what a beauty his wife was—they started 52nd Street Jazz. They used to have jazz jam sessions at different little clubs all up and down 52nd. They were part of that movement, on the music level. They opened up Jazz in the Park—every Sunday free jazz, big bands, small bands. It was all free. He never took written credit for anything. He's made fortunes and given fortunes away, anonymously. He'd say, 'You can build my building after I'm gone.' We spent a lot of time together at Birdland."

Another neighbor was "a famous old dyke named Trude Heller." Trude ran a renowned club in the Village, with a very good Chinese chef. "She was older than the rest of us. She was probably in her early fifties. She was a godsend because she was the only one who ever had any fucking money. Joanne used to say, 'Come on. We're all just poor little actors.' Trude was nice. She treated me good. She was a member of the inner sanctum of club people. Trude had a car, which made it easy for us to get around."

They would go to the theater when they could, and to the movies. Coburn was deeply affected by Kurosawa's *Seven Samurai* (1954), the story of seven mercenaries who save a village from bandits. "It opened in New York, and that's when I saw it. I must have seen it, oh, seven or eight times in the first two or three weeks. I took everyone I knew to see it, because it was such a brilliant film and it was made so well. Everybody loved it, of course. It was the first Japanese film I had ever seen."

In October 1960 he would even introduce a screening and discussion about the film back at Compton Junior College, part of the "Evenings at Compton" series. He was especially attracted to the character of Kyuzo, the master swordsman played by Seiji Miyaguchi, and the irony that "it was the end of an era where a half-blind bandit can kill the greatest swordsman of the time, with one of those old muskets."

Coburn was next cast in a small role in director Walt Witcover's 1957 off-Broadway production of *Red Roses for Me* by Irish writer Sean O'Casey. The cast was primarily people drawn from both the Actors Studio and the Adler Studio, including Warren Beatty playing piano. Witcover employed a lot of improvisation in the rehearsal period. He described Coburn as a "tall and amiable young novice," incorrectly believing this to be his first theater role.[19] Stella Adler loved the production, which involved many of her students, and subsequently hired Witcover to teach improv at her studio.

It was heady and fun—without anything serious in Coburn's life except his acting work.

"They couldn't figure me out. They knew I wasn't gay, because everyone in town was hitting on me, unsuccessfully. I like girls a lot. I was surrounded by them. I just wasn't sleeping with any of them. No, I never did. I liked my platonic friendships with girls. I liked it that way. We'd hug and kiss, but I just wasn't serious about any of them. We were all just playmates.

"The long-lasting friendships I've had with women have always been of a philosophical nature rather than a sexual nature, and they've lasted a long time. I don't have many—Joanne Linville because we escaped that trap of Compton together and we took some other ones with us. We were jazz babies together. All of us used to share the joint. We'd get high and listen to music, and [I] got turned on to some great American music. We did a lot of things under the influence of marijuana. It was fun and open and free and great. Sensational. Fun. Very little of it was sexual. All of us, we'd have separate girlfriends and boyfriends outside of this group. There was this nucleus of us, and I'm sure if I called them up tomorrow, they'd say, 'Come on, let's go get high.'"[20]

New York in the late 1950s was an extraordinary, vibrant time for actors and theater, for all the arts. "We used to go to the Met and look at all those great paintings and look for the genius, look for the style of the painter, the style of what they were painting."

Aside from Stella, other legendary teachers were offering classes—Sandy Meisner, Lee Strasberg, Elia Kazan, and Bobby Lewis. One of Meisner's students was Steve McQueen, "kind of an infamous rogue in New York." Coburn met him in a bar in the Village, introduced by a mutual friend.

"He was leaving, and I was just going in. He said, 'How you doing, man?' revved up his motorcycle, and went roaring off. A lot of people knew him, and a lot of people really detested him. A lot of people liked him because of his audaciousness, and everyone knew that he was either going to be a really interesting movie star or die trying."

Another great teacher was Harold Clurman, whose classes started at midnight to accommodate the actors who were appearing in productions. Attendees included George C. Scott, Colleen Dewhurst, Kim Stanley, Marlon Brando, and Luther Adler, Stella's brother. Joanne Linville also attended this class. It was here that she met her future husband, Mark Rydell, who would be another of Coburn's lifelong friends. Coburn and Rydell's first meeting was unusual, however.

"He came to take Joanne on a date. He rang the doorbell, and I came to the door in my underwear, since it was a very hot day. I introduced myself. 'Joanne said she'll be ready in a few minutes. We're friends from Compton. Come on in and have a drink.' I could see that he was ill at ease, wondering, *Who the fuck is this guy?* It was the first time I'd met Mark. He was an actor then, and I had seen his work on all the live television shows, which was quite big time. We waited, and I got dressed. About twenty minutes later, her usual late self, Joanne came in. Mark wanted to know who I was. Joanne came up with her line about all of us being 'poor little actors' just sharing a place."

Soon all three were hanging out at the local jazz clubs. Rydell recalls, "I mean, it was just amazing, you know. You could go listen to Miles Davis in one place and next door you hear Charlie Parker and then Art Tatum and Oscar Peterson. We loved it. New York in that period was so full of passion, so full of idealism."[21]

It was in this spirit that Coburn and some colleagues attempted to open their own theater company. He was on the board of directors, and for about six months from late 1957, all the money he made on commercials went into this venture called the American Theatre and Drama Society. It was to be housed in the Pyramid Theatre on St. Mark's Place in the Bowery.[22] Their idea was to create something like Luther Adler's now-defunct Group Theatre.

"We formed a failure, but nevertheless it was a try at a theater. Tried to be something like the Group Theatre but a little different. It was a place where [actors] could come to this theater to work out, you know, and have plays done and scenes done. All the graduating students, everyone who had studied with Stella, came to the opening night. Luther Adler, who gave the keynote address, said, 'What are you all doing here? They don't want you. They don't want you.' He told us the truth. It was wonderful."[23]

Unfortunately, the company collapsed, imploding under philosophical differences. Coburn withdrew himself and his money. "The guy that dreamed this up, who was the visionary of this thing, wanted to establish a standard for actors in order to join, like an engineer, you had to pass a certain kind of test of knowing all these things before you could join. He held the whole thing back. We opened it, and I closed it. I finally said, 'No, I can't take it anymore.' It was an absolute failure because of this guy. He wouldn't relent. He wouldn't say, 'Let's get people down here. We'll have improvisational theater.' [He'd say,] 'No, not until we get this thing down. We gotta have a charter. We gotta have all this bullshit.' He wanted to make it a kind of democratic thing.

"You can't have democracy in the theater. It's totally dictatorial. It's not democracy. You gotta have a leader. A guide. A director is what it's called, a producer. And everybody works around this. Everybody devotes their attention, time, and everything they have to whatever it is that they are doing. Sometimes it's a play; sometimes it's organizing an event of some kind. But you have to have these kinds of people. And they'll turn up. Somehow they always turn up. But not in our case!"

This was the same idealistic sensibility and work ethic that Coburn brought to his later work in films, an appreciation of the auteur's vision and a willingness to give everything he had to support it.

Spiritually he continued to devote attention to esoteric writers. He had read Khalil Gibran in junior college, without realizing that Gibran was a Sufi. He had learned of the Hindu swami Vivekananda during his time at City College—not from his classes but from a young lady friend. He was searching for a spiritual philosophy that was practical and accessible rather than merely a matter of faith.

"I was looking for a point of view. I was never religious. I could never cotton on to Christianity. The Bible is a doctrine that you can change any way you want to make it. It depends on how good you are at getting people to believe it and interpret it. That's why it's so cryptic. The Bible is probably the most cryptic piece of work that anybody has been able to gather together, and nobody knows how to read it. It doesn't *do* anything.

"People would say, 'Well you have to have faith.' I never really had faith. I wanted something that was doable, that I could take care of. In the Catholic religion, you have the greatest invention in the world, the confessional. It seemed weird to me. The control was left up to faith. That wasn't something I could do. The problem is all religions, with the exception of maybe

Buddhism, are based on belief systems and don't have anything to do with doing. There is a little something wrong with that, I think. Buddhists find out what it is like to live the life of an ascetic when they are about thirteen or fourteen, and they chant. I went to study Buddhism [at] a little place near Stella's studio, a little Buddhist temple. They would tell stories. The place was very small. I did that for a while."

Then some friends introduced him to the writings of George Gurdjieff and P. D. Ouspensky, who was the former's protégé. Gurdjieff's story enthralled Coburn, especially his twenty-one-year journey throughout Eastern Europe, the Middle East, and North Africa beginning in 1888. Gurdjieff studied the esoteric wisdom of as many traditional spiritual paths as he could find, including traditional ritualistic dances and movements, which he appropriated into his own movement designs. His writings reinterpreted the universal themes he found in all these ancient religions.

Gurdjieff devised diagrams to help his devotees understand his ideas, which he called "The Fourth Way." Coburn especially appreciated his "Food Diagram." At the bottom level is biological sustenance, food and drink for the physical body. This is followed by a series of steps leading to the "Food of Impressions," needed for the inner growth of the soul. Impressions—gathering them, offering them to audiences—was a repeated theme in Coburn's own rhetoric. He was always seeking new impressions.

Coburn also bought into the teachings that man is an automaton, and that all our feelings, thoughts, and deeds are merely mechanical, unconscious responses to stimuli. However, consciousness can be awoken by introspection.

The first Ouspensky book he read was *In Search of the Miraculous*. It was a revelation. It felt "like a cookbook," he says.

"It really turned me on because it was a technique you could do. It was a technique about how to become conscious. He called it 'the Work,' and it was the work on yourself, and I've been doing that ever since. I still have all the books because it works in you and you have to give it attention. The first thing you learn is that you can direct your attention, instead of having your attention taken from you by this, that, or the other things scattered around. You can direct your attention toward whatever it is you want, lock onto it, and receive the benefit of it. 'Life is only real when *I Am.*' This is something that has been working in me all along.

"When I became conscious that there was such a thing as consciousness, my aim was to become more conscious. To wake up. To wake out of this dream of whatever it is we're involved in and start paying attention to what life is. And if I'm not real, then life just continues on, and I'm in this dream state that can't take me anywhere. It might be a nightmare, sometimes a bad dream, or a very good dream. Nevertheless, it's just a dream. It's not real. To make it real, to be real, to be now and be who you are, not what you think you are, what somebody thinks you are, but really who you are. And you really get mixed up a lot. I do.

"If you are able to resolve what you are after, what your life aim is, your major aim, a lot of little aims come in along the way to boost it up, help it out, or take it away and distract you from going on with it. All of those things you have to deal with, but you deal with it by observing yourself. Don't forget to remember yourself. Gurdjieff talks about the many selves we have within us, and each one of them wants their time. Doing is being. Being is doing. In order to be and do at the same time and be aware of that and be in touch with it and remember to do it, that's the chore. That's the aim.

"It has to do with being able to remember your Self. Getting conscious. Getting more conscious to see things from many points of view without having to identify with any of them, or being able to identify with all of them. Seeing things as they are without having to like them or dislike them.

"One of my favorite phrases is from George Bernard Shaw: 'Forget about likes and dislikes. They are of no consequence. Do what must be done. This is not happiness, but it is greatness.' It has to do with objectivity."

Slowly Coburn was honing his craft with classes, commercials, and small parts on live TV series, especially with production company Studio One. He spent a season doing stock in Detroit in a play with Eva Gabor. He had a theater actor's sense of superiority, believing television at that time to be an inferior product but a useful means to an end—food and rent.

"We did a lot of live television back in the joint. Studio One mainly, because a lady casting director was a friend of Stella's, and she would come to class every once in a while, and see what was happening there, and she would give the ones who she thought were good gigs, so they could pay their way. Maybe it would be a walk-on, maybe just a line or two, or maybe just be an extra."

By 1958 television production was starting to move to the studios of Hollywood, and many of Coburn's friends were going back to Los Angeles. He packed up and joined the exodus returning west.

4

That's the Part I Want to Play

Well, I figured she knew how to do it.

—JAMES COBURN, 2002

In late 1958 Beverly Kelly was a pretty, dark-haired divorcée with a razor-sharp wit. She had beautiful, almond-shaped eyes, and she had traveled.

Born Beverly Ann Funkhouser in 1934, her grandparents, the Kellys (sometimes spelled Kelley) had traveled from Louisiana to Texas to Oklahoma in one failed farming venture after another. A few years earlier than the Harrison Coburns, they too fled the incipient Dust Bowl down Route 66, finally settling in Pomona, California. Beverly's free-spirited young mother, MaryAnn, worked as a fruit packer. She was on the first of what would ultimately be six marriages. Beverly's father, Jack Funkhouser, was a big, handsome man who resembled Robert Mitchum. He was from a large clan, and when his marriage came to an end, he had hoped that little Beverly would come to live with him. But she preferred to stay with her mother. He spanked her, something she would resent to the end of her days.

Beverly grew up in Pomona, maturing early. Records show she married a former Marine at the age of fifteen in July 1950. The couple honeymooned among the redwoods in Northern California. Perhaps her husband was suffering from post-traumatic stress disorder (PTSD), which was rarely acknowledged then. He turned out to have a temper and hit Beverly.

"I would not stand to be beaten, so I ran away," Beverly confided many years later.[1] She divorced him, then married another man who took her to Acapulco. There she secured another divorce, before she took up with a very much older man, whom she called "the General." As his mistress, Beverly was to sit quietly, beautifully dressed, and perfectly made up, and adorn the man's home—an objet d'art for the admiration of his guests.

Naturally, this quickly became boring for someone as alert and smart as Beverly. Soon she was having an affair with a young local man, which necessitated a swift escape when the pair was eventually caught. Beverly made her way to Las Vegas, where her poise and good looks attracted the attention of Leon Goldner, who also used the name Lee Grayson, a man vaguely connected with the Jewish mob in that town.

He taught Beverly how to be a casino shill, entertaining and distracting gamblers with her conversation, always under his watchful eye. They were married in 1956, and their daughter, Lisa, was born in early 1957. Goldner seems to have been a devoted father, enjoying taking snapshots of his toddler daughter, who strongly resembled his pretty wife. As might be expected for someone in his line, however, he was eventually arrested, convicted, and sent to prison for a long stay. Beverly again ended her marriage and returned to her mother's home in Pomona, somewhat more prosperous than when she'd left.

By late 1958 she was using her mother's maiden name and attending swanky Hollywood parties while little Lisa was home in Pomona, being babysat by her affectionate grandparents.

It was at one of these parties that a mutual friend introduced diminutive Beverly Kelly to tall, lanky, up-and-coming actor Jim Coburn. There was an immediate sizzle between them. They left the party together, and took off and drove to Joshua Tree, in the California high desert, where they spent all weekend under the stars, as she says, "smoking, drinking, and fucking."

Coburn was sincerely in love. Beverly's checkered past didn't bother him. He was attracted to her beauty *and* her sharp mind. They shared a deep interest in esoteric religions and Eastern and Middle Eastern art. He was pleased to share his knowledge, reading list, and ideas. In turn Beverly was a fun traveling companion, a playmate, and later an astute adviser about career matters. They were married in Tijuana, Mexico, in November 1959, and shortly after that Coburn legally adopted Lisa, saying, "Why not?" The couple moved into a little two-bedroom place on twisty St. Ives Drive, above Sunset Boulevard.

Professionally things were going well. In one of his early auditions in Los Angeles, Coburn had walked into the studio to be greeted with delight by none other than the episode's star, Eva Gabor, calling out, "Hello, darling!" It was *General Electric Theater*, an anthology show produced by Motor Club of America. He got the job.

Many years later he credited Hume Cronyn from that shoot as one of the people who helped him master acting for the screen. "Hume taught me an acting process for film in about two days. Learning to act is a technique all its own, but film technique is different. With a close-up, you have to use this much energy, with a full shot this much. He taught me a lot of little things, simple mechanical techniques I didn't know anything about."[2]

Those two days with Hume were on that same May 1958 episode of *General Electric Theater*, with Eva Gabor. Cronyn played the title role of the episode called "Ah There, Beau Brummel."

From then on, Coburn was extremely busy as a character actor playing guest roles in TV series, usually the villain, primarily in the ubiquitous and highly popular westerns, as well as police procedurals, in the late fifties to early sixties. He performed seventy-seven guest roles between 1959 and 1963, plus had starring roles in two admittedly short-lived series, for a total of ninety-four appearances in half-hour episodes. Additionally, in the same period, he worked on five feature films and took the occasional recreation trip to New York to visit Sid Shaw and Birdland.

In between gigs, until the early sixties, he continued to drop in to Jeff Corey's Professional Actors Workshop classes, there meeting a whole new generation of younger actors, including people like Sally Kellerman and Jack Nicholson.

Many of the big movie stars of the era got their start in television. It was a common practice in those days for character actors to appear more than once in the same series, playing different roles. Coburn appeared in *Wanted:*

Dead or Alive three times as different heavies between 1959 and 1960. The show's star was Steve McQueen.

"The first thing he asked me was 'Do you want to smoke a joint?' I said, 'Sure, why not?' Everybody at that time, making all those westerns, we were all stoned most of the time. Acting in those things was fun. If you were stoned, your imagination took over. We weren't sloppy. We did not have really strong grass back then. It still gave you a buzz and made you feel good, and made you hungry. We ate a lot of sweets. That was Steve's downfall. He had a sweet tooth.

"[One day] we said we'd go somewhere for lunch together. He had been chatting up this chick, one of the extras, who was kind of cute. When I went over to his dressing room and knocked on his door, he says, 'Yeah?' I say, 'It's Coburn, man.' He says, 'Yeah, well listen, man. Let's do that tomorrow. I'm kind of busy right now.' He was in there schtupping this extra. That was one of his favorite things to do in the afternoon. His wife, Neile, called him a 'male nymphomaniac.' He was kind of like that."[3]

Off the set, newlywed Coburn grabbed the opportunity to be part of a social experiment. In 1954 Dr. Oscar Janiger, a psychiatrist researching at the University of California, Irvine, began a long-term study of the effects of LSD. It was a relatively new psychotropic chemical that many psychiatrists believed could be useful in treating various mental illnesses. Janiger was interested in the effect on healthy people, particularly on their creativity. Over the next few years, he administered controlled amounts of the substance (based on body weight) to selected volunteers in many professions, including creative and performing arts. It has been noted that Dr. Janiger was inundated with more volunteers than he could use, despite charging participants around thirty dollars for each dose.

Coburn was one of the people accepted into the study. His first LSD trip was on December 10, 1959. Prior to starting, everyone filled out paperwork stating their reasons for participating. Coburn recalls that he wrote, "To gauge present consciousness (where I am to where I can possibly go)."

"Oscar was an osteopath. He got this government grant to do experiments with LSD, to see what was really happening. He would charge thirty dollars for the Sandoz pills, and you would go to his office in Hancock Park, you would drop the pills, and then you would go have a little bite to eat, because you had fasted the night before. You didn't have any coffee. And then you would come back. . . . I had taken [peyote] a few times already. This was a little stronger. It lacked the spirituality—the realness of peyote. It did not have the purity of peyote. It was a very interesting trip. I had a wonderful time. In a place where you think there was nothing in there, under the influence of acid, your consciousness raises to such a degree, you can find joy in the simplest thing. It was great."

The participants stayed in a quiet room at the doctor's Hancock Park office. They were supplied with paper, writing implements, and art materials, and encouraged to record their impressions of the experience. Nurses observed closely, standing by in case of any problems but not guiding or interfering.

"There was this little hand mirror, about three inches in diameter. It was just on the table, and I was smoking a cigarette, and the ashes kept falling down, so I put the mirror down and watched the ashes fall on the mirror. Then I picked the mirror up, and I could see this ancient, prehistoric land, bubbles. As I held it close to my eye, I saw this pterodactyl looking right back at me. Hooo, wow! 'Hi there.' What a stunning impression that was. Because the acid is consciousness provoking, you are very aware of what is happening, and you never forget it.

"It is said that the more conscious you are, the more you remember. I started Ouspensky back in New York. Because I had been doing Ouspensky work, it gave me a standard to look for, a way to direct my attention toward something. One thing I had learned to do was to direct my attention. Whew, thank God for him.

"There were other people in this room, doing whatever came into your mind. Nobody was guiding or helping. Just you. After you came down, you would write a little something and give it to Dr. Janiger. He had you do a thing with cards, a mind-reading kind of thing. Then all of his research was sent back to the university.

"My wife came to pick me up afterward, and we got in the car and drove through Hancock Park. I saw each of these houses as characters—each of them had a characteristic of its own. You could see the old man who had built the house, with dark and brown. All of them had characters. It was wonderful. I've never forgotten that, and I still see those things when I go over there. I repeated the trip a couple of times, but not with [Janiger]."

A few years later, Coburn caused a stir when he admitted to appreciating LSD when on *The Tonight Show Starring Johnny Carson*. It affected Lisa's social life when some of her friends' parents refused to let them come over anymore. Years later still, he remembers the experiment fondly and openly when interviewed in *LA Weekly*, "It was phenomenal. . . . I loved it. LSD really woke me up to seeing the world with a depth of objectivity. Even though it was a subjective experience, it opened your mind to seeing things in new ways, in a new depth."[4]

Meanwhile Coburn was cast in his first feature film, a western that shot in one week starring Randolph Scott for Ranown Pictures. He portrayed "Wid, a simpleminded sort," Pernell Roberts's sidekick. "I got a job with [director] Budd Boetticher, who was doing his CinemaScope film called *Ride Lonesome*. A bunch of stunt men, I met a lot of them. Budd was a strange cat but a good director."[5]

Coburn may not have realized how fortunate he was to be in a Randolph Scott picture. Boetticher recalls that actor's generosity: "I don't think there was ever a finer gentleman in the picture business than Randolph Scott. . . . Randy would say, 'I sure like that young fellow,' like James Coburn, 'Let's give him more lyrics.'"[6] Boetticher also recognized the Coburn charm early on. The original plan was for his and Roberts's characters to be killed at the end of the movie, but Boetticher persuaded the studio head, Sam Briskin, that "people are going to love them" and to let them live.

Coburn's second feature film was in a minor villain role in *Face of a Fugitive* (1959), a now nearly forgotten western vehicle for veteran actor Fred MacMurray. It also starred Buzz Henry, who would become another of Coburn's close friends, cast as a henchman. Then it was back to TV shows for Coburn. "My rate went up from $750 to $850 a week."[7]

Not long after his last appearance on *Wanted: Dead or Alive*, he ran into Robert Vaughn coming out of a market. Vaughn had just been cast in an upcoming western feature film, *The Magnificent Seven*, being directed by John Sturges. It was to be a remake of Kurosawa's *Seven Samurai*, about seven gunslingers hired to save a village from banditos, who each have personal reasons to risk their own lives. Vaughn had mentioned Jim Coburn to Sturges, and the director had asked him to have Coburn call in, but quickly, because an actors' strike was imminent. In the event of a strike, only projects with completed casts could continue into principal photography, which is the filming of the script with the actors and main crew, called first unit, as compared to getting shots of exterior locations or vistas, typically done by the second unit. Vaughn had been looking for Coburn for some days.

At the same time, producer Walter Mirisch was considering who might fill the need for cowboys. Coburn had worked for his company on the recent shoot for a series called *Wichita Town*: "The first segment was an episode entitled 'The Night the Cowboys Roared,' in which James Coburn played the heavy. This was the first time I'd met Jim, and he was so good in the show that I remembered him later when we were casting *The Magnificent Seven*."[8]

Either way, the fates were moving for the excited actor, who immediately directed his agent to get him an appointment. With two recommendations, Sturges was keen to meet this guy.

"There's a character I wanted to play in that movie, and I hope it's not cast. I'd done a couple of things for the Mirisch Company, and they liked me. I met John. He had these big thick glasses on. He said, 'Okay, Jim, you got a part in the show, at the railhead. But there's also one of the seven [that] hasn't been cast yet, but I won't know about that until about three in the afternoon because they're arguing about billing and money and stuff like that.' And I said, 'What part is that?' And he said, 'Britt. The man with a knife.' And I said, 'Is that the character who was the greatest swordsman?' And he says, 'Yeah, that's right.' And I said, 'That's the part I want to play, John. I want to play that character.' And he says, 'Well if these guys haven't come to any conclusion by three, you've got the part.'

"I went home feeling so excited and told Beverly, 'I've got the opportunity to play, Jesus, I might get to play—' And the phone rang. It was John saying, 'Come on over and pick up your knives.' I just about went through the roof."[9]

Of all seven characters, it was with the laconic swordsman that Coburn most empathized. He'd felt a deep attraction to the character ever since he dragged his friends to screenings of *Seven Samurai* in New York. Britt only had eleven lines in the movie, but he had presence. This was a perfect example of Coburn's philosophy of acting—of letting go of his own ego and allowing the character to come to the fore. Other actors might have turned down the role because it had so few lines, but Jim Coburn saw that silence as the essence of the character.

"My character was so filled with action. He was Mr. Action, or asleep. I didn't have anything to say, so if I was in the background, I'd sleep. He was very, very loose. He'd be totally relaxed, then pop into action. He didn't waste any time messing around. That was my idea. There wasn't anything else to do. When it was necessary for me to do something, they'd wake me up and I'd do it, then go back to sleep. That was the nature of the character. He practiced his craft a lot, and he did what was necessary to do and nothing else beyond that. He was like a samurai, and his craft was killing. Otherwise, what good is a gunfighter unless you're killing somebody or shooting somebody?

"That was one of the great things about that character—he was a realist and didn't have anything to do with any of the bullshit. He went ahead and did what must be done. And that was the joy of him because he was so pure, so slick, so clean. He was a knife."

Coburn worked with stuntman Richard Farnsworth to learn how to become adept at the unusual fast-draw throw Britt used. "We had to invent the underhand throw. I got so I could stick a knife in a board anywhere, anytime—if it was seven feet away. The underhanded way was tough, but we made it look real. On film it looked real."

This was the first time Coburn got to travel abroad for a shoot. The production was shooting for twelve weeks, mostly in Tepoztlán and Cuernavaca in Morelos, about fifty miles south of Mexico City. The locale has been appreciated for several hundred years for its mild climate. The shoot was physically comfortable. Of course it was more comfortable for the main stars, who had air-conditioned trailers, while the rest of the seven managed with grass huts as dressing rooms. "The cast and crew stayed at the Hotel

Jacarandas, described by Vaughn as a 'glorified motel,'" while the production rented Yul Brynner a comfortable villa.[10]

"Yul Brynner was recognized. He was the star. Consequently, everyone was riding on his back. But they didn't know what kind of film they had. John Sturges was a wonderful director. Yul was the king. He had a gofer that would travel with him all the time. When he would snap his fingers, they would put a Gauloises in his hand. I liked him. We had a lot of fun together, then and thereafter, because he was such a liar, but such a good one.

"He lied about everything. Where he was from. What he did. How he got to where he was. You never found out the truth of how his life really was. It was so complicated. He complicated everything. He would intersperse incidents of reality into the stories he made up, so it had a touch of reality, so no one could doubt it. Why doubt it anyway? It was a good story. I don't think he gave a shit if anyone believed him—he just like telling them, all very good stories. But he was the king, and he acted like the king."[11]

There was ongoing tension between Yul Brynner and Steve McQueen, and between Brynner and villain Eli Wallach. It all started when Sturges and the cast went to Mexico City to watch the rushes of the previous week, which they did most Saturdays. Rushes are the shot scenes printed quickly from the developed negative but not color corrected. The idea is that the director can see and hear how the performances, rough edits of scenes, and cinematography are working in time to reshoot or make changes before moving on to another set. It also helps to discern if more shots are needed that would help the edit. When at a distant location, the film negative was often flown express to Los Angeles weekly, and then the rushes returned by the same plane to be projected for evaluation.

Wallach, then primarily a theater actor, had worked hard to develop his character. He had gold teeth made and bought red silk shirts and an oversized sombrero to display the wealth the bandit leader had accumulated from oppressing the farmers. Coburn recalled that Wallach described his character as "a dandy spendthrift." His idea was that the menace would be very subtle.

"Eli—now that was an actor. He was great. He took his image from Khrushchev, back from the time he pounded his shoe heel on the table, and he used that image for his character. He made the opening of the film when he rides to the village, with his Mexican sombrero and forty banditos—he rides into it like he owned the place, like he's the master returning from the hunt, like Khrushchev making a big splash in America. People loved Khrushchev. They took him to the cancan.

"He was very benevolent, calling everybody by their first names, saluting everyone. He got off his horse and went over to Carol who ran the cantina, not badass at all, just smooth. 'How much wheat do we have today? How much grain did we make this year?' They were going to pick up their winter supplies, and they did this every year, but they took what they wanted, which was a bit more than anyone wanted to give them, but nevertheless they took it and rode off, and that was the opening of the film.

"[Ferris Webster, the editor] put together this beautiful scene, which worked really well. He was so pleased. The opening made it really happen. Afterward, Yul said, 'We'll have to shoot it again.' And there was quiet, just absolute silence in the room.

"And John said, 'What do you mean, Yul? I think it was fantastic. Everybody thinks it's wonderful. What's wrong with it?' Yul answered, 'He doesn't give me anything to play against. He's Mr. Nice Guy.' Yul didn't know how to play it or build on that, or he didn't want to or whatever.

"So it became a great feud between Eli and Yul, all of us really, because we all appreciated what Eli had done and really hated the idea that someone could say, 'You have to shoot it again because it doesn't give me anything to play against.' Each one of us would have found something to play. It wasn't that fucking difficult. So immediately, there was an animosity built up around that particular thing. But that was the only thing. Otherwise Yul was very congenial, and he was the king. But he was that kind of slimy king sometimes."

John Sturges was "this old-time moviemaker" because "in John's mind, if your star wants something, you give it to him. That's the way it was done from the time movies began, and John was going to give it to him." They shot the opening again, "with Eli Wallach snarling a bit."

Meanwhile McQueen enjoyed upstaging Brynner by playing with his hat in the background or doing fancy gunslinging. Reportedly, Brynner hired someone just to keep count of the number of times McQueen touched his hat during his, Brynner's, speeches. Brynner would stand on a mound of dirt to look taller than McQueen, a mound that McQueen would surreptitiously kick and diminish between takes.

"Steve, in all of this, I guess he was always paranoid about anybody who was in a film with him, because he wanted to be in the picture by himself. He'd always try to get to people he was playing opposite so they would not look better than he did. He'd teach people how to do things, but he would not teach them how to do it well. With Brynner, it didn't matter one way or the other, because Yul would just pin people with his big round eyes, and it didn't matter whether he could swing the gun around, or twist it, or do any of the fancy crap that Steve liked to do. Steve liked to show off a lot with that stuff."

Eli Wallach, who gallantly never mentions the reshoot in his biography, did note that Sturges appreciated the tension that the silent competition between his two stars gave to their scenes and "never chastised his actors for it."[12] According to the director's biographer, Glenn Lovell, his feelings were stronger. "Sturges was excited by how each actor fought for his turf" and savored the memory, saying, "Oh, it was a big rivalry—they were at it day and night."[13]

Occasionally during the shoot, Coburn and McQueen would get some grass and get stoned in the afternoon. One day they were setting up to film part of the final shoot-out. McQueen's character "had been shot in the leg, wearing these chaps, and there was blood coming out of it—he was dripping around."[14] The pair thought they had plenty of time and went to sit in McQueen's air-conditioned trailer in comfort.

"Steve and I smoked a joint. All of a sudden someone says, 'Okay, Steve, we're ready.' So we jumped out of the trailer and walked over. I was going to watch the scene. It was after the major fight and everyone was coming out of different places to see what had happened. I had been killed, and I was down there lying on the floor. Steve comes out of the building where he had been shot and is kind of standing there, and then he starts to make a move, and they say, 'Cut, cut! Steve, would you take your shades off?' And

I mean, they had to reset the whole scene, which took about an hour to set up. He was inside a place. Nobody noticed [his sunglasses] until then. There was nobody else there. That broke me up."

Beverly joined her husband on the shoot. She drove down from Los Angeles in their new brown Jaguar 3.4 sedan, which was duly admired by the cast, including Robert Vaughn. Later that night, he joined the Coburns, dining late at the fanciest restaurant in town, "the only place in town where you wouldn't get the runs," according to Vaughn.[15]

After the meal, Vaughn was horrified when the parking valet crashed the car while returning it. "The hood went up, smoke came out, flames came out. The driver fell into the street. I stood there absolutely stricken just looking at this car. I looked at Jim, he looked at me, he looked at his watch and said, 'Man, we are never gonna get a cab this late.'"

The truth was, Coburn hated that car. It had already been in a fender bender at home, even before Beverly had set off for Mexico. After the valet incident, he had it repaired so that he and Beverly could drive it home at the end of the shoot. But that was not the end of the brown Jag misadventures.

It had been a long day driving toward the coast near Los Mochis. "All of a sudden, the road just ended; the cement ended. For about forty yards, it was like the road had been washed away. Crash, boom—[we drove across] onto the other side. My tailpipe section was dragging. I couldn't figure out what to do. We were in the middle of nowhere.

"Along came this man, I'll never forget him. Mr. Bird had a pickup loaded with about five guys. 'Looks like you're having a little trouble here. Is there any way I can help you out?'

"I explained my problem. He called one of the guys over, who cut out a length of barbed wire, got under the car, and wired the whole tailpipe section up into the thing. 'Now that should get you to a little motel about forty miles down the road,' he says. 'Don't drink the water. Don't even look at the water, but you can stay there overnight, and then in the morning, drive into this little town and there's a mechanic there. Tell him Mr. Bird said you'll fix the car for me.'

"We arrive at this motel, and there is this one big heavy light shining down on millions of cockroaches. In order to get our little cabin, we had to walk across all these cockroaches, and I had sandals on. The proprietor was a little upset at having to take care of us so late in the evening, so he just gave us the key and pointed. We turned on the faucet, and the water that came out was all green, totally algae. Fortunately, we had some bottled water and beer, so we had something to drink anyway. We finally got into bed, which was okay. It wasn't filthy. The sheets were clean.

"We got up really early in the morning, paid for our room—the cockroaches were all gone by that time—drove into this little town. We went to the little garage, told the man what Mr. Bird had said. Twenty minutes later he fixed it, and another problem the car had. It cost about eight pesos. I gave him a twenty-dollar bill, and he about fell through the floor. That was the most money he had seen in a long time. We finally made it to LA. 'Next time, Beverly, we fly.'

"So that New Year's Eve, driving home from a party, in front of the Pantages Theatre, late, two or three a.m., I stopped at a signal. I hear this screech, then *blaff!* and someone plows into the brown Jaguar. That Jaguar was totally destroyed. All I could say was, 'Thank God!' Jesus, I hated that car, and for good reason, you could see."[16]

The Magnificent Seven initially opened in October 1960 with little promotion. It looked like the picture would fade into relative obscurity. However, when it opened in Europe in February 1961, it did very well. It was suddenly a big hit, especially in Germany, England, France, and Spain, where Coburn received great reviews, which reflected back in good publicity and an uptick in attendance back home. It soon made back its two million–dollar budget, and then some, spawning some less impressive sequels. The film received an Oscar nomination for Elmer Bernstein's score and a Golden Globe nomination for Robert Vaughn as Best Newcomer. It has since gone on to be regarded as one of the great classics of the western genre and is still popular. It has had a couple of rereleases over the years, in France and Japan. And the story was reimagined yet again in 2016 with a new cast.

After filming *The Magnificent Seven*, Coburn went back to the grind of TV. He continued to be an in-demand guest star on lightweight dramas, always trying to rise above the material with his acting. "I tried to justify the character. Here's the baddest cat in the West, faster than anybody, and he runs up against a guy, and he gets defeated right at the end. How do you justify that? You have to justify it somehow. So I'd always give him a flaw of some kind. A twitch or something, or maybe fading eyesight, or some giveaway that most people would recognize. It was always cut out. Whatever it was, was cut out. The editors didn't give a shit. We had a half hour to get it over with. It was frustrating. It used to piss me off, but I got over it. I did my job. It was there. If you don't want to use it, that's not my fault."

Then he was hired as the hero's nemesis—"a gambler of reptilian repute"—in a period adventure series about the Alaskan gold rush. The head writer of *Klondike* was a young, up-and-coming writer—Sam Peckinpah. In the pilot episode, he introduced Jefferson Durain, Coburn's character, playing a high-stakes poker game.

As described in the script, "Jeff is a quiet-spoken man of enormous charm. Cat-moving, wiry, a Southerner of apparent culture, a fine sense of humor, and a profitable understanding of the illness affecting so many of his fellow men: the constant desire to get something for nothing. While a born gambler and superb bunko artist, Jeff is not a bad man as bad men go. He has no more sense of right and wrong than a hungry tomcat, but he does have an understanding of human frailty and very soft spot for the helpless, the old and innocent. As long as they are poor. Very poor. In some ways he is a humanitarian, but always with a heart for other people's gold. A charming 14-carat thief with a strong appreciation for life in general, human nature in particular, and the very human and very lovely girl now seated beside him."[17]

This was the kind of layered, complex, character-driven writing that inspired the ongoing artistic collaboration and friendship with Peckinpah that defined much of Coburn's working life. The series was written with a developing through-line story as well as weekly self-contained adventures, which make the scripts feel very contemporary. Peckinpah wrote at least five episodes alone and collaborated with or supervised the writers on the rest.

He gave Jeff Durain some great one-liners too, like "It's not the principle—it's the money."

Eventually *Klondike* was axed in its second season after poor ratings, but in a much-hyped move, the two stars of the show immediately segued into a contemporary buddy-comedy series as the midseason replacement with the same sponsor. In those days the sponsors paid the production costs rather than merely buying airtime for commercials, which gave them a great deal of pull regarding stars and content. They wanted to take advantage of the evident chemistry between the two stars.

Acapulco was fluff, with plenty of women in bikinis to add a visual appeal that the wintry *Klondike* lacked. Although it was not renewed after its first short run, the series was useful for Coburn's career in that it gave people the opportunity to see him as a lighthearted hero with a much greater range.

Not long after *Acapulco* ended, in May 1961, Beverly gave birth to the couple's only son, James Harrison Coburn IV. At the time the family was living on Warbler Place in a little district called the Bird Streets in the West Hollywood hills, right above the Sunset Strip.[18] Soon they wanted to own their home. Coburn took his earnings from his next few pictures and purchased a nice four-bedroom, two-bath 1936 home on Outpost Drive in the hills overlooking the Hollywood Bowl. Very private from the street, the house was built around a shaded inner courtyard filled with plants and overlooked by a wooded hillside. French doors linked the living areas through the garden.

The last time this house had been renovated was in 1944, some sixteen years earlier. So the Coburns invited Beverly's dear friend, interior decorator Eddie Tirella to redesign the little place as a showcase for the beginning of their Oriental antiques and fine art collection. "He tore it apart and put it together again. He did a wonderful job. He would put out great French bouquets with lots of flowers. Eddie was a gay guy. He was an Italian so he made great spaghetti, and he loved to sing."[19] Tirella went on to design for other stars, including singer Peggy Lee, before the 1966 car wreck that ended his life.[20]

The Coburns enjoyed gathering eclectic groups of artists, writers, actors, musicians, and art dealers for small parties at home. One of those friends was Edmund Kara, a fashion-designer-turned-sculptor, who would soon find fame as the creator of the Elizabeth Taylor sculpture in the movie *The Sandpiper* (1965). Kara was Tirella's partner at the time, sharing a home in West Hollywood along with a giant poodle that Lisa Coburn remembers fondly. Kara hand-carved a high wooden bed for the Coburns' master bedroom and helped with the decorating.

Kara had in common with the Coburns a fascination with the East, especially India. As a teenager, he had studied at New Jersey Arts High School. "We got a very well-rounded education—all of the usual subjects in relation to art."[21] This educational philosophy made a strong impression on Coburn, who agreed with the idea that students would gain greater understanding of any society's culture and history through the study of its art. Years later he expressed the same idea whenever the conversation turned to education. "I was bored by history [in school] because it was all about crime. But if you taught history from the point of view of art, you'd have a hell of a lot more people be interested in it. And it would probably be far more true than the history of crime."[22]

The presence of a new baby in the house made little dent in Coburn's busy work schedule. He was uncomfortable around babies and young children, not only without any knowledge of child development but also without any desire to explore it. "I certainly was not cut out to be a parent. I said it to every woman I was ever with since Beverly that I didn't want children. I didn't know what kind of parent I would be, and I know I was a terrible parent when Jimmy was around. The truth is I didn't care [what they did]. I just thought, *Do what you want to do. Just don't get caught.* I don't know if I ever told them that, but that's how I felt. I gave them hugs and kisses and all that kind of stuff. I loved to get out of the house and go on location and be involved with something else rather than the familial stuff. I was out of the house as much as I could possibly be."

He had the opportunity to spend some time out of the house when he was cast in the Steve McQueen World War II movie *Hell Is for Heroes* (1962). This was shot in the towns of Cottonwood and Redding in Northern California, where the rolling farmland and sparse woods doubled for the war-torn French countryside. Despite the Sacramento River, which runs through the center of town, the climate this far inland is typically hot and dry. The mountains to the west block any chance of sea breezes reaching the interior.

That year, 1961, the temperatures during the late summertime days soared as high as 117 degrees with such regularity that many scenes originally planned for daylight were changed to night shoots. Happily, this added a film noir atmosphere of menace and isolation.

The film was promoted as a true story of bravery and sacrifice, with what was purported to be gritty realism based on actual events on "Murder Hill," where a small squad held a hill against the enemy by the daring ploy of pretending there was a whole company encamped there. It was mostly noted as the feature-film debut of comedian Bob Newhart and for Steve McQueen's generally irascible behavior. The shoot was troubled by creative conflicts. It is never a good sign when a new writer and new director come on board mid-production. Coburn's character, the mechanic or tinkerer of the squad, was signposted as brainy by having him wear spectacles.

Bob Newhart, in his autobiography, noted that Steve McQueen distanced himself from most of the cast, intentionally echoing his character's relationship with the squad. Like several of the cast, Newhart himself begged to be killed off early but was denied.[23] Many contemporary critics dislike the phone call scenes that were a nod to Newhart's signature comedy routine, although there is a weariness to his delivery that makes the ruse plausible in context.

Eventually, due to cost overruns, the studio refused to pay for more film stock, leading the production to run out before finishing the planned finale. Director Don Siegel made the best of the footage he had, creating the abrupt, ambiguous yet effective end of the story in the middle of the action, with "no feeling of positive affirmation."[24] It has since been hotly debated among film fans. That and McQueen's brooding, slightly wild-eyed characterization are the main reasons for the film's enduring cult popularity.

Coburn had nothing much to say about *Hell Is for Heroes*. He showed up and did his job, staying out of the acrimony between some of the cast members.[25] He brought a subtle depth to his character, Corporal Henshaw, particularly in his interactions with McQueen's character, Reese. Under proper regulations, Henshaw would have been next in the chain of command, outranking Private Reese. But the force of Reese's personality overcame the weaker man. Coburn has a particularly wonderful silent moment of inner debate and capitulation in the scene just prior to their foray into the minefield.

The next time Coburn had the opportunity to work with his friend Steve McQueen, it would be on a bona fide summer blockbuster, one of the most beloved and enjoyable war movies of all time.

However, before that happened, it was once again back to TV and, in an unusual turn, Coburn's last professional theater appearance. He starred as the Communist in Edna St. Vincent Millay's *Conversation at Midnight* at the Coronet Theatre, opening in November 1961. The play had received staged readings before, but this was the world premiere of a full production. Coburn got good reviews for his six-week run, including from David Bongard of the *Los Angeles Herald-Express*, who wrote, "James Coburn is outstanding. His keying makes the role come alive with tremendous conviction, which causes a bit of sadness in view of his convictions. We are made to want better things for him."[26]

The play was brand new when Coburn joined the production. "Edna had just finished the play and was overwhelmed with the joy of just finishing what I think is a minor masterpiece. Just great fun. We went to her home in upstate New York to rehearse it. We became friends.

"We opened at the Coronet Theatre. Halfway through the play, the kid who was playing the advertising executive was supposed to light a cigarette and sit at the edge of the black wings. [The first night] the spark of the cigarette hit this black stuff, and it went straight up to the ceiling and burst into flames. The whole audience saw it, thinking it was some kind of trick. We announced that everyone should get out of the theater immediately because we have a fire backstage. The material was supposed to be flameproof—black duvateen on a board. Out the doors everybody went. We had coffee and sandwiches out there. We waited for the fire company to put the fire out. When everybody came back in, [the director] Bob Kiss got up and told the story of Edna St. Vincent Millay.

"After finishing the manuscript, which was a long poem, with every character having a different way of expressing themselves, she went to Florida, put down her suitcase, took out her clothes, the manuscript, left everything on the bed, and put on her bathing suit, went for a swim. Jumped in the water and was swimming around out in the sea, looked back, and saw the hotel on fire. Everything burned to the ground.

"All she had left was a bathing suit. Friends took her in, and she went back to New York and rewrote the entire play by memory. She was extraordinary. The irony was that the first night of the first staging, the theater went up in flames. It worked really well. I was pleased to be in it. In fact, it was a joy."[27]

He continued to be extremely busy with TV gigs at the same time. Sometimes he had to race from the set on one of the filming ranches in Valencia or North Hollywood to the theater in Beverly Grove, just east of Beverly Hills. "We were working four nights a week. I was always pleased when I didn't have to get up early in the morning to play some stupid thing on television, some bad guy. Sometimes I would be working right down to the wire, cutting it to the nitty-gritty before that eight o'clock curtain. I'd always show up, and sure enough I had to go on. We all had understudies—we were all working actors. The studios tried to make provisions for you to get to the theater on time, but sometimes things just didn't work out that way. I was always really on the edge."

Luckily he never missed a performance. At the end of the run, he considered joining the Broadway production, but the movies got in the way.

Hell Is for Heroes was in the theaters when John Sturges called. As Coburn later retold, Sturges said he was "going to make this movie with Steve, and Bronson, German actors, and English actors, Richard Attenborough's going to play X. I was supposed to play the Australian guy. John sent me the script, and I said, 'Sure. When do we go?'" He traveled to Germany to film *The Great Escape* over the summer of 1962.

Glenn Lovell in his book *Escape Artist* describes how the production team had come out in May to scout locations, attracted by German film incentives. When rain and early spring snows delayed the exterior shoot, the interiors were shot in studios in Munich. Nearby University of Munich, "with its English-speaking exchange students, was a handy source for extras."[28]

The camp was created in a stretch of forest in Bavaria. For permission to clear the area for the camp, the company would be required to replant double the number of trees taken out for the shoot. Nor were the removed trees to be wasted but were instead to be offered to locals for replanting. Sturges notes that not everyone was pleased with the arrangement, recalling "one proprietary forest ranger" watching with some enmity. "We took out ads, and hundreds of people showed up to take the trees that had been dug up and bundled in burlap. And we did replant after we built the set. But that one guy never forgave us, because they had lost a year's growth. He spied on us throughout the shoot, cursing and shaking his fist from the tree line."

The movie was based on the true event of an Allied POW mass breakout during World War II. With one of the original tunnel kings, Wally Floody, on board as adviser, the attention to realistic detail was extraordinary. You know it feels real when your adviser reports having nightmares. Most of the events in the script, such as the escape attempts in the logging truck and the potato distillery, had actually occurred. The dirt problems faced by the diggers were also historically accurate, as were the solutions they devised.

Many of the cast called on their own memories of military service, including James Garner who was a scrounger for his Marine company during the Korean War. David McCallum was a lieutenant in the British forces in postwar Africa. RAF flying officer, Donald Pleasance had spent time imprisoned in a Luftwaffe-run POW camp during World War II, where he reported being tortured.

The company met in Munich before principal photography. "We had a big preproduction party on one of the soundstages, and we were all meeting each other, the Scotsmen, the Irishmen, the Englishmen, the German actors. We had a great cast, a wonderful cast.

"Charlie Bronson is standing with these little German girls. He was drinking a bourbon, and he asks them, 'Why don't you shave under your arms?

Why don't you do that?' And they had never been asked that before. Otherwise they were quite beautiful chicks, and all a little embarrassed about Charlie even asking that. That was the first thing he said. Charlie stole the show with that question. But it was weird. 'Hell, Charlie, that is the culture here.' He didn't care."[29]

The shoot was planned for twelve to fourteen weeks, meaning there were long stretches when various actors would not be needed. After the grueling pace of the last few months, it felt like a vacation, especially once Beverly and little Lisa arrived for a visit. (Jimmy stayed home with the nanny.) Coburn and Beverly spent much of his free time tooling around Europe. "It was a good thing, because I got to travel all over Germany, Switzerland, Austria, France. Every night we'd check in with the first assistant director, Jack Reddish." Reddish would give the actors notice of when they were due back on the set.

Beverly especially loved Zurich, "a great city—all of Switzerland is marvelous," while she found nothing to like in Germany, describing the food as "a huge bore" and the people "unspeakable."[30] However, Coburn's imagination was captured by some of the fairy-tale castles built by Ludwig II in the 1870s and 1880s near their location, not least because Ludwig was a patron of the arts and music.

"The things King Ludwig built have lasted. He gave [composer Richard] Wagner such a big lift, made great halls for him to play in, a beautiful place on a lake. It looked like Versailles. He fashioned himself as a guy who took care of the artists and gave the artists, architects, musicians, dancers, sculptors an opportunity to work their number, which I think is probably far better than building a lot of fucking guns, ships, and bombers that everybody else chooses to do with their money. And they called him mad!"[31]

On the set, problems arose with Steve McQueen, almost from the start. "It was a really congenial group. Everyone was really together, except for Steve. Steve was unhappy. He didn't like his role, and he wanted to be written so that he was all alone. And then when you see the movie, you see what happened. He was always alone. The only friend that he gets is little Ives, the Scotsman."

McQueen, who had yet to shoot anything, stormed off when he saw dailies that included James Garner in his costume, an attractive white turtleneck. He threatened to leave altogether. This led Sturges to consider rewriting the script to focus on Garner's character as the lead. Garner himself felt this would never work, since he appreciated the ensemble nature of the production. He and Coburn invited McQueen to come out to Garner's rented house in Munich, and they somehow persuaded him to stay with the picture. Garner notes in his memoir that he "would have been happy to give Steve the turtleneck" if that is what it took.[32] That all three men shared an affection for marijuana may or may not have factored into the discussion.

Returning to set, McQueen worked with two top writers brought in from LA to develop his character, give him a heroic path, and add in the motorcycle sequences for the climax of the film. These turned out to be some of the most memorable scenes. "Strangely enough, it is really the thing that made the movie, and made all these people want to go see the movie again and again, Steve McQueen jumping the fence, which *he* never did."[33] McQueen's wife, Neile, devised the cropped sweatshirt costume and encouraged him to keep the baseball and glove props, while his friend Bud Ekins brought over two converted Triumph motorcycles from the United States and performed the final stunt.

McQueen had several brushes with local police due to his speedy driving. The set was often besieged by fans of *The Magnificent Seven* who were keen to catch a glimpse of McQueen, Bronson, and Coburn. That movie had been a huge hit in Europe only the year before. "We were all big heroes over there. We were all famous movie actors, which was kind of nice. It was the first time I'd seen [*The Magnificent Seven*] all together, in Germany. All the voices had been dubbed. I probably could have learned the seven lines I had in the fucking movie in German, and they wouldn't have had to dub it, but that was the way it was."

Meanwhile during filming, Bronson fell in love with Jill Ireland, who was married to David McCallum at the time, and with him in Germany for the shoot. Ireland was admitted to the hospital in Munich for a sudden miscarriage, while McCallum happened to be back in London for a few days doing postproduction work on *Freud* (1962). She had almost died. "Charlie started taking care of her. He was with her night and day, every place we went. He couldn't stay away from her. David was so happy that there was somebody who cared and would take care of her while he was working, and he always thanked Charlie for that. They just grew together. By the time the movie was over and everyone went back to California, [Charlie and Jill] moved in together in Bel Air and [eventually] got married—but they all remained friends. [Charlie and Jill] had a beautiful relationship for a long time until Jill Ireland passed away in 1990.

"Charlie was a little bit older than all of us. Hell of a guy. You can't not like Charlie Bronson. . . . He had a great sense of humor, very funny guy, just that no one understands his humor. I don't even understand his humor, but I sense it. They bought a place in Vermont. I asked him, 'Do you like Vermont?' He said, deadpan, 'Jill loves it.' There will never be another Charlie Bronson."

McCallum remained a gentleman about his wife's affair, telling Glenn Lovell, "There was an awkwardness about it, but at the same time, one had to have a stiff upper lip, and keep things as polite as possible for the sake of the children."[34] He would soon go on to star with Robert Vaughn in the iconic series *The Man from U.N.C.L.E.*

The Great Escape opened on the weekend of July 4, 1963, in the United States but not before a special London premiere had been arranged for POW veterans. These men gave the film a hearty seal of approval.

Over time the film has only increased in popularity. It is one of the films always mentioned whenever a journalist needs a pop bio to introduce any article about James Coburn's career. His part in it was quite small, and his Australian accent dubious, but he did have some good lines and humorous moments.

Sturges recalls a scene regretfully cut from the final edit that reveals the mysterious contents of the case Coburn's character, Sedgwick, carries everywhere: "Sedgwick, who's Joe Organization, stops by a stream, opens the thing and in it he had food, wine, a change of clothes, a compass, and a book. He starts nibbling the cheese, drinking the wine, reading the book. Got a big laugh. But it had to go. Length."[35]

It was in the next few remarkable movies that Coburn moved from a minor character to important supporting roles. These set the stage for his stardom. In his personal life and spiritual journey, he was embarking on the explorations that would forever mark him as one of Hollywood's alternative thinkers.

1. Mylet Coburn with baby James in the town of Laurel, Nebraska, 1928. This is the only known image of James Coburn as an infant. Courtesy of the James Coburn Archives.

2. James (*indicated*, ca. 1941) was the team manager for several sports teams while at Roosevelt Junior High School in Compton, including the basketball and track teams. Also pictured, standing to the left, Coach Rex Dixon. Courtesy of the James Coburn Archives.

3. James and his mother, Mylet, May 1944. Jim, fifteen, wears his Roosevelt High School "Yell Leader" uniform. Courtesy of the James Coburn Archives.

4. Early portrait of James, ca. 1948–49. This could be a senior class photo or an early photo from Compton Junior College. Note the wide lapels. Courtesy of the James Coburn Archives.

5. In Germany, ca. 1951–52. Coburn wrote "Ground Pounder" on the back. Courtesy of the James Coburn Archives.

6. In Germany, ca. 1951–52. Coburn wrote on the back: "Me and the boys, at work, on maneuvers." Playing a hand of poker, which he usually won. Courtesy of the James Coburn Archives.

7. PFC Coburn in his casern in Mainz, Germany, wearing the moustache that was to become a problem, ca. 1951–52. Courtesy of the James Coburn Archives.

8. Coburn early professional photo during the New York era, ca. 1956—a natty dresser in suit and tie. Photographer unknown. Courtesy of the James Coburn Archives.

9. Early Coburn headshot from his New York days, ca. 1956. Photographer unknown. Courtesy of the James Coburn Archives.

10. Coburn during the New York era, ca. 1956, in a professional shot with a pensive attitude. Perhaps he recalled when his car was wrecked and he threw the fender into a telephone pole. Courtesy of the James Coburn Archives.

11. A 1956 image from a studio shoot. Though the photograph was not chosen as his professional headshot, it captures the way he looked when talking about something interesting to him. It's remarkable the difference a good haircut can make. Photograph by Gene Howard. Courtesy of MPTV Images.

12. Snapshot taken during a break on the 1963 shoot for *The Great Escape* in Germany. From left appears to be Carey Loftin, Lisa Coburn, James Coburn, Beverly Coburn, two unidentified women, and actor John Leyton ("Willie, the Tunnel King"). Courtesy of the Beverly Coburn Archives.

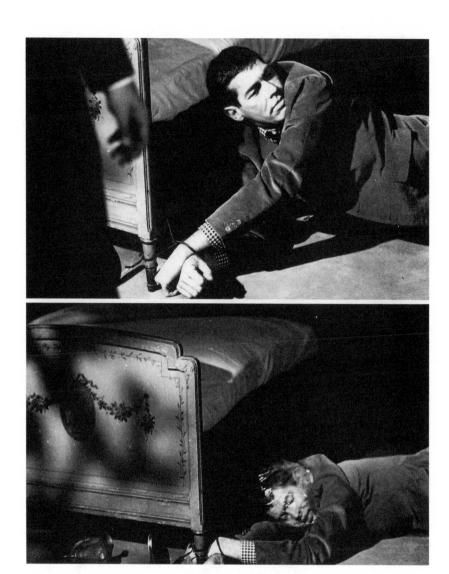

13. Publicity shots of James Coburn as "Tex" on the set of *Charade* (1963)—first preparing for his death scene, then suffocated with a plastic bag. Actors often have to hold their breath for long periods of time. Courtesy of Universal Studios Licensing LLC.

14. Coburn with Lisa and Jimmy at their bungalow during the shoot for *A High Wind in Jamaica* (1965). The kids loved going on location with their dad. Photograph by Lynda Swarbrick. Courtesy of Twentieth Century Fox Film Corporation.

5

Gladly and Willingly

I asked him, "What's *Charade?*" He said, "It's a film with
Audrey Hepburn and Cary Grant." My pants about fell off.

—JAMES COBURN, 2002

In October 1962 Coburn had just finished shooting *The Great Escape* in
Germany. His manager called him in Munich and told him to hurry to
Paris, that he had a job there called *Charade*. Forgetting about his plans to
visit Egypt, he immediately set off for Paris, driving, as he describes, "in this
old Mercedes made of cast iron, I believe, because you couldn't destroy it. I
kept running into things, and it didn't even bend. I scratched it but it didn't
bend—so I learned by getting lost in Paris."[1]

Thus began his relationship with the city for which he would hold a lifelong affection. Driving in Paris was different from Los Angeles. "It's a hard
city to drive in until you learn the rules. When you learn the rules, then it's
easy. Then it's push and shove, push and shove, *bomp, bomp, bomp.* You let
them know you're not a patsy. You let them know you're a Parisian."

In his enthusiasm, he arrived in Paris a little early, before they were expecting him. Associate producer James Ware, who spoke fluent French, found a
place for him to stay. It was a three-bedroom apartment on rue du Colonel
Moll, in the 17th arrondissement, close to the Pont d'Iéna (which crosses
the Seine virtually at the foot of the Eiffel Tower). "It was just a hotel until

79

Beverly could get there." Shortly thereafter Beverly flew in with toddler Jimmy and five-and-a-half-year-old Lisa. They promptly enrolled Lisa in a bilingual school and set up house. The couple hired a governess and a maid, who only spoke Spanish. Both were marvelous cooks.

Their little apartment, which Beverly describes as "a rat trap—quite good by French standards" was in a row of pale stone buildings adorned with carvings of flowers and heavy carved balustrades.[2] Inside there were "water pipes and very many other fixtures predominately fixed. It was filthy—it is now just dirty—I like it. We have beautiful marble fireplaces in each room, which had been unused for many years until the Americanos moved in."[3] In the typical French style, tall, narrow French doors opened onto shallow balconies, protected by ornate wrought-iron railings. But windows were not opened much that winter.

In October the weather was still pleasant, but in November snow started to fall. For the next five months, "we only saw the sun once, as we were leaving. The snow that fell in November was still blowing around the streets in April," Coburn remembers.[4] As it turned out, December kicked off the coldest winter Europe had experienced since the Little Ice Age in Elizabethan times. In Britain it was known as the Big Freeze. Beverly wrote, "Now we have icicles hanging off our fingers and noses."[5] Snow and ice storms interfered with everything—except filming in Paris.

Charade is a sophisticated, intelligent mystery-romance. Three old friends harass the innocent widow of a fourth friend, seeking the proceeds of a hoard of stolen wartime gold, while a charming rogue, played by Cary Grant, tries to help the widow escape their clutches. Also in the mix is a mysterious FBI man, played by Walter Matthau, and the local police detectives.

Coburn had never before met Cary Grant, Audrey Hepburn, or Stanley Donen, the director, until they were "all thrown together in this ice cream maker."[6] The film's costar, Audrey Hepburn, eventually confessed to Coburn that it was she who had discovered and recommended him for the role of Tex Panthollow after admiring his performance in *The Magnificent Seven*. "How do you thank someone for that?" He also had a friend in the director of photography, Charles Lang, who had shot *The Magnificent Seven*.

Early in the shoot, Coburn came to the set and found Cary Grant in his dressing room—"It was just a green box on the set. We all had one."—and was invited in to chat. Walter Matthau was shooting the scene in the office with Audrey Hepburn, and he strolled over. "Walter said, 'Hi, Jim, how you doing?' Then he looked over at Cary Grant, and he said to me, 'Did you ever see someone do a better Cary Grant than this guy?' And he walked away. He was a funny guy—he had a strange sense of humor, but funny. That was the only time I ever saw Cary Grant off balance."

Coburn enjoyed watching how smooth Grant was when he worked, even though off the set they did not spend much time socializing. "Cary Grant, now he had style. He was the tip of the iceberg when it came to style. A groovy guy too. I kinda liked that guy. He was totally on balance all the time. He'd do three takes, one up, one down, and one right down the middle. Three takes and he would have it. He only had one front tooth, which he managed to conceal by the way he held his mouth. He was a groovy guy, and we had a lot of fun. Unfortunately, I didn't get to spend too much time with him there, only on set when we were shooting. He was in that whole other level of stardom. He and Stanley Donen would go to the parties given by Darryl Zanuck, and I'd be home taking care of the kids and doing that shit. We weren't invited anyway. I was jealous. Sure, I'd love to be there too."

At the start of the shoot, Coburn was called to the Megève ski resort, where they shot the scenes when Hepburn's character, Reggie, and Grant's, Peter, first meet. A dreary fog had rolled in and lasted for days, hiding the spectacular mountains that were the whole reason for the location. Coburn was to shoot what is called a "weather cover," a scene that can be set up indoors, when the planned exterior scene is delayed by bad weather. It is the scene when Tex menaces Reggie with matches in the telephone booth—"I felt really bad about burning Audrey. It went against my nature." That scene has become one of his highlights in the picture, although at the time it was disturbing to some of the international censors, who insisted that it be shortened. The timing of the shoot was great because he got to hang out a little there at the resort during what editor Jim Clark recalls was "a week's hiatus, the last quiet time for six months."[7]

Every now and then there were dinners, like celebrating Grant's birthday. There had been a cake at the soundstage. Then later some of the cast dined at the Rothschild Hotel and sat around the pool. "[Cary Grant] was just starting to get gray. We were sitting around a heated pool after dinner, having some champagne, and he says, 'I'm too old for the part. I'd never be seen with anyone who dressed like that. I'd never go out with a kook like that. She looks like a kook wearing that Givenchy stuff.' What a guy."[8]

Coburn spent a great deal of time with Audrey Hepburn. They had plenty of topics of conversation and mutual friends. Hepburn had recently filmed the somewhat controversial *The Children's Hour* (1961) with James Garner just before he started *The Great Escape*. Ironically, given the weather, her most recent film was *Paris When It Sizzles* (not released until 1964), which she completed filming in October, just days before *Charade* began. She also had her son, Sean, with her, who was about ten months older than Jimmy. Sean was tall for his age, taking after his father, Mel Ferrer. Coburn asked her what had attracted her to Mel. She replied, "The way he just looked me in the eyes—the way he penetrated me with his eyes."[9]

"I'd go talk to her all the time. She was really sweet, really a lady, and one of those people you meet now and then and wish all people were like or want to be like. She was great. I loved her. I thought she was just fantastic, and we had a lot of fun. I'll always remember how she worked all night when it was so cold."[10]

Beverly describes one of those long, cold nights: "The movie is proceeding on schedule! In spite of a snow storm Tuesday nite, which was one of the most beautiful things I've ever seen. The flood lites allowed us to see the mad swirling of millions of glittering flakes, blown in gusts of wind in all directions."[11]

Meanwhile the biggest challenge was keeping warm at home. Coburn describes it this way: "Our flat had five fireplaces and a little man who came around and begged us to buy his firewood. Every week we'd buy a little more. As it got colder, the guy didn't show up. We were running out of fucking wood, and our concierge wouldn't turn the heater on until December, one of these strange rules. I kept bitching and yelling at him, screaming, 'Turn on the fucking heat! We have a baby.' He'd say, 'Put a blanket around him.' The only place that was really warm was the car where we had a heater, or the studio. Even when I wasn't working, I would go to the studio anyway to get warm. We finally had to go out and buy wood and carry it back up ourselves to the apartment, each one of us—Lisa, the old lady, Beverly—so we had enough to heat one room at least. We were breaking things up, tearing up the phone books, trying to get the fire started. And the flue was always stuck. It was terrible. That was not pleasant."[12]

Beverly felt it too. "We have been truly freezing here. Nothing can keep me warm." But she also notes, "This city is worth it. The beauty is so intense it almost pains the eyes. I have a love affair with Paris."[13]

It wasn't all work. Just before Christmas, Orson Welles's film *The Trial*, based on the novel by Kafka and starring Anthony Perkins, opened in Paris. It was screening at a little theater next to the drugstore near their apartment. Coburn and Beverly stood in line in the snow to see it. "It was freezing cold but worth it," Coburn says. "It was about a man who knew he was innocent but did not know of what. Cinematically it was brilliant."[14]

They also socialized with some of the crew, including Jim Clark and Laurence Méry, assistant editor and Clark's soon-to-be fiancée. As Clark recalls in his autobiography, "James Coburn was a different sort of guy. With his wife Beverly in tow, Laurence entertained them in her bijou flat one evening, which was a tight squeeze. James was into a number of Californian fads at the time."[15]

The happy shoot came to an end. The Coburn family flew home to beautiful Los Angeles. "It was like summertime," Coburn remembers.[16] "In fact we went to the beach the following day." *Charade* has gone on to be one of Audrey Hepburn's most beloved films, and the beauty of Paris, the snappy pace, and sparkling dialogue make it feel ageless.

In LA Coburn had a brief respite from film work, filling his time with a few TV roles—some of his best TV work, including a classic *Twilight Zone* episode, "The Old Man in the Cave," and an episode of *Combat!*, which has become a highly regarded military action series. He also filmed a supporting role in a TV pilot that was not picked up but was released to the theaters at the same time as *Charade*. The low-budget western *The Man from Galveston* (1963) gained some traction from his presence. He played the marshal, a sympathetic character, but no one was fooled by the marketing. The reviewers clearly knew that it was originally meant for TV.

Coburn could not have realized it at the time, but in the last months of 1963, he was about to act on the last TV series episodes he would shoot until 1980. He traveled to Minnesota to shoot exterior locations for an episode of *Route 66* and to his old Studio One stomping grounds, now the Filmways studio, in New York, for an episode of the provocative courtroom drama series *The Defenders*.

He also used his downtime wisely to do some voice training with Giovanna D'Onofrio. He met her through his friend Ted Maitland, another actor and LA City College alumnus. D'Onofrio taught voice in New York and Pennsylvania, in the midthirties, before moving to Albuquerque, New Mexico. She visited Los Angeles every now and then to work with different performers. She was known for combining the use of the bel canto technique with modern science, and she had studied with Douglas Stanley, author of the seminal work *Your Voice*. Not content to stick to opera singers, D'Onofrio also worked with blues and jazz performers as well as actors.

"She built a whole upper register for me. Pretty soon I had over a three-octave range of tones I could use for singing or talking. Her technique for building a voice was exactly the way my voice developed on its own, naturally. It had to do with breaking down and building [the voice] back up again. She called herself a voice constructionist. She had the opportunity and did clean nodes off of opera singers' vocal cords through exercise.

"I worked with her for four or five years. She must have been in her fifties. She had very thick glasses and couldn't see without them. We would work on the piano, doing scales, breaking through. She taught me a technique of how to break through and get the voice working. I had a deep voice, but I didn't have an upper register. She gave me a little over a three-octave range. She didn't charge anything. We just worked together a couple of times a week. I was her only natural product. My voice had developed naturally, from coughing my voice away. She'd had to work for years with people to have a lower register or a register that goes up and down. [My lower register] wasn't a problem. I could use the voice.

"[When you act] you express through the sound of your voice, through the words you can use, and where you can take them. And how you use the words, saying what you want to say, with the words. The wider the range of your vocal technique, the better you can express.

"I lost contact with her, but she was also an astrologist and told me that I would not be with Beverly for a long time and that it would dissolve, and it certainly did. . . . She also told me that poor man Kennedy would not survive his second term, that he would die in office, and that my biggest success would come late in life, and it certainly has."

D'Onofrio's prediction about President Kennedy came to pass during principal photography of Coburn's next movie, *The Americanization of Emily*, about the romance between an American naval attaché and a British widow who is reluctant to start a relationship with someone who might be sent into battle.

Coburn was attracted to the script because he appreciated the screenwriter, Paddy Chayefsky. "When I read the script, I knew it was something special because of the words." James Garner agreed with the assessment: "I've never had finer words to say on a movie screen. . . . His dialogue is like fireworks, it *crackles*."[17]

Originally Garner had been cast in the Paul "Bus" Cummings role, with William Holden tapped to play the lead, Charlie Madison. Holden backed out of the picture, and the part was offered to Garner. But now finding the right actor for Bus Cummings was a challenge.

Garner takes credit in his book, *The Garner Files*, for the casting coup. "I'd worked with James Coburn in *The Great Escape*. He was a good guy and a terrific actor. When I recommended that Jimmy take over the Bus Cummings part, Marty Ransohoff and his assistant, John Calley, agreed. It turned out to be a great choice."

The characters were dog robbers, staying out of combat through being of service to their admiral. If they didn't have whatever luxury he wanted in their private Aladdin's cave, they knew where to find it, including pretty women for their parties. Once again Coburn's military experience was help-ful to him, as indeed was Garner's. "We'd all witnessed the kind of snafus, interservice rivalries, and insanity portrayed in the film that cost people their lives."[18]

The actors had a wonderful time for most of the shoot. Coburn says, "The story was the thing that [we] tripped off. James Garner and I had such a ball doing it, a great time playing those two characters, Bus and Charlie. It was an antiwar movie of the best kind of content. Why make a glory out of war? Why build statues to great soldiers? You know, [Charlie's] argument was perfect. And I was the most dangerous man—that's the way I played [Bus]. I thought he was really a dangerous man to have around. He would go for anything. If this is what the major wanted, if this is what the captain wanted, this is what they're going to get."[19]

In hindsight the only thing the pair disagreed on was Arthur Hiller. Gar-ner had worked with him very recently, on what was Hiller's second feature film, and found that "he has a gentle demeanor but knows what he wants."[20] But Coburn was frustrated by that same demeanor: "Arthur Hiller, generally he's going to say, 'Uh-huh,' because he doesn't have a strong opinion about it, whatever we came up with."[21]

Arthur Hiller had been directing episodic television for as long as Coburn had been acting in it. They had even worked together on a couple of shows in 1958, an episode of *Suspicion*, written by Stirling Silliphant, and later an *Alfred Hitchcock Presents* episode.[22] Hiller says of Coburn, "This was a young man that was already a fine actor. I always say he just oozed charm, and in that oozing of charm, he could play almost any kind of role. Like he could play a villain with a sort of gentle charm also. Yet the character stayed a villain. And he was very good at satire. . . . I discussed his character with him beforehand, or talked about his scenes sometimes ahead of time, but always just to point out why I wanted it a certain way to fit the story. But then left him alone. He just did it. My directing then was just touching a button. I didn't have to really direct him, so to speak."[23]

Coburn felt that the director brought his television sensibilities to the film. "He tried to do some long camera shots, some really long takes, doing kind of like television walking down stairs, into a room and not giving himself a chance to cut anywhere. If you missed something, you have to do the whole thing over again. I had to do one take seventeen times because of that. I kept saying, 'Arthur. You can cut right here. Bang! Let's make some cuts. We don't have to have this in one. What's the point?' He was trying to have something all in one like *Citizen Kane*, I guess, those long takes that Welles did. They were all very good, and they were all necessary. All very timed and perfect. Things were happening in there. [Welles] was telling the story within the shot. There's got to be something to tell if you're going to use a shot like that; you tell a story in that shot."[24]

The film shot primarily at Selznick International Studios and used Santa Monica Airport and Mandalay Beach near Oxnard. But the production had started in London for two weeks in October to capture exteriors around the city and at MGM British Studios in Hertfordshire. Dukes Avenue in Muswell Hill in London was used for the exterior of Emily's house and still looks very much the same now as it did then. "We could have shot it anywhere, actually. We just wanted to go to London. We were in London for a week or two, staying at the Savoy." Beverly joined her husband for the trip. The couple got in some shopping, including in the up-and-coming counterculture area of Charing Cross Road, where they visited the trendy bookstore Better Books in search of poetry by e. e. cummings.[25]

Two notable events happened during this trip to London. The first was when Coburn met Petey Kameron's friend Herbert Kretzmer, who was a lyricist and the theater critic for the *Daily Express* in London. He and Coburn enjoyed many similar interests, such as the music of Charlie Parker and smoking grass, but their main shared passion then was the 1957 Kurosawa film *Throne of Blood*.[26] Kretzmer picked up Jim and Beverly at their hotel and drove them to his country house, to party safely in private .

"When grass was just becoming popular in London, it was really kind of an underground thing since you could not smoke it openly. Herbie had this little thatched-roof place out in the country. We called it the Flying Club. We got it together over *Throne of Blood*. We both did it, acted it for these people who were there that night. We did the scenes we enjoyed the most, and we knew it backward and forward. That Flying Club, all right, it was a lot of fun."[27]

Herbie Kretzmer drove the Coburns back to the Savoy that night. He later recalls, "I had found a friend for life. For the last forty-one years, I have pretty regularly picked up my telephone in London and heard that wonderful, instantly recognizable voice announcing the identity of its owner in a single unadorned word, 'Coburn.' And then I knew Jim was in town again, and it was almost always playtime."[28]

In turn Coburn continued to admire Kretzmer's multiple talents. "He has this ability to write songs, to write journalism, to write essays, to not only just do it but do it with such grace and such intention. . . . He would do stories about all of the great composers of the time. They talked about everything. He had this ability to capture the essence of these guys and put it down in a way that made you love them."[29]

In time Coburn would attend Kretzmer's second marriage, to Sybil, and the gala opening of the musical *Les Misérables*, for which Kretzmer wrote the lyrics, in 1985 in London. There were gaps in their friendship caused only by distance. It was the kind of friendship that immediately picked up wherever it was left off.

The second notable event was the beginning of Coburn's little side business in purchasing and reselling luxury sports cars with producer John Calley. After *The Magnificent Seven*, Coburn had purchased a Morgan. "It was a four banger, four cylinders, and it had this great drophead and looked English, a convertible. I sold it to Eddie Tirella when I got my first Ferrari. That was a 250 GT that I paid about $1,500 for. It came from Brussels, red with a black top. That was a dream of a car.

"John Calley and I started importing sports cars. He was a really groovy guy, funny man. He took over the studios and became a billionaire. Ferraris are very fast when you have somewhere to string them out—140 to 145 is the fastest I've gone. We would buy European trade-ins on new Ferraris—we'd buy three or four at a time for fifty thousand dollars used [in the early sixties], he'd make them work and gussy them up, and then we'd sell off all but two, one for each of us. We had two

Ferrari F-250 LM with rear engines. Sold one to Haskell Wexler. He still has it [as of 2002]."

One of Coburn's cars, his famous California Spider Ferrari, would go on to set a sales record, unfortunately some years after he had sold the car.

But that was many years later. Meanwhile work continued on *The Americanization of Emily*. The admiral was portrayed by Melvyn Douglas. "He was cold most of the time, but he was good in that film, and he was a wonderful actor." Douglas told him a great story about Greta Garbo. As Coburn retells it, "When you do an over-the-shoulder or close-up shot, you have to stand off to the side, and then you play to each other. [Garbo] didn't want anybody to do that. She wants them behind a mirror, because she wanted to play to herself in the mirror. So she played to herself, and [Douglas] had to stand behind the mirror saying his lines."

On Friday, November 22, 1963, they were shooting a party scene filled with gaiety, laughter, and double entendres. Marty Ransohoff barged into the set with the news that President Kennedy had been shot. Stunned into silence, no one could continue filming that day. Instead they crowded around the transistor radio someone had brought into the soundstage, desperately hoping the news was a mistake. In the end the production shut down for almost a week. It had been Arthur Hiller's birthday, but no one celebrated.

Filming restarted with a somber mood. Work continued into the middle of January, making it a chilly time to shoot action sequences in the ocean. Hiller describes the weather as "bad . . . all the better to simulate the other side of the English Channel."[30]

The editing process took nine long months. All the actors were proud of the finished film, which opened to mixed reviews. It didn't garner much action at the box office. "We had a big ending to the film. Paddy wrote a great ending, but it was never in the film. It was too controversial, I guess. The studio didn't want to have it in. I was now an admiral, and they were having a big parade. I was sorry it didn't get more of a play. I don't know why it didn't. Maybe because it was in black and white. That was to get the feeling of the 1940s. I'm not sure, but Kennedy was assassinated during the making of the film. That may have had some emotional effect on it."[31]

Perhaps, but some critics had the opposite opinion from the actors about the script itself, noting "long winded, full-blown speeches" and "diatribes. . . . The picture is inconsistent, lacking in tone, in balance. It has bite and it has action and it has drama, but the underlying attitude is lacking in taste. . . . The film has things to say but it is too wordy."[32]

The film may also have suffered from following too closely several other noted antiwar pictures from 1964, including Stanley Kubrick's enduring satire *Dr. Strangelove*, John Frankenheimer's drama *Seven Days in May*, and, released only few weeks earlier, the chilling Sidney Lumet drama *Fail Safe*. Since two of these were also black and white, it seems the real reason for *Emily*'s tanking was that the public had consumed its fill of wordy antiwar movies. Even an enthusiastic review by Bosley Crowther in the *New York Times* couldn't save it in 1964.[33] It has, however, gained something of a cult following today.

While Arthur Hiller labored in the editing room, Coburn shot his first movie with Sam Peckinpah. They had become friends after crossing paths every now and then around the studios. In addition to *Klondike*, Peckinpah had been knocking out interesting scripts for various television westerns during the late fifties. He also got his start directing in the same milieu.

Coburn was heading into the commissary at MGM when he bumped into Peckinpah coming out of the barbershop. Peckinpah told him that he was about to start on a new project shooting all around Mexico. Coburn's experience in Mexico on *The Magnificent Seven* had been very positive, and he'd enjoyed Peckinpah's most recent release, *Ride the High Country* (1962) starring Randolph Scott, whom Coburn remembered fondly from *Ride Lonesome* only five years earlier.

Coburn had lunch with producer Jerry Bresler in early January 1964 to discuss Peckinpah's project and communicate his enthusiasm for being part of it. Bresler sent a memo to Peckinpah: "[Jim Coburn] is extremely bright and conscientious, extremely excited about doing a picture with you. . . . Coburn will finish his present assignment on January 15, THE AMERICAN-IZATION OF EMILY, and will immediately be fitted for wardrobe and then start practicing riding a horse with one arm."[34]

In addition Coburn would "gladly and willingly" do rehearsals off books—that is, without cost to the production—for the opportunity to be part of the show. There would be no rest between gigs, no vacation, just continual work—the work he loved more than anything else.

He was cast as the one-armed, part-Indian scout Samuel Potts, number four on the call sheet, a supporting role to Charlton Heston's title character in *Major Dundee*. Joining the cast as Dundee's antagonist was Irish actor Richard Harris, who had recently won the Best Actor award at the Cannes Film Festival for his work in *This Sporting Life* (1963). Also in the cast were many familiar faces from Peckinpah's movies, including another of Coburn's close friends, character actor R. G. Armstrong, as a fighting preacher.

The *Major Dundee* shoot was an enormous undertaking—exhausting, frustrating, lengthy—that exposed all the actors and crew to the best and worst of Peckinpah. Starting in spring of 1964 and shooting for seventy-four days, the company traveled around the areas of Durango, Morelos, and Nuevo León in Mexico. They shot interiors at studios in Mexico City. It was hot, dirty, and uncomfortable.

Scrutiny from the moneymen back at the studio became increasingly intrusive. They continually attempted to shorten the schedule and reduce the budget. Filming finished on April 30, 1964—from the point of view of the studio, fifteen days and $1.5 million over budget, but almost exactly at the original roadshow budget that Peckinpah had first proposed. Ultimately their greatest conflict came in the editing room, when the studio was determined to trim the film with little regard to the artistry or the narrative.

On the surface the story of *Major Dundee* was a simple rescue and revenge tale. But Peckinpah made the story into an epic by treating the title character's emotional journey as the heroic struggle of a man diminished by failure trying to redeem his life and rediscover his pride and purpose. He wanted the production to have the same quality, and he apparently wanted the physical discomfort of the characters to be mirrored in the general discomfort of the company. Peckinpah continued with the same working method that Coburn would see each time they worked together, which was quite a contrast from his last gig.

"Sam Peckinpah could handle men really very well. He was a real man's man because he understood who men were and how to treat them. He was not some namby-pamby 'Darling, would you move over here for a minute' kind of director. He was a working alcoholic. We'd have to drag Sam out of his room. 'Come on, come on, man. Time to get on the set.' 'I'm just working on this.' 'Jesus Christ, what's the matter with you? Come on.' 'Okay, okay, don't get your shit in an uproar, for Chrissakes.'

"So we'd finally get him out on the set, and we'd shoot the scene. We'd look at the scene and rehearse the scene. He'd then make groups—he'd put one over here and one over there, and then he'd put me in the center of the group, or whoever was in the center of the scene, and people would come forward from each group and enter the center of the thing. The cameras always stayed where they were. That way he had the whole thing covered all the time, and he had three cameras all the time. So they would never cross that way, or they would always cross the line. It didn't matter. He would do it all that way. If he wanted to, he would take it all the way over to the side and shoot one master this way, and he would get everything. And he could do that very simply by telling the guys what to do, because he gave them all pieces to do that were [worth] doing.

"He'd never tell actors what to do. He'd say, 'Do it again.' He paid such close attention to what was happening. He'd be in the middle of the scene, shooting a scene. He knew what was going on, everything was going well, and he'd say, 'Say that line again!' The camera's still rolling. 'What?' I'd say. And he'd say, 'Say that goddamned line again!' So you'd say it, and a different attitude would come out. And then you'd have to justify everything from that attitude. The first time this happened, I was shocked!

"That's what I mean when I say he'd shove you over into that abyss—from knowing everything to not knowing anything. Then something real is taking place. Hard work—but great stuff came out of that. He never talked about the characters or what was happening. That was all in the script, and he expected everyone to know that stuff. How you did it was up to you. If you were doing it too mechanically, he would guide you. He got some great performances out of people.

"He'd say, 'Make it mean something. Let's see some balls, man. Yeah, that's it.' Even if it was a shitty little scene, somebody who was just responding to someone else, he'd give that actor a chance to work. Everybody. He gave them a chance to really work. And they all did. When they learned how to do it. He got everybody going on that trip. Everyone expressed their personality, the reason they were hired to play that part."[35]

Peckinpah was a difficult and challenging man; his complexity was reflected in his difficult and challenging movies. In his stars he often raised ambivalent feelings. Charlton Heston was famously so enraged at one point during the *Major Dundee* shoot that while on his horse, he charged at Peckinpah, brandishing his sword. Nonetheless, later during the shoot, when the studio planned to replace the director, Heston sacrificed his own fee on condition that Peckinpah stay.

It wasn't all work and struggle. During the shoot in Durango, the stars had the opportunity to attend a splendid *corrida* and watch a renowned Spanish bullfighter work. Juan Jimenez, known as "El Trianero," dedicated his bull in that tournament to Charlton Heston, a national hero in Spain for his portrayal of El Cid in the 1961 biopic. Unfortunately, that first bull gored El Trianero very badly. He was rushed to the hospital. Heston, Richard Harris, Jim Hutton, Slim Pickens, who had been a rodeo bullfighter, and Coburn went to see him there some days later.[36]

As Coburn describes, "There he was, sitting up in bed, and he had his entourage, his girlfriend, there, and they were drinking champagne. He showed us his wounds and his scars. We were leaving for Mexico City and told him we'd see him there in a few weeks after he healed up.

"We were shooting inside the Churubusco Studios. I saw him come in. He was limping. We greeted him, and he invited us to a *corrida* at a ranch where they were testing the young bulls. We went up on a rainy, drizzly day, to have a kind of barbecue and watch the activities in the bullring. A road filled with potholes, he had this big long-tailed Cadillac. Chuck [Heston] had already arrived. He was out in the middle waving a flag around, a cape attached to a stick. He kept asking me to get in the ring. I told him it was his thing, not mine, and I'd just watch. Finally, Trianero came up to me and said, 'Come on, Señor Coburn. This will be good for me in Spain.'

"The next thing I know, I'm standing in the bullring holding this wooden sword and cape, and so I started acting like a bullfighter. He said, 'Just follow his eyes,' so I did as I was told. To find yourself in the middle of a bullring playing with a calf that had been knocking people down, and you're actually dancing with it—it was fun.

"I won two ears, by showing courage. They just cut off the tip of the ear. The impresario of the ring in Mexico City came to tell me I was the best out there that day, but that it might be wise to give one of the ears to Chuck. He could've had them both, as far as I was concerned. 'No no no, we will give him one.' We had the whole ritual with the *pulque*—a beer made from cactus; it's the ordinary drink of the Mexicans that work in the fields—and chorizo. It was fun."[37]

During the shoot, Coburn became quite friendly with Richard Harris. Harris was frustrated by Peckinpah's inconsistent working methods and made very tired by the physical demands of the production. When Beverly arrived in March, for a four-week stay, Harris's wife, Elizabeth, also came to visit. As Coburn told Harris's biographer, Michael Callan, the four of them would go out to bullfights and "the social circuit in our time off. [Harris] was an original, with everything that connotes. He was very clear about his position in the movie industry—clearly someone who was straddling two worlds of art films and blockbusters who felt conflicted. That conflict came out in drink. When he wanted to, he could hit the liquor like no one I knew."[38] Harris spent a lot of time analyzing his own career with Coburn and "anyone else with a sympathetic ear and a strong liver."

For fun the couples shot some 8-mm short films as an essay on Mexico. Coburn shot bulls while others in the project shot landscapes or the peasants. Harris shot a child's funeral. "He could be morbid, especially when he was tired. At that time, he seemed mostly utterly exhausted."

Despite these interludes and a second visit from Beverly, who was hunting pre-Columbian art, by the end of the seventy-four-day shoot, Coburn and most the rest of the company could hardly wait to leave. At the final call of wrap, after nearly twenty-four hours of filming, there was an immediate exodus to waiting cars to dash to the airport. "See you later, motherfucker."[39]

They probably feared Peckinpah would find something else to shoot. Coburn immediately called his manager, Hilly Elkins: "James instructed me that if a script came in that was to be shot in Mexico, not only should I not tell him about it, but I shouldn't read it. He said, 'Hill, I'll do a picture in Mexico as soon as they finish the country.'"[40]

Peckinpah didn't feel the same way. He stayed behind a little while longer wooing his future wife, the luminously beautiful young actress from the scenes in the village where the troop rested on the journey. Then began his battle to hold on to his vision in the editing room, a battle he would lose when he was ultimately fired by producer Jerry Bresler.

Coburn and Beverly were with Peckinpah, Heston, and a few others from the shoot, lurking incognito in the back rows of the February 5, 1965, screening of the wrecked movie. It was barely comprehensible, with arbitrary cuts and incongruent music. The audience laughed at it. Coburn related this story to Peckinpah biographer David Weddle: "We came out of the Egyptian and Sam was absolutely rigid. He reached in his pocket for this pint of whiskey and he was shaking so much he dropped it and broke it on the sidewalk. My wife put her hand on his shoulder and said, 'Sam, Sam, easy baby, it's just, just, it's just a movie. I know, we all feel that way, but Jesus, don't let it hurt you.' She calmed him down a little bit, but if Jerry Bresler had been there at that moment he would have fucking killed him."[41]

Eventually the movie would be somewhat restored closer to Peckinpah's original vision for it. Current versions, at least, have an understandable story.

At that screening the Coburn family had recently returned from what must have felt like a vacation, shooting *A High Wind in Jamaica* (1965) on location in Jamaica for two months, with a month in London for the interiors. Coburn had been to London for tests and rehearsals, then flew into Kingston, Jamaica, on June 25 to be joined by Beverly and the kids about a week later. They then spent July and August of 1964 enjoying the tropical climate while he portrayed Zac, the cranky, wily second-in-command to Anthony Quinn's Captain Chavez.

At the time, the shooting location, Rio Bueno, and the nearby beach villages had only recently been discovered by tourists. The area could certainly be described as an unspoiled tropical paradise—lush greenery, turquoise waters, pristine white beaches, and a nearly uninterrupted skyline in every direction. Most of the structures dated from Colonial times. It was perfect for shooting a Victorian-era period film.

The movie was based on a 1929 book, *The Innocent Voyage* by Richard Hughes, about a colonist's wild young children who, on their way to school in England, accidentally stow away on a pirate ship. It is often compared as a kind of bookend to William Golding's 1954 *The Lord of the Flies*. Both deal with themes of children as naturally savage beings who need the firm control and direction of adults to become or remain civilized. According to a 1986 documentary produced by Scottish Television about the director, Alexander Mackendrick was enthralled by the book, considering the "dark" novel a work of genius.[42] Some years earlier he declared that he "desperately wanted to make this movie." After finishing the picture, he was less enthusiastic about the result, having learned a valuable lesson: "Second-rate books, you can make films of, but true masterpieces never should be transferred to the screen." The story had been considerably lightened and sanitized in an attempt to skew it toward a family film.

Coburn was interviewed for the same documentary about his experience working with Mackendrick. "It was wonderful to watch him. He was producing the thing, helped build the sets, moving. He was doing more than anybody could ask because he wanted this thing to be really good. And he was very responsible to it. He'd dreamed about it, he told me, for twenty years."

He went on to speak admiringly of Mackendrick's ability with the child actors. The director had often worked with children and "learned more about working with adult actors from working with children." He maintained an amazing level of patience. "He was superb with them. He never raised his voice to them. He would turn around, after this little girl who kept looking the same all the time, and [make a face then turn back smiling]. 'Yes, darling. Just right.' He would go after her and just . . . He knew how to do that. I don't know how to do that. I would lose my patience with the children. But he wouldn't lose his patience with anybody."

Working with Mackendrick reinforced Coburn's profound commitment to his art form. "I think he taught me the value of film, of the honor of making film, of dealing with the magical instrument, the realization of certain visions, the solidifying of dreams—that responsibility . . . Ah . . . I don't think there's anything anybody can do that's more important than make films."

A little hyperbole, perhaps. At the time of the documentary, 1986, Coburn seemed completely sincere in his beliefs about the cultural value of movies as a force for social change. It was an idea that had long percolated in his thinking, and one that Beverly shared. She had written about it back in 1963: "Movies are the greatest propaganda we have, also the greatest setters of style and attitude, and I feel we should use the responsibility positively."[43] Back then, as a couple they were discussing ideas that would soon influence the next stage of his career. But in the meantime *A High Wind in Jamaica* was an opportunity for him to really show his charisma on-screen.

With six young children in the cast, most of whom had their whole families with them on location over summer vacation from school, the hotel must have resembled a playground. Coburn was likely relieved whenever he could board the sailing ships—rented for the shoot and shipped in from Miami—and sail off across the bay.

One of the children was portrayed by thirteen-year-old Martin Amis, who would grow up to be a celebrated novelist. In his memoir, he recalls playing chess during the shoot both with "avuncular" Anthony Quinn and "the divinely pretty daughter—Lisa Coburn—of my other costar, genial James, who was in love with me and followed me everywhere, even down into the deep end of the pool of the hotel on Runaway Bay. I loved her too but I wanted moments of reprieve. She was seven."[44]

Deborah Baxter, playing the central character of Emily, was much busier on the film, but she too enjoyed playing in the pool with the Coburn kids during those eight weeks in Jamaica.[45]

The child actors survived a near disaster on the London set when a longboat broke loose and crashed down the sloping deck, narrowly missing several of them. In addition Baxter survived almost being blown away by the enormous fans brought in to re-create the hurricane at the start of the story.

The film was released toward the end of May in 1965. Unfortunately, it was a commercial failure, with reviewers confused. On the one hand, those familiar with the dark, uncomfortable themes of the amorality of childhood from the book found the film too light, while people expecting a family film in the Disney mold found it disturbing. One infamous *Newsweek* review says, "Alexander Mackendrick's direction is a paragon of taste and restraint. . . . It is as if Shirley Temple between choruses of 'On the Good Ship Lollipop' were dismembering a puppy. . . . These children, being father to the man, are the monsters within everyone."[46]

Mackendrick liked the review, saying, "Of course the producers were appalled. But for my money it's very fair—that is exactly the quality in Richard Hughes's strange little masterpiece."[47]

For Coburn the film was especially valuable because it was the first time that his name appeared on the same title card as the lead star, below it, but in letters the same size as Anthony Quinn's name, marking a definite step up from his prior supporting roles.

Interviewed not long after he finished shooting *A High Wind in Jamaica*, Coburn discussed his own versatility in looking for "the brass ring of a leading man"[48] rather than character roles.

"Everybody has a different idea of what my potentialities are. Every director has a different idea of what my qualities are. It's probably beneficial for me. There aren't any doors closed to me. Producers can think of me for many things. I'm not carrying the ball yet. I'm ready to accept the responsibility but I don't know if people think I am ready for it."

People did think that very thing. In 1965 he was on the cusp of stardom. But first there was the small matter of his contractual obligations, as well as the family's growing desire for a larger home.

6

The Brass Ring

Going through the sixties the way it was, kept me healthy.
There was a lot going on, but I never got hung up on anything.
Work was the only thing I got hung up on.

—JAMES COBURN, 2002

Beverly passed through the arched porch and the heavy front door. Jim Coburn and close family friend James Logan, who had found the place, followed her through the entryway into the spacious foyer. The kitten heels of her shoes clicked on the green tiles. She looked up to the dark wood beams on the high ceiling. The central tiled fountain was dry, but it took only imagination to visualize it working and filled with flowers.

The Spanish Colonial–style house had a mazelike quality. They walked through one archway to discover a vast empty living room with an over-looking balcony and an enormous fireplace. The windows soared almost to the ceiling, letting in light filtered by greenery and elegant wrought iron. Off to the other side, they found an interesting octagonal room shaded by old trees. Upstairs in one wing, they explored bedrooms and sitting rooms overlooking a garden, while the opposite wing they found looked down on a sunny tiled patio. But the colors of the walls were dreary, and the garden was filled with strange cement sculptures.

From the back of the main house, a tree-lined path led to a charming guest-house, a swimming pool, and grounds filled with fruiting avocado and citrus trees. In the front a driveway curved to a multicar garage. The whole thing was set a good fifty yards back from the heavy wooden gate to the street, but much of the front yard was overgrown and the circular garden plot nothing but dirt. The round gatehouse was almost overcome by bougainvillea vines.

Beverly knew at once that this was the perfect home for them. Wide expanses of plastered walls waited to be filled with art. It was a perfect house for entertaining, both large gatherings and intimate soirees. It was at the top of the hill with nothing directly above them, thanks to the hairpin curves of Tower Road. The whole Los Angeles Basin sparkled below. The mansion was a blank slate waiting to be made into a comfortable, welcoming, and above all private, retreat.

The Coburns paid $250,000 in late 1965 for the 1927 Spanish-revival mansion on 2.5 acres in Beverly Hills. The prior owners called it a white elephant—too many rooms, too many nooks, too many echoes. They didn't live there, allowing it to be used as a filming location instead. Coburn called it his monastery.

They hired flamboyant jewelry and production designer Tony "More Is More" Duquette to design the "whole downstairs" and promptly left for a trip, "leaving him to his own devices."[1] When they returned, they found the home filled with the vivid colors—turquoise, deep ruby, his custom-mixed hot pink—and the painted trompe l'oeil details that were the designer's trade-marks. He had added shimmering mother-of-pearl to every wood surface, including the ceiling beams, and plenty of mirrors to catch and reflect the light, including on some of the ceilings.

"Tony Duquette decorated it, so it looked like a temple. He collected all sorts of brilliant things—his choices in texture and taste. Over the fireplace we had a white bird of paradise. Gorgeous. He did a lot of extraordinary things for us."[2]

The bird of paradise was a one-of-a-kind sculpture using found objects, created by Duquette himself. Collaborating with Duquette, Beverly hand-decorated small pieces, like stools, boxes, and frames. She disliked the gray or bland off-white plastic cases of electronics like TV sets. She would paint trompe l'oeil leopard patterns or decoupage printed velvet or cotton fabric to the outsides so they blended in to the wild mix of textured wovens, printed cushions, and soft furnishings.

The octagonal room was turned into the gong-and-drum room, piled with multitudes of large pillows made from antique *suzannis* from Kazakhstan and Indian *kilim* rugs. In the drum room, Coburn would play his rhythms and invite his guests to join him in the exchange of energy that came from drumming together. He was creating drum circle meditations long before the idea became mainstream.

He loved their art collection and had a special affection for Persian rugs. "Islamic art can be very, very beautiful. The first time I had some money to buy something real, I bought some fourteenth-century Eastern art for Tower Road. Rugs became quite a thing too. I bought a ton of rugs. To know a rug is to know a friend, because that friend will take you on a long carpet ride. Gurdjieff was a carpet seller. Because he knew so much about carpets, he kept his whole school going buying and selling carpets, his whole trip. He had a room that he used to do interviews in that was totally covered in carpets—ceilings, all the walls, all the floors—totally covered."

On each trip abroad, the couple sought out Afghani textiles, Middle Eastern bronzes, Central American ceramics, and Persian and Indian wood and plaster figures. Often Beverly flew back from international trips carrying delicate embroideries or woodblock prints on her lap. She was also well known among art dealers. "Beverly had a good eye for bronzes. She would buy three from a dealer, then tell him he would have to give her the one she really wanted, the best one. Nine times out of ten it worked. She would get what she wanted. She coveted anything sacred. We probably had $1.5 million worth of art in the house. [The dealers] used to call Beverly 'Shanghai Lil, the Dragon Lady.'"

The eclectic style had an underlying theme. The home was photographed by Eliot Elisofon in 1969. He captured the rich colors and warmth, while Beverly described the philosophy behind the decor. "Because the house, with its white stucco walls, Spanish tiled roof, and rounded turret, is decidedly

Mediterranean—even somewhat Moorish—in appearance, they chose this to provide a unifying motif to the interior decor. The Moors, as Mrs. Coburn explains, provided a bridge between the Mediterranean cultures and the Far East, and hence carefully selected pieces from as far off as Thailand and Japan can be artfully mingled with fabrics and furnishings from Italy, Spain, and by extension, Mexico. . . . The home is at once distinctive, original and harmonious."[3]

It was good that Coburn had a place to rest that was harmonious and serene. His professional life continued at the same blistering pace he had set for himself ten years prior.

The 1960s were an exciting time to be working in Hollywood. Young people were especially restless. Public dissatisfaction with the ongoing war in Vietnam, the increasing tensions of the civil rights movement, and the new technologies, especially in medicine and computing, were all combining to make the mid-1960s a volatile period. Feminism was challenging the masculine domination of culture, and the Cold War was inspiring paranoia.

Stories of spies and superspies were popular at the time. It wasn't a new genre. Espionage stories had been around since the silent movie days. In the 1960s the James Bond franchise captured lightning in a bottle when Sean Connery took over as the debonair British not-so-secret agent. His government-issued license to kill freed him from the consequences of his behavior. Other spies of the era made in a similar mold were counteragent Matt Helm and, on TV, the men from U.N.C.L.E. and the comedic Maxwell Smart with his smarter sidekick, Agent 99. But it was the James Bond series that solidified the genre conventions, including the scene when the wonderful high-tech gadgets are explained to the hero and the villain monologues.[4]

Then there was Derek Flint. He was a decidedly American individualist character, a true eclectic renaissance man, able to maintain evenhanded, balanced relationships with and "satisfy" four ladies in his household ("I don't compete with them"), while being adept at numerous arts, sciences, and physical practices, including martial arts. It was the perfect vehicle for James Coburn's first ascent to leading man status.[5]

Three years earlier Beverly had written to James Logan from Paris to discuss the state of the film industry. Her letters reflect the kind of deep conversations about her husband's career that the couple was having. Beverly wrote about a new kind of film for the future: "Maybe it's time to stop showing sickness and violence and inhumanity and go on to the possibility of perfection as a theme." She describes a character that could well be the genesis of Derek Flint: "I want to see live, living, disciplined, thinking, growing, swinging characters in movies, full of love & energy & ambition & making it as these sort of people do.... Let's give them something new, something that makes forward movement, the great & only thing to be desired. God, I'm such an idealist. I make myself sick sometimes."[6]

In this spirit, Coburn's newly formed production company, M.O.F.F. (Mother's Old-Fashioned Films), joined with director Daniel Mann and producer Saul David to develop *Our Man Flint*, which 20th Century Fox hoped would be a megahit and possible franchise for the studio.

Coburn says of the process, "Every chance we had, we would put our two cents in and take ideas on a trip. We were all able to contribute. That was the fun of it. We had an open end. We didn't have any literature to follow, so we took the theme of the ideal individual, doing, learning. Everything he knew, he learned how to do. It wasn't one of those magical things where you were endowed with powers."[7]

Cowriter Hal Fimberg evidently felt the actors' contributions were less central to the collaboration. "[It] was not only the collaborative writing effort of Ben Starr and myself, but drew on the talents of Saul David, a former book editor with a splendid story mind. We worked not as writers against producer but as a team and even our arguments were most helpful.... Stars James Coburn and Lee J. Cobb ... offered pertinent suggestions."[8]

But first Coburn had to deal with his multipicture contract with producer Marty Ransohoff (*The Americanization of Emily* [1964]). He took a cameo role, along with many other actors, in Ransohoff's production, the pointed satire *The Loved One*. In later days he dismissed this as "a bunch of shit. It was Tony Richardson's getting back at Hollywood. It was just junk."[9] Then he negotiated a buyout of his contract, instead signing a multipicture deal with 20th Century Fox.

Our Man Flint shot on the back lot of Fox, in the San Fernando Valley, and at the airport in Washington DC. Daniel Mann storyboarded the whole thing, and his script notes show his attention to detail and planning. Coburn spent time with karate and fencing instructors, practicing the fight scenes. These were choreographed by Buzz Henry to take advantage of Coburn's special abilities, including a good side kick. "I did all the stunts I could do, up to a point. Buzz designed it around what I was capable of." Flint's apartment was luxurious, while much was made of his hip clothing. The bespoke designs by Ray Aghayan and Edward Wyngear featured "costly fabrics, including raw silk and cashmere."[10]

Of the character, Coburn often repeated in interviews that he was a true individualist. "After all, Flint trained himself. We wanted to make it the antithesis of Bond. Bond was really in bondage to the British government. We wanted Flint to be his own man. Flint was the antithesis of Bond. Bond was in bondage, and Flint was a free man. That was the theme. The ideal individual. The American. Individuality is what America was based on, becoming individuals within the confines of the society. The society grows stronger with individuals than it does with a bunch of total followers. Each individual can express itself in positive ways towards the antithesis done by order or higher government or whatever."[11]

There is an easy naturalness to Coburn's portrayal of his most recognizable alter ego. Flint persistently refuses to be drawn into the business of government spying, until his friends' lives are threatened. He demonstrates his superior personally designed tech, including the now-iconic lighter with eighty-two different functions, "eighty-three if you want to light a cigar,"[12] superior fighting abilities, and superior observational skills that rival those of Sherlock Holmes. (Flint: "I noticed they were wearing Battle of the Bulge ribbons." Cramden: "There *is* no ribbon for the Battle of the Bulge." Flint: "Exactly!")[13]

The production was not without challenges. For example, while the casting of the four household beauties was easily accomplished, the casting of the main villainess was a longer process. The studio hoped to make a star of Israeli beauty Gila Golan, provided she could overcome the surprising Brooklyn accent that producer Darryl Zanuck noticed in her screen test.

Meanwhile Motion Picture Association of America (MPAA) censor Geoffrey Shurlock, nemesis of producers everywhere, voiced several concerns, including insisting that the painted nudes in Flint's art collection be of good taste. His main ire was reserved for the concept of the reward room in secret organization Galaxy's island lair and the notion of women as pleasure units. The compromise was to ensure that female companionship was only one reward option available; other rewards were to include luxury cars, dancing, and gourmet meals. It is doubtful that anyone was fooled.

Saul David fought hard for the reward room scenes. In a letter to Darryl Zanuck, he writes, "I propose to make the reward room sequence, and everything else in the picture, tasteful, amusing and ironic." Such scenes were important to show the peril to Flint's women and elucidate the theme. After all, Galaxy is an evil organization. "Our film does not endorse them. . . . We attack both in word and deed, everything Galaxy stands for and wind up destroying it and all its works. For all its amusing tone, the film has some pointed and hard things to say about reducing people to units. . . . Its essential attitudes are satirical. But we cannot attack what we're not allowed to show. . . . We can't dramatize the fall of evil men without looking at them."[14]

As usual the censors were far more worried about offending people with sexuality than with violence. Although there was little blood in the movie, villain Hans Gruber did meet a rather grim end.

Meanwhile the script allowed Coburn to reveal the character and himself as urbane, erudite, charming, and cool. *Cool* meant both "calm and ingenious under pressure" (such as when Flint converts his dinner jacket and a hand towel into a disguise) and the "ultimate in effortlessly hip."

His eyes, his smile, his rangy, long-legged physique that suited the Mary Quant chic of the day—all these were seen as attractive because the women in the movie found him so. Like the slightly craggy Sean Connery, Coburn was the perfect embodiment of a mature man rather than a teen ideal. His fans were grown women, not teenyboppers. "I made the character of Flint fit me because he was the character I want to be. He could keep four women happy at the same time. They could all do what they want to do, and not have any of them be jealous, and he could do it very well, doing it in a way that is noncombative. In Tangier the guys would say, 'Hey, Flint, where's your harem?' Flint was very loving. He had to save those girls' asses all the time."[15]

The movie opened in mid-January 1966, not usually a popular time of year for adventure pictures. It was a genuine hit, both domestically and overseas where the fan base was already vigorous. Coburn appeared on *The Tonight Show* to promote it just days after it opened, before setting off on a whirlwind publicity tour, accompanied by Beverly, in the same Learjet that Flint apparently flew in the movie, provided by Bill Lear himself. "[*Our Man Flint*] made me a star. Put me out there. I did a fifteen-city tour in five days in a Learjet. That was fun. Boston, New York, Chicago, Kansas City, Cleveland, Cincinnati, Dallas—we worked our way up and ended in San Francisco."

The way newspaper journalism worked in those days is interesting. A few well-known staff writers in the major centers, usually New York or Los Angeles, would write reviews, interviews, or profiles, and then the articles or portions of them were syndicated to all the smaller regional papers via the several wire services. In this way the entire country essentially received the same message. It was rare for a local paper to write its own film review, and even rarer for them to have access to a star to write a special interview. Even when promoting screenings at local theaters, they would simply lift the description from the promo packages.

For example, Patricia Davis wrote a feature about Coburn as Flint, and it traveled by United Press International (UPI) to all corners of the country. The article mentions that "he says he doesn't have time to do television anymore."[16]

This inspired dozens of headlines in papers all over the country such as, "Coburn Lost to Television." Other papers glommed on to his enthusiasm for the Learjet, as described by Davis: "He admitted to being nervous at first, but said his enthusiasm for the sleek little plane quickly overcame his nervousness. Now he says, 'It's the ONLY way to travel. We made it from New York to Boston in less than 30 minutes. . . . Why, it took longer than that to get from La Guardia Airport to midtown Manhattan!'"

Coburn returned from promoting the movie to settle into his new home as a star, firmly clutching the brass ring of leading man, ready to carry the movie.

His newfound status was on display as the headliner on his next job, which was also his first collaboration with director Blake Edwards, once again for the Mirisch Company. *What Did You Do in the War, Daddy?* (1966) was a World War II screwball satire about an Italian army battalion ready to surrender to the G.I.s, as long as they are allowed to hold their annual village wine festival first. Coburn portrays Lieutenant Christian, a world-wise soldier just trying to get home, who manipulates the neophyte captain into essentially saving everyone who matters once the real enemy, the German army, shows up and puts a damper on the festivities. Dick Shawn, as the captain, had the lion's share of screen time, but it was the lieutenant who devised the climactic trick-the-enemy sequence.

As usual, censor Shurlock was on watch for obscenities, complaining that there were just too many "damns and hells" in the script, and most especially that they should remove the "damn it all to hell."[17] He also expressed concern about an obscene arm gesture, which turned out to be somewhat warranted when the Legion of Decency also complained about the gestures in their review.

The picture was shot on a purpose-built set in Lake Sherwood, in the then-sparsely populated Santa Monica Mountains northwest of Los Angeles. This allowed the stars to come home every night, which made for a nice change.

By the time *What Did You Do in the War, Daddy?* was in theaters, Coburn had already completed work on his next movie. Originally titled for main character Eli Kotch, *Dead Heat on a Merry-Go-Round* (1966) filmed in Los Angeles and Boston for Columbia Pictures. It was about a slick con man and his schemes to rob a succession of women.

The script drew its share of ire from Shurlock, who in addition to the usual points about strong language, was particularly concerned about the amorality of the character. He says in an early letter that the movie was "antisocial in nature. It creates the impression that evil is inviolable and triumphant, so long as it is clever and painstaking."[18] It is a little hard to take him seriously when he also proposes that the belly dancer in one part not be "offensively suggestive" but "decently clothed." She's a belly dancer, for goodness' sake.

Vital to the production code was that evildoers must be punished and miscreants must always be caught. In addition the visitation of morality upon those who deserved it was also a necessary part of the theme. If there was redemption for a character, it was only for the spirit—never for the body, which could still be subject to execution. The problem here was that "the leading man is a successful and clever criminal who remained relatively unscathed because of his ingenuity."

By the mid-1960s the understanding of morality in the country had become less simplistic. The death of President Kennedy reminded everyone that good people sometimes died. Morality was not as black and white as it seemed. It was even becoming possible for a woman to have sex before marriage and still be considered a good person. Moreover, the vise grip the MPAA once had over filmmakers was loosening. Emboldened by the local success of foreign language films, which were released without the MPAA approval stamp, more and more filmmakers, and even the studios, were demanding a level playing field. Increasingly they chose to release certain titles without the stamp. The censors' work would soon shift from code enforcement to the nascent ratings system.

In the meantime Shurlock got twisted in knots, trying to ensure that if Kotch was not imprisoned for his deeds, it should at least be clear that he was in a mental and spiritual prison of his own making, that whatever else happened in the movie, he should *not* be happy. Rather than merely lay down the law, Shurlock offered increasingly convoluted creative solutions. He proposed that the story include "the suggestion that Eli Kotch is a victim of his own cleverness to the point of being diseased by, and unable to free himself from, its compulsions."[19]

The writers kept reworking the script, fine-tuning it to show that "this criminal is in the grips of destructive fever." In the end Shurlock had to allow the film to go forward despite his opinion that the writers' attempts were "somewhat thin, making their point."[20]

Filming for *Dead Heat* began in early February 1966, starting in relatively warm Los Angeles before moving to chilly Boston. Coburn, notably, had a piece of this film, 10 percent on the back end. Another fun piece of trivia is that the film marks the screen debut of Harrison Ford, who was paid $150 for a day's work on February 16, portraying a bellboy.

Despite Shurlock's efforts, the inherent charm and charisma of James Coburn left audiences approving the character more than disparaging him. Shurlock's worst fears may have been realized, once he saw the reviews.

The *New Yorker* 1966 review by Brendan Gile says, "An extremely clever melodrama. . . . Debonair and heartless wretch. . . . Surely there is a certain fittingness in the fact that a movie which, almost unprecedentedly, permits evil to triumph, itself triumphs."[21]

However, Gile also intuitively understood Shurlock's point. "In an adroit anti-climax [the film] warns that this life has such wanton tricks of good fortune up its corkscrew sleeve that even the most gifted crook is well advised to go straight."

Richard Schickel wrote about it and another contemporaneous release in *LIFE Magazine*: "Moralists will observe that in neither film is crime punished with the traditional Hollywood retribution of jail or death. This may represent a breaking away from the strictures of the old code, but in the context of films that are essentially fantasies, it may merely be seen as just the right touch—at last—of truth about the ways of our world."[22]

Of the major publications, only *Time* magazine did not have a good review, calling the picture "flaccid."[23]

The truth is that people like rogues, and the public was tired of being babied by the censors.

With this short string of successes, Coburn and Beverly were living the kind of life he had always hoped for. Instead of being on the outside watching costars head off to the fancy parties, they were part of the in crowd. In April, days before Jim presented at the Academy Awards for the first time, Beverly was matron of honor at her very good friend Elizabeth Ashley's wedding to George Peppard. The guest list included stars of the day—Gregory Peck,

Debbie Reynolds, Eli Wallach, and Roddy McDowall, while George Hamilton escorted Lynda Bird Johnson, the president's daughter.

Coburn had two Ferraris in the garage—"His and Hers; every family should have them"—and was being profiled as the man who "collects drums and Chinese gongs, and wants more than anything to direct pictures."[24]

The Coburns were becoming known in Hollywood as wonderful hosts. As Coburn describes, "Tower Road was a famously infamous place to come to just have a ball. There were drugs, and there were girls, and this and that and the other thing. The kids loved it. All my daughter's girlfriends and boyfriends made it a party house when we were out of town, and it was a party house. Great location, nice views.

"It was a kind of Moroccan-Spanish-style house. It was a great house. The living room was this long, wide room that went down three steps. We had a niche with a big bronze Buddha mask. Off to the right, there's a great big round table, a big armoire filled with candles and incense. All the walls were covered with beautiful *thangkas*.

"The house was an attraction. We'd have a lot of people over. People were there most of the time."[25]

One visitor was Dick Webster, who had co-founded the original Source restaurant with Jim Baker. Webster was "the first hippie. He was better than the first hippie—he was the first hipster." A staunch vegetarian, "into grass and peyote, into meditation, into chi," he earned just enough money as a bit player and extra to support his frugal lifestyle, living in a little shack behind what was the original Hamburger Hamlet.

It was he who first introduced Coburn to playing the gong, one day in the midsixties when he stopped by to visit Webster for a cup of tea. "He had this gong there. I said, 'What's that?' He played it for me. Then he said, 'Here, try it. It is a wonderful instrument.' So I played and he played the flute. Then Beverly, for a Christmas present, got me a gong. Our friend built a hanger for it, and I've had it ever since. I've turned a lot of people on to the gong."

It was with Webster that Coburn had first tried peyote a few years earlier. "Dick soaked some dried peyote buttons overnight or for a couple of days. We got up early one Sunday morning, drank the juice—that incredibly weird, awful taste, blech. We drove out to Palm Springs and out into the high desert at Giant Rock, where there was this gathering of people on a space trip, looking for UFOs, and we walked around and everyone was looking at us like we were aliens. It was so alive and electric. Everything was just poppin'. It was afternoon. I'd never been past Giant Rock before. There was a little road that leads off behind this big rock, and we drove and drove to the end, and the stars were coming out. It was a full moon.

"We stopped at this rock quarry. It looked like all these rocks had tumbled out of the great side of the mountain. It was just wonderful with the full moon and the stars peeping out around it. We decided to play drums. I had a little conga, and he had a big conga. He walked up into the quarry where it was nice, and I went out to the fender of the car and started pounding out different rhythms. We got this whole thing going.

"I heard this strange sound and realized a bunch of bats had started flying around. One of them popped me right in the forehead, and I'm going, *Wow, what is this?* I got stormed by these bats! So I got into the car, and they were hitting the roof. What a trip that was. After about ten minutes, the drumming stopped and the melee stopped. Dick came down and got into the car. I said, 'What about those bats?' And he said, 'What bats?' He wasn't fazed by the bats at all. He was just walking through. I knew I could see them—the lights were on. I could see all these bats flying all around him, but they never attacked him. We evidently broke their radar with our drums. It was very exciting."

Coburn and Beverly welcomed houseguests. Family friend James Logan was a frequent visitor on his trips from his home in Rhodesia (now Zimbabwe). Beverly's family, her half sisters and brother from the Funkhouser side, often came to visit as well, along with Beverly's father, Grandpa Jack, who was a heavy equipment operator and operating engineer. He had helped build the Hoover Dam.

Jerry Chapman, who was married to Beverly's half sister Karen, recalls the time he and Jack were building a tree house on the Tower Road grounds for the kids. "There were two-by-fours and four-by-fours. We were building this tree house for little Jimmy. And we're out there working, and Big Jim comes by, and he's talking to us, you know, and we're just shooting the bull, and he's gonna help. So Jack looked at the situation and said, 'You never worked a day in your life.'

"So Big Jim was talking about how he had this job, and he had that job, and how he got into acting because he didn't want to have to work for a living, and he's laughing and having a good time. So he says, 'Jack give me something. Give me something to do.' And I'm down here with Jim, and Jack's up there doing something, and Jack says, 'Where's that blankety-blank hammer?' and he turns and [his elbow] knocks it down. And it went on top of Jim's head.

"Big Jim said a couple of words, and then said, 'I'm not going to help you anymore.'"[26]

One of the constant pastimes at Tower Road, aside from drumming, was playing pool. There were always competitions between guests. Coburn was not above using his relatives to his advantage. Jerry Chapman recalls a time when some producers were playing pool while the family was visiting. "So we walked in, and they were playing pool and talking the big stuff, and Jim says to whoever this guy was, 'Let's play for more money.' And the guy says, 'Okay. We'll play, but who's going to play with you?' Jim says, 'I'll have my father-in-law play with me.'

"You had to know Jack. Wherever Jack went, it was just work boots, Levi's, and a shirt. And his hat. He always had his little ball cap kind of thing on. He didn't dress up for anybody. He looked like a country bumpkin to them. They were posh people.

"Jack says, 'Okay, but are you sure you want to play for money?' It was quite a bit of money. But Jim says, 'Don't worry, I'll cover your stake. No problem.'

"They were playing eight ball. So they set it up, and they said to Jack, 'We'll let you break.' And then Big Jim had a smile—my God, you'd think he just won an Oscar.

"They were really giving Jack a hard time. 'Do you want us to help you pick your pool cue, old man?' He says no, and he throws me the car keys, and he says, 'Go out and get my stick for me, will ya?'

"His wife, Jean, had just bought him a really nice pool cue. So I went and got it, and he put it together. They still kind of laughed a little bit. But he's eyeing it up; he's really playing this thing. I've played pool with him. I knew they were in trouble the minute he said okay.

"So he lines it up, and he eyes it, and he says to Jim, 'Well, what do you think?' And Jim looked at him and says, 'Are you sure you want to do that?' And the other guys are going, 'Oh, oh.' Jack sunk the eight ball on the break, which means he wins.

"And Jim says, 'Do you want to play two out of three?' And they were done and they left."

They probably went down to Hollywood to warn all their colleagues about the pool shark Jim Coburn had staying at his house.

As entertaining as life in the house was, the architecture also enabled physical separation between family members. While Lisa didn't mind it, over the years it particularly hurt Jimmy. "[Lisa and our parents] were always off in their rooms doing their thing, while I was left alone with the cook."[27] It was easy for the parents to dismiss the kids to their own wing. Coburn seemed oblivious. "We had a housekeeper and a kind of a nanny. [The kids] were home alone but taken care of. I had no worries about them at all."[28]

Jimmy often felt abandoned, unable to hold his father's attention for long, even when Dad was at home. One day when Jimmy was about five, before he had learned to swim, he and his dad had walked down to the pool. Jimmy was playing near the edge while Dad lay down to sunbathe.

Some maternal instinct alerted Beverly, and she came out to see Dad snoozing on a lounger and Jimmy's tiny body inert at the bottom of the pool. She screamed. Coburn jerked awake and immediately dove to the bottom and pulled his son out of the water. He gave first aid, and fortunately Jimmy was revived.

Unfortunately, the main result of the scare appeared to be that Jimmy would get even less time alone with his father. Perhaps, after this accident, Coburn didn't trust himself to supervise the little guy. "I don't know what to say about [the kids], actually. I was never a good parent. It's hard to tell the truth about the kids because they don't believe it. We always had a housekeeper and a nanny. My son used to think that I went up in an airplane and came down again three months later. 'What do you do up there, Daddy?'"

Then in late June 1966, the whole family went up in an airplane, or more accurately two airplanes, with the kids and their nanny following their parents two weeks later. They were all off to Jamaica to film *In Like Flint*, the less successful sequel to *Our Man Flint*. The company took over the historical and prestigious Round Hill Hotel on Montego Bay, where many of the cast and their families stayed. The Coburns lived in a Victorian villa up the hill with a wrap-around veranda to take advantage of the views. It was beautiful in Jamaica in midsummer.

Jimmy was suffering at the time with a cast on his ankle. He had jumped off a balcony at the Tower Road house and tore his ligaments. While in Jamaica, they healed and the cast had to be removed. Coburn and Buzz Henry, stunts director on the movie, had a tough job trying to cut through the rock-solid material with whatever they had at hand, and they broke several pairs of scissors before they could eventually pry it off.

Bill Lear had a cameo role in the film as a pilot, and everyone had fun on the set—except when Coburn jumped from a boat and injured his foot, ironically in the same way that Jimmy had. He couldn't have a visible cast on his foot in the film though. So to prevent him from walking, he was carried around on a stretcher between dressing room and set, set and home. Most of the publicity stills from the shoot show him seated or reclining.

Coburn was frustrated by the script and felt the studio had rushed into production without enough input from him. "We didn't have a chance to really finish the script, because they wanted to get it out. We had to start shooting before we wanted to, and we never quite got the ending right, but it turned out okay. The ideal individual versus the women, taking over the world. They don't even use hair dryers anymore."

The ideas were supposed to be bigger, yet the whole thing—Flint's redone apartment, the villain's lair, even the crowds of pretty women running around in swimsuits—seemed smaller. The locations were beautiful but often look overcrowded. It appeared that the extras wore their own beachwear, which is not an unusual practice, but in this case it makes the crowd scenes look inconsistent. And the extraordinary egg-shaped hats worn by the older ladies were indeed a curiosity.

Meanwhile Coburn's wardrobe, designs for which had been a talking point for *Our Man Flint*, this time came from Martin of California. This was clearly a promotional tie-in. Martin of California was a manufacturer of men's ready-to-wear outdoor wear and sportswear. Ironically Martin's slogan was "If you're an overreacher . . ."

The plot of *In Like Flint* was somewhat convoluted, involving a surgically enhanced impostor posing as the president and a goofy women-take-over-the-world plan using a satellite, which seemed a deliberate attempt to ridicule contemporary feminism. If that was not clear from the script, it was made explicit after the movie came out.

Critic Clifford Terry claimed that the film included "latent Lesbians" [*sic*],[29] while reviewer Harry Haun describes the villains as "beauty-cosmetic tycoons by profession and veiled lesbians by inference."[30] In response, Saul David, Hal Fimberg, and Gordon Douglas wrote an open letter to the *Hollywood Reporter* and *Variety* debunking this "lesbian angle" as unintended and unintentional, referencing their intention to critique or spoof current feminist writers and scholarly works.[31] They cited Ashley Montagu's *The Natural Superiority of Women*, Simone de Beauvoir's *The Second Sex*, and "the more contemporary moans of Betty Friedan, etc." They ended the letter with, "I'm dismayed that the implication was drawn." This controversy certainly served as a nice distraction from the genuine plot holes and absurdity, and probably attracted curious viewers. Manufacturing controversy, especially around perceptions of obscenity, is a marketing technique that goes back to time immemorial. Today's audiences might find that aspect of the story offensively sexist.

On the other hand, actress Jean Hale, who played Lisa, the femme-fatale leader of the women, felt very positive about the script as a feminist statement. She told pop-culture author Tom Lisanti that she was excited to be part of it. "I can't tell you what I had to go through to get this role. It was a very sought after role because *Our Man Flint* had been such a big success. From what I heard, Fox head Dick Zanuck wanted Catherine Deneuve. But producer Saul David thought I was just right for the part. Since Zanuck wanted a Grace Kelly–type, I had to screen test doing a scene from one of her movies.

"*Flint* was brilliantly written in a satirical, farcical way but played straight. For a mid-sixties spy spoof, the film was pretty aggressive in the way it tackled the issue of oppression. We were women who loved men but were tired of being oppressed by them. We were trying to exert our dominance over men while staying feminine at the same time. But I think the studio got scared that the film went too far and pulled in the reins. They cut Flint's speech to the women about the nature of the oppressed."[32]

That speech was in the climactic confrontation scene, a whole section of dialogue that nicely elucidated the theme as somewhat more universal:

> FLINT: "I'm sure all your facts are accurate but, like every other underdog
> in this world, you know more about the sickness than you do the cure.
> What you propose merely turns the coin over. It's the same old coin.
> If it's a slug on one side, girls, it's a slug on the other. Now, forget it!"[33]

This was cut to just "Forget it!"

This antifeminist rhetoric was something of a betrayal of the humanistic qualities of Flint. Hal Fimberg wrote that this time the screenplay was "a solo task, I started with nothing but the central character," along with a nice trip to Jamaica that allowed him to "tailor the action to the actual situation."[34] Promoting the writing was all part of the marketing process.

One ingenious publicity stunt was devised by the production's publicist, Leo Pearlstein. Riffing on the health-and-beauty theme of the story, he set up a health food bar for the set. The snacks included "natural treats like honey, boysenberries, certified raw milk, and prunes."[35] The story was promoted in movie magazines.

Jean Hale was often asked about her costar: "James is adorable and easy, yet challenging to work with. He is a very sweet, gentle man. When I went on tour to promote the film, the big question was always, 'What was it like to kiss James Coburn?' I'd respond, 'It was lovely but all in a day's work.'"[36]

In Like Flint was nothing like the runaway hit of the original, but it still made money. The producers hoped to continue the franchise, but the scripts that were proposed were so awful that Coburn had one response—forget it.[37]

Instead he directed his attention to his next collaboration with Blake Edwards, who was producing the comic western *Waterhole #3* for Paramount. The story is about a supposedly charming rogue who learns where a bandit has hidden a cache of gold stolen from the U.S. Cavalry. Unfortunately, a bunch of other people find out about it too. Hijinks ensue. The director was William Graham, making his feature-film debut after a decade directing TV.

This script went through many iterations, starting in March of 1966. Reading between the lines of certain production department memos ("many arguments will be advanced that you can't go by the script.... You put your money on the creative talents despite the negative report from the pragmatic analysts"), it sounds like the script had problems from the start that were never really resolved.[38]

Eventually the producers determined that "much, so much, depends on casting." Apparently, they planned to rely on the Coburn charm and charisma to make a fundamentally unpleasant individual likable. Filming began in early October 1966 in Lone Pine and Red Rock Canyon State Park in Central California. If not the Mojave Desert itself, the region is certainly adjacent to desert. It was dry and dusty. Still, after three months at home between films, with only a quick trip to Jamaica for *In Like Flint*'s opening, Coburn was pleased to be on a set again.

Once again Shurlock had particular concerns with the language, and more. "The problem lies principally in the presentation of the rape, as well as the reprise of it in this serial-comedic style."[39] Eventually he proposed that the only way around it was for this film to be one of the very first released with the brand-new designation: Suggested for Mature Audiences.

Unlike Coburn's early classics, this movie has not aged well when subjected to modern sensibilities. Today's audiences would likely find the same part of the movie, including the dismissive attitude from the rape victim's father, to be discomfiting and certainly not funny. It's as if the filmmakers couldn't decide if it was a caper film, a buddy road film, or yet another satire about stupid military brass. Even usually delightful Joan Blondell couldn't save her own dialogue in the remarkably poorly choreographed shoot-out in the whorehouse. The geography of this scene is so confusing, it looks as if everyone expects their bullets to curve in the air.

Most contemporary critics agreed, with the best reviews finding the humor inconsistent. The whole thing suffered from invidious comparisons to *Cat Ballou* (1965), which also includes a narrative in the form of a ballad.[40]

The critics generally liked the chemistry between Coburn's and Carroll O'Connor's characters much more than the chemistry between Coburn and the sheriff's long-suffering daughter played by Margaret Blye.[41] Apparently the movie was more fun to shoot than to watch. The *New York Times* reviewer blamed the script—"the tangled twistings and turnings of the strictly hoo-tenanny plot. . . . Mr. Graham must have lost his script away out there . . . [and] just made it up as they went along."[42]

Roger Ebert was the harshest, saying the film "is approximately as hilarious, as a pail of limp grits." He did not like the "disproportionate amount of dirty stuff. Subtle, filthy little double meanings." He put the blame squarely on the star, "who comes across on the screen as one of the most self conscious [*sic*] actors now in movies. Every wink and twitch is calculated."[43]

At this time, Coburn *was* self-conscious—intentionally so. He was still as fascinated by the teachings of George Gurdjieff and P. D. Ouspensky as he had been when he first was turned on to their writings ten years earlier in 1956. He was actively engaging with what Ouspensky called the Work, at least to the extent that it was possible from just reading about it by himself, as opposed to studying the concepts with a teacher or group. Plus he was reading everything he could find about Sufis.

He was especially interested in using these ideas to improve his own acting ability and refine his process. "Everything is always changing. If you get stuck, believing one thing about one thing, you're stuck there, instead of seeing all the other possibilities. One of the things I learned was the ability to direct my attention.[44]

"One day I was sitting in the movie theater, and I found my attention being taken, so I stopped it and directed my attention to the exit sign, then to the back of the head of the person sitting in front of me, and then I redirected to the screen and watched the film consciously, instead of just sitting there letting it roll over me, like we all do. In fact, that's what we want to do, to go through all of the emotions they give us vicariously. That's what motion pictures and art are really about, to give emotions to the layperson, the person without the ability to consciously display their emotions.

"That's what acting is, just a conscious display of emotion. Sometimes real, sometimes unreal but nevertheless, it makes the audience feel something. It's about getting to the point we were free enough to let it go, let it happen. I couldn't possibly prepare for the scene if I was trying to *do* something. It would never happen. If I just turn it on and let it go, it always comes out okay. Sometimes it's better than other times, when I may have to do it again and goose things up a little bit. A little more energy. Be guided that way. But you just have to let it go, let it out. Then it's a joy. It's a hell of a lot more fun. Find the blockage and work. That's part of the whole trip, relaxing and letting it go. You keep the body and the ego out of it. You can't act with an ego, and you can't work with an ego. Get rid of the ego. The ego blocks everything. The ego stands in the way of anybody taking in anything real, except what the ego wants to be real. And that ain't much."

Apparently Coburn was able to reconcile the concept of not preparing with his Method training. He had certainly read the seminal text by Konstantin Stanislavski, *An Actor Prepares*, which was still on his bookshelf at the end of his life. He first learned the idea of knowing the character's needs and intentions in any scene from Jeff Corey.

He thus sums up his process of acting and developing his characterizations: "I call it telling the truth for a living. It's not lying. You try to tell the truth. To talk about acting—you can't just do it. What you have to do is *do* exercises, improvisations. Then you can get something going. You put two people together, put them in conflict, and see how they, as people, overcome it. Make the conflict work, then make it art. How do you make art? You show them. You just don't get up there and start fighting with each other, which is what a lot of people do.

"But to talk about it is not possible. Stella used to explain what characters do and why they did it. But how do you get to the place where you can actually do that? Experience. You just have to build up experience based on certain principles. The rules of engagement. Working with dynamics, like listening to Count Basie's band. The principles of knowing who you're talking to, as well as knowing who you are that's doing the talking. In other words, the acceptance of being a character, of being another person other than yourself. Find out what a person talks like, what he wants, and what he does, and *do* it. Act like you know what the fuck he's talking about.

"Acting has to do with in between the lines, not on the lines. It's in between where you're listening. Listening—that's the key to the trip. You can't respond unless you know what the person said, and how he said it—tonality. Is he pissed off? That's dynamics. Feed that dynamic.

"Spencer Tracy said, 'Just learn your lines and don't bump into the furniture.' The absolute worst thing you can do is learn the lines by rote. Then it sticks so that every time you do the scene, you do it the same way. The key is trying different ways. Don't be locked into anything. Try attitudes you can move into.

"Every *character* isn't trying to be conscious. You can tell—to a degree—how conscious they are by what they do and how they do it, much as you can yourself. How much do I take in? How much can I absorb from an impression? And what do I do with that impression? Does that impression just work in me? You don't have to do anything to take in an impression. Impressions just work in you, but you have to be conscious and open enough to be able to take in an impression."

Some of the mental processes Coburn described might just as accurately be called mindfulness today. He described the period as "very intense and very good. I was incorporating some of the things [from the Work] into my films, like in the Flint films. Subtle things. My aim was to show things people didn't see.

"*Waterhole #3* was an esoteric western, like the gold was the light and we were seekers of the light. The last line of the film, I was looking over my shoulder and said, 'Maybe we pay too much attention to the gold.' Then I look over my other shoulder and say, 'Then, maybe we don't pay enough attention to the gold.' That was a fun movie."

Actually the line was "Maybe we take gold too seriously. Then, maybe we don't take gold seriously enough," just before he escapes to Mexico with a comet's tail of others with equal, or better, claims to the spoils. Hindsight is supposed to be 20/20, but it seems like willful denial to pretend that this particular film was imbued with spiritual or intellectual significance, or at any rate that such significance was made visible to the audiences.

Gurdjieff lamented "the endless pursuit of social recognition [and] sensory pleasures."[45] Coburn needed recognition to succeed in his occupation, even while he presented the persona of a philosopher to journalists, like syndicated columnist John Kent: "James Coburn is given to such statements as: 'I strive to balance myself, to strike the exact center of life, from which point I can depart as an actor to points of extreme—but not live them. I am concerned with mental and emotional balance, all my parts equaling each other. . . .' He thinks he has made progress in himself except that 'I'm too dogmatic. I cannot accept contrary views on the subjects I feel strongly about. That is an extreme I am working on. I must correct it.' That last line comes with thunderbolt intensity."[46]

At the same time, he was perfectly happy to spend his leisure time with his wife and their friends in the pursuit of sensory pleasures—whether it be through the recreational use of alcohol and drugs, or through his enjoyment of music, drumming, and his gong. He told Kent that he used drumming to work out his frustrations. "Sometimes I go into a room at home and work up a frenzy on [the drum]. I don't think; my hands just take over everything. The drum responds, and you integrate with it. The more the drum vibrates, the more tension drains out of you."

It may be that his quest to eliminate ego had the effect of, ironically, making him more self-involved, more self-centered, rather than less. Coburn's next film gave him the opportunity to explore the things people don't see, in a much more direct way.

7

The Horse's Mouth

I wanted to direct motion pictures, and I wanted to learn how to do
that, and I figured just watching films is not the way to do it. Everybody
else thinks that is the way to do it—just watch a lot of films, you will
know exactly what to do. Well, that's untrue because you have to learn
lenses; you have to learn blocking; you have to learn acting and actions.
You have to learn the psychology of getting an actor to do one thing
when he doesn't want to do it and make him happy about it. You have
to make a scene happen, building the dynamic out of something that
is really just words. So, you know, you have to do a hell of a lot more
than just look at a film to know how to do it.

—JAMES COBURN, 2002

Sharp wind gusts buffeted James Coburn, nearly sweeping him away while he
gripped the metal railing for dear life. Just below, out of frame, an assistant
clung to his legs. The pair was close to three hundred feet above the ground,
in the torch of the Statue of Liberty in New York. "Nobody had been up
there in forty years. We had to get special permission. Quite an experience."[1]

The film shoot was for *The President's Analyst* (1967).

Five years earlier, during the filming of *Charade*, one of the frequent visitors to the set had been Ted Flicker. He was a friend of that movie's writer,
Peter Stone. Some years later, back home, Coburn ran into Flicker at a party

at George Peppard's house. Flicker had just completed a new screenplay called "The President's Analyst," a political satire. "The idea turned me on immediately, and I asked to read it. I fell in love with it." The story and the character fired his imagination and percolated in his head while he worked on other projects.

Waterhole #3 had been produced and distributed by Paramount Pictures. That studio had a beleaguered recent history. For several years after the collapse of the theater-ownership system, Paramount management had struggled to stabilize the studio's income. Foolish financial investments had been made. They sold off many of their hard assets, such as buildings, land, and their TV station, attempting to stay solvent. Then in late 1966 the company was bought by Gulf + Western Industries, headed by Charles Bluhdorn, who hired a young—some would say, upstart—producer, Robert Evans, to take charge as vice president of production. At the time, Evans was still (but not for long) married to Camilla Sparv, who had costarred in *Dead Heat on a Merry-Go-Round*, which was still in theaters. Evans hired Peter Bart as his second-in-command, and the pair set about looking for scripts and projects. They were hurting for hits.

Even while shooting *In Like Flint* and *Waterhole #3*, Coburn had stayed excited about Ted Flicker's youth-oriented script. At the end of those shoots, he left his production company, M.O.F.F., and formed a new one, Panpiper, without a bunch of partners, to co-produce the project. During the promo campaign in March 1967 for *In Like Flint*, he laid the groundwork for the upcoming film, commenting on the contrast between generations. "I think the kids get it.... They see the result of the aim of this generation and they want something different ... not to die on some battlefield in some war we never should have been involved in."[2]

One sticking point was that Flicker wanted to direct his own script. "I asked him if he could direct. He said he had directed some television. I'd been working at Paramount, so I gave it to Peter Bart. He fell in love with it and told Bob Evans they had to make it. They asked me the same thing, 'Can he direct?' 'Well, if he can't, we'll fire his ass and get someone else.' That was the way it had to go. Ted was a good guy, very intellectual."[3]

Most of Evans's attention was directed toward *The Odd Couple* (1968), but he was happy to support this other picture. In his memoir, *The Kid Stays in the Picture*, he says, "James Coburn was the perfect leading man for the late sixties. Rugged but irreverent. I thought it was a great coup getting him for an anti-establishment black comedy."[4] They put together a strong, experienced production team, a mix of film and TV people from Paramount and the freelance crowd—"all the right people."[5] The producer brought on was another old friend from the *General Electric Theater* days, Stanley Rubin. His beyond-solid credits include having won the very first Emmy for a movie made for television in 1949. The art department head was a Desilu Productions stalwart, Pato Guzman. Some of the cast were tapped from Ted Flicker's improv group, Compass Theater.[6]

The film shot in Washington DC and around New York as well as at the Paramount lot and ranch over the summer of 1967. The company had to gain special permission to shoot a running chase scene in a Manhattan city street. Hidden cameras were mounted high on buildings, making ordinary passersby de facto extras. The local police precinct was kept in the loop for the evening shoot, with the local beat cops ready to be part of the scene. Given the word, Coburn dashed out of a Chinese restaurant and took off running down the sidewalk with two actors hot on his heels. He slipped between random pedestrians milling around before turning a distant corner. The character was supposed to jump into a van and hide, leading to the next part of the story.

Unfortunately and unknowingly, he crossed into the neighboring precinct. An officer, seeing a running man and his colleagues in the distance, thought Coburn was a suspect and whacked him in the face with his billy club, stopping him cold. The shoot had to be delayed for several days while the swelling in Coburn's face subsided.

"We wanted to know who this cop was. I said, 'I want that guy outside my trailer guarding me from now on.' But nobody would cop to it. Mayor Lindsay sent me a great bouquet of flowers and half a case of champagne, saying, 'That will teach you to run around the streets of New York at night.' I was walking in the park the following day, and I saw a couple of cops, and they said, 'Hey, Coburn, what happened the other night?' I told them the story and said the guy had hit me in the goddamned nose. They said I was lucky I didn't get shot."[7]

The movie's plot has the title character becoming increasingly paranoid and delusional. Upon discovering that his fears are justified, he runs off and eventually hides out in a hippie commune with a rock band.[8] Coburn spoofed both Flint and his own public persona, playing a gong with the band in a wild, drug-fueled love-in scene, before being grabbed by one of the international agencies desperate to learn the president's secrets. The climax of the movie has the chillingly prescient concept of the true bad guys being "TPC," which stands for The Phone Company, their cheery robotic representative happily monologuing about their plans to keep everyone under constant surveillance.

In another prescient sequence, the Russian spy Kropotkin (Severn Darden) notes that the United States is becoming more socialist, while the USSR is becoming more capitalist, and "soon they will meet in the middle and shake hands."[9] Both the CIA and the FBI are lampooned (although no more than any other nation's espionage apparatus), and the end credits specifically note that neither group helped the production in any way.

Geoffrey Shurlock, whose voice was certainly fading in influence, was concerned about the portrayal of the American agents as well as the sexual content, as usual. There was to be no rolling in the bed during a bedroom scene, and the view of a naked girl's rear end was to be from a distance.[10] The script called for this latter shot to be a wide reveal in any case. The censors were apparently not groovy enough to get the pointed drug references in the song lyrics, which they passed without comment. The song "Inner Manipulations" (aka "Changes") includes the lyrics "the changes that rearrange my mind."

The censors were not the only ones concerned with disrespect of authority. The notorious head of the FBI, J. Edgar Hoover, pressured Paramount to sanitize the film. Evans revealed that two G-men had visited him to tell him that "Mr. Hoover did not appreciate the FBI being made fun of."[11] After some resistance, Evans caved and changed the letter names to FBR and CEA, making sure the press knew why.[12] As the story goes, after even more pressure was applied directly to Bluhdorn, Ted Flicker was prevented from making his final edit. However, he sneaked back to the editing room and cut the negative as he wanted it—and the extremely tight deadline meant the completed film went out that way with elements of biting satire and much humor.[13]

Hoover, not renowned for his sense of humor, was angry. He made another call, and despite the largely positive reviews—"a bright, original idea developed with jaunty good humor and real flair . . . some amusing buckshots at bureaucracy, professional liberalism and poor Freud"—the film disappeared from theaters after a very short run.[14] The overseas openings were canceled or delayed, with the film showing up only on TV in the UK. Even though Ted Flicker was nominated for a Writers Guild Award in 1968 for his screenplay, the film was relatively obscure for a long time. It was not released on DVD until 2008.[15]

Viewing *The President's Analyst* today, the parts about the spies and the government agencies feel very light, more along the lines of gentle irony. The parody representation of the liberal middle-class family, with their house gun and car gun and oblivious privilege, and the moving story of childhood racism from CEA agent Don (Godfrey Cambridge) feel far more topical and incisive. The scenes in the hippie commune, the least appreciated bits in 1967, are now some of the funniest. The film has been rediscovered and enjoyed at revivals and festivals, even being included in the book *Last Word: Final Scenes from Your Favorite Motion Pictures* by Josh Gross, which also includes *Charade*.[16]

Even while all this drama was going on in the editing room and Hoover's office, Coburn was already off filming his next picture on location in Spain and London. It was during this trip that he had his first opportunity to travel to Tangier in North Africa, another part of the world he and Beverly came to love.

It is hard to grasp the pace of his life at this time, shooting two or three major starring roles in movies each year, sometimes with two films overlapping in the theaters in their first run as well as second runs of recent pictures in regional theaters. It was possible to see double features of the two Flint movies in some towns, even while *Waterhole #3* opened in a neighboring cinema. Add to that his appearances on talk shows, like *The Dick Cavett Show*, and his public service announcement promoting Christmas Seals for the 1968 holiday season that showed in theaters nationwide. Coburn's face and image were certainly in front of the public nearly constantly in the late 1960s. Around this time he announced his ambition to direct someday. "I may be terrible at it, but man, I've got to try!"[17]

Coburn spent the late summer and early fall shooting *Duffy* on the beautiful Costa del Sol in Malaga, Spain (birthplace of Picasso and Antonio Banderas), and across the straits in Tangier. The plot was about two disaffected sons planning to rob their own wealthy father with the help of Coburn and his convoluted plan, but of course the caper goes awry. He played what was coming to be his typical groovy, turned-on cat—a metalworker of strange mixed-media sculptures, a hippie and playboy who also happened to be a part-time professional thief. His character resides in a crammed studio near the beach in Tangier, a part of the world renowned at that time for a high level of acceptance of alternative lifestyles. George Gurdjieff and some of his followers had lived in Tangier, as had the leaders of the Beat Generation, Allen Ginsberg and Jack Kerouac, for a time. It was also an important stop in the education of painters Delacroix and Matisse. It was the perfect setting for a counterculture character's home, and perfectly plausible as an American artist's residence.

The director, Robert Parrish, was an Oscar-winning editor and director of many westerns, among other films.[18] He had started his career as a child actor for John Ford and later worked for Ford as an editor. By the time he got to *Duffy*, he had just come off two stressful turns directing notoriously challenging actor, Peter Sellers.[19] By comparison, this project was quite literally a day at the beach.

The rest of the *Duffy* cast were British. The casting had been completed in London before the company traveled to Spain in late July. Coburn had pushed for singer/songwriter/actress Marianne Faithfull for the leading lady, having recently met her and Mick Jagger, who were dating at the time. That didn't happen—Susannah York was cast in that role. Faithfull did have some recommendations for eateries in Tangier, however, as the Rolling Stones had also visited there not long before.[20]

Initially Coburn felt worried about James Mason's performance. Working with him in front of the camera, he couldn't see Mason's reactions, so he kept trying to force something—until he saw the production rushes. "He was effervescent. Sparkles were coming out of his eyes. Everything was happening. I felt like such an asshole, trying to make something happen with this guy, when it was already happening. I just didn't know how to look at it. He was great, a wonderful man. It's great to work with great actors. [James Mason] was a consummate actor, a great actor, a great *film* actor. A great film actor does very little, and the camera does the rest. James could raise an eyebrow and tell a world of things."[21] Coburn would enjoy working with James Mason twice more in his career.

The company was in the historically cosmopolitan city of Malaga during the annual Feria de Málaga religious festival in the first week of August. The Coburn kids came, with their nanny, for two weeks on their summer vacation from school, but only in time for the last day of the festival. Audrey Hepburn was there at the time too. The Coburns were not in the city but were staying in a more isolated house in Almería, down an unpleasant twenty-mile dirt road. The house had been used by Anthony Quinn during the shoot of *Lawrence of Arabia* (1962). A reporter for the *Daily Express* wire service came to the location, ostensibly to interview Coburn, but ended up writing rather more about Beverly. "She manages her husband's affairs, travels with him almost everywhere and, with splendid wifely enthusiasm, shares his interests. . . . 'I got our gong for him for Christmas. I seldom play them but I share Jim's enthusiasm for them. It can be very soothing. It takes all of your attention and [is a] great focusing point.'"[22]

The reporter of course noticed that the actor "seems to be getting pretty passionate with some of the girls on the beach" and notes that "unflappable" Beverly did not seem to be bothered. "Anybody who has been on a movie set, and seen all those beautiful girls with their makeup dripping under the hot lights, will know it's strictly work."

Beverly may have been watching the scenes "affectionately," but film sets are boring after a while, especially for people not working on the film. Spending time with her children also held little interest for her. Just as the kids arrived, she took a trip across the straits to Tangier on a quest to find a Sufi. "We had been reading all the Sufi lore," Coburn says of the time. "It's like the old Indian story—let's follow the coyote and hope he'll lead us to water."[23] Most recently they'd read a book on the subject by someone called Idries Shah.

After looking at some carpets and antiques, and telling all the people she met that she wanted to find a Sufi, one of the dealers finally suggested that Beverly see "the Professor." Her taxi driver took her to this mysterious professor's house.

Coburn recalls, "So he says, 'Yes, madam, what can I do for you? I am a professor of Oriental religion.' He was a professor emeritus at Oxford. She says, 'I've been reading a book called *The Sufis.*' He said, 'Who wrote that book?' and she answered, 'Idries Shah.' He replied, 'Idries Shah is my son. You have come to the horse's mouth.'" Beverly spent the next week going to his house for daily meditations and hearing his wonderful stories. "Then she came back, and after hearing her stories, I was so jealous."

Soon when the Spain-Tangier unit wrapped and the company had a short hiatus, the whole family spent a week at the Minzah Hotel in Tangier. Coburn says of the first time he met Shah, "We just grabbed each other, hugged like we were very old, old friends for about three minutes, in a wonderful exchange of energy. From that point on, it was like I had come home." Lisa was particularly interested in the Professor. "He would tell her stories, and she would be enthralled. Then he would lean over and spit."

From then on Coburn considered Professor Ali Shah his *murshid*, or teacher. They had an intense relationship for the next two years, in various places. Shah stayed with him for a month during the shoot of *Hard Contract* the next year in nearby Torremolinos.

"He was my first real teacher of any esoteric significance. We spent a lot of time laughing and carrying on. He was a member of and stayed at the Royal Over-Seas League in London. They had the greatest scones, and we would have tea in the afternoon. He had written seventy-five books, esoteric stuff.

He lived on the receipts of these obscure books that were in libraries. He had access to the inner sanctum of the British Museum. One day I was going to pick him up. He was going to study some ancient Rumi manuscripts that were there. I showed up in my red Ferrari 275 GTB. There he was, skipping down the stairs in his gray djellaba with green trim, and I opened the door and strapped him in, and he was very excited. 'I've found it! I've found it! I've wondered all these years why we do it.' I asked, 'Why do we do it?' He answered, 'Immortality.' It took me a long time to figure out what he meant by immortality. I can see him now—skipping down those steps at the front of the British Museum."

Shah was full of insights and humor—"all the stories he told were filled with humor, the ones about himself especially." He taught Coburn "to play but play seriously" and how to do a proper seated meditation. They discussed fate and the need to take responsibility for oneself.

"I've been a serious student about things that seem to have a way of doing things, a way of doing yourself, a way of becoming something, a way of making you less habitual and more conscious about how to do things. It's been both a help and a hindrance. Sometimes you just need to leave it alone. After a certain point, you can't just leave it alone—you have to give it attention; then you have to give it action; then you have to suffer whatever that means. That's what I'm doing now.

"We have to learn how to regulate our machines. We are under the law of fate or under the law of accident, and it's up to us to find that out. And we're under the law of accident until we become conscious enough to become under the law of fate. Then what happens? There are fewer laws, but they are more difficult to deal with.

"And you *have* to take over. There's no magic involved. You can say, 'Well, fate will take care of it all.' Bullshit! Not after that. Not if you've decided to take care of it. Then you have to take care of it. It's a responsibility to yourself if you decide to take that on. I decided to do that a long time ago and look where it's got me.

"Obviously, I wasn't ready, because I didn't have a school; I didn't have anybody to guide me. Ali Shah was the only one that guided me toward anything, and that was the mystical side. If he [had] lived longer, and I'd been with him more, I probably would have taken that trip to more of a degree than I did."

Unfortunately, Professor Shah was the victim of fate. He was killed in a tragic and somewhat absurd accident, crushed by a soft drink truck in November 1969.

After the first week with Shah, the children flew home again while Coburn and Beverly made a quick detour to Brussels to collect his next new Ferrari, before heading to London to finish up *Duffy*. There they were interviewed and photographed for *Woman's Own* magazine. Both were wearing garments that they had likely picked up in the Tangier bazaar, for Beverly "a psychedelic housecoat," while Coburn wore "a long kaftan and lounged back in an armchair, smoking French cigarettes through a holder."[24] Evidently, hippie and tribal fashion styles hadn't made it to the mainstream quite yet.

Coburn spoke eloquently about love. "Man must be here for self-evolution, a development of the mind. We've still got a long way to go, but I feel I found the key to our purpose. In a few words, I would say it is to understand ourselves and to learn to love. Yes, love is what it's all about."

He talked about working on *The President's Analyst*. "There was a great crowd of people involved—really grooving. All giving off vibrations and sparking each other's ideas. We all understood each other. We all knew what we were doing. Everyone's energy was going towards the same thing. We were all so involved—it was a rare experience. I want to go on working in these kinds of conditions."

He described his marriage and their relationship. "She balances me. . . . We have our disagreements. I might see things one way and Beverly another. After all, people are individuals. But there is something between us—a feeling that surrounds us, which I think is love and which I think is a good kind of unity. . . . Since I met Beverly, I realized that it isn't unmanly to talk about love and say what you feel. And our marriage has got better and stronger as the years have passed. . . . Marriage is both people working for the family unit. The physical side is just the beginning of a relationship, not the all in all. You have to relate on all levels or try to.

"I didn't have a great vision of romantic ecstasy, but I wanted a partner who could share my existence with me. I wanted a marriage through which we could evolve together from plane to plane—as a growing process, together. The important thing to us is that it's a productive relationship. We grow. It's love that counts. And we hope to go on together—loving—forever."

They certainly had a strong commitment and strong feelings. The article notes that Beverly traveled everywhere with him, to which Coburn added, "Well she has to, she's the one who cuts my hair!"

Notwithstanding, shortly after this, Beverly did go home first, prompting Coburn to write her a beautiful poetic letter, as usual addressed to "My Love."

"Since you went away, it's rained and rained. Beautiful rain splattering the gray Thames rejuvenating its tired waters and mine. We are working in an old boat works on the small eyot in the middle of the stream. It's marvelous and lonely, I wish you were here. To touch, kiss, smell, to feel, to love, to look at, to marvel with, to bite, to hold your hand, to fill the empty place in our midnight bed. My heart seeks your presence and spins in circles with your image there. I love you. I've just finished my exercise with you and Murshid. My letter to him follows this to you, my love."[25]

He clearly missed her presence when she wasn't with him.

Other than the *Woman's Own* profile, the press was not kind to the movie *Duffy*, one British paper calling it "unmitigated tosh."[26] James Mason rather mildly responded that it was tosh, "but not unmitigated." He notes, "It must have been the hippie stuff which so upset the English critics." Today it is a film that is appreciated by a cult audience more for the time capsule glimpses into a lifestyle than for the fairly thin story. For lovers of campy, vintage hippie style, the scenes in the nightclub are worth the price of admission. They are scored by R&B musician Ernie Freeman with organ music, and feature some of the most blissed-out dancing since the reward room in *Our Man Flint*. The main song, in what seems to be a response to the Rolling Stones's hit, is "I'm Satisfied." As James Fox's character opines, "It's gonna be a groovy little happening, man."[27]

After being away from home for more than three months, Coburn flew home in time for the opening and fast closing of *The President's Analyst*.[28] Then in February 1968, the pair was off again, to a shoot in Rome, followed by an extended vacation trip starting in Egypt and going through Southeast Asia.

Candy by Terry Southern and Mason Hoffenberg was a deliberately provocative book, with highly graphic erotic language, and considered very funny at the time. The story followed a series of episodic vignettes in the journey of a callow young woman whose clueless charm and beauty raise the interest of a succession of men. With her catch phrase, "Good grief," and her belief that she somehow incited all the lascivious attentions of everyone from a college professor to a homeless hunchback ("Well it's my own fault, darn it") and was doing a service for humanity by giving in, today's readers might consider the book laced with a grating misogyny. When it was released in 1958, it rose to number one on the bestseller list as a satire on sex and sexual repression.

If ever there was a film project that defined the term "cult movie," *Candy* was it. The director was Christian Marquand, "who was a friend of all of ours, and that's why we were doing it."[29] The screenwriter was Buck Henry, although he and Coburn both wondered at the time why Terry Southern was not writing it. "Terry Southern was a friend of mine. I met him through some musician friends. With one book, he had become a cult figure. We hit it off. He called me 'Big Grand Guy Jim.' He called Beverly 'Bev Beauty.'" The answer was that Terry Southern "wanted nothing to do with it, having withdrawn when they insisted on taking out the hunchback."[30]

The cast was a collection of luminaries, including Walter Matthau, John Huston, and Marlon Brando. The leading lady was Swedish newcomer Ewa Aulin, a former Miss Teen International, 1966. "Young and stunning, about twenty or twenty-one years old, and a beautiful posterior Brando just couldn't take his tongue off of. He could just not think about anything but this beautiful thing. She had never acted before, and she was just thrilled to do the film. She was sexy and cute, all those things you wanted her to be."[31]

Actually, she had only just turned eighteen, two weeks before the Coburns flew in.

Marlon Brando portrayed a guru obsessed, as all the characters were, with the title character. However, he was also personally interested in Aulin. His single-minded pursuit of the girl—one might call it sexual harassment in modern parlance—caused her to become utterly overwhelmed. She went into hysterics. She was unable to speak due to laughing uncontrollably. As a newcomer and very young, powerless in a system that always favored a star, her laughter was her only defense.

When the Coburns arrived in Rome for the shoot, Aulin was in a clinic by the sea in Ostend, supposedly taking a sleep cure.[32]

"They put her in for a week but had to keep her there for two weeks. When she [had first] arrived, Brando in his brilliance started making her laugh. Brando in his prime was probably one of the funniest human beings I've ever met. He makes you laugh. He kept me in stitches a lot. A very funny guy. I don't remember anything [about the movie] because I was laughing too hard. It was always something about himself. The joke was always on him, and that was what was so funny.

"Because Brando had such big eyes for her, he was always trying to make her laugh. The maharishi-type character he was playing had to wear this long fright wig, so every time they had a scene together, every time he would say anything, she would break up laughing. She started laughing every time she saw him on the set.

"Poor Ewa, she was a sweet little thing. She finally came back, and still she saw Brando in the fright wig again. Everybody broke up, and so did she. She kind of calmed down, and they shot some scenes that were necessary. Then when they needed her to do her scenes with Brando, Christian played the role on the other side of the camera and they just shot her so she wouldn't laugh. That's the way they solved that problem."[33] It must have been a relief.

Coburn met John Huston for the first time in the makeup room and asked him what he was doing. Huston replied, "They fired me off *The Madwoman of Chaillot*. That bald-headed guy didn't like me." He was talking about Yul Brynner. On *Candy* Huston was playing the head of the hospital while Coburn was portraying "the greatest surgeon in the world. We shot the whole scene in the studio where I had my thumb in the back end of John Astin's head. . . . All the extras in the operating theater were all Italian royalty—dukes and counts and what have you, princes. There were a lot of them, evidently."

In Coburn's spare time, he and Beverly saw the sights of Rome. "We were going through St. Peter's, and I walked in there and saw all these marble crypts with past popes on top of the caskets. They are all carved by these great artists, and they all look quite heroic. I wondered what they had all done to get put here. There was some kind of ceremony. I don't know what it was. We saw all the old cardinals. You could almost see the dust bounce off their shoulders, and they all looked like they were sound asleep, walking in this line, swaying back and forth. Some of them had incense, and it looked like they were ninety years old. I think, *Where did they find all these sleepy old farts?* And then they sit down across from the choir, and someone, an Italian cat with a big loudspeaker, gets up to announce the cardinals. Some big honcho does about ten minutes in Latin; then the choir begins out of the speakers. These old cathedrals are like sound generators, but they had sound coming out of these big speakers until it was such a cacophony. Then the cardinals get up and leave the same way they came in. Their robes were silk and brocade and looked like each garment cost thousands of dollars."

After the shoot, Coburn and Beverly flew to Egypt, at last. It was their first time there. Cairo was not what he expected. "Cairo was like a ghost town. No one was there. Even the dust in the streets of Cairo was lying flat on its back. Pure sand flies. And we'd drive by these housing projects, and it smelled like the worst kind of diarrhea you can imagine. From the Hilton Hotel, where we were staying, to the great mosque, which I wanted to see, we'd have to pass them. For ten minutes of the ride there, it was like a dysentery odor of pure shit. It was awful. And it did not clear up until you got on the other side of the mosque. Whew! In Cairo, I expected something great and magnificent, strange, exotic."

This was not long after the Six-Day War between Israel and Egypt. There was still a great deal of tension, and since the United States supported Israel, while the Soviets were with Egypt, American visitors were looked on with some suspicion. There were still soldiers in "ragtag uniforms" visible around the city. The museums still had blast tape on their windows. The hotel was almost empty, with just a few locals sitting around drinking coffee. As tourists the Coburns stood out.

As it happened, that night was a full moon. Coburn wanted to see the pyramids at night. They drove out with a guide, and when they arrived, Coburn determined that he would walk around the Great Pyramid while Beverly waited in the car. He set off into the silence, the light from the moon casting deep shadows. "While I was walking, I was hoping for some kind of esoteric flash to happen. I walked all down one side. I turned to where all the little buildings were. I hear this noise. There was this guy, an Egyptian soldier with his rifle, a guard. I said, 'American, tourist!' over and over, and he just stood there and looked at me, with his rifle. The car finally pulls up, and the driver gets out to talk to him, and we were told to get the hell out of there. Evidently, we were not supposed to be there at night. Did they think anyone was going to steal the pyramid? So it was half an esoteric experience."

After this scare, Coburn visited the mosque and noticed the contrast to St. Peter's. "The echo inside the mosque—it magnifies—it's exquisite."

Next the couple spent two days in India starting in New Delhi, to visit some friends, the Kumars, who were renowned art dealers. They went from there to Agra to the Taj Mahal. "That was fantastic. Walked around at night with flashlights. That was a trip. It looked like really dark slate—a gray black. The closer you get, the more magnificent it is—that white alabaster with all the unbelievable colors. There you can learn a little bit about love. Talk about devotion."

Then they went to Bangkok and on to Cambodia. In late February 1968, they were some of the last tourists allowed into the country before the United States started bombing perceived Viet Cong bases there, as the Vietnam War escalated. The general mood was becoming a little hostile toward Americans, but the Coburns stayed at an old manor house and went on bicycle carts to see Angkor Wat.

"We saw things that don't exist anymore. Gorgeous six-headed *nagas*, making the body of the bridge, palm-lined streets. We were the only ones there. We went into one of the *wats* and heard this chanting from all the young monks and some old ones. The begging bowls, given by a benefactor, were out in front. I said, 'Who gave you this?' 'My father.' 'What does he do?' 'He's a fisherman.' But they were living this way—they were chanting. There was something real happening, an air of reality happening. I was very impressed with reality. They all smoked cigarettes."

Their last stop was to spend a few days in Japan, to buy antique Hiroshige and Hokusai woodblock prints.

Coburn and Beverly were home again for spring in Los Angeles. They immediately carried on with the Hollywood lifestyle they enjoyed, reading esoteric texts and a pile of scripts, and inviting friends to visit for fantastic meals, long sessions of drumming and philosophical discourse, playing snooker and pool, drinking high-end booze, and smoking grass.

"Most of the entourage was people who Beverly had picked up who were either like drug dealers or ethnic art dealers from Kathmandu and India. They were constantly coming over to sell stuff. We'd just invite a bunch of people over and have a good time. Sometimes we served food. We'd just bring out stuff. We had a lot of cocaine. We smoked good grass, bad grass, but mainly good grass. That was part of the attraction. We were open with that but careful. Nobody ever busted us because we were careful. We weren't blowing smoke in people's faces. We didn't proselytize. It was too dangerous. I didn't let those guys come around. It was really illegal."

Some of those guys were associated with Peter Coyote and the commune group called the Diggers, later known as the Free Family. They were soliciting for funds to buy a property, Black Bear Ranch in Northern California. They planned to create a new commune and had a delegation led by Michael Tierra and Elsa Marley, visiting all the stars around Hollywood who were known to be into alternative lifestyles. As Coyote puts it, "Michael had a list of celebrities who were either sympathetic to their goals or terrified of invasion by his wild friends and paid them to leave."[34]

Coburn was neither, particularly. He was possibly on the list because he had attended the notorious summer soiree at Jennifer Jones's home where the Esalen Institute gestalt therapist Fritz Perls had infamously spanked Natalie Wood.[35] Coburn and Beverly often visited the Esalen retreat center to relax in the spa. "It's really a meditation center. You just lie in the baths, watch the stars, and relate to yourself and other people."[36]

Or it might have been because at the time the Coburns were strong supporters, including financially, of the Los Angeles Free Clinic, run by another friend and Digger sympathizer, Murray Korngold, on Beverly Boulevard. Newly reopened in 1967, this was a place where the indigent, including runaway youth, could come for medical care and addiction counseling free from judgment. The Coburns may have been careful about not using weed in public, but they were outspoken about the foolishness of the drug laws at the time. They told reporter Kimmis Hendrick of the *Christian Science Monitor*, "The Establishment, if we can call it that has lied about drugs. It has maintained a double standard. It says that alcohol is all right for you but marijuana isn't. So youngsters don't believe that anything the 'Establishment' says is bad is really bad. If they heard people telling the truth about marijuana, they'd believe them when they warn against methodryne [*sic*]."[37]

Beverly had also been involved with assisting a group of impoverished California indigenous people in the mountains south of Tijuana by giving them food and other goods.[38]

Coburn was not interested in supporting the Black Bear commune, and he sent the delegation on their way, whereupon Tierra set fire to an American flag in the tiled fountain in the foyer. The smoke damaged the foyer and parts of the adjoining rooms, necessitating another call to Tony Duquette.

The great irony was that in those days, Beverly Hills was far from being a hippie or counterculture enclave. It was more a well-to-do suburban neighborhood than a glitzy tourist attraction, even the shopping center around Rodeo Drive. You could eat at a family-run diner and browse the small local toy store. Like any other family neighborhood at the time, the kids would run around in and out of each other's houses and play in each other's backyards. It's just that in this case, the neighbors were people like Donald Sutherland and Jack Lemmon, and the backyards were acres of lush landscaping with fruiting avocado and citrus groves. And cats, lots of cats. There were times when Beverly was feeding twenty-five free-roaming cats outside the kitchen door.

Jimmy went to school at El Rodeo Elementary, and in years to come would ride his bicycle to school or down into Beverly Hills for food. He also liked skateboarding. One day he broke a front tooth while riding, causing Beverly to ban skateboarding for both the kids. When he was a little older, Jimmy spent several of his school vacations with his aunts and Grandpa Jack in Parowan, Utah, learning to fish and plant corn. Along with James Logan, these relatives were part of a core group of people who were stabilizing influences in the kids' lives.

One of the people entrusted with the care of the children was Alcencia Salazar, the cook. She went by the nickname of Chencia. The kids grew up on a combination of home-cooked Mexican food and the traditional American recipes that Beverly taught her. There were always fresh corn tortillas, warmed over the open gas flame, spread with butter, and rolled, as a fast snack, and *chilaquiles* for breakfast, eaten in the kitchen at the end of the nine-foot wooden table. It had been purchased in a props sale from Warner Bros. Studio. Rock solid, it was one of three made for the pie fight scene in *The Great Race* (1965). That film's star, Natalie Wood, once stood on that table, covered in whipped cream.

Coburn and Beverly had a short three months at home until the end of May 1968, during which time they celebrated Jimmy's seventh birthday, before it was off to Torremolinos and Tangier to shoot *Hard Contract* for Fox. Coburn portrays a cynical hit man transformed by the love of a blasé woman, who happens to be traveling with his next, and final, target.

The heat was blasting in the middle of summer. Spooky Stevens, the studio publicist, tried to make a virtue of necessity by talking up the professionalism of the cast working through the horrible heat and dust and, in costar Lee Remick's case, two bouts of food poisoning or stomach flu, which sent her to a Madrid clinic for several days in August.

The white-plastered buildings, lovely on the screen, only added to the glare. "The earth in the area is of a red-clay variety common to this region of the Spanish southern coast. Firemen were required to wet it down intermittently during the shooting, but even this did not prevent the tired cast and crew from returning each night covered in red dust."[39]

Coburn and Beverly lived in the top floor of the villa that was being used as a shooting location and brought Professor Shah over from Tangier to stay with them for the two months in Torremolinos. "He charmed everybody on the set. He was a charming man. That voice! 'Zorah!' That was his maid's name. And she would make this chicken curry for lunch, which was unlike any curry I had ever tasted before. It was like chicken that was boiled in this red sauce, thin as vinegar, but it tasted just great, wonderful on couscous. He would be in the middle of a meditation, and she would be talking with all the other ladies. I guess she was about forty-five to fifty years old, big, and round, and very jolly. And she and the girls would gather at the hammams," the Moroccan steam baths.[40]

Finally the Coburns returned home. They did not leave the country again for a little over a year. Coburn had a short respite from working before preparing for a film in Louisiana, and he spent his time reading and socializing, catching up on listening to music.

In early November 1968, he went to a party at the Candy Store, the nightclub owned by celebrity hairstylist Gene Shacove, to celebrate Steve and Neile McQueen's twelfth wedding anniversary during a break in the shooting of McQueen's picture *The Reivers* (1969). A mutual friend, writer Stirling Silliphant, asked Coburn if he wanted to meet a truly remarkable martial artist, the man who had played Kato in *The Green Hornet* television series. This was the first meeting between James Coburn and Bruce Lee, who was to become one of his dearest friends.

Coburn told Lee that he had learned some screen fighting for the Flint films. "He told me he had seen me do some martial arts in my films and commented that 'you looked too flicky, not powerful enough.'" He was skeptical when Lee told him about the now-famous one-inch punch. Coburn put a pillow over his chest and stood in front of a cushy chair. Bruce Lee stood and positioned himself, held out his fist, and suddenly moved it just an inch. The focused power knocked Coburn backward head over heels until he was sprawled in a corner. He jumped up and said, "When do we start?"

In the early days, they trained at Lee's house where there was plenty of equipment, but as time went on, the *sifu* (master) helped Coburn set up some punching bags, and the pair would work out on the back patio at the Tower Road house. "We would get together a couple of times a week for lessons, and we'd have lunch down in Chinatown once, twice a week whenever Bruce and I were in town together. I'd try to catch him and couldn't catch him. We'd break boards and stuff like that. I got pretty good at it. I never had an opportunity to have to prove it by fighting anybody, and even today when people know I've been taught by Bruce Lee, nobody fucks with me. Isn't that great?

"If I had known Bruce when I made [the Flint] films, the fight scenes would have been fantastic. Bruce was a great teacher. He taught from your perspective, from your talent, which would then become the center of your technique—whether you had a good side kick, speed, a good punch, whatever it was. That's what a good teacher does. They have you work with your particular point of view or talent. My talent was a strong running side kick. I had a pretty good punch too. That's all good teaching really is—teaching from your talents."

Lee's wife, Linda, notes in her book *Bruce Lee: The Man Only I Knew* many conversations between the two men. On one occasion Coburn bought a new punching bag, over one hundred pounds, and hung it from an industrial-strength chain. Lee felt the bag was too hard but determined that he could soften it some. "So he took a running kick at it and broke that chain and broke a hole in the canvas—it flew up in the air and fell out in the middle of the lawn out there—busted, dilapidated—a brand new bag."[41]

Lee's business associate M. Uyehara recalled the first time Coburn came to Lee's office to collect him for an outing. "Coburn impressed the office staff that day. He was extremely humble and took his time to shake each person's hand. He even went out of his way to greet shy individuals. He returned to our office a few more times with Bruce and was always the same—gracious and humble."[42]

Coburn was Lee's second celebrity pupil, the first being Steve McQueen. Lee called Coburn a philosopher and described McQueen as a fighter. Lee had been honing the philosophy behind his own unique martial art, Jeet Kune Do, with as much focus as he used when he worked to keep his body in incredible shape. He and Coburn enjoyed philosophical discussions.

"His method of teaching was not teaching at all in the accepted sense—it was evolving through certain ideas; teaching you tools; finding out your strong points, your weak points. . . . We talked about life in general, and also its esoteric values that we were both trying to get at. . . . Bruce was constantly relating everything in life to martial arts and martial arts to everything in life—which kind of staggered me a little bit because I didn't know how to do that—how do you relate everything to martial arts? But Bruce was the personification of that."[43]

Bruce Lee was also interested in learning about tai chi, which he thought was "wonderful and great exercise. Marshall Ho'o and Bruce met at my house one time. They were talking, and Bruce was testing him. 'What would you do if I did this?' And Marshall did that. Marshall Ho'o was the best, and Bruce was the master of Jeet Kune Do. No defensive moves at all, it was all attack. Speed was the only defense he had. Marshall was a little concerned—he thought he should not be questioned.

"Bruce was always testing these martial arts guys. Tai chi is not a physical combat—'the inner school of martial arts.' Start external and go in—you have to. After an hour with Marshall Ho'o, he liked him and liked what he did."[44]

For all his charm and enthusiasm, Lee could also be a little conceited, even cocky. "Bruce created himself. He read a lot, started off as a street fighter in Hong Kong. Jeet Kune Do is really scientific street fighting. That's what he called it, anyway. He made up that title. People built a whole mythical thing around Bruce's death, that it was because he was giving secrets away. All the secrets he gave away were only things he put into practice. He just said all this other bullshit was bullshit. He broke down all the crap that people were practicing, just to get some kind of ego gratification, out of something they thought was martial arts.

"Bruce was brash. He would not do any kind of demonstrations. He would go to these conferences and meetings, which were noncontact events so it was really hard to judge talent. He kept saying, 'It's bullshit. How can you have a fight when you have to miss somebody?' He got them to start using gloves, which made it a full-contact sport. A real sport. He brought all of that about. He would come to be a judge. I went with him a few times. Whenever he was asked to do demonstrations, he always refused. 'What does it mean to crack nine pieces of cement with your head, except that you can crack nine pieces of cement with your head? What do these things prove? What do they have to do with martial arts?' This is what he would say.

"So he was a judge on this television program. During the demonstrations, when asked what he thought of these board-breaking feats and so on, he said, 'Well, all that proves is that a man can break a board with his fist, he can break a brick with his head, and he can break a block of ice with his ass.' He put everybody down. 'Well, Mister Lee, are you afraid to show us what you could do? Are you all talk?' So he asked them to tape three of those boards together, he held them out to his side and dropped them, and pow! He side-kicked them, and they just shattered and went up into the flies and broke bulbs, and everything was raining down sparks, a real show. It was just pure luck. Everyone was in shock, and he pulled me aside and said, 'I had no fucking idea that would ever happen.'"

Bruce Lee was constantly working on improving himself, his physical fitness, his mental acuity, his ideas, and his plans for a brilliant career. Coburn told Linda, "Each time I came back, I was astonished to observe how Bruce had evolved even further in the meantime."[45]

Coburn's workouts with Bruce Lee were interrupted by the shoot for *Last of the Mobile Hot-shots*, shooting over April and May 1969 in Louisiana. Based on the Tennessee Williams play *The Seven Descents of Myrtle*, which had premiered on Broadway in May the year before, it was a turgid melodrama containing all the usual elements of sexual tension typical of Williams. Undoubtedly, the producers hoped to repeat the success of other recent, sexually charged adaptations of his plays including *Cat on a Hot Tin Roof* (1958), *Suddenly, Last Summer* (1959), *Sweet Bird of Youth* (1962), and *The Night of the Iguana* (1964). That some of the screen's great actors—Elizabeth Taylor, Katharine Hepburn, Richard Burton, Paul Newman, Geraldine Page—had appeared in these films only added to the possibilities. The film that started it all was *A Streetcar Named Desire* (1951), which had made a star of Marlon Brando.

As well as being based on a Williams play, *Hot-shots* appeared to have all the right elements: the eminent Sidney Lumet directing and producing, Gore Vidal writing the screenplay, Oscar-winning director of photography James

Wong Howe, music by Quincy Jones, Coburn himself, and the new British sensation Lynn Redgrave, who had won a Golden Globe and had been Oscar nominated for *Georgy Girl* in 1966 and was fresh from a daring, antiwar British production, *The Virgin Soldiers*. This was Redgrave's first American movie production. The third star, Robert Hooks, was also a serious actor and writer. He was part of the police procedural TV series *N.Y.P.D.* and one of the founders of an off-Broadway repertory theater group. The project had potential as a dark character study with a strong ensemble.

However, something went wrong, starting with the literature. In this case the play itself had been unsuccessful, running for only twenty-nine performances despite the lead actress, Estelle Parsons, being nominated for a Tony Award. The plot was somewhat puzzling, with the common Tennessee Williams theme of a love triangle hampered by the three main characters' lack of likability. The *Mobile* of the title refers to the city in Alabama, Mobile Hot-shots being a disbanded all-girl singing group in the story. That the group had been topless was only the start of the tawdriness around this film.

Louisiana in the late spring was sticky hot. The actors stayed in Baton Rouge at the Bellemont Hotel, at the time a famous luxury hotel, where Redgrave had to get up two hours earlier than everyone else for her 6:00 a.m. makeup call. For authenticity, the movie shot at a St. Francisville antebellum mansion, described in the local paper as "an old house, in the state of disrepair . . . [with] thick bushes and trees on the grounds." Its name, authentically evocative of Tennessee Williams, was Rosebank.[46] The same newspaper showed a surprising lack of discretion and printed the address of the location. Locals were tapped as extras.

Rated "X—no one under 17 admitted," presumably for sexual situations (although not what is considered X-rated today), the film puzzled reviewers. People were decidedly uncomfortable with the vague, implied suggestions of homosexual incest and the generally unsympathetic characters. At first it seemed to be a satire on the cultural dysfunction of the TV generation, but soon it became a wordy misfire. *Time* magazine called it "difficult—or impossible—to sit through."[47] The most interesting review came from the *New York Times* describing Coburn's character as "a man who seems oddly muscular for someone suffering from terminal cancer of his one lung."[48] Evidently, the concentrated workouts with Bruce Lee were making a visible difference.

Coburn didn't talk about that movie, most likely understanding that it was going to tank despite everyone's best efforts. Instead he turned his serious attention to developing a new movie idea with Bruce Lee and Stirling Silliphant. Lee had come up with the concept for a film based on a character's journey to enlightenment through martial arts. The three men would get together several times a week, "having pledged to each other that they would allow nothing to interfere with that schedule, beyond family and work" until the script was finished.[49]

"We wrote a wonderful screenplay together, Stirling, Bruce, and I, called 'The Silent Flute.' Nobody could understand what the silent flute was. It's the one that plays inside you. Nobody can hear it but you. It was about a man whose martial art was his yoga, and his nirvana comes at the end where he's seeking the book, and he goes through all of these trials in order to get to this place where the book is, and he opens the book, and it is a mirror."[50]

The original plan was to shoot in Thailand, Japan, and Morocco. For the next two and a half years, whenever he was in town, Coburn kept to his promise and worked on this script assiduously.

But in the meantime it was back to work and jet-setting around the world. In late 1969 Coburn went to Brazil for a week to join his friend Henry Mancini at the International Festival of Popular Song in Rio de Janeiro. That time he brought James Logan with him, while for once Beverly stayed at home, looking after the new addition to the family.

8

A Different Kind of Man

I am not a good parent, I must admit. I was a failure at all of that stuff because I didn't have that kind of tendency to be a father. To dole out discipline certainly was not my cup of tea. I hated doing that. They didn't know any better. They were just trying to express themselves—not in a good way or whatever it was. Jimmy would take things apart without any intention of putting them back together again. "What are you doing? Put it back together again." "Why?" He got really interested in electronic things. I guess he finally learned to put them back together.

—JAMES COBURN, 2002

One of the ways Beverly and Jim Coburn would pass the time during those many long flights while they were traveling the world was to play cards. They would always keep things interesting by betting. One of the things they played for was a Rolls-Royce for Beverly, which she subsequently very much enjoyed driving around. Another was a pet monkey.

"Beverly and I were flying back from London, and we were playing gin. She was a great gin player. She taught me how to play, but she always beat me. So we were playing for a monkey, because she wanted a monkey, not knowing anything about having a monkey. She just had this desire to have a monkey. We played and played and played, and finally, she won two monkeys. And I thought, *We'll never have a goddamn monkey.*

"So it was a few months after that, it was around the time they landed on the moon, Beverly was at the pet shop getting something for the dog, and they had this little, tiny guy—a woolly monkey. He reached his little fingers out of the cage and took hold of her finger. Woolly monkeys are the cleanest, most beautiful, perfect monkeys. They don't have hair around their balls, or under their arms, but the rest of them is covered in this short, very fine hair, and they are very clean. Their feces don't smell.

"Monkeys were legal at the time, but the way they were caught was not, and if we had known, we never would've had them. The mothers would be carrying the babies on their backs, and the Indians would shoot arrows at the mother, and she would fall from the tree. If the fall didn't kill the baby, they would take the baby and sell it to the importer. All those people that sell those things could buy them and put them in the stores.

"We named him Moonbeam because we got him on the day man first walked on the moon [July 20, 1969]. We got him and took him into the house, and he didn't know what the fuck was happening. He was crawling all over the snooker table, and I was astounded and so was Beverly. What are we going to do with this monkey? I started reading up on woolly monkeys and found out a lot.

"Because they are primates, they have to learn how to do things. So I became his mother. He would ride on my back, pulling my hair. We kept him in our bedroom, and our bedroom became an absolute, total mess, a total disaster. When we first left him alone, we put him in the bathroom, but he learned to turn the water on, especially the hot water, which he really liked. The water was gushing out of the shower, the sink, the bathtub. We had to take the faucet handles off. We built this huge monkey cage underneath the bedroom with ropes and swings. I had to teach him how to swing, even how to pee in the toilet. I took him in the bathroom and showed him.

"Moonbeam was really a lover. I loved him! I had to teach him how to climb. I took him to the big avocado tree and climbed up the tree with him and ripped him off me and climbed down as fast as I could. He had this prehensile tail he used instinctively, and it would wrap around a limb. After three times, he'd beat me back down and laugh at me.

"Later we got another, older woolly monkey that we named Coco, but she was more mature. She had spent more time in a cage, and she had to regenerate herself. She was strange. Coco was a female and more standoffish."[1]

The monkeys became somewhat famous in their circle of friends and would often surprise people by jumping on their shoulders or scampering about. Once Beverly's sister Karen was visiting them. "Chencia brought in this huge plate of wonderful fruit—papayas and avocados. We were sitting there, just starting on the fruit, and this monkey came and set his butt right down in the middle of all the fruit. I thought, *Oh my gosh*, but Beverly didn't think anything of it. She just said, 'Oh well.'"[2]

Karen's husband, Jerry, recalled the mischief. "One of those monkeys was pulling [Jim's] ear and grabbed the fruit, and Jim said, 'That's it! Either they go or you go.' He didn't say, 'They go or I go,' he said, 'They go or you go.' He said that to Beverly."

By this time the monkeys were becoming a handful, and the master bedroom was a disaster. Despite Moonbeam learning to pee in the toilet and climb trees, the monkeys were not well behaved. "If you put anything down, they would just snatch it, and rrriipp!"[3] Coburn never made the connection that possibly the creatures were reacting to his long absences and unpredictable (to them) returns, just as human children might. Eventually they were taken to a loving exotic animal sanctuary in Buellton, California.[4] Beverly made yet another call to Tony Duquette to revamp the bedroom and convert the big cage back to a solarium.

Once the monkeys were gone, however, Coburn missed them. "It was like putting your child in jail. We grew fond of these animals—we brought them up. To have to give them up was very difficult, and I did not want any pets after that because I didn't want to get so attached."[5] Eventually he rediscovered his love of cats, "so easy and playful and fun," but the only dog in the house was Jimmy's. Jimmy did not miss Moonbeam and Coco at all, but rather was glad to see them go since he felt that the monkeys had received the lion's share of his parents' limited attention when they were at home. They had only been around for a few years, but they still loom large in his memory.

Lisa was growing up fast. Her parents allowed her to travel to Morocco alone when she was fifteen. "We'd been there together. She was never very long by herself. Lisa was always singing, dancing, carrying on. Always had a lot of boyfriends." Given her own history, Beverly saw nothing problematic about allowing Lisa to be independent. For years she also insisted that Lisa babysit her brother, apparently so that she need not look after him herself, including on their travels. This imposition caused enough resentment in Lisa for Jimmy to feel it.

Coburn remained oblivious about the conflicts between the kids and was baffled about why his preteen son seemed troubled and was a handful. Even years later, he never made the connection between his lack of availability and his son's attention-seeking behavior.

Coburn describes, "Beverly would bust Jimmy for doing some silly little thing and really overcompensate on the punishment and tell me I had to go in there and spank him. I'd say, 'Why don't you go in there and spank him yourself? I don't care what he did there. It wasn't that bad.' 'But he's grounded for a month.' I felt sorry for him, but he brought it on himself because of his attitude about going to school. They finally kicked him out of public school because he wouldn't play the game. He wouldn't study. Toys and things he wanted, he took them from other people. 'I want that.' He was just awful. I don't know [about nature or nurture], but I was out of the house as much as I could possibly be."

Meanwhile he and Beverly taught Jimmy how to mix drinks and thought it was perfectly appropriate to have him serve as a barman to their guests in their small soirees with their close friends, held in the upstairs sitting room off their bedroom. After dinner the boy would pour one last round then be dismissed so that the adults could smoke joints and snort cocaine. A few years later, once he realized what was happening, Jimmy would sneak into the room early in the morning and pick the roaches out of the ashtrays before the maid came to clean up.

In February 1970 *Playboy* magazine devoted almost sixteen pages to a riveting moderated panel discussion called "The Drug Revolution." Coburn joined eight other authorities—all white men—antidrug law enforcement officials, doctors, artists (including William S. Burroughs and Baba Ram Dass), and social commentators. He met Alan Watts, the Zen philosopher, another influential person in his life, during this panel.

During the discussion, the most conservative speaker became increasingly reactionary and downright insulting, advancing the same tired tropes that are still used against drug law reform today. The progressive thinkers demonstrated a level of erudition that would allow men to claim with perfect sincerity that they "read *Playboy* for the articles."

Coburn was likely included on the panel because by this time it was common knowledge that he had been part of the LSD experiments back in 1959. He refrained from admitting his own continued use of marijuana, probably a wise move, confining his contributions primarily to the use of LSD and its influence in popular culture. "There are plenty of psychedelic themes in rock songs. . . . The real significance of the LSD trip is not the experiences that you can put into words because you know they are all drug-induced; it's something else that lets you go inside your head and find the real center of gravity of your being, as in Oriental meditation."[6]

He also spoke of the "meth heads" that he and Beverly had seen while volunteering at the Los Angeles Free Clinic. "Speed really fries your brain." Many distinctions were drawn up between alcohol and the use of other drugs, and government policy dealing with them. Coburn agreed that smoking cigarettes was harmful. "I know I can't really justify my smoking, since I realize it's physically harmful to me. Certainly, it makes us adults look pretty silly to kids. The way we throw fits over marijuana and ignore tobacco problems really shows up our hypocrisy."

One of the issues discussed, as might be expected given the publication, was drugs as an aphrodisiac. Coburn was more concerned with "the new dimension of love that these drugs open up." He remained hopeful that drugs could be used to control negative passions "revenge, hatred, greed and lust." His idealism included the hope that LSD would not be left in the hands of doctors, but that "policies for psychedelics should be controlled by a panel of educated citizens," not unlike the *Playboy* panel itself. His last prophetic words were "the drug revolution, like the social revolution, isn't over."

He did manage to squeeze in one reference to *The President's Analyst* but did not mention *Last of the Mobile Hot-shots*, which would have been newly in theaters by the time the panel was published. Probably just as well. The hedonism displayed by those characters would surely have played into the hands of the antidrug contingent.

As a matter of fact, that was the last Coburn movie to open in theaters for the next year and a half. A number were still playing, most particularly *Hard Contract*, and many of his older films were showing on TV. The turn-around time from big screen to small was short. One reason was the common practice of shooting a TV version of certain scenes, usually to eliminate swearing in the dialogue, during principal photography. This facilitates the swift editing process and saves the actor from having to come in and loop awkward overdubs. Even Peckinpah would shoot TV cover scenes, all the while grumbling at the necessity.

Between sessions working on "The Silent Flute," Coburn was in preparation for his first movie with Sergio Leone. A few years earlier, Leone had approached him to star in the spaghetti western *A Fistful of Dollars* (1964). "I turned him down because I didn't know who the fuck he was. I was his first choice. And the second one too—he wanted me to do that one too. And by that time I was into Flint and movies that I wanted to make. Well anyway, he finally came up with something that was interesting to me. It wasn't such a clichéd character. The others, he had them playing the harmonica and a cigar sticking out of the side of their mouths, and all that crap.

"[Those] stories were all about revenge. This is a little different. The character was good. He was a guy who was a revolutionary. He was fighting for a cause that he believed in, and he was betrayed by his friend."[7]

Duck, You Sucker, which is also known as *Once Upon a Time, the Revolution*, had a difficult start. Thomas Weisser in his 2000 study, *Spaghetti Westerns*, wrote about the lead-up to the shoot. Initially Sergio Leone planned on simply supervising the production. Early on he intended to have Eli Wallach starring with Sam Peckinpah directing, but Peckinpah was busy and the studio wanted Rod Steiger for that role. Then Leone approached Peter Bogdanovich, who was still a new director. They had creative differences in their approaches around camera work and editing style from the very beginning. That did not work out. At one point, Monte Hellman was considered. Finally Giancarlo Santi, one of Sergio Leone's editors, started the film.

Almost at once, this meant trouble. "After shooting began Coburn and Steiger (feeling compromised and claiming they had been hired to make a 'Leone' film) refused to work. Leone took over the helm."[8] Coburn was certainly pleased about that. "Sergio was one of those guys, making a movie was like a toy to him. He had grown up in a rich family, and his family always provided him with enough."[9]

The shoot began in Dublin for a few days, to shoot flashback scenes, and then Coburn arrived in Barcelona in the first week of June 1970. The shoot continued throughout the hot summer in Spain. Beverly split after only a brief visit. The locale was just not comfortable. He wrote to her of his feelings and of missing her, still starting his letters with the same two words—*my love*. Whenever they were separated, his letters and poems tended to be romantic, full of erotic yearning. He was still deeply in love. Beverly kept these epistles for over forty years, through all the turmoil that followed.[10]

Sometimes his letters contained actual news. This production was plagued with all the nuisances that come with shooting in rural locations and some unusually severe disasters, none of which seemed to make the papers.

"My love, I'm somewhere between Madrid and Barcelona. The communication problem here is very bad indeed, so I'll try to get into Madrid before going to Rome to call you. Since you left, our camera operator was shot in the leg by Rod with a wooden bullet from a machine gun, the special effects man broke two ribs and knocked his teeth out in a running, tripping, falling thing; the second unit camera op was driving speedily and plunged off the road into the sea on the aqua dulce road killing his focus puller, breaking the shoulder of a makeup man, and is in a coma himself with less than good chances of making it out. The full moon took its toll."[11]

One of the big challenges was hauling around a cannon. "The carriage was so big and so heavy—four horses couldn't pull it to the top of the hill. We became kind of friendly enemies."[12]

Through all this Leone was pleased with the actor's level of professionalism and reliability. In an interview he said, "Coburn, that's something else. With him, it's the star system. You explain the scene to him, he says 'yes, Sir,' and off he goes and does it."[13] The director needed facile actors, because he was modifying the script as they went along, using improvisation.

Duck, You Sucker has become one of the most studied and written about of Coburn's films in recent years, both for its place in the history of European cinema and for the extraordinary score by Ennio Morricone. The score was not only an artistic triumph but also a technical one. They made use of a then-new simultaneous multitrack technique in post-sound for fluid mixing, turning down the volume of the music or background ambiance when an actor spoke.

Despite being set during the revolution in Mexico, Leone was creating a commentary about the current situation in the world. He saw the various contemporary revolutions and the Cold War as being inherently class conflicts—put simply, the wealthy elite trying to hold on to their wealth. The movie becomes a dissertation on revolutions as circular and on the dangers of violence—as one scholar puts it, "*Duck, You Sucker* actually questions the value of revolutionary violence rather than celebrates it."[14]

In promotional material for the film, Coburn notes, "It soon becomes terrifyingly apparent that the character's hang-up is simply destruction for destruction's sake. . . . Mallory is really more interested in the power which a revolutionary covets rather than in changing society for the better. And that just about sums up the problem with revolutions. . . . Things haven't changed much, have they? Today's revolutionary is tomorrow's establishment."[15]

Duck, You Sucker opened in October 1971 in Italy, to popular acclaim, but took a long time to get to the United States. By the time it opened in late June of 1972, Coburn's next two features were already in theaters—*The Honkers*, where costar Slim Pickens shone, and his Blake Edwards collaboration, *The Carey Treatment*.

Coburn was described as having "a large following of young people between 15 and 30 thanks to his dapper, zany portrayals" in the Flint movies, but those were rapidly fading into the past.[16] He hoped that *Duck, You Sucker*, his groovy mysticism, and the remarks he would often make in the press in support of "young people" and their aspirations would reignite his young adult fan base.

According to the American Film Institute Film Facts of that year, the critical consensus for *Duck, You Sucker* was six favorable reviews, four mixed, and only two negative. Of the favorable reviews, Judith Crist, the eminent critic at *New York Magazine*, gave one of the raves about the movie itself—"a luscious movie-movie," "a big, sprawling adventure"—and about Coburn— "he gives the best performance of his career. We didn't know the stars or the director had it in them; the discovery is pure pleasure."[17]

One of the lasting results of the film was that the following year, Sam Peckinpah reportedly screened the picture for writer Rudy Wurlitzer, to convince him that James Coburn would make a great Pat Garrett for their upcoming tortured masterpiece, *Pat Garrett and Billy the Kid*.[18]

Well before that shoot, in 1970 Coburn returned to his work with Bruce Lee and Stirling Silliphant during the week and spent some Sundays driving the kids down the crowded freeway in one of the Ferraris to Palm Desert, to visit their grandparents in the home he had bought for them. Jimmy remembers the excruciating boredom of these outings, especially sitting in the heat in the convertible, stuck in gridlock: "It felt like it was every weekend."[19]

When that got too dull, Coburn made quick trips abroad, such as making a fall shopping expedition to buy the English-made clothing he favored. Beverly would slip across the Channel to Paris to pick up beautifully tailored blouses and dresses from Yves Saint Laurent and Coco Chanel to complement the custom-made black silk pajama sets she wore ubiquitously around the house. In winter, instead of overcoats, she favored dense black or navy wool flannel capes she had brought back from the souks of Tangier. She was tiny, and by now Lisa had grown tall enough that the two often shared clothing. Back home the couple was still happily married, still being photographed together out and about at premieres of their friends' movies and at industry functions, costume parties, and charity events.

The Tower Road house was still a mecca for cool cats and partiers. One visitor was Petey Kameron, at the time managing The Who as the less visible partner in their record label, Track Records, which had also just released Jimi Hendrix's latest (and, as it turned out, last) album. Petey had long since moved on from the left-wing folk music scene of the 1950s and instead was hanging out with rockers and gurus, people like Scottish singer, songwriter, and musician Donovan and various Zen masters and maharishis. The Coburns would often invite East Indian musician Ali Akbar Khan and composer Ravi Shankar over. "We had good music, big speakers, loud music, all the jazz."[20] Coburn was living the life he'd always wanted, surrounded by the kind of fascinating thinkers and artists whose presence and influence he cherished.

They hosted a *satsang*, or "sacred gathering," at their house with Baba Muktananda when the guru made his first tour of the United States at this time. "They knew I had this big house and I was susceptible to the teachings because I knew Alan Watts and several other people. Beverly was also interested in the association with these people."

The main sponsors were Ram Dass and Swami Rudrananda, usually called just Rudi. Rudi (born Albert Rudolph in 1928) was a Coburn friend, and they in turn were his customers. He was a dealer in sacred Asian art, with a hole-in-the-wall shop filled to the brim with art from Japan, India, and especially Tibet—essentially smuggled out of the country to save it from "destruction at the hands of Chinese communists."[21]

Rudi was a spiritual teacher of what he called Kundalini Yoga, based on open-eyed meditations and formed from a fusion of many traditions. He had studied with the George Gurdjieff and P. D. Ouspensky self-development group in New York in the midfifties, before trips to India changed his focus. His spiritual teachings were grounded in practicality and being in the world rather than being secluded from it.

"Rudrananda had an antiques store in the bowels of New York, where Broadway and First cross over. He had studied with several gurus. He had a really dirty mouth. 'Look, damn it. I have been studying for twenty years, and I want to be made a pandit.' Okay, but you have to give up sex. 'They want my balls, I'll give up my balls. I've given up everything else.' So he got the teaching."[22]

Indeed Rudi was known for using colorful, contemporary language with his students. He had met Muktananda in India, on one of his buying trips, and studied with him intermittently over about five years whenever he went back—all while still managing his well-known shop.

Muktananda's entourage for his visit included his translator, Gurumayi, as well as Rudi and a crowd of followers. "We put out food, and it was gone in ten minutes—everything. Just gone. We had this big spread laid out—cookies, cakes, stuff to eat. Everything was gone. These guys were supposed to be ascetic. I didn't even get any. Muktananda didn't eat either. He didn't need anything. He lived on air. I found him very strange but very, very warm.

"I sat at the table with Muktananda, and we held hands throughout the entire afternoon. He was doing interviews. They were asking him questions. He always gave the same answer. 'The blue pearl of wisdom.' He sat there with his dark glasses and this orange stocking cap, and every time he said it, he would squeeze my hand and laugh. I was getting a lot of energy from him. He did not speak any English as far as I know. We related perfectly to each other.

"And the students would say, 'Ah, the blue pearl of wisdom.' No one asked, 'What *is* the blue pearl of wisdom? How do you get it, and what do you do with it once you've got it?' Nobody said that. And then they would go away, and then they would ponder it for a bit and go off and play golf or go operate on somebody."

Soon after this event, Rudi would sever his ties with Muktananda, disturbed by the latter's insistence that he be considered an actual god by his followers. Slowly Muktananda's sect took on more and more characteristics of a cult, isolating initiates from their families and friends. Eventually, after his death in 1983, in an echo of *Candy*, Muktananda would be accused of sexual abuse of teenaged girls within his ashrams. He was also accused of misusing funds and ordering the physical intimidation of any critics in the sect. Rudi did not live to see this tarnishing of his former teacher, as he was killed in a small plane crash in 1971.

Another regular visitor to Tower Road was Alan Watts, the scholar and philosopher who had been part of Dr. Janiger's earliest mescaline experiments and the *Playboy* panel. He believed that Buddhism should be thought of as a form of psychotherapy rather than a religion. "He was a lot of fun. He was great. We used to play the gong and chant. He knew that he was always welcome to come and hang out whenever he came to town from San Francisco, and whenever I was there, I would go to his houseboat in Sausalito. We'd get together once or twice a year, telling stories and jiving. I'd play the gong, get a kind of rhythm going, and he would start a chant; then he'd change the chant. It seemed like an esoteric rap. One time he brought this great script he'd written, really good script, about an English guy who comes to Hollywood and becomes a guru."

Then in December of that year, 1970, Coburn was invited to be part of the inaugural World Conference on Scientific Yoga, in New Delhi, along with his friends Murray Korngold, who also happened to be Ted Flicker's analyst, and Dr. Sidney Prince, both connected to the Los Angeles Free Clinic.[23] The conference brought together several hundred Indian swamis of different traditions with about fifty Western experts.

"People were invited who had written books or who had some kind of reputation, psychiatrists, socialists, people interested in esoteric subjects from America, to mix with Yogis from the East—a coming together of East and West on an esoteric level. Beverly said, 'Why don't you go?' So I went."[24]

One of the main organizers was Christopher Hills. Hills was an art gallery owner and an activist for Rastafarians in Jamaica, and a businessman who later created spirulina and pioneered multilevel marketing. He also founded the University of the Trees in Northern California to study esoteric topics. At the conference, psychologists and counselors, including some connected to the Esalen Intitute in Big Sur, gave demonstrations of group therapy sessions and presented research papers while Yogis created a meditation circle outside in the beautiful weather.

"Sidney and Murray were not believers. They were doers, experimenters. We had a great time. Really a lot of fun. We went to the Almora, and Sidney was chased by one of those wandering bulls that walk around the streets. I don't know why. It knocked him down and bruised him, and he said, 'What the hell. They're sacred animals.' I said, 'They must have known you were Jewish, man.' That was a good trip, a lot of fun, very enlightening.

"A lot of hippie types there were filling their egos but not their hearts. Some of them came to my room at the Oberoi one night for a shower, and they were so filthy, the walls were caked with mud afterward. I ordered some food—they brought up a big Indian tray, and everyone scarfed it up in no time. The brothers Kumar in New Delhi, they were there, and Nik Douglas, who was responsible for a book called *Sexual Secrets*. He was a scholar, learning to speak Tibetan. He traveled with the Karmapa."

Coburn met a guru lama doing *pujas* (prayer rituals) to raise funds for a lamasery. The man said he needed three or four hundred dollars, which seemed like a very small amount. Coburn pulled out the cash he had in his pocket, about six hundred dollars, and handed it to the lama, saying, "There you go, man, take it." Somewhere in Almora there is a lamasery built thanks to James Coburn.

On the final day, he and his friends went to see the Dalai Lama bless a lamasery nearby. "We were there waiting at a bridge between New and Old Delhi, watching every type of locomotion. It was like watching time pass. I had slain my ego, and it was swinging, watching elephants, camels, Mercedes, dogs, bicycles, people carrying things, beggars, a rich man with his entourage following him. We followed [the Dalai Lama] to the new lamasery or whatever. It was hard to get to him because there were so many people. We saw a glimpse of the Dalai Lama, and that was it. We felt we had been uplifted."

At the end of the conference, they had a "big bash" in the auditorium, with music and dancing. Then later that night, the whole event was capped off with an address by Krishnamurti. "In this gigantic tent set up on the same grounds as the school, but right next to it like a football field, a soccer field I imagine, Krishnamurti came to speak. We felt we had been uplifted, and we were in the back of this huge tent. All the seats were filled. There were a few thousand people, Krishnamurti had this loudspeaker, and his first words were, 'What is this yoga?' And it broke me up. And it took him a few minutes before he said anything else. Then he went on to explain, 'What is the use of this? Why do you do all of this? What is the use of these practices?

You're already who you are. You are perfect. You just don't realize it.' He went through his whole trip, and it just brought everything down from wherever it was. And I've been fighting my way through the whole thing ever since. I'm not a believer. You either do it or not do it. But believing is not going to get you anyplace.

"That was Krishnamurti's message. He did it in one night. It took the rest of them a week. Some of those gurus had some of the biggest egos you've ever seen. They reside in their egos. Krishnamurti knew who he was. He knew what he was talking about, and he knew how to tell it."

Coburn arrived home just in time for Christmas, feeling enlightened and spiritually refreshed. Unfortunately, he managed to catch some sort of bug, which put a damper on the holidays. It started to hit him when he was on his way home through Hong Kong, and once he got home, he was "totally exhausted and sick as a dog." He says, "It took me a couple of weeks to recover from it." In one respect it's not really surprising that, having gone through a spiritual experience of such intensity, the body would react. His mind and spirit were in such an open state, and his body would have been equally open, and susceptible to being hit. Or it could simply be typical of what happens when you travel and live among huge crowds for a time, in hotels and on airplanes. Incidentally, that January their home won the Travel Reflection category of the annual Burlington House Awards, which saluted American taste in home decor and furnishings.[25]

Not long after his return home, Coburn met the man he would consider his best friend and closest confidant for the rest of his life. "Frank Messa has been a friend for, I don't know how long, maybe thirty years. He came over to the house with somebody, and all of a sudden, he was there. Frank was a bit of a poet and liked to play drums, so we just got together and started playing drums every chance we get. We still do that."[26]

In 1971 Messa was a local artist and musician, who made flutes by hand in the Japanese style. "I was painting down here in Long Beach," Messa describes.[27] "A friend of mine, Doug [Bergeron], said, 'I want to take you to meet somebody who wants to meet you. Bring your harmonium.' A harmonium is an Indian thing that I got that I had taken apart and remade so that it made a fantastic sound.

"He didn't tell me it was James Coburn, just a friend in Beverly Hills. We drove and drove and drove—this was up on Tower Road. It was like a mansion up there, like a big castle. I thought, *Wow, who's living here?*

"I walk in, and the first person I meet is Beverly. She's *very* beautiful. She meets us at the door. The whole place was magnificent with the foyer. It was a beautiful place for my first impression. Then when we went in, there was a bunch of people that I recognized. There were about twenty or thirty people in there. Bob Dylan. I had to maintain myself from not being too star struck.

"And suddenly I meet Jim. And at that time, he was one of my favorite people, because he played the gong and I liked him in *The Magnificent Seven*. I knew who he was, and I really liked his flute playing. So I was thinking, *Oh my God, this is James Coburn*. He's very elegant, as he always is when he's meeting people.[28]

"And I got to play for everyone. When I got done, I was accepted. Then Jim takes me into a room off the living room—it was a big place that was full of drums and the gong, and we started playing. And he left all the guests. Some of them came in and picked up drums and began to play. We played in there for about an hour and a half, just having a grand time. And when it got later and later, he said, 'You don't have to go home. There's a guesthouse down the bottom of the hill. Stay there so we can talk in the morning.' So that's what I did. I was elated. Wow, this is fantastic. He was a great guy."

Messa stayed a few days after that first meeting. Then he kept coming back to drum, play flutes, and have discussions. It got into a pattern where he was up there three or four days a week and eventually had a room in the place. Coburn liked him, as did the kids. It took him a little longer to be accepted by Beverly. "I knew the children. But Beverly was the most elusive of all. She was almost like this person who was like an angel who overlooked everything and didn't really befriend me. And then after about three weeks of me being there a few times and having some dinner with them, Beverly takes me alone. With her eyes, she has this magical quality about her. She grabs me by the hand, and she says, 'You know that you and my husband have a rapport together, and I think that's very good. He needs somebody to play with,' and I said, 'Great.'"

From then on Messa was a fixture in their lives, upon whom Coburn came to rely. "Our friendship has lasted so long because we give it attention. Friendship is something you constantly want to flower, constantly want to give to, fertilize to make it more—so that it may grow, so it will be a place where you can reside any time you need to. You're going to walk around in the garden of friendship. The Sufis call it a rose garden, and they call each other 'friend.'

"Frank's always been there. I hired him to take care of a lot of things I couldn't do because I was working. He's a handyman around the house. He has lived in Long Beach ever since I've known him. He goes up to the woods every year on his birthday. It's a venture that requires a lot of stamina to go up there. I was never a nature boy. I hate going camping. Frank's become one of those guys you can always count on if you want to go camping or something like that. He'll work out the whole thing for you."[29]

There were always little chores Messa could help with. He would notice something that needed doing and go ahead and do it. For example, he tended the bamboo groves, which always need attention to prevent them from overgrowing other plants. He was meticulous with small construction. He helped build the cedar-lined rug room, where the carpets not in use were kept. Messa said, "It was a massive room, with shelves all cedar, and the rugs were known. I mean Beverly didn't mess around. She knew that was worth thirty thousand dollars, that was worth fifteen thousand dollars, it was from that province, it was from that village. She didn't depend on the rug dealer. Sometimes these rug dealers would come up, and she'd let them tell her the story—and it was bullshit. And she didn't interrupt. She'd wait until they finished, and then she'd tell the guy, 'Get out!' [pointing] 'You lied.' And he'd go, 'But, but, but . . .' And she'd say, 'You know exactly what I'm talking about. Get out.' And she'd pick out one of the rugs and give the whole history about it, and the guy would go pink and run out the front door."[30]

The valuable collection was cared for with regular maintenance. This was one room that was off-limits to pets—cats or monkeys.

Messa also made instruments for them to play with, including replicating an unusual log drum that had finally become unusable from so much use. Coburn considered it one of his favorite percussion instruments. "I had a log—it was kind of like an *H*. It was a very old, old piece of wood. Pieces kept breaking off, and each time it would give another sound. I'd play it like a xylophone. It was from someplace in South America. Beverly bought it in an antiques store. She asked what it was and was told it was a musical log. We had that thing for a long time. It made all kinds of sounds, and the dynamics on it were great. It was really a lot of fun, until it broke completely to pieces. Frank and I would play rhythms for hours at a time, and it was great fun. Sweat would be coming off us. I broke two watches. My rings were smashed."[31]

During these years of the early to midseventies, Coburn and Beverly were what Messa called tight. "Anybody who saw their relationship would not even think about seeing one against the other, because you would get your ass kicked. Especially Beverly. She had a sense about her. These guys would come in puffed up with all their power, all their Hollywood power, and she would *zzzzzzt*. You would watch them wilt after they talked to Beverly. Because she also had power. Beverly knew how to handle these guys without intimidating them or making them feel unmasculine. She had a super way of just talking to a man and making him melt. I've seen it.

"In fact, she told me one of the secrets. She said, 'Watch my pupils'—and then she made her pupils go big, and I said, 'How did you do that?' It was one of her secrets; then she would laugh. And she'd tell me, sometimes, 'I'm gonna make my pupils big when I'm talking to these guys. Watch their reaction.' And sure enough they'd melt. You could see them just kind of change their minds because they really didn't know what was happening there. She had a way of making herself up. She was absolutely gorgeous. During that whole time when they were having all those parties up there, there wasn't any woman who could come in and stand her ground with Beverly. It was out of the question. It wasn't because she was so fabulously beautiful. It's because of the way she handled herself. She had a way. She understood it."[32]

Beverly understood the movie business and the stock market. The house had a telex machine, where Beverly could communicate with people all over the world, including her Swiss lawyers. She would also periodically surprise the Coburn accountants by going on what Messa called raids. "She was brilliant. She knew things. She was very, very intelligent. She was extremely well read. She was smarter than anybody else who showed up there, including the agents. I used to go down on raids with Beverly every now and then. Beverly's tenacity and how smart she was—it was her and Jim's money. [The accountant] was supposed to take care of the stuff, and that's fine, but she'd say, 'Do I have to trust him without checking up on him? No.' A raid would be in the middle of the afternoon, on a Tuesday. She'd suddenly get in the car. Sometimes I'd go with her, and we'd just show up, knock on the door, and walk right in, and Beverly would say, 'I just came to check up on the books.' And he had to stop whatever he was doing and go down the line, bomp, bomp, bomp, and talk about their investments. And if there was something Beverly didn't know about, there would be a problem, and if there was something that he didn't know about, that he didn't do, there would be a problem.

"She played a lot of stocks. She was not a wimp. She took it very seriously—she was reading that stuff. She had brokers she would be able to call up and change things around. She was very smart. She played with oil when it was ten dollars a barrel."

At this time Coburn was still talking things over with Beverly, who would read the scripts sent to him and give her generally astute opinions. He chose his projects based first on the character—whether the character himself had a unique or unusual point of view, something different to say about the world. Sometimes the Coburns would seek the opinions of trusted others in their circle, like James Logan, who would happily read scripts and write down his thoughts, such as when they were considering an unnamed Cold War spy actioner.

Logan certainly understood what was wanted in a script and character. "This can be a very successful picture, and I take that seriously. It is vastly superior to *Where Eagles Dare*, *The Big Bounce* and *[The] Bridge at Remagen* and features on which millions are being spent at this very moment but I am against it for the following reasons: 1. It isn't a truthful picture. The personalities and all the action a[re] distorted out of all reason for theatrical effect. It can't be taken seriously. It's Derek Flint again only not so freelance. 2. The part does not have individuality. The man is an operative, handsome, sexy, strong, successful, audience pleasing but he's a fantasy cloak and dagger spy first and personality second. He's not real. It's formula all the way, well done, but it's still formula all the way."[33]

Evidently, Coburn declined this script. It was still some years before he would start taking anything offered him, either for the money or just to get out of the house. In general he would rather be working than not, and he sometimes chose projects based on their location and the chance to travel. He had the freedom of choice that comes with stardom. Thanks in large part to Beverly's assiduous attention to their stock portfolio, they were in good shape financially. Coburn seemed drawn to antiheroes—Eli Kotch, Duffy, the assassin John Cunningham, Jeb Thornton, Sean Mallory—rather than the good guys. Some of these characters were fundamentally cold and distant. The superiority that his charm had rendered attractive in the Flint movies and *The President's Analyst* could appear as hauteur in some of these unscrupulous characters. Others were merely self-centered rogues, but the defining element of almost every character was individualism.

Lew Lathrop of *The Honkers* was certainly part of this mold. He was an aging rodeo cowboy, estranged from his family, desperately trying to hold on to past glories but with the emotional maturity of a teenager. He was irresponsible, immature, and charming, but rather unlikable. He ignores his wife and son, and takes his best friend, played by Slim Pickens, for granted. Although Coburn and Pickens had worked on many of the same TV series back in the day, it was always on different episodes. The first time they worked together had been on *Major Dundee* (1965). They were friendly acquaintances.

It was the first studio directorial effort from actor-writer Steve Ihnat, who had acted in *In Like Flint*. It had originally been intended as a small personal picture, but United Artists liked the script and wanted to jump onto the rodeo film bandwagon, a current minor trend. Unfortunately, as often happens, this meant that *The Honkers* was somewhat overshadowed when the Steve McQueen picture, directed by Sam Peckinpah, *Junior Bonner*, came out a few months later. They even both include a parade down Main Street of a country town. Roger Ebert notes this visual similarity between these rodeo pictures: "lots of dusty roads and pickup trucks and rodeo footage cleverly edited to make it look like the star was really in the arena."[34] In a widely mixed critical response, reviewers debated whether *The Honkers* or *Junior Bonner* was better. Some critics considered both to be inferior to the Cliff Robertson starrer, *J. W. Coop*, which had started the trend.

Cowriter and wardrobe man Stephen Lodge recalls speaking to Coburn when he was first cast, about his costumes: "I had some leather chaps custom-made for him by a lady in the San Fernando Valley. I made the appointment for him to be measured and then called him up to let him know. I was worried that he'd expect the lady to come to him. But he was very nice and just said, 'Where do I go?' He went out twice, first in a gray Ferrari, and the second time in a red Ferrari. The seamstress was amazed that he had two Ferraris, one for each foot.

"He had never done a modern western—set in present day—before. He and Slim Pickens came in to try on wardrobe at the same time. When Jim pulled his pants on, he pulled the waist up all the way. He looked in the mirror and said, 'This doesn't look right.' So Slim Pickens went over and tugged them down to show him how to wear them, and that's how he kept them. The best thing for me was when I heard one of the locals in the country town say, 'There's Jim Coburn. He looks just like one of us.' He was very serious at work."[35]

The Honkers was shot in Carlsbad, New Mexico, for a few weeks in late April and May 1971, employing local townspeople as extras and bringing in many actual rodeo stars, including the current world champion, to create an authentic atmosphere around the competition. It was a happy shoot. In all the local and neighboring towns, the company advertised for extras for the big parade scene, with the promise of some nice raffle prizes, including color TVs, as enticements. On parade day, May 15, about seventeen thousand people came and lined both sides of five or six blocks of the street. There were four or five cameras, and the parade kept going around and around the blocks all day long to capture all the action. There was a nice festive atmosphere. It worked so well that the company put out a second call for people to bring their entire families for the rodeo sequences to be shot over Memorial Day weekend, promising the chance to meet the stars (and throwing in a plug for the Carlsbad Caverns).

Coburn tended to stay in his hotel room rather than join the evening parties, working out with the hand weights he brought along and enjoying an all-too-brief visit from Beverly. She didn't stay for the whole shoot, and even during her visit, she stayed away from the set. There wasn't a whole lot going on around Carlsbad at the time. Once you had seen the caverns, that was it for local attractions.

The filmmakers devised an ingenious way to shoot Coburn participating in bronco and bull riding in the absence of either process shots or present-day computer-generated imagery (CGI). The mechanical-effects crew rigged a bouncing fulcrum onto a six-wheel ATV. They added a faux horse body, complete with tail, something like a saddle on springs, and did the same for the bull. It drove around over ground dug up to be very bumpy, with the actor on the back being shot in close-up from afar with a very long lens. This had the effect of capturing both his performance and the blurred background of the rodeo atmosphere. Coburn spent the better part of a day on the bucking "horse" and longer on the "yellow bull." His level of physical fitness undoubtedly helped.

In the end the performances of Slim Pickens, as the rodeo clown and Lathrop's only friend, and of Lois Nettleton as his ex-wife almost ran away with the picture (as indeed did Ida Lupino and Robert Preston in *Junior Bonner*). Lodge was disappointed that a very sweet romantic scene between Nettleton and Coburn was cut from the final print.

He reveals that the ending of the film was also not as originally planned: "There was a whole sequence at the end where Lathrop goes back to ride that yellow bull. We wrote the bull that kills Slim as like the whale in *Moby-Dick*. In the original ending, Lew goes back to the empty stadium at night, and turns on the lights by himself, and rides that bull to a standstill, and *then* he walks away. But they came out from the studio and wanted us to just end it without shooting that last sequence, with him just walking away as you see."

The missing scene and the original ending would have cast Lathrop in more sympathetic light. Apparently the studio's idea was to save a little bit of money, although at just over one million dollars, it was certainly a low-budget picture even for 1971. Being isolated in Carlsbad meant that there weren't dailies. The shot film was sent away for processing. Still, there was plenty of time for editing before the May 17, 1972, premiere.

Unfortunately, United Artists had just spent a lot of time and money promoting their latest Bond film (*Diamonds Are Forever*, 1971), leaving little energy left for promoting *The Honkers*, much to Lodge's disappointment. Coburn did give a promotional interview for the press release, calling the film "one of the most exciting I've ever made."[36]

He went on to say, "The rodeo rider is a dramatically different kind of man. They're the last, perhaps, of the great individualists in the American tradition. They're mavericks. In a sense, they're like the youngsters of today who are unable and unwilling to conform to the demands of the establishment, who need freedom and self-expression and who need to maintain their own individuality. . . . You might call it a tragi-comedy—of a cowboy, me, who's really over the hill. But in keeping with his philosophy as a Westerner, who'll have no responsibility but to himself, he's still on the rodeo circuit, because to him and his kind it represents the last frontier. . . . Slim Pickens is remarkable, a walking—maybe I should say riding—Encyclopedia of this field. The background we got from him is not only fantastic but helped us all in getting the realism we needed and wanted."

Then Steve Ihnat suffered a sudden fatal heart attack at the Cannes Film Festival, sadly cutting short what everyone expected would be a very interesting career as a director. The film had a short run in cinemas then was somewhat further cut for TV, where it played frequently throughout the midseventies and eighties. Now it has disappeared with only rare reappearances on the Westerns Channel.[37]

The Honkers was a pleasant experience that took just over a month of Coburn's life. He had started the year excited about "The Silent Flute" screenplay, which was now completed. It had taken three years between jobs, but having polished the script, Coburn, Bruce Lee, and Stirling Silliphant took it to Warner Bros., who liked the idea but insisted that the film be shot in India because the studio had a bunch of blocked rupees there—money sequestered in India that the government there refused to remit out of the country. Panpiper Productions and Silliphant's company, Pingree, had formalized a joint venture to produce on April 5, 1971. Now that *The Honkers* was done shooting, Coburn had time to join his two colleagues on a trip to India to scout locations.

That trip to India was something of a disaster. It was hotter than expected and uncomfortable. Bruce Lee was disgruntled when Coburn received the star treatment wherever he went. It was challenging to find the right locations, and the Indian martial artists, who had their own traditional practice, would have needed "at least three years to train to the right level," according to Bruce.[38]

Eventually Coburn was convinced that it was not possible to make a film about Chinese kung fu in India, at least not a good film. He said so, firmly. Warner Bros. backed out of the project. Bruce Lee was very disappointed and blamed Coburn for the delay, and it almost caused a rift in their friendship. Silliphant, having more experience with the script development process at Hollywood studios, was more sanguine about it, figuring there would be more opportunities. He rightly understood that it can sometimes take years to shop a script around before it finally gets sold. For the moment, he continued to write parts for Lee into his ongoing TV projects and to send "The Silent Flute" script all over town. He even approached James Aubrey at MGM. Aubrey declined, which was fortunate for reasons that will become apparent.[39]

Lee and Coburn reconciled, and it was not long after this that Lee went to him for advice, which turned out to be a crucial professional turning point. "I actually talked him out of doing the television series *Kung Fu*. Bruce was not an actor; he was a martial artist, and he always let his ego take him on that trip, and you can't have an ego and be an actor. You've got to sublimate that thing down there. I knew if he took on the character in *Kung Fu*, his career would be over. His talent was as a martial artist.

"I suggested he go back to China and do those films that were just perfect for him, that made him such a huge star. He really wanted to do television. I said, 'Man, don't do it. Television limits you.' 'I can act,' he told me. 'Well, you can act well enough, but the films will show off your art more.' He thought about it, and thought about it, and finally decided to go back and make those Southeast Asian films. And he became Bruce Lee, Martial Artist."[40]

Coburn arrived home from India just in time for the network television premiere of *The President's Analyst*, which received a modicum of publicity. It had been four years since it was in the theaters, about double the usual timing. It was a nice beginning to another intense period of back-to-back movies, with much travel around the country and overseas. He was back at work preparing for his next film almost at once. This would prove to be one of the most frustrating experiences of his career.

9

Boom, Boom, Boom

I never looked for fame. It comes on as a rush, and you just deal with it, whatever happens. You're asked to sign autographs and do this, that, and the other thing. Sometimes it was fun, sometimes it was boring.

—JAMES COBURN, 2002

Coburn chose his next film because he liked the story. It was a medical murder mystery based on the Edgar Award–winning book *A Case of Need* by Jeffery Hudson, the mystery genre nom de plume of Michael Crichton. It was Crichton's fourth novel, published the same year he graduated from Harvard Medical School. He clearly drew on his hospital experiences while studying.

The script looked good. It had some changes from the book: instead of being a long-term member of the community, Dr. Carey was a newcomer; instead of being privy to the ongoing secret trade in compassionate abortions, he was an outsider; rather than being a family man, he was alone, which allowed a romance blackmail subplot. But the underlying story of a pathologist turning detective was a precursor to every medical-examiner-investigating-murder procedural to follow. Michael Crichton's earlier sci-fi novel *The Andromeda Strain* had recently been adapted into a successful film of the same name by Universal Studios. Coburn was looking forward to playing the hero in this adaptation, *The Carey Treatment*, for MGM.

The idea of working with director Blake Edwards again was icing on the cake. Edwards approached the project with cautious optimism. His last film had been at MGM, under the auspices of film executive James Aubrey. It had not been a good experience.

Like Paramount Pictures a few years earlier, MGM was struggling financially. Unlike the strategy implemented by Paramount's Bluhdorn-Evans dyad of making hit movies to save the studio, MGM's businessman owner, Kirk Kerkorian, and his appointed studio head, James Aubrey, chose a radical cost-cutting, asset-liquidation strategy. The latter was tasked with unloading $62 million in company assets.

Aubrey brought his nickname "The Smiling Cobra" with him from his tenure at CBS. Immediately upon being hired, he canceled twelve films that were in preproduction. Over the next several months, he closed the British MGM studios and the New York offices. He personally fired either 3,200 or up to 3,500 individuals, depending on the source. Vincent Canby in the *New York Times* described the situation as "the realization of everyone's worst fears of what would happen to Hollywood when the money men take over."[1]

Certainly Coburn distrusted the studio moneymen, often calling them shoe salesmen. On the other hand, the studio was in imminent danger of closing altogether.

Aubrey's greatest outrages were probably the sell-offs—starting with the auction of the props, decor, miniatures, and costumes that had been stored in various places on the studio back lot, including vehicles and vintage set pieces. He sold the entire lot of items to the David Weisz auctioning company for a tiny $1.5 million for an on-site auction in 1970. In hindsight it was a massive miscalculation, which did come back to embarrass him, since the auction itself ended up making between $8 and $10 million. In those days there was not the market for movie memorabilia that there is today. Some things were being sold as useful rather than historical, particularly contemporary wardrobe items. But Dorothy's ruby slippers even then were remarkable, and one pair fetched $15,000 at the auction and is now in the Smithsonian.[2]

The second notorious sale was that of Lot 3, which included three western streets, Tarzan's jungle, and the lake that doubled for "Ol' Man River" from *Show Boat* (1951), to a developer for an apartment complex, followed shortly thereafter by the sale of Lot 2. Debbie Reynolds hastily formed a consortium of actors and directors and tried to buy Lot 2, with the idea of turning it into a theme park tourist attraction.

Obdurate perversity was at war with parsimony. Spite won. Aubrey turned the group away, selling to another business for barely more money. They planned to demolish the site to recover and recycle copper wire from the electrical grids before building new housing. Reynolds bemoaned the situation in an interview. "The farsighted geniuses that were now running MGM couldn't see why anybody would want to tour the Studio's back lot.... They were only interested in selling the property for real estate development, and they were not interested in preservation only money.... They had to leave it to Lew Wasserman and Al Dorskind at Universal to show them."[3]

After several years of legal wrangling and fighting with Culver City over the lots' zoning, these first real estate deals both fell through. Despite a small income in rentals to other movie shoots, Aubrey allowed the streets and "homes" that were part of the public's collective consciousness—for example, Andy Hardy's house, and the street where we met Judy Garland in *Meet Me in St. Louis* (1944), as well as Verona Square, the exterior set used for Norma Shearer's *Romeo and Juliet* (1936) and many other classic movies—to fall into such a state of disrepair that eventually MGM realized $1.5 million *less* than if Aubrey had just sold Lot 2 to the Reynolds consortium at its original offer.

At the same time, new lending practices in film finance were being implemented, where the banks would lend on a picture-by-picture basis, with the film itself being the collateral, rather than make a block loan to a production company. This led to a new premium on careful preparation and prompt release. Aubrey agreed with this method, which, applied thoughtfully, could produce good pictures. However, limitations require enhanced creativity. He was known to have "contempt for creativity.... Like many of his peers, he tended to blame the industry's financial crisis on creative self-indulgence and its recent appeal to counterculture values."[4] One of the last films produced under the old guard was *Zabriskie Point* (1970), a financial and critical debacle that can only have added to his disdain. The last thing Aubrey was interested in was pandering to the "youngsters of today" who so intrigued Coburn.

Aubrey set a cap of two million dollars as the production budget for any film at MGM, enforcing the limit with drastically shortened shooting schedules and decimating the post schedules, leaving little time for editing.

In the biography of the director by Sam Wasson, Blake Edwards recalls the negativity around his most recent MGM film, *Wild Rovers* (1971): "There was no discussion—an integral part was simply removed. It was my best film, and he butchered it. I'd beseeched them; they still butchered it."[5] Edwards considered leaving Hollywood. "But then I did a foolish thing. I allowed myself to be coerced or seduced or whatever. Aubrey got me in and he even apologized and he said, 'but here's this project—*The Carey Treatment*—that I know you're right for and we'll stay out of it.' He was lying through his teeth—he was actually out to crucify me."

The project started out well with refinements on the script going into September, as is usual. Principal photography began in Boston on October 4, 1971, with plans to shoot most of the picture there, including a high-energy ending sequence. It was winter, and the costume design reflected the season and a very hip, contemporary sensibility. The sartorial elegance of the costumes was noticed by some of the reviewers including Vincent Canby at the *New York Times* who wrote that Dr. Carey "affects the kind of slash pocket, casual clothes worn mostly by male models for Esquire."[6] It's hard to tell whether he approved or not.

Edwards attempted to reflect the genre-bending switches in the narrative between a hospital procedural and a murder mystery through shifting between different camera styles and lighting, what Wasson calls "the kind of genre turnaround he loves."[7]

Then disaster struck. Aubrey broke his promise. He ordered the company back to Los Angeles for the staged interiors before filming the climactic sequence in Boston, using bad weather as an excuse. He excised about ten days from the planned shooting schedule. Edwards was forced to rewrite and rework on the fly, while Coburn was dismayed at the loss of the planned climax. As he told interviewer Joseph Leydon, "We had a great design for the ending, but they didn't know a goddamn thing about it! We were really going to build that thing, so it had some kind of marvelous—boom, boom, boom—real impact."[8]

In addition Aubrey "set a release date that made it impossible to finish editing, and utterly mutilated the ending."[9] The fact that his own daughter, actress Skye Aubrey, was number four on the call sheet evidently made no difference to him. The time allotted to post was ridiculous. *The Carey Treatment* was in theaters about six weeks prior to *The Honkers*, which had shot six months earlier.

Edwards was dreadfully disappointed as well as suffering physically. "His back had given out on him in Boston. He shot it in incredible pain for the rest of the film."[10] At the conclusion of principal photography in mid-December, he walked away from the impossible editing schedule and moved to Europe with his family. He told Wasson, "Like a lot of directors as angry as I am, I believed Aubrey wanted to turn MGM back into a movie studio. I eventually realized nobody at MGM was interested in being in the movie business at all. Certainly, no one was interested in making good movies. Nobody knew how. In fact, MGM executives were antagonistic to artists. They wanted, demanded mediocrity."[11]

Coburn never forgave Aubrey. He still complained about him years later, telling Leydon, "The thing he got his kicks off of, is destroying films that other people have made. You can't imagine, you really can't imagine the kind of ability that this cocksucker has! For a man to deliberately destroy a film . . . We had a couple of real nitwits for producers on that, old buddies of Aubrey's . . . who's just an arbitrary, evil man, who cuts it out either because it's too good, or because it's some particular personal quirk that he didn't want in there."[12]

Coburn took time in November for some self-promotion. He appeared for the first time on an episode of *The Tonight Show*. "I played the gong on Johnny Carson twice. One of those times, Don Rickles was on the show. I really played the fucking thing—when I finished I got a big hand. I came over and sat down. Rickles was already sitting there. Johnny asked me where I got the gong. 'Well, my wife gave be my first gong.' Don Rickles took it—'Your wife gave you your *first* gong?'—and turned it into a sexual entendre. And we laughed and laughed for half an hour. It was funny, and ever since Don and I have been close friends. Whenever I see him, we remember the gong.

"The first time they thought it would be just a silly thing, and Johnny was standing over me when I started playing it, and he really started listening to it, and it took the bloom off his jokes that he was going to make about me playing the gong, so he had me back to play again."[13]

This scenario would continue to be repeated for Coburn's entire career, whenever he appeared on a talk show to demonstrate the gong. Jocular skepticism always transformed into wonder while watching his elegant playing.

The visit to Johnny Carson and an appearance on *The David Frost Show* the following week were bright spots in a frustrating time. By the end of principal photography on *The Carey Treatment* (at that time still being called *A Case of Need*), Coburn could barely contain his anger, which he unloaded into the press. In an interview with Marilyn Beck, he charged that the "budgetary pressures from MGM's head offices were so absurd they've squelched our creativity."[14] He grumbled that the pecuniary focus affected everything from the script to the shooting schedule. He also added, "As difficult as it was on the cast we didn't see half the pressure. As producer, Blake Edwards was the one it hit hardest." He was upset at the skewed priorities of those in charge who would "throw away money on absurd things instead of the thing that counts—on the film!"

Coburn saw the tensions between art and commerce as something that would plague the industry and his own life. He considered the big studios "so laced with greed they can't see straight" and resented that he felt like he was drawn into that whole acquisitive philosophy. "The worst part is that once you've acquired all those possessions, you're pressured to keep them." In addition he was bitter about the tricky bookkeeping that he believed essentially swindled himself and others who supposedly had a share of the profits. He was particularly upset about this at the time because he was about to file a lawsuit against the producers of *Candy* alleging that he was owed money from profit participation.

Coburn also made a dismal prediction about the reviews of *The Carey Treatment*, which was largely realized. While he himself generally received compliments, criticisms of the film seem to reflect the result of randomly taking out ten days' worth of work. One reviewer describes it as "an extraordinary ragbag of a movie,"[15] while another suggests that Coburn was the "only salvation" of the film, which "goes nowhere."[16] Vincent Canby of the *New York Times* believed the whole thing was written as, and meant to be, a high comedy—"absurdly entertaining. . . . I don't think we have to take this too seriously."[17]

After a short break, at the start of March 1972, Coburn went to Kansas City to the annual convention of the theater owners' group, the United Motion Picture Association. He was honored as the Show-A-Rama Male Star of the Year, a title that reflected his status as a box-office draw, at the time.

He used the occasion to announce a new project, the creation of a loose affiliation of directors, actors, producers, and others who wanted to help get quality films made outside of the big studio framework. The idea seemed an intelligent reaction to his frustration over *The Carey Treatment* shoot and a reflection of his belief in taking action. Rather than just grumbling, he formed a consortium to do something about it.

Coburn called the group Minder Bender Pulp, or MBP. "We're not a producing organization, but catalytic organization. It's something that's never been tried before as far as I know, and it's really very simple."[18] The plan was that creative individuals with ideas get together—with each other and with the financiers who will support the film projects. He put together a glossy full-color comic book brochure to promote it.

"We're bringing together a group of twenty proven film talents who feel that films should be made by writers, directors and actors working together, rather than as hirelings of car rental–shoe manufacturing industrialists. . . . The goal is to create a positive environment for inspiring new impressions in the state of filmmaking for profitable self-fulfillment. . . . The purpose of the system is to put the total entity of the film from concept to theatrical release in the hands of film talents."[19]

It was a notion both ahead of its time and hearkening back to the original impetus behind United Artists in 1919. It would partially work like a networking group. For other projects, the group itself would act in a similar way as some of the big agents today, who create film production packages—scripts with director, producers, and stars already attached—to raise independent financing. MBP intended to have its own financing in place for members to access when they were ready to begin. The project would have a fund from which up to five medium-budget films (as $500,000 was considered then) would be made, with MBP owning a portion of the films and some profit participation. For the financiers, it was asserted that there would be "less risk in investing in a group of films made by different film talents rather than in just on the film." This was moving in the exact opposite direction of studio film lenders, who were increasingly lending on a project-by-project basis.

Additional grand ambitions included creating a resource of production information, such as locations and a pool of production teams as well as a public relations/publicity department and a distribution "consulting department." Finally, there were other plans including motion picture and theater-restaurant complexes, mobile film libraries, more comic books, record production and distribution, and TV production and syndication. Some of the individuals connected with MBP were Francis Ford Coppola, Faye Dunaway, Sam Peckinpah, and Katharine Ross and her husband, Conrad Hall.

Coburn was keen to point out the fiscal savings: "A film made independently with MBP help can be budgeted at half of what the same film might cost under studio auspices. The waste, greed and staggering overheads of studio filming will be avoided.'"[20] One principle in the overall plan was that the filmmakers themselves were the only ones to determine whether their project was worth doing.

Coburn claimed that five film projects scheduled to begin shooting that summer had grown out of the MBP program. The brochure asserted that the first was to be *Ward Craft*, to star himself and Tom Skerritt, and written by Jeb Rosebrook, who had just written Sam Peckinpah's recent movie *Junior Bonner*. *Ward Craft* was to have started its shoot in Arizona in January 1972.

That project never materialized. MBP as an official organization was never mentioned in the public record again.

The creation of the group reflected Coburn's intense desire to control his own career and not be part of projects that were subject to the misapplied priorities, as he saw them, of the studio bigwigs. He was proactive when he saw an existing problem that he could solve through ideas. Throughout his professional life, he attempted to influence independent production through the formation of his own companies to develop projects in which to star. He had done that with M.O.F.F. and Panpiper. A few years later, he and Beverly would create a production company, Scarab, and an international corporation based in Liberia, that was a deferred tax shelter for overseas income rather than a production entity, Pyx Quartation.

Hilly Elkins, Coburn's longtime friend and manager, called him an "ideas man" rather than a producer, although he had not yet given up his ambition to direct. "I tried to capitalize on the entrees that were available. But producing wasn't his joy. He liked putting ideas together. But then he wants to go away, have someone write it and get on the stage and do it. Basically, he did not want to be a producer. He was very happy being an actor who occasionally produced."[21]

Still, when possible, he liked being hired early so that he could influence the development of the script and characters. "We have no one but ourselves to blame for typecasting. I tire of playing similar characters, doing a series of the same kind of roles over and over. It's very dull for me and, I'm sure, for the audience. I like to space and vary the parts I play. [We hope] it will be a concert. That's the ideal, with no competition between artists, but rather a rapport. It doesn't always happen, but it's marvelous when it occurs—when you're devoting all your energy toward the scene rather than ego trips."[22] Nonetheless, he was still very clear about his preferences and the commonality underlying all his roles. "They represent strong individualists with a touch of the bizarre. . . . I don't know why, but I'm attracted to bizarre, mysterious, unknown qualities in people and characters. I like to find out what the mystery is in a character and not reveal it too far—every character should have something not revealed."

The year 1972 would be intense. In spring Coburn would go back to Spain for the first of four feature films he would shoot within twelve months, with four unique characters. These films were released to the theaters in exactly the reverse order that they were filmed.

But first the year started with Coburn shooting a precursor to many of today's reality shows, an ABC Sports special titled *Challenge*. The premise was to train a celebrity in a new outdoors skill, something of interest to him or her, and record the person's process and reactions. Then the challenge itself would be a test of the new skill set. In this case it was a car-racing challenge. Coburn enjoyed training for five days at the Bob Bondurant School of High Performance Driving at the Ontario Motor Speedway. "The challenges of racing were increased daily to prepare for the actual competition: a race against other amateur graduates from the Bondurant school."[23]

The other half of the episode featured host and outdoorsman William Shatner learning to white-water kayak. The program debuted in the popular Sunday afternoon family time slot, 4:30 p.m., on April 9. It was initially planned as a series that became a single special, although Coburn's footage was reused in a different ABC Sports special the following year.

Of the experience he says, "It's like cliff walking to the edge and then looking down. When you come through it you feel more, rather than less." He worked through a maze, a slalom course at ever-increasing speeds, and an accident-simulator setup to learn braking. He also learned the toe-heel professional acceleration method and how to manage skids.

Coburn's son, Jimmy, remembers going out to the speedway to watch his dad train. It was intense. The irony of all of this is that as much as Coburn loved driving fast in his Ferraris, he was not into racing. "I just like to drive. I was not competitive like Steve McQueen and Jimmy Dean, all those guys who really liked to race."[24]

Soon after this shoot, Coburn arrived in Barcelona for another historical western set in the Civil War era.

A Reason to Live, a Reason to Die filmed in central Spain, including at a still-standing western set dubbed "Mini-Hollywood." The pic also starred Bud Spencer, with Telly Savalas in a villain role. Coburn's character, Colonel

Pembroke, had echoes of Major Dundee in his quest to redeem himself from charges of cowardice, although his true quest was revenge for the murder of his son. The story has been compared to the conceit of *The Dirty Dozen*—a ragtag group of soldier criminals are promised amnesty in exchange for service and, in this case, are literally rescued from the gallows. Their quest is punctuated by meeting dishonest schemers at every turn, making one ask, just who are the criminals?

Bud Spencer steals the picture with an endearing portrayal of a quick-thinking trooper who goes undercover in the fort. There are some nice action sequences too, especially in the finale. The shoot was relatively fast, and the film had a staggered release in Europe over two years before eventually coming to the equivalent of the art house circuit in the United States. The film was dubbed with other actors for the European releases, a process that always bemused Coburn.

He only had twelve days between the end of his shoot in Spain and the commencement of principal photography on his next film, *Harry in Your Pocket*. He was paid $150,000 with an additional $50,000 deferred, plus a portion of the profits and $1,000 per week living allowance, to start with rehearsals and preparations on June 19, 1972, in Los Angeles.

This included wardrobe fittings and training with a former professional pickpocket, Tony Giorgio, now going straight as an actor and sleight-of-hand magician. The stars learned all the tricks, movements, and most importantly timing, as a group, as well as the lingo. The process begins with a "stall"— someone who distracts the victim (the "mark") by jostling them—allowing the "cannon" to lift the wallet ("poke"). The cannon then passes it to the nearby "cleaner," someone whom the mark would not even have noticed in the background.[25]

Harry in Your Pocket was produced by Cinema Video Communications, an independent production company put together in late 1971 by director Bruce Geller, agent Alden Schwimmer, Blake Edwards, and author Harold Robbins.[26] They appeared to have a similar ethos to MBP with the intention of avoiding studio waste, as Schwimmer elucidated in a letter: "We feel that in composite we represent a body of experience, accomplishment and ability that no major studio can match, and we have been and shall continue to utilize those abilities so that 95 cents out of every dollar spent goes to the project as opposed to the major studio operation where 75 cents on every dollar goes anywhere but the project."[27] This was surely a concept that Coburn could get behind.

The working title of the film was *Harry Never Holds* after the one cardinal rule of Harry's team, a cannon mob. Principal photography began in Seattle on July 5, 1972, and included shooting on the monorail there. The company moved from Seattle to British Columbia and then to Utah.

Sometimes filming on location was hampered by the crowds of people that gathered around Coburn wherever he went. Once again he portrayed a very slick, mature man in his prime, an emotionally guarded character, very well dressed, very good-looking, undeniably cool, even in the heat of summer. His character's success in the game came from maintaining his distance, avoiding sentimental entanglements, even with one of his oldest friends and colleagues. Eventually his undoing was in breaking his own rule, holding both the wallet and his emotional attachment to his protégés.

The shoot extended over the summer vacation from school, and eleven-year-old Jimmy spent much of his vacation traveling with the company during the shoot. He became friends with the less busy costar, veteran actor Walter Pidgeon. "He was my buddy. We walked around Victoria, British Columbia. We hung out, had tea, and chatted."[28]

When they traveled by ferry to British Columbia, they took the opportunity to shoot some scenes on board. Then in Utah they apparently shot in the same hotel in which the stars were staying. In August in Salt Lake City, the production took a page out of *The Honkers*'s book to fill a stadium with background people, inviting the public to watch the filming of an equestrian jumping event at the Salt Palace arena, employing local riders for the show. Once again the company offered free raffle drawings for a color television, cameras, and bicycles to participants, along with free admission. The final day was August 19, 1972, leaving just over a year for editing. At one point they had to ask for a special favor from the company producing Coburn's next movie, *The Last of Sheila*—getting Coburn to do some looping while on location in late October. Looping, or additional dialogue recording (ADR), is the practice of recording an actor's dialogue separately, having them lip-synch to the already-shot film, when the production audio track is unusable for some reason.

Just before setting off for that next gig in the South of France, Coburn endorsed the campaign for Proposition 19, a ballot initiative to legalize marijuana. The campaign was struggling to get people to publicly donate and endorse the effort. The lawyer for the campaign, Robert Ashford, claimed that stars "that smoke marijuana every day . . . are hiding behind their wealthy attorneys, realizing it's just the poor people who get arrested for smoking marijuana."[29] The only other celebrity to endorse the campaign was Tommy Smothers.

Ashford lamented the hypocrisy in Hollywood but failed to take into consideration that studio film contracts still contained a serious morality clause. Even Coburn's contract for *Harry in Your Pocket* contained far-reaching language enjoining him to "conduct himself with due regard to public conventions and morals" and to "not do or commit any act or thing that will degrade Artist in society or bring Artist into public hatred, contempt, scorn or ridicule, or that will shock, insult or offend the community or violate public morals or decency."[30] He risked being fired, unpaid. Seen in that light, supporting the proposition at all was a small act of bravery.

The Last of Sheila shot on location in the beautiful Côte d'Azur—the Mediterranean coast close to Cannes. The publicity made much of the ironic fact that the luxurious yacht that supposedly belonged to Coburn's character, a film producer, belonged to a real-life film producer. However, this was just a stroke of good publicist luck. The company had originally leased a slightly larger yacht belonging to a private individual with no connection to the business. It had foundered off Mykonos two weeks before rehearsals were scheduled.

The shoot stretched over late September through the middle of November, not the usual time to enjoy the Riviera weather. There was a lot of rain to contend with. Producer-director Herbert Ross jokes, "They call this the Overcoat d'Azur."[31] Even when the skies were clear, chilly winds and tidal currents caused the yacht itself and others in the background to drift around, playing havoc with the continuity. The entire cast and crew (of thirty-one) spent twenty-eight days on the yacht, much of it at sea.

In general it was a happy and enjoyable shoot, and when they did dock, they were in beautiful locales. Frank Messa visited and recalls it as "a lot of fun."[32] Some of the stars rented villas, such as Dyan Cannon's near Grasse. Actor Richard Benjamin and his wife celebrated their wedding anniversary toward the end of the shoot in October, with a dinner party and evening of disco in Cannes hosted by Cannon's manager, Allan Carr.[33]

Coburn and Richard Benjamin became good friends, even though Benjamin was initially startled because Jim was a hugger. "Very early on when I first saw him and went to shake his hand, when we first met on this picture, he wasn't having any of that shaking-of-the-hand thing—it was a full embrace. I had not embraced a man before. Embracing wasn't exactly my thing. I may have embraced my father early on at some point, but a stranger, another actor—it just wasn't in me, that embracing thing, you know? But somehow with Jim it was all right. I felt better for it.

"When you act with somebody, something happens or it doesn't happen. And acting is a high-wire act. I think it is two aerialists on trapezes and yes, you're saying the lines, and yes, there are emotions or whatever, but there is a trick going on. There is something happening in the eyes, and there is a challenge, and there is a 'Will you catch me if I really take a risk? I'll catch you if you take a risk.' And when I acted with James in that picture, I saw it in his eyes. I saw that we were flying. I could see the spirit in there. When that happens it elevates you. You play a better game because you're playing with someone who's really good."[34]

Coburn picked up a new silver Ferrari Dino, in which he enjoyed tooling about, putting his lessons with Bob Bondurant to good use on the twisty corniches up and down the coast near Cannes and Nice. Benjamin has often told the story of the unforgettable outing they had together on one of their days off. Coburn picked him up outside the Carlton Hotel on La Croisette then suggested they head on over to Italy, which worried Benjamin since he didn't have his passport.[35]

"So we're out on the auto route, and it's really nice and smooth, and I'm looking over to the other side, and the cars seemed parked. I wondered why they're stopped, and he said, 'How fast do you think we're going?' I said, 'Oh, I don't know but fast, right? Like eighty or ninety?' He said to look at the speedometer. So I looked down. It's 135. So I said, 'Kilometers right?' He said, 'No, miles per hour.' Well in fifteen minutes, we are in Italy."[36]

They got to the border and were naturally stopped by the guard who came out and demanded to see their *passeporti*. "Then I see this star thing happen. I hadn't quite ever seen this before. Jim turns to the guy, takes off his dark glasses, smiles at him, and a light comes out of Jim, a star light, something that glows so bright that it hypnotized the guy. This is what a real movie star is. I have never seen it when a movie star turns on the light. The guy is in a kind of daze, and he says, '*Passare commendatore*,' and the next thing I know, we are in Italy. I said, 'What happened back there?' and he said, 'Oh, you've got to have a little faith.'"

They drove around Italy and saw the local sights around there, and finally it was night so they decided to head back. "There's a Porsche behind us flashing the lights, and I said, 'Hey, Jim, I think he wants to pass us.' Jim says, 'I don't think so.' Well, I'm a Jewish kid from the west side of Manhattan. I'm sitting next to Derek Flint, and we're going 130 miles an hour playing fender tag with a Porsche. We get back to Cannes in about ten minutes. It's a trip I'll never forget."

From then on, Benjamin was another friend who would periodically come over to the house and hit the gong. As he said, "That's on another plane for someone like me."

The plot of *The Last of Sheila* was intriguing, with plenty of twists and turns and surprises. It was a whodunit, with a touch of hubris and irony, that required close attention. It was written by friends Stephen Sondheim and Anthony Perkins, and according to author Craig Zadan as quoted by Douglas Braverman, it was "inspired by the elaborate party games which Sondheim and Perkins often designed to entertain their friends."[37] Herbert Ross had been a guest at one of their famous Halloween treasure hunts. Each writer focused on their favorite aspect, for Sondheim the puzzles and clues, for Perkins the suspense of the narrative, drawing on his experience working with Hitchcock. They wrote the script separately and then mailed their pages to each other. There was a whole level of in-the-know humor, such as Dyan Cannon's lovingly on-point representation of her own agent, the somewhat notorious Sue Mengers. Mengers also represented Coburn and Richard Benjamin.

Sondheim, who had been instrumental in bringing British crossword puzzles to America, "obviously takes great delight in devising these multi-level brain teasers. [The movie demonstrated] an intricacy and a delight in the cerebral which sets it apart from most other screenplays."[38] Some of the critics found it too convoluted. Actor James Mason was disappointed in the reviews, saying, "It was intriguing and funny and deserving of an audience's attention. Granted it called for a great deal of attention, more than the critics were evidently prepared to lend."[39]

Certainly it is one of Coburn's movies that has held up well over time. It is just as intriguing and clever today, the glamour and location just as alluring, as in the summer of 1973 when the movie first appeared in theaters. In *The Encyclopedia of Film* it is described as "one of the most significant inside jokes ever played on the movie going public."[40] One of the fun lasting effects from this movie was that Herbert Ross used Coburn for a jokey uncredited cameo in his film *California Suite* in 1978.

Meanwhile, back in Los Angeles, Sam Peckinpah was in preparation for the movie that Coburn would, for the rest of his career, name as one of his two favorites, *Pat Garrett and Billy the Kid* (the other being another Peckinpah film, *Cross of Iron*). Peckinpah had been working hard with Rudy Wurlitzer to complete the script and casting.

When author Garner Simmons interviewed Coburn for his Peckinpah biography, *Peckinpah: A Portrait in Montage*, Coburn said, "Rudy wrote a beautiful script. I thought it was one of the best scripts I've ever read. And Sam destroyed it. But the script has to crumble and die in order to be reborn in the form of the film. Now I've worked on films where the scripts were not destroyed. But then those films were never really anything special. Creation involves the destruction. It hurt Rudy because he didn't understand that process."[41]

Coburn's involvement was touch and go for a while, as the original schedule had filming beginning about a month sooner, while he was still shooting on the Côte d'Azur. Since everyone, including himself, was very keen on him playing the role of Pat Garrett, Herbert Ross did all he could to shorten his schedule. In the end Peckinpah had to shrug off the delay, stop pretending to interview other actors, and push the start date to November 13, 1972.

For Coburn it was quite a jarring change from cosmopolitan Cannes and Nice to the dusty, chill aridity of Durango, Mexico—a part of the world that he had once sworn he would eschew forever. Katy Haber, Peckinpah's assistant, recalled that the location was chosen because of the existing standing western sets that could be adapted to the film. It was isolated with nearly unmarked railway tracks passing through the township. "There was a train that comes once a week and causes fatal accidents because people forget about it."[42]

So much has been written about the disasters and challenges around the creation of *Pat Garrett and Billy the Kid*. It was amazing that the film got in the can at all, given the destructive internal and external forces at play, including that the production company was MGM, still under the supervision of now-notorious James Aubrey.

The internal forces were Peckinpah's alcohol-fueled inconsistency and raging inner misery, exacerbated by the personality clashes between Aubrey and the equally notorious director. Aubrey seemed to bring out the worst in Sam, who sometimes acted like a gleeful child spoiling for a fight, like when he said that he had purchased a single share of MGM stock and planned to call for a vote of no confidence at a stockholders meeting.[43] Then at other times he would retreat into morose and hostile, incoherent drunkenness, far worse than on *Major Dundee*. He was deep in an alcoholic's typical denial, where he was never in the wrong and nothing was ever his fault. However, in this case, there were some problems that were *not* his fault, even if dealing with them was his responsibility.

The biggest problem was when an undetected fault in a camera flange resulted in weeks of work being unusable, at least as far as Sam Peckinpah was concerned. James Aubrey didn't care and refused to allow the time for reshoots, even though these particular costs would have been covered by insurance. In a case of maddening irony, Peckinpah had requested an on-set camera technician be assigned to the crew from the start but had been refused because of the budget.

Coburn was equally contemptuous of the Smiling Cobra, as he told David Weddle, Peckinpah's biographer. "What an evil mother-fucker this Aubrey was! All the masters were out of focus. We couldn't use any of the masters and Aubrey kept saying, 'Nah, nah, nah, the people will never know.' He really didn't give a shit, he didn't care. He had no respect for the public. His trip during that time was to sabotage films. Evidently, he hated people with talent."[44]

Peckinpah was determined to reshoot the out-of-focus scenes, even while the shoot was falling ever further behind schedule. The external problems that caused delays started with poor weather. At one point gusting winds were strong enough to smash windows in the sets and rattle the roofs. Recording sound was impossible. Repeated illnesses eventually affected the entire cast and crew. Plus, a John Wayne picture was shooting nearby and had already appropriated most of the available local crews and resources. This remained as a friendly rivalry even after the Peckinpah team won the intercompany soccer match. Coburn was a spectator.

Aubrey sent a succession of his people to Durango to try to wrest the project back under his control. These included veteran, Oscar-nominated, art-director-turned-producer Lewis Rachmil, who had a reputation as a problem solver. Rachmil had worked as a watchdog for Walter Mirisch at United Artists on many more films in both Mexico and the UK than are credited on his IMDb listing. As he explains in a 1975 interview, "This job isn't just knowing the numbers. At times you're like a psychiatrist or a confessor, trying to put everybody's heads back on. This is a business of personalities."[45]

He knew Peckinpah from the editing process of *Straw Dogs* (1971), but as a representative of the studio, he was unlikely to be considered as an ally by the director—this despite being a reasonable person who absolutely understood quality filmmaking in a way that eluded Aubrey.

Rachmil could not prevent Peckinpah and the rest of the company from colluding to reshoot the unusable scenes at all kinds of odd times—over lunch, at the end of the day, when they were purporting to be rehearsing, or while setting up for a different scene. Inconsistencies between the call sheets and the daily production logs seem to reflect that reality. Coburn describes it as "exciting filmmaking. Fuck it, why not? You've got to go for it as long as you're into it."[46]

Even without reshoots, the shooting schedule was absolutely crammed, with numerous setups and many pages to be covered each day. Peckinpah worked in his usual multi-camera method. It was hard work, but not impossible. Generally each scene would have only two or three long takes—a few times the production log noted six takes, but that was rare. Of course it would have been a great deal easier had Peckinpah been fully present for the entire day instead of only the "four hours when he was a genius" in the middle, as Coburn describes.[47]

Coburn explained how Peckinpah would start the day with a glass of vodka. Then he would hold on to a glass of seltzer dashed with Campari, which would gradually become a deeper and deeper cranberry red as the liquor ratio increased. Then later in the afternoon, when the daily decline began, the Campari would become paler and paler, as it was mixed with increasing proportions of vodka.

The assistant directors injected humor into the call sheets, with inside jokes and stories, like the time the fog machine went awry and created such a roiling miasma that shooting had to wait for the wind, for once absent, to return and clear the air. There was a humorous remark, toward the end, about needing an extra truck just to haul away Peckinpah's infamous memos. They also made sly but good-natured remarks about Bob Dylan and Kris Kristofferson's music.

Bob Dylan had been cast once Peckinpah heard his songs, without considering Dylan's lack of film experience. He would wander off between takes and lose track of time. He sometimes went jogging through the distant background of the shots, not realizing the scope of the setting. Katy Haber recalls, "Bob Dylan had no concept of continuity, no concept of what making movies was about."[48] He would even take it upon himself to change his costume between setups in the same scene.

Haber also recalls the boredom of the off hours: "We each had a house. There was nothing to do in Durango except sit and listen to Kris and Dylan singing. Every night, that's all we did."

A little way into the shoot, a sympathetic reporter visited the set. He wrote a remarkably positive article about the production. At that time Peckinpah was still feeling optimistic. "Peckinpah seemed magnetic but not terribly controversial. Intense and engrossed, he carefully scrutinized his crew setting up a shot. . . . Then satisfied that everything is under control he permitted himself a moment to relax to discuss his work. 'This film smells good,' he said. 'I like the feel of it. And the actors are so completely into their parts. . . . Coburn is so into Garrett I'm beginning to think he *is* Pat Garrett.'

"Some cows refused to go in the right direction. 'Feed 'em hay on that spot for a few minutes,' he would instruct a wrangler. 'Then chase them away. When the cameras roll they'll go back to it. . . .' Peckinpah is a serious craftsman and artist whose success lies in his ability to re-create on film a time and place that are long gone."[49]

Coburn went to Los Angeles for Thanksgiving and for a few days in mid-December. When he returned to Mexico, he brought Jimmy with him, on his break from school. The company had time off over Christmas too. When MGM refused to pay for flights home, the rest of them celebrated Christmas with a riotous Mexican-style barbecue, entertained by a mariachi band hired by Peckinpah, while Jimmy and his dad flew by private Cessna to Mazatlán, a resort city on the west coast. They bought fireworks, which they set off from the balcony of their hotel, right over the ocean splashing a hundred feet below.

For eleven-year-old Jimmy, the shoot was tremendous fun. He was paid scale to perform in several scenes with groups of children, most of which were cut from the movie. But one of his scenes from early January is there, at least in the contemporary version of what has come to be called the director's cut of the film; Jimmy portrayed the young boy who ducks down on the river raft.

Once Jimmy ate some bad steak that made him sick for a day or so, but at least he seemed to escape the lung infections that laid out most of the cast and crew. Peckinpah himself had a bout of some kind of dysentery in

December, causing long delays that were noted in the official production report, but the flu that hit almost everyone in January was even more devastating. Generations of ancient cow dung mixed with fine silica in the topsoil had swirled into the air with the wind and lodged in the visitors' lungs. Coburn discovered only after the fact that he had shot a scene in the saloon with Walter Kelley—everybody was so sick that day that nobody remembered shooting the scene until they saw the rushes. Katy Haber, who was accustomed to giving Peckinpah vitamin B_{12} shots, found that everyone wanted one. "They all stood in line, stuck their arses in the door, and I shot them up with B_{12}."[50]

Peckinpah directed with the philosophy that there was no drama without conflict. He seemed unable to maintain a distinction between his work—his art—and his life. Ignoring all directives from Los Angeles, he began the same kind of passive-aggressive strategies that he had used to good effect on past productions—billing the company for all kinds of extraordinary costs. Disputed invoices include one for "refreshments" for his camper for $2,250. For comparison Coburn's camper only required $750. Other expenses included heating oil for various actors' homes on location, indicating how cold the weather was, and damages of various kinds to the rented house where Peckinpah acted out some of his increasingly frightening rages as the shoot grew more and more grueling. He took to carrying a gun around all the time, and one night he shot his own reflection in the mirror in his house.

Nightly rages aside, Peckinpah was pleased with the film and Coburn's performance in it. For his part, Coburn loved working with him, despite his inconsistencies. As he told reporter Joseph Leydon, "Actors like Peckinpah so much, because he places them in these situations and takes all their crutches away, and leaves them naked there and allows them to work in a way that keeps the creative flow going all the time. He takes all the clichés away. . . . It brings a new kind of intensity to it that brings you through the rest of it."[51]

Finally they came to the climactic sequence. Coburn told author David Weddle for *If They Move . . . Kill 'Em* that he was ready to fight for what he felt would work for the character and the scene. "When we were rehearsing [Billy's death scene], I saw the mirror there by the door. I saw myself in it and I said to him, 'After I shoot the kid, I want to shoot myself in the mirror.' Sam said, 'No, no! No, no, no, no!' I said, 'Yes, God dammit, I want to shoot it! Fuck you, man! That's what I'm gonna do, I'm gonna do that! Now set that fucker up!' We were yelling at each other and he was adamant. He wasn't going to do that, didn't want that to happen! . . . And then, somehow, we rehearsed all that night, but we didn't shoot. We came back the next night. I said to him, 'Are we going to shoot the mirror?' He said, 'Fuck yes, you're going to shoot the mirror! That's what you want to do isn't it?' That's the way he was. Of course I knew about him shooting himself in the mirror at his house. It was just another kind of thing. Shooting the ghost."[52]

Filming ended on February 6, 1973, in El Sauz, Durango. One of the last scenes shot featured Peckinpah himself acting with Coburn. Then it was home to the editing room, where the schedule was almost impossible. The release was set for May 23, before either *The Last of Sheila* or *Harry in Your Pocket*.

Paul Seydor, in his treatise, *The Authentic Death & Contentious Afterlife of Pat Garrett and Billy the Kid*, describes Peckinpah's method: "Editing is often called 'the final rewrite' or the 'final directing.' For most directors this is at least quasi-figurative, but for Sam it was quite literal: 'the dailies are just the beginning,' he said. The cutting room is where he found his films, where he shaped the performances, where he built those complex structures of shots and images. . . . The editing was an integral stage of a process of development and exploration that began with the script and ended on the final mixing stage."[53]

Aubrey had a contractual obligation to screen two public previews of Peckinpah's preferred cut. Amazingly Peckinpah made his deadline, with the help of a team of editors. But Aubrey had no obligation to release the film that way. With history repeating itself, he had the film trimmed, losing many minutes and what Coburn saw as the entire thematic justification for his own characterization, the framing scenes. He was very disappointed, to say the least, as he told author Garner Simmons: "There are three scenes that justify the film that are missing from the MGM version. . . . It was to be told from Pat Garrett's point of view, rather than from Billy's, and it was done so purposely. The Studio didn't understand that at all. They apparently wanted some sort of balance going. So the Studio eliminated . . . those the scenes that place Garrett in his quandary. Garrett had made a choice, and the film portrayed him working his way through that choice. He had to deal with his own conscience, and he suffered greatly."[54]

The studio's cut focused on the action sequences and Billy's character, which created the idea that Garrett was nothing more than a sellout. Once again Sam Peckinpah made a losing bid to have his name removed from the credits.

It forever baffled Coburn why studios would bring on Sam Peckinpah, knowing how he worked, and then squander the possibilities for extraordinary film art that he represented. "He was not an ordinary guy making movies. He was a unique human being—enigmatic, strange, far out, hateful, disdainful, and crazy and loving and genius, all at the same time. Sam, I think, was the best director I ever worked with. Because he could handle more people in a very balanced way, when the studio didn't interfere with his work, which they usually tried to do. He used the dynamics of actors putting things together. That's how he made the movie, and that's a difficult way to go—difficult in the editing room. He would justify things according to what was there. And everything in all his movies was always purely justified. But from a point of view that was not an ordinary one. That's why I say he was enigmatic. You can't put your finger on him. He had facets that most people wouldn't even consider. Most people try to be one thing. He would turn the light on to lots of different sides of him. I guess alcohol helped that, helped him open up.

"Sam was cutting the film the way he wanted to, and they wanted something else. Then they should hire some mechanic. If you hire Sam Peckinpah, you're going to get a Sam Peckinpah film. That's what you pay your money for."[55]

Even in 1973 critical opinion was quite diverse, with most seeing at least flashes of brilliance and some suspecting the truth. Critic Jay Cocks wrote a lyrical review for *Time* magazine. Bear in mind that he likely saw the Peckinpah preview cut before the film Aubrey eventually released.

"As played superbly by Coburn, [Garrett] is a dead eyed cynic, a man who can slither neatly from one moral position to another. . . . The changes ordered by the studio are mostly stupid but not disastrous. Even in the maimed state in which it has been released, *Pat Garrett and Billy the Kid* is the richest, most exciting film this year. There are moments and whole sequences here that stand among the best Peckinpah has ever achieved: a raft moving down a muddy River, a ragged family huddled on board; the final meeting of Garrett and Billy back at old Fort Sumner at night, with men moving like apparitions and dust blowing like a rasping fog. The whole film has a parched eerie splendor that no one could really destroy."[56]

An even shorter version of the film played often on television in the late 1970s. But in recent years there have been meticulously researched restorations made of what is presumed to be closer to Sam Peckinpah's vision, which is what is available on DVD. While opinion is still wildly divergent, most people regard the film as a tortured work of genius, and Coburn himself believed it was some of his best work as an actor. "That was a good film. There's a lot of really tasty things in there, whether you like what it's about or not."[57]

Meanwhile Aubrey lasted at MGM until 1974, when he resigned to become an indie producer—disappointed that Kerkorian sold the distribution arm. The MGM logo and library were the last assets that the studio had at the time. There was more financial finagling with stock options and buybacks and international loans. Someone was making money, and the hotel in Las Vegas was a profitable concern. But the fact remains that the products released under Aubrey's tenure tended to be bad and badly promoted, and that did not help the studio regain solvency. In what might be considered an epic fail, Aubrey said no to *Jaws*. Lewis Rachmil outlasted Aubrey as a production VP and later would lecture on producing for UCLA Extension.

After an exhausting year, Coburn took some time off to travel. In April 1973 Pingree–Panpiper Productions made a deal with 20th Century Fox to produce "The Silent Flute." Tentatively the shoot was planned to start sometime between June 15 and December 1 of 1973. Coburn and Stirling Silliphant flew to Hong Kong to meet with Bruce Lee, hoping to revive the project. By then Lee was too busy working on his masterpiece, *Enter the Dragon*, to be able to consider it.[58]

Coburn then spent some time in Japan. After that, in the early summer, he took another trip with Beverly, traveling to Turkey and Iran, looking for art and being photographed at the Cannes Film Festival. He had no film in the festival, but it was a joyous place to visit. It was the last big trip the two took together.

Just weeks after they returned, on July 20, 1973, Coburn got a call from Stirling Silliphant to tell him that Bruce Lee had died in Hong Kong. "I just couldn't believe it. I had just spoken with Bruce on the telephone three days before when I got the call from Stirling. I asked what had caused it, and he said it was something about his head. I knew exactly what had caused it because it had happened once before [on May 10, 1973]. He was tired, and they told him to take it easy for a while. He wouldn't listen to anybody anyway. Because he had it all worked out. But it didn't scare him. I had just come home from Japan, and he came up to the house and told me the whole story of what had happened to him. It upset him enough to get on a plane the following day and fly to LA from Hong Kong and take a full physical, and they couldn't find anything wrong with him. He was in perfect condition. Everything was perfect on him. Because they couldn't see the aneurysm growing in his head. And that is, of course, what killed him."[59]

Coburn was one of the pallbearers and delivered the final benediction at the graveside near Lake Washington, as requested by Lee's wife, Linda. He spoke extemporaneously. "I just stood up and spoke. If you write a eulogy, you get all fucked up with rhetoric and junk people already know. I just said something simple."

Linda Lee recorded what he said: "Farewell, brother. It has been an honor to share this space in time with you. As a friend and as a teacher, you have given to me, have brought my physical, spiritual and psychological selves together. Thank you. May peace be with you."[60]

But it is Coburn's words close to the end of his own life, looking back, that showed the depth of his friendship. "Bruce was brash. He was beautiful. The last time I saw him, his skin was like velvet, every muscle in his body was tuned. He was like a violin. He was just gorgeous. I had a part in his life as well as he had a part in my life. I am very proud to say that I knew him very well and loved him a lot."[61]

15. Coburn and Terry Southern talk over *The Loved One* script, ca. 1965. Photograph by William Claxton. Courtesy of Demont Photo Management.

16. Coburn and Beverly playing cards at the table in their upstairs sitting room at the newly purchased Tower Road house, 1965. Photograph by David Sutton. Courtesy of MPTV Images.

17. Coburn reclining on a sofa on the balcony, with Beverly looking pensive, 1965. Photograph by David Sutton. Courtesy of MPTV Images.

18. Coburn playing the gong in the music room at Tower Road, 1965. Photograph by David Sutton. Courtesy of MPTV Images.

19. Coburn having a tender moment with Jimmy during a publicity photo shoot, 1965. Jimmy thinks he was hoping to go for a ride. Photograph by David Sutton. Courtesy of MPTV Images.

20. Coburn playing a gong on the roof of a Park Avenue building, New York, New York, June 27, 1967. Photograph by Jerry Schatzberg. Courtesy of Getty Images.

21. Coburn and Richard Benjamin "play croquet" during *The Last of Sheila* shoot for publicity (1973). Licensed by: Warner Bros. Entertainment Inc. All Rights Reserved.

22. Coburn quietly reading a newspaper during *The Last of Sheila* shoot, on the dock beside the yacht, renamed *Sheila* and used as the main shooting location for the movie (1973). Licensed by: Warner Bros. Entertainment Inc. All Rights Reserved.

23. Coburn and Sam Peckinpah discuss a scene from *Pat Garrett and Billy the Kid* (1973).
Licensed by: Warner Bros. Entertainment Inc. All Rights Reserved.

24. Coburn in the trenches with Sam Peckinpah and Katy Haber on the set of *Cross of Iron* in Yugoslavia (1977). Haber recalled that they were wearing masks because they were burning tires to create black smoke, a dangerous and toxic method that would be entirely illegal today. Photograph by Lars Looschen. Courtesy of STUDIOCANAL.

10

The Only Reality

One of the great things about being an actor, especially in this business, is that you run across these strange characters, men and women who have extraordinary imbalances, and personalities that go along with that. Instead of going to jail or something, they become actors and exploit this aspect of their characters, of their personality.

—JAMES COBURN, 2002

After Coburn's busy year, his several trips abroad, and the emotional stress of losing his close friend Bruce Lee, it is hardly surprising that he felt exhausted. He spent three months resting, doing very little promotion for *Harry in Your Pocket* other than local interviews. He admitted to being very tired in one of those interviews at the Beverly Hills Brown Derby restaurant, and to feeling like a stranger. "I've been away so long I hardly recognized my neighbor, Jack Lemmon, running down the road walking his two standard poodles—or looking or whistling for them."[1]

Jack Lemmon's poodles did tend to get away from him, and they often made a beeline for the Tower Road house, even if it happened to be the middle of the night. Lemmon's son, Chris, related the night he and his dad were looking for the dogs, Walter and Virgil, while somewhat inebriated. They were basically trespassing in Coburn's courtyard and turned to see him, in his robe, glaring down at them from the picture window above. They fled.[2]

At the same time, Coburn continued to be outspoken in his opinions about the business, grumbling about "the current management" at MGM, "mutilating the results by unbelievably cutting and hacking the pictures," and complaining that television lacks creativity because it is a selling medium, perhaps conveniently forgetting his own start in commercials.[3]

"Creative work simply does not exist on TV. How can it when the mood is constantly interrupted by someone telling you to shave closer or brush your teeth?" He reiterated his belief that "the motion picture medium is vitally important" and once again mentioned his eagerness to continue writing and "eventually to get into direction." It had been awhile since he had publicly expressed that desire.

Despite all of this, by the time the interview was published, Coburn was two days away from leaving for another overseas location. He went to shoot the British film *The Internecine Project* in London, starting in mid-October. Internecine means "mutually destructive." Coburn plays an entirely amoral character who manipulates four associates to kill one another in a highly choreographed sequence over one evening, in such a way as no suspicion would fall upon him. The character was the ultimate individualist, someone who had become so detached from other people that he used them as tools. He spent much of the film sitting at his desk in his home, speaking on the phone, as the ultimate puppet master. But rather than being dull, it was an intense and absorbing psychological thriller.

On October 28, 1973, Coburn participated in the photo shoot for the cover of *Band on the Run*, Paul McCartney and Wings's album, by the coincidence of his simply being in London at the right time. He joined an odd collection of individuals, including the legendary British actor Christopher Lee, world light-heavyweight boxing champion John Conteh, and popular talk show host Michael Parkinson, once again cementing his cool cat credentials. Photographer Clive Arrowsmith described the six celebrity escapees as "iconic people of the time ... all people that were easily recognizable," while Paul McCartney said that they were all invited "just for a lark."[4]

The following year Coburn did not see any international travel, but that doesn't mean he was at home. Instead he worked on one of the most physically grueling shoots he had ever done. *Bite the Bullet* started shooting at the beginning of March 1974, after several weeks of horse-riding preparation and rehearsal, and went on until the end of June. The film was a period piece (1906) about an endurance horse race, and for the first time in a long time, Coburn was not the lead.

The star was Gene Hackman, who portrayed an animal lover, an unusual enough take for the period of the film. One of the goals of producer-director Richard Brooks, was to show that it was possible to make a movie about a horse race, even with some painful-to-watch but simulated animal cruelty, without mistreating any of the animals. "It was my intention to make a movie that would show the positive side of life—that would dramatize human dignity and loved animals—that would show 'winning a race' is not as important as 'how it is won'—certainly *not* at the expense of the animal."[5] The production was lauded by most animal rights groups. Brooks made a particular effort to show uncut original footage to anyone who expressed concerns. Two of the actors, accomplished equestrians in private life, Ben Johnson and Mario Arteaga, even brought their own beloved horses to ride on the screen, effectively proving the assertion.

Brooks was a meticulous researcher. He found newspapers from the period of the film to re-create for props, like the *Police Gazette* from 1906. The props and settings had many tiny details, including re-creations of vintage-style packaging and signage. He researched laudanum and its use, and referenced historical books about American folklore. This is the level of preparation that Coburn appreciated in his directors.

On the other hand, Brooks was notorious for not giving his actors the entire script, either because he was still writing it or, as in this case, to keep them surprised. He did not want to reveal the winner of the race in advance, saying in an interview with reporter Dorothy Manners, "Spontaneity in improvisations can be gems unless a player has already made up his mind about what he's going to do."[6]

The film shot in some beautiful, if rugged, locations, in New Mexico and Colorado. But it was the White Sands National Monument of Alamogordo that was familiar to Coburn, where he had stopped as a child. He, and some other actors, got in trouble with the Teamsters union for driving their own cars to the set. He had taken the opportunity to drive from Los Angeles to New Mexico, undoubtedly making the trip in fewer hours than it might take a regular driver. The company was fined, but the two parties did eventually come to an agreement to allow those cast members who wanted to drive themselves to do so. Journalist Bridget Byrne, who visited the set, wrote that Coburn drove her back to town "at well over twice the speed limit in the Ferrari he got as part of the deal for making *The Last of Sheila*."[7]

In interviews from this period, Coburn expressed two contradictory stories. Periodically he would talk about being a homebody and not wanting to attend a lot of Hollywood parties. He would speak of a desire to be alone with his family, at home. "My idea of a relaxing evening is to not have anyone around! In my life there is always someone around, particularly when I'm filming. Friends or family, or just people who happen to be there. So when I'm home I become a very private person. My home is like a monastery, and I use it that way. Sometimes I don't leave that place for a week. . . . I've got so many hobbies—and they're always changing. Last time I was trying to learn the tabla—it's an Indian drum."[8]

Then by contrast he would talk about making movies as "the only reality" and seems to dismiss his time at home as the interludes between what was really important. "When you are not working it's fine, easy, you're home, looked after, but making movies is the real thing."[9]

It is easy to suppose that after a sequence of two or three movies, he would see the attraction of taking a break at home. But then after a short period at home, he would feel restless and want to return to the stimulation of a movie project. Perhaps his true quest was to find the balance in himself between that outward-focused urge to be actively creative and his inward-focused studies and personal journey.

He sometimes announced grand plans and projects, but then it seemed nothing further developed. For example, nothing concrete came of the Minder Bender Pulp scheme. And at the end of *Bite the Bullet*, he told Dorothy Manners, who interviewed him many times over the years, that rather than rest at home, he was planning to go on a grand tour of Paris, Marrakech, Cairo, and the Sahara Desert with a group of friends. It was to be a kind of personal development pilgrimage. "We are just investing some time in ourselves. . . . Families can go along if that's desired. Our objective is to observe, listen, learn. We aren't even setting any time limits such as a tour. We hope it will become sort of a perpetual journey, that is always going somewhere."[10] But there is no evidence that this group odyssey happened.

This was all part of Coburn's ongoing mythology. In private his social life was very active, with an entourage and visitors almost constantly at the house. There were two types of parties at Tower Road. The first were for his closest friends, private parties in the master suite upstairs. The second were more work related. Producers and directors, potential colleagues and costars, would come to grand events held in the main living room, on the patio, and in the foyer. There was often drumming and gong playing, and always wonderful hospitality and fine food and drink. But there was also a certain guardedness. No one had yet guessed that there was any trouble in the Coburns' relationship.

Katy Haber, Sam Peckinpah's assistant, attended some of these parties. She describes Beverly as "like Elizabeth Taylor," and says, "She was very gregarious, and she was very present. You felt her very much present. When I was there, I felt that there was a very strong relationship. She was definitely queen of the palace. Definitely."[11]

These parties were work, not relaxation. Coburn would use his movie star charisma to impress the decision-makers and moneymen from the studios. He called it the dancing bear. Frank Messa describes being invited to watch from above, sitting unobserved in the little nook that overlooks the living room: "Jim used to say, 'Sit up here in the balcony and watch me. I'm gonna go down there and schmooze around. You can watch the action from up here.' It was a beautiful spot. Jim was one of the gracious hosts of all time. Don't forget off the side room, there was the snooker table and the pool table. There was always some kind of contest going on."[12]

Coburn was still actively reading works by George Gurdjieff and P. D. Ouspensky. He attempted to introduce his son to their writings. Jimmy was thirteen at the time. "He gave me this book to read, but I just couldn't get into it. I tried, but it wasn't interesting to me."[13]

Once during summer, Jimmy and his friend John were planning a trip to the beach. John remembers they had to earn the privilege: "It was a Saturday, and we wanted to go to the beach, and his dad told us, 'You have to mow the lawn first before you go to the beach.' So we did a half-assed job. We were kids, you know. He came and looked at it, and we had done a terrible job. He said, 'This isn't right.' So he showed us. He had a big cigar in his mouth, he was wearing a white linen shirt, and he was out there like dancing with the lawn mower. It was one of those self-propelled mowers. He was out there dancing and mowed part of the lawn, and then he said, '*That's* how it's supposed to look.'"[14]

Coburn's goal that day was to express the mind-set he had learned working at the Tower Theatre in Compton when he was the same age, the mind-set that continued to inform his work. Whatever work you do, put your whole focus and attention—your best effort—into it, and make it as joyful as you can.

Coburn still enjoyed an intellectual debate, just as he had in college. It was something that many of his friends noted over the years. Friend and manager Hilly Elkins says, "We shared passionate and lengthy arguments we both enjoyed."[15] Frank Messa spoke of it too: "[We discussed] everything, you know, life. It wasn't an argument. It was a debate. And then we'd get the books out to prove the point and look down the lines. It was a very fun time. It wasn't a contest. It was an expansion of brain. We'd start at one place and end up thousands of miles away."[16]

Interesting people continued to visit the Tower Road house, everyone from family to actor friends to esoteric authors. They would come for the wide-ranging conversations and to enjoy the drum circles. Actor Seymour Cassel, a friend since they'd met on *Hell Is for Heroes* (1962), says, "I'd go over there, and we'd smoke something, and he started playing those bongos, and I started laughing. And he says, 'It's good, isn't it?' And I said, 'It's loud, James. It's really loud.' And he said, 'Aw, but if you get the rhythm to it, you got something going.'"[17]

Cassel was one of a group that frequently contributed toward bail money for another mutual friend and frequent guest, the troubled scion of the Barrymore acting dynasty, John Barrymore (Drew's estranged father). Messa remembers him being something of a fixture at the house, having returned to Hollywood in 1974 from an extended stay living the life of an ascetic in the California High Desert. Sometimes Barrymore would hang out on the roof of the pool house.

"He was a little snapped, so to speak, off the deep end. He'd come down and steal the milk from Beverly's back kitchen. She knew what was happening. She didn't care. She loved him. He was a very special person in their life. Beverly also had a relationship with the older Barrymore family. John absolutely adored Beverly. Beverly and he were like bonded."[18]

He would bring over various items from his father's home at the Barrymore estate, Bella Vista, including esoteric books with the Barrymore bookplate. Other items that the Coburns acquired from Barrymore include a set of antique fireplace andirons and a set of low slipper chairs, which Tony Duquette reupholstered in his signature dark-pink fabric.

Coburn had less patience for Barrymore, however, noting that he liked him, but "I didn't like to put up with his bullshit. He was always high on something, more of a pill freak. He had this enormous talent, but he didn't feel that anyone else deserved it, so he wasn't going to sell his talent to anyone because nobody would appreciate it anyway. He wanted to go to India, and he wanted all the people he knew to pay for him to go to India. He came to me to get some money. And I said, 'All you have to do is go to work. You could work for one way or round-trip—it would only take you a few days to get the money.' He said, 'That's your way. My way is begging.'"[19]

Coburn said Barrymore had a habit of going to a restaurant and after dining, "he would just leave and not pay for anything, so they'd give the check to someone he knew and everyone paid for him. He scammed everyone. One time he said, 'I'm mad, you know. It runs in the family.' Being around him was like living in a pressure cooker, with someone who was half-insane."

Coburn and Beverly had mutual friends as well as their own friends. For example, Beverly was friends with Atlantic Records founder Ahmet Ertegun. Messa remembers, "Ahmet used to come over there and play backgammon and get his ass whipped, because [Beverly] was a very good player. And they would bet sometimes up to ten thousand dollars, and Ahmet would have to write a check out at the end of the evening."[20] Ahmet drank gin and tonic. Jimmy would fetch the Tanqueray from the downstairs freezer and mix the drinks for the pair at the small bar in the upstairs sitting room.

In October 1974 Coburn began his third film with his friend Charles Bronson. It was called *Hard Times*, about a street boxer (Bronson) and the hustler who takes up as his manager. The company shot in New Orleans and environs starting on October 14 and going through the beginning of December, with a few days off for Thanksgiving. Bronson's contract specified that he finish shooting at 6:30 p.m. on daytime shoot days, without deviation, and he would simply stop and walk away at that time.

It was a busy shoot with many nights in the schedule, with everything, including interiors, shot on location mostly around the French Quarter, which still had the period vibe that this Depression-era story required. During production there was a burglary and at least three accidents. One sent an electrician to the hospital. Maybe he was made nervous by Bronson's behavior.

"Charlie has always been enigmatic. You can't get a reading on him. He is a great observer. A strange guy. Charlie has never been very outgoing. Quietly desperate. Not very emotional. When we were doing *Hard Times*, he intimidated everybody on the set. He was the intimidator. He really did intimidate everybody, not by doing anything, simply by watching. Just a sigh and—a strange fact—he'd roll his eyes. And sit on the set and smoke and watch everybody work. All of the grips, all the electricians. Just sitting there, legs crossed, watching them work. Intimidating just by watching. As soon as people caught on, he would start hitting on a different way, picking on things he had been observing. He is a fighter—strong, cold, chilling."[21]

Professionally things were going very well for Coburn, although there was the aborted Richard Burton project, *Jackpot*, which folded owing money to everybody involved. At least he got a quick trip to England out of it. *Hard Times* was popular and in the theaters a long time once released, and it had very long legs on television. For now Coburn was almost constantly in the public eye.

For this reason, Helen Gurley Brown considered him for *Cosmopolitan* magazine's first male nude centerfold. Photographer Guy Webster considered that image "one of my favorite photographs. She wanted sexy actors almost cheesecake. That was done in the style of Caravaggio, a famous Renaissance painter who painted with great shadowing and detail. The fun thing about James Coburn was he was really up for it, for the shooting. He was such a good sport. That was done at his house. When I was there shooting this picture, a beautiful girl friend of his was in the backyard of their estate teaching yoga, naked, with all the people naked, all the students naked. I'm going, 'God I love it. I love Beverly Hills.' What's behind these walls, nobody would know.

"These were really neat people. Avant-garde people. Most of the show business people were really, really square during this period. He was one of the hippest. He was more like rock-and-roll. The others were really uptight and square. He was cool. He was like what we all were in the sixties. He was relaxed and open, and not afraid of sexuality."[22]

Apparently Gurley Brown deemed the photos from the test shoot too artistic, and she used Burt Reynolds instead.

From the early seventies through the end of the mideighties, there would be at least one of Coburn's movies, from *The Magnificent Seven* onward, playing on television each and every week. Most weeks there would be several on different networks. His first-run movies would be supplemented at the theaters by his movies from the past year or two in double features and at drive-ins. Hardly a week went by when he was not mentioned in the press, even if only the capsule reviews of the week's movies on TV. He was absolutely a sought-after figure in the United States, and even more popular in Europe.

His personal life was less satisfactory. The problems in his marriage slowly became more and more obvious to the couple, if not to the public. By this time not only was Beverly not coming with him to movie sets, or even visiting, but she was also not joining him in public at events and parties very often. "Beverly was off on her own adventures that didn't have anything to do with me, and I was off making movies. We were always separated. She was home and I was off, or I was at home and she was off. Beverly started traveling on her own. Or she would travel with somebody like Frank. She'd take the first-class tickets I was given and travel all over the world, India, all the places we'd been."[23]

It was a bad idea to leave Coburn unattended. As Katy Haber notes, "Film sets are dangerous places. It was a men's fun fair. On every picture, there were girls around. Crew members would walk through the lobby of the hotel with their key on a string and say, 'Any takers?' It was not a good idea to leave a fantastic-looking superstar on his own on a set. Every man is a kid, you know."[24]

As time went on, Beverly left the house less and less, holding court in her bedroom instead. Coburn was less inclined to take her professional advice, losing confidence in her judgment. "She got to be a pain in the ass. Doing a lot of cocaine. Lack of emotionality, no sex. We didn't do anything. All these people coming around. I'd come home from location, and the house would be filled with all these people I didn't know. All these assholes, drinking my wine, probably fucking my old lady, or doing whatever it was. I was like a stranger. They would have to straighten everything up so I'd have a place to sit. It was a drag."[25]

When he went out to Hollywood parties, he tended to be alone. Actress Josette Banzet, nodding acquaintance at that time, remembers him coming to a party her friend Bara gave at her home in Malibu for Stella Adler. "I saw that long, long, slim James come in because I was facing that way. Tall, all in black—black sweater, black pants. I had met him briefly at parties, but I had never been attached to him as a friend. He was always alone when he went someplace, I noticed that."[26]

Eschewing Beverly's advice while at the same time strongly desiring to stay out of the house that felt increasingly unwelcome, Coburn made some questionable choices—*Jackpot* being a case in point. He also took a small role in the all-star ensemble of the World War II movie *Midway*, with Henry Fonda, in the spring of 1975. The film was a major big-budget undertaking, given the full publicity treatment over a long shoot and longer time in post. Coburn's small part was shot quickly on the USS *Lexington* in the Gulf of Mexico. The role felt rather stiff, and critic Rex Reed described the actors as "like soldiers from the Hollywood Wax Museum."[27]

Then Coburn made the fateful choice to shoot a film over the summer in Greece, *Sky Riders*. Until recently, Greece had lived under "a very rigid, very militaristic" government who had taken over in a junta in 1967. "For some reason, they wouldn't let them make movies there during the regime. This was the first [foreign] movie made in Greece after those guys."[28]

It was to be a lightweight adventure thriller, heavy on stunts, reuniting Coburn with his *Duffy* costar Susannah York. While the kidnap-rescue plot for *Sky Riders* was fairly silly, the movie was notable for featuring the then-newly popular sport of hang gliding in what was advertised as (and proved to be) an exciting climax. Hang gliding aficionados continue to enjoy the film because of the spectacular flying. The flying sequences were choreographed and performed by the renowned Wills family and their friends. Bob Wills and his brother Chris, the flying stunt coordinator, had traded first and second places in the national hang gliding championships for the last few years. Bob's wife doubled for Susannah York in the film.

There was a long, rather lyrical sequence of a flying circus, filmed near the resort of Kamena Vourla. The flying for the exciting rescue at the monastery location was genuinely dangerous. Changing weather conditions often caused delays. According to Chris Wills, interviewed for the magazine *Ground Skimmer*, "That particular location is about as unsafe as you can find for safety. It is about 100% treacherous."[29] This was *before* glider pilots used safety parachutes, and obviously before CGI.

The team also helped with training the actors and setting up a circular crane rig for shooting the stars' close-ups. Coburn, whom Wills describes along with Robert Culp as "really nice guys," did as much stunt work as the insurance company would allow, including lying perilously along a helicopter landing skid, flying over an alarming cliff drop-off. Footage of this stunt was later used in the opening credits of the series *The Fall Guy*, starring Lee Majors, along with some of the hang gliding footage. In fact some of the time the company was waiting on pinnacles with thousand-foot drops on all sides. Again Wills notes, "If you fall in any direction, you could roll off the ledge."

Glider pilot Dean Tanji recalls, "James Coburn loved to hang out with the stuntmen. . . . [He] and the other actors had many of their meals with the hang glider stunt team. They did this to learn about hang gliding and to gain flight insight, pilot mannerisms and pilot chit-chat."[30]

Charles Aznavour, incidentally a close friend of Coburn's London buddy Herbie Kretzmer, was also in the cast. Coburn says, "We were in a bazooki one night, and they were introducing us, and they asked Charles Aznavour to come up and sing, and he said, 'No!' and they kept applauding. He explained that ten years ago, he sang there, and 'they did not pay me enough, so I am not going to sing now.' He's a funny guy."[31]

It was during this shoot in Greece that Coburn met a pretty, young Greek woman named Angela and embarked on a serious affair that would have long-term repercussions in his marriage.

Angela was a public relations person at the Athens hotel where the company stayed. Coburn's daughter, Lisa, then eighteen years old, accompanied her father on this trip. She had been photographed by the press on arrival and mistakenly identified as her dad's girlfriend, which inhibited her social life in Greece, until she met Angela. She found Angela to be "a darling."[32] She says, "We became friends, and then they did too." According to Lisa, her parents had developed an understanding once Beverly stopped coming to sets. She didn't want to know what happened while he was alone on location, provided he was discreet and didn't involve his family. However, this was more than a quiet on-location fling. The press assumed Angela to be Lisa's companion.

Somehow Beverly learned of the shenanigans and was enraged that he would use his daughter as misdirection. She got on a plane for Greece, intending to express her displeasure to her husband. Lisa collected her mother and Frank Messa from the airport in Athens and could immediately sense that Beverly was furious, so she escaped to the resort island of Hydra in the south. She was shortly joined there by Frank after he escorted Beverly to the Meteora monastery filming location near Kalambaka, in the central mountains of the country. What kind of new agreement the spouses reached is not known. Lisa notes that "Mom didn't stay long," but Lisa herself remained in Greece until the end of the shoot. Coburn extended his time abroad with a trip to London before flying home at the end of August 1975.

Almost immediately upon arriving home, he left again to play the heavy in a hard-edged western with Charlton Heston, *The Last Hard Men*. It was about a vengeful chain-gang escapee tormenting the lawman who sent him to prison by kidnapping the latter's daughter. It shot on location in Utah and Arizona, starting in September and going through early October. As a shoot it was neither unusually tough nor especially easy. To say that the character was unpleasant is an understatement. Early in the story, Coburn's character, Zach Provo, appears to have some kernel of goodness inside. But soon it becomes clear that this man is an absolute reprobate. The downbeat ending reveals an unrelenting dark character. The movie inevitably draws comparisons with the work of Peckinpah. "Following the violent trend of Sam Peckinpah's *Wild Bunch*, *The Last Hard Men* is long on violence.... The dramatic effect of continuous bloodbaths wears thin quickly."[33]

Shortly after Coburn wrapped the picture, his father was hospitalized. He had been taking care of his parents financially ever since becoming wealthy. He purchased a home for them in Desert Hot Springs and another later in Garden Grove, in Orange County, near enough to visit but not so close that they would drop by. "They lived far enough away that I didn't have to be around them all the time. I always detected a bit of envy, and then . . . I started buying him houses and paying their way because he had contracted arthritis really badly and couldn't work. I had to pick up the pieces. He appreciated that but never really liked that. He would have liked to have been able to do that himself. He didn't get any kick out of it, you know. He was too racked with arthritis. He came down with it when he was fifty something, working all the time in the garage, on those cement floors, and having that Scotch-Irish gene that took a lot of us down. He didn't know how to fight back. He didn't know what it was. He took gold shots. He did whatever the fucking doctors told him to do. 'We'll give you some of this. If it doesn't work, we'll give you some of that.' And they didn't know. They still don't know. Unfortunately, they have no idea."[34]

Harrison Coburn died in the hospital on December 24, 1975. "And my father's last words were typical. The nurse told me this. I arrived at the hospital just after he died, and the nurse says, 'Well, he certainly was a son of a gun,' and I said, 'Yeah, why? What did he do?' And she answered, 'Well, his last words were *goddamn it!* And it embarrassed my mother. 'He really didn't say that, did he?'"

Even at the end, Coburn had never reconciled fully with his father. Therefore he was more worried about his mother and her feelings. "She was a happy lady, until things really started turning to shit and my father started dying. Because of arthritis and his heart. I paid a lot for that." He could hardly wait to escape again. He flew out to London within a month, ostensibly to start prep for *Cross of Iron*.

Cross of Iron was Sam Peckinpah's only war movie, and the second of Coburn's favorite movies. He was very proud of the film and his work in it. "It's certainly an antiwar film. And it's a film about the heroism of men who fight war. I think that's one of the things that Sam was concerned with, but all soldiers are going out there to fight for something. It's their own personal heroism of getting through that awful, awful thing called war. . . . It was like playing in a jazz orchestra where everybody is swinging, you know. Like when everybody is right there on top of it. He would generate a kind of attention that would just be invigorating. It was sensational. . . . Because he brought out the best in you. He brought the thing out in you that you didn't know existed."[35]

The *Cross of Iron* shoot was one of the most extraordinary debacles in the history of cinema, yet it produced one of the most compelling antiwar pictures ever made. By working with an independent financier rather than with one of the main studios, Peckinpah thought that he was finally going to have the kind of creative freedom and positive working experience he desperately desired. There could be an entire book written on the backstory of this bizarre production.

It started well enough with Peckinpah and Coburn visiting the producer, Wolf Hartwig, at his home in Germany in January 1976. Hartwig had been a pornography producer and, as it turned out, was accustomed to dealing primarily in cash. He was interested in moving into legitimate filmmaking, especially if there was a part for his wife in the script.

Peckinpah embarked on extremely thorough research and highly detailed preparation. His notes on the script drafts, and his notes from meetings with

Coburn and such people as the production designer, Ted Haworth, show him drawing out the important themes and fine details. He was especially anxious that no piece of business, or prop, should be unjustified—he would ask questions in scribbled notes in the margins like "Where did this [prop] come from?" He also continued his habit of crossing out any acting notes and most descriptions of actor business—that is, physical activity with props or set pieces—intending that these should arise organically in the moment.

In the last few days of January, he and Coburn were in London, where Lisa joined them. They celebrated Lisa's nineteenth birthday at the Trader Vic's in the bomb-damaged Hilton that had been attacked by the Irish Republican Army four months earlier. Then they flew to Munich. Coburn and Peckinpah spent the flight working on the script together. Making Munich home base, they drove around Germany, including to Wiesbaden to study archived war footage and the propaganda films of Leni Riefenstahl. "In a castle in Germany, we saw this pristine version of *Triumph of the Will*. It was so clean and so pure. It was devastating in its power. . . . I have never seen that done in film before. Leni Riefenstahl had all this evilness thrust on her. But her greatness lived beyond that. All she was doing was making movies."[36]

They also noticed that some of the same frontline conflict footage was in both the British and German World War II archives, yet it would be cut differently to be used as propaganda by both sides.

At the same time, Coburn squeezed in the making of a fun documentary about the Winter Olympic Games in Austria, *White Rock*. It seemed Coburn was avoiding going home and was not deterred by Beverly's disapproval from doing precisely what he wanted. His lover, Angela, joined him during the shoot. "We found Angela in Paris because I kept calling her house with my number wherever I was. She finally called, and we picked her up at the airport at Eagles in Innsbruck. She gleefully came, running into my arms, and I gleefully surrounded her with mine. And so she was there throughout the time we were there."

Coburn especially enjoyed the opportunity to learn the fundamentals of different sports, including the unprecedented chances to take some runs down the track in a two-man bobsled with the Austrian team and to demonstrate his shooting prowess in showing the biathlon. "I played hockey. They put me in a goalie suit. That was really a trip. I could never skate very well in the first place. I was always falling on my ass—bang, bang, bang. The puck would be coming at me in different places. I didn't know what the fuck to do. It was bouncing off me. Then it was the skiing. Got to the high jump. I said, 'Well, if my fear of falling wasn't greater than my love of flying, this would be what I would like to do.' Then they showed a guy—*whoosh*—flying. We did the luge. They put me in a luge thing. Then we did the two- and four-man bobsled, up and down, dozens of times.

"Lisa and her boyfriend Robert were there, and Angela at this time. We got to do all these things together, which was fun. It was great fun. The bobsled was really interesting. First time you go down this bobsled, you go *prang*. Your head bounces off the bottom. Of course you've got your helmet on, so you don't feel anything other than bobbing around. But by the third time, you get in tune with the curve, and it is wonderful—it's just really fantastic. We knocked about three seconds off our time."

The narrated segments of *White Rock*, which Coburn wrote, were light and effective. He looked relaxed and happy. His enjoyment carried forward into the continuing prep for *Cross of Iron* since Angela was still with him.

"The affair continued for a while. She came to Innsbruck and stayed with me. Sam came over to do preproduction for *Cross of Iron*. Then I came back home. Then I went to Yugoslavia for the shoot, and she was there for most of the film. She wanted to get married, hot to trot to do all of that. Warm, lovely, sexy, beautiful thing, the affair.

"During the last part of shooting, we were getting along really fine, and she mentioned to Sam that she would really like to marry me, and Sam said, 'Well, you're not going to do that because there's a little lady named Beverly who seems to be attached to him, and I don't think that will ever happen.' And that just broke her heart. And she asked me about it, 'Why did he say that?' I told her I'd rather be with her than Beverly any time, and she just sort of marched away, and that was the last time I saw her on the set. Sam was such an asshole sometimes, to do dumb things like that. Maybe he was just jealous. That was probably it, the son of a bitch." Coburn laughed as he said that.

The shoot was originally planned to begin in March 1976, but a financial squeeze, language difficulties, and communication breakdowns made it increasingly difficult to get started. Ted Haworth sent repeated notes and memos asking for the promised money to pay for construction materials and tools, for equipment to be delivered, for locations to be finalized, and for the funds to hire sufficient people to safely build the sets that Peckinpah envisioned. Coburn cooled his heels in London, with some anxiety, as he was booked to start another film, *Diary of an Assassin*, with a Swiss production company later in the year. He finally flew into Slovenia to begin shooting *Cross of Iron* in mid-April.

The production documents and the slew of memos going back and forth between Peckinpah and Hartwig reveal the almost constant chaos. Even without Peckinpah's paranoia, health issues, heavy drinking—he was too terrified of arrest to use cocaine in Slovenia—and constant tinkering with the script, the shoot would have been a fiasco.

Part of the conflict had to do with the way moviemaking appeared to be done in this part of the world. The budget was broken down in a very different way from what Peckinpah and his team were accustomed to in Hollywood. Rather than each department having a separate line item—such as art department, props, camera, locations, and wardrobe—there was a single large sum allocated to the Yugoslavian company, Jadran Film, for "facilities." From this sum, the Yugoslavian carpenters and production workers were supposed to be paid, and all production costs drawn. The main problem was that the budget included no monies for preproduction or preparation. The financiers intended to pay for production only—that is, starting with principal photography.

This meant it was especially difficult for the art department to build the sets and for wardrobe to acquire costumes because rentals needed advance deposits. As production continued, hardly anything was delivered as promised. They were making do with the best they could find at the time and constantly rewriting. Originally Hartwig had promised twenty vintage tanks—but in the end he could only secure three. Meanwhile many of the department heads continued to need "a hundred vital items one must ask for forty times before you get it."[37]

Coburn recalled, "On the first day of shooting, the set wasn't ready. When asked why, they said because they didn't have any nails. That nails were not on the list. Bobby, a great prop man who worked with Sam a lot, drove across the border to buy two dozen hammers and a big amount of nails. We never had a finished script. We had blueprint and that was it, in order to keep the chaos rolling. The ending was completely improvised."[38]

The cast and crew were often not paid their wages for long periods of time until Hartwig would show up with a briefcase full of cash. He also made deals with various hotels and other locations, which sometimes worked to the detriment of the production and ended up wasting money. At one point, in an unprecedented move, Coburn threatened to refuse to continue shooting until crew back wages were paid.

Coburn liked to sum up a film experience with a clever epigram. He would develop these little sayings and forever after trot them out whenever there was an interview situation. For *Cross of Iron* press, he would always, for years after, say, "The Yugoslavians promised us everything, delivered half, and charged us double."

But according to Katy Haber, who personally typed every Peckinpah memo at the time and kept on file a copy of every note, letter, memo, invoice, or scrap of paper with a mark on it, this was incorrect. They were as much victims of the process as everyone else. "He's wrong about this saying it was the Yugoslavians. It was the German, Wolf Hartwig. The Yugoslavians only had what Wolf Hartwig paid them to have. On the first day of shooting, Sam said, 'Okay, I want you over here, and I want Jim over here. Okay, would you mark 'em?' And they all stood around and said, 'What?' They didn't have anything. They didn't have hammer or nails."[39]

The shoot was an incredibly stressful time. Eventually Coburn and Haber decided to drag Peckinpah to Venice. His clothes were in tatters, and he was exhausted.

"It took cajoling him—he really didn't want to go," Coburn says. "So when Saturday came, Katy and I stuffed him into the car and said, 'You're coming to fucking Venice, man. This is it. Get in the car and shut up.' 'Goddamn it, you can't talk to me like that.' 'Get in the car!' We arrived in Venice and got in one of those boats—putt, putt, putt, putt, putt—and went going down the canals, and he was like a captain, standing up with his head in the air and looking at Venice. And someone would be singing, there'd be music, and he would say, 'Goddamn, son of a bitch,' and he was commenting on the beauty of Venice.

"Sam loved Venice. He took to it like a duck. There's no place in the world like Venice. All the houses are empty; no one can afford to live there. People live on the mainland. It's too expensive to live on Venice. If you have dinner at Harry's Bar—a couple of Bellinis $50, I usually have *pasta e fagioli*, a fish, and then some wine, naturally—$250.

"We stayed at the little hotel that I like there, up in the Piazza, next to the theater that burned down, Hotel La Fenice. We took him out to dinner, Harry's Bar, had a bottle of champagne, and put him to bed. The next day we were going to take him shopping and buy him some clothes.

"We went to pick him up, ten o'clock. He didn't want to go; he wants to stay in bed. So Katy and I went out for coffee and went down to the lobby, and here was Fellini. I had met Fellini in Rome a couple of times."[40]

Here Haber takes up the story: "Fellini was wearing a fedora hat and a big cape. Jim saw him and said, 'Signor Fellini,' and he went, 'Ja-mes Co-burn!' And they hugged each other. They absolutely knew each other. I spoke to him in Italian. I said, 'Signor Fellini, I want to introduce you to someone, but I want it to be just as much of a surprise for you as it is for him. Will you accompany me upstairs?' It was a chance encounter for both of them. That's what made it so rich.

"Sam didn't want to get up and open the door. It was locked from the inside. I said, 'Sam, open the fucking door.' And finally he opened the door, and he was standing there naked. Fellini went, 'Sam Peckin-puck,' and Sam went, 'Oh my God.' Fellini actually picked him up and threw him on the bed, and I said, 'Jim, I think it's time for us to go.' We came back in the afternoon, and they were still chatting."[41]

A little later Fellini was still in the lobby working with his writers when Peckinpah finally left his room and came downstairs with Coburn. "And Sam says, 'Listen, Mister Fellini, if you ever need anybody to shoot second unit for you, I'm your man.' That would have been . . . phew . . ."[42]

After this refreshing break they returned to Yugoslavia. By the end of the shoot in early August, the relationship between Peckinpah and Hartwig had completely broken down. The only way the shoot and subsequent editing continued was through an injection of money from the English distributor EMI. The ending of the film, which had been planned as a spectacular, grim battle, was unaffordable. Instead of spending several days on the climax, they spent one afternoon. Then there were a few weeks off. In early September Coburn shot commercials for the film in London before doing reshoots of the romantic scene with the sanatorium nurse, played by Senta Berger, at EMI Studios in London. Luckily for Coburn's schedule, by this time the *Diary of an Assassin* project had crumbled, although it led to lots of back-and-forth over monies owed to Coburn through Pyx Quartation.

Beverly was still hostile toward Jim, but she was also resolved to continue to help her husband with his work. It was, after all, their main source of income. She was in London from the last week of August to help with those commercials. She also started making notes, prepping for a legal challenge to Wolf Hartwig for such shares of the gross as would be expected. Talk of the production getting audited had begun months before. The editing process had less studio interference than Peckinpah's other films had, but it was still challenging. Coburn stayed in London until mid-October.

After the grueling *Cross of Iron* shoot, his and Beverly's relationship was certainly not what it was before. The very first gossip of an impending split appeared on New Year's Eve, and it was announced, somewhat officially and belatedly in January 1977, that the couple was having a trial separation. A property settlement agreement had been drafted by Beverly's lawyers and agreed upon as early as November 1976. It included the explanation: "Unhappy differences have arisen between the parties and they intend to separate and live separate and apart as soon as possible,"[43] It was also noted that there was still one minor child in the marriage. The documents stipulated that the house was to be sold as soon as possible. Beverly had second thoughts about this process, and in later proceedings the official date of separation was pushed to sixteen months later, which had the advantage to Beverly of increasing the overall value of the community property. By waiting they also did not have to deal with any custody or child support issues. She also rethought the idea of being obliged to sell the house, where she continued to live for some years after the divorce.

Escaping Beverly's simmering resentment, Coburn took the chance to go to Japan for a week in early February 1977, accompanied by Peckinpah. This was the first of two trips he would take there with his friend. It was a good opportunity to do some work on the script for Sam's next film, *Convoy*, which would see Coburn working as second unit director. They stayed in the Hotel Grand Palace in the center of Tokyo.

"Toshiro Mifune gave a party for Sam and me. He had this whole house in Ginza, an entire geisha house come to take care of us. It was at a hotel. A woman chef. The food just kept coming, [for] about twenty people. The Japanese and Sam and I, and his cousin Walter Peter. We were all there. The geishas were so cute. They would sit down and tell you little raunchy stories. They'd flirt with you. You'd get all hot and bothered, and then they would move on to the next person.

"Everybody was doing different things. Mifune only drank scotch. We were all drinking sake, getting smashed on sake. This started about six p.m. All the working girls had to be off the streets by eleven. At ten thirty it was over. Each geisha had a talent, some singing, play koto, play the flute, the harp, dance. For some reason, the *mamasan* picks me to do this dance. We really got into it. It was great fun. It was like doing an improvisation with somebody who is really great at improv. This semi–martial arts thing.

"These girls were all trained. All the girls had such a sweetness about them and were very well managed. The dinner that night probably cost Mifune $25,000, maybe more. It was really expensive to take this room and have the whole geisha house come over."[44]

At home there was an uneasy peace. Jimmy was away at a boarding school in Massachusetts while Lisa was sanguine about the impending split. "[The kids] didn't seem to mind too much. Lisa was old enough to say, 'Well, that's the way it is in Hollywood.'" To their friends and the public, the separation seemed a natural consequence of Coburn's continuing blistering work and travel schedule, but the divorce was put on hold for the sake of a very special visitor to Tower Road.

II

Shoe Salesmen

The real work is the practice that works in you, that you gained from the understanding of the tales, and whatever that might be. You may get one thing from it, and I might get something entirely different from it, yet it's all valid. But it works *in* you. All the Gurdjieff stuff works *in* you, after you establish it. Being the observer, watching yourself. Observe yourself day and night, night and day, all the time, from that particular point of view. You find yourself asking, what the fuck am I doing? Where am I? And then you'll know.

—JAMES COBURN, 2002

His Holiness Rangjung Rigpe Dorje, the 16th Gyalwa Karmapa, known as the Black Crown Buddha, was born in Tibet in 1924. The Karmapa is second only to the Dalai Lama in Tibetan Buddhism and is the embodiment of the Kagyu lineage. In 1959 with the invasion of Tibet by China, the Karmapa escaped to live in exile. He settled in Rumtek, India, to form his *sangha* (monastic community) where he built a monastery and a monk retreat and training center. He also built an outstanding aviary to house his collection of small birds. Then starting in the mid-1970s he was inspired to make trips to the West, Europe and North America, to spread the dharma—the teachings of the Buddha that practitioners believe create cosmic order and joy.

In early 1977 he embarked on a trip to the United States, beginning in upstate New York and then coming to the West Coast. The trip was organized in part by Erhard Seminars Training (EST) transformational instructor Werner Erhard, and His Holiness stayed in private homes with his entourage, including spending part of his time in Southern California at James Coburn's Tower Road house. It was kept relatively quiet that he was staying there, with gatherings for private blessings happening by invitation only. The Karmapa also performed public Black Crown Ceremonies, one on February 5, and another for Erhard's EST students on February 26, 1977, in Los Angeles.[1]

While in town, the Karmapa took the opportunity to visit Disneyland, which he seemed to enjoy, before running north to Santa Cruz for a few days then circling back to Beverly Hills to Tower Road.[2] Rather incongruously he also called on Hugh Hefner at the Playboy Mansion to see Hef's collection of exotic songbirds.

Despite the increasing stress of their disintegrating relationship, Coburn and Beverly were united in their desire to host the remarkable Karmapa and his party of eleven monks, translators, and helpers in their guest suite. For Coburn it was one of the most meaningful encounters with a spiritual guru of his life.

Coburn had many conversations with the Karmapa, via his translator. "I didn't want to waste time talking jive. I had some good conversations with him. I asked Karmapa, 'What about the dharma? It's been locked into a crystallized state up in Tibet. Do you believe it was necessary for the Chinese to come, to take all your people and get all of the dharma moving again around the world in various places and other seats?' He said, 'Yes, of course, it was absolutely necessary.' Then I asked, 'That means maybe the next Karmapa will be a Scotsman or American or a Canadian?' And he said, 'Oh, not yet.'"[3]

Aside from formal ceremonies, the Karmapa enjoyed the smaller private activities, including eating some meals in the Coburns' favorite private sitting room upstairs and casual al fresco dining in the wonderful Southern California early spring.

"I taught him to sing 'Happy Birthday.' We were having a big picnic at Tower Road, on the patio and out on the lawn, with all the monks, the *rinpoches*, Werner Erhard, and Karmapa. Frank was chasing a cat up a tree, actually climbed the tree and got the cat down, and everyone stood around and applauded. One of Werner's associates was having a birthday, so we sang to him. Afterward, Karmapa didn't know what we were doing. The Karmapa said, 'You teach me song?' I said, 'You don't know what happy birthday is? Date of birth, when one is born?'

"We translated for him, and, 'Oh, yes, we have birthday.' He understood, and I taught him the whole fucking song. And we all clapped. He had the best time learning a silly song like that, and I had a wonderful time teaching it. We had a really special relationship. Just one-on-one, which is very rare to have with those high guys. He really was something special. Every time he would see me, he would put his hand on my head. He never blessed me—he gave me a zap of high energy on the back of my neck."

One evening Coburn and Frank Messa got all the *rinpoches* playing drums. Drumming is part of the funeral rites of the Kagyu tradition, as shown in the biographical documentary about the Karmapa that Coburn narrated some years later, *The Lion's Roar* (1985). It was not proper for the monks to be playing the drums casually. But apparently they heard the beats one night and were curious. They tiptoed down to the drum room. Coburn and Messa were playing and persuaded the monks to try the instruments. "They only played one beat, and we kept trying to get them syncopated to what we were doing, so we were showing them how to do that, and they were having the best time. They had a great time doing that."

Messa also recalls the same event: "They can't speak because they only speak Tibetan—we had translators there the whole time—but Jim offers the first one the drumstick, and I get up, and we had all kinds of drums there—we had a set of everything.

"So suddenly we got six of these monks with mallets in their hands beating all these drums, because we are playing together creating more and more of a racket. It started out pretty soft because they were timid, but Jim and I were playing, and pretty soon we looked up at each other. With a little smile, he gave me that look like 'These guys are into it, man'—and they were.

"Then all of a sudden in the doorway—the Karmapa. Nobody even heard him. He came out of his room, and he's standing there just looking at his monks beating the shit out of these drums. He didn't say anything. One of them happened to glance over, and he saw the Karmapa and—blam—put the sticks down, then there was silence. Then—*prrrrrrt*—like little mice upstairs. And the Karmapa just looked at us, turned around, and walked to his room again. Jim and I just cracked up. It was so funny."[4]

Messa was there on another day when the Karmapa impressed the assembled with his own musical ability. "We were in the living room downstairs. Jim had an original Tibetan horn. They telescope out. It was sitting next to the fireplace down there. One of Jim's friends, a saxophone player, not one of the monks, opened it out and set it up with the end resting on some furniture, and blew into it. He made a few feeble sounds. The Karmapa didn't say anything. He just gets up, and he walks over to the guy standing there, and the guy gives him the mouthpiece. The Karmapa grabs that horn, and he takes one big breath, and he blows into that horn. It was so loud, it was like thunder came out—*woooo*—and the windows shook, the drapes were moving. And Jim said, 'Now *that's* how it sounds!' This blows everybody's mind—this was tremendous. Of course he knew how. This was a mountain horn."

But the highlight of the Karmapa's visit, both for him and for Coburn, was the private outing in Coburn's favorite car.

"I took the Karmapa for a ride in the Ferrari, because he wanted to go for a ride in the Ferrari. Does he want me to really stand on it, or just go for a drive? Driving up Benedict Canyon, no other cars were coming. Sitting in his robe, we were both strapped in, and—*whoomph*—I took off. He says, 'Oooh, very good.' Down Mulholland, over Coldwater. One hundred miles per hour. The next day he wanted me to drive him to his next meeting. I asked his assistant if he wanted to go in the Ferrari or the Mercedes. 'Oh, I think the Mercedes.'"[5]

Messa recalls that Beverly and the Karmapa would "physically fight" over precedence whenever they were leaving a room. He would watch them race "to the same doorway. Some of the doorways are big enough, they can both walk through, but when they got to a doorway like the bedroom doorway—only one can go through at a time. They'd both hit at the same time—and Beverly would always win." Usually the Karmapa was careful of his dignity and status. "If you didn't bow down, he had a bad habit. If you stuck your hand out, he'd grab your thumb and pull till you'd have to bow, whether you'd like it or not. I adored him. I had his picture up on my wall for a long time."[6]

Coburn felt a deep affection for him as well. "When the Karmapa stayed with me, he was up all the time, walking around, dictating to one of his aides. He was diabetic. If he was in pain, he certainly didn't show it. He had a wonderful sense of humor. Deep belly laughs, bumping heads." When the group was finally leaving, Coburn did not bow but instead wrapped the Karmapa in a great hug. "And he gave me a big hug back. That was nice, and the last time I saw him."[7]

The visit had lasted ten days. "It was great. I loved it. I moved out right after the Karmapa did. He left and so did I. It was like I put that together for Karmapa. I knew there was never going to be anything more than the Karmapa coming to Tower Road."

As nice and symmetrical as this idea feels, it wasn't quite accurate. Coburn continued to come and go, using this address as his official home base. In the meantime, Messa, who loved both Jim and Beverly, decided to take himself out of the uncomfortable situation and split for a while to focus on his own painting career, and be out of range of difficult questions. "I wasn't going to be played as the middle. I made this agreement to both of them, that I didn't know where Jim was."[8] By this time his ink drawings—for which Beverly had once paid fifty dollars just to be kind—were fetching two hundred dollars in galleries.

Coburn was peripatetic for a while, busying himself with the publicity for *Cross of Iron*, traveling to major cities to promote the movie. The film was a marketing challenge. He felt that the film had been deliberately buried in the United States because it was from the German point of view. Many interviewers wanted to focus on Peckinpah's reputation for portraying violence, forcing Coburn to defend the film.

"If you're doing a war film, it needs violence because that's what war's all about. I think the drama in the film has to do with facing violence: it has to do with facing one's self and has to do with overcoming and purging the violence from one's self. . . . You don't have to be violent to be affected by [violence]."[9]

He was very busy through April, May, and June. On May 1, 1977, his first commercial for Schlitz Light aired. He made *The Guinness Book of World Records* for the highest payment to an actor, $250,000 per syllable. Then there was the preparation for his job as second unit director on *Convoy*, which took up his summer when he wasn't doing talk shows in New York and Chicago. In Chicago he took some time out for acupuncture treatments, something he had found helped him with the pain from gout attacks in the past. This time it was an ache in his elbow. For the first time, he publicly mentioned arthritis in an interview, without thinking it was anything serious.

"It's some kind of arthritis I think. See there's this little sac in here, between the bones, and the fluid is supposed to flow right through. But for some reason it's getting stuck, and swelling up. . . . See this squishy lump?"[10]

But he also reiterated his enjoyment of acting and the process of working. "It's a lonely thing, making movies. But it's a distraction from life too. You can't do anything else once you've started a role. You can't leave it alone once the juices start. It takes all your attention. A production is like an encapsulated organism and keeps growing. You give it total attention and it grows and grows and becomes everything. It evolves as long as you keep feeding energy into it."

Convoy, filmed over the summer of 1977 in New Mexico, was going to suck a lot of everyone's energy. The production was close to an utter debacle. It was based on a country song, a thin story that Peckinpah was determined to enlarge into an epic antiauthoritarian fable about a truck driver leading his associates to protest new road taxes by driving a convoy of trucks to create a blockade. In an early script meeting with Kris Kristofferson, Peckinpah declared, "This should become a protest picture, Cesar Chavez, Kennedy. [Ali MacGraw's character] pushes him to protest about numerous things, a revolution from the silent majority."[11] He gathered many of his usual staff and familiar stars. Coburn was somewhat bemused by Peckinpah's choice of material but was keen for any reason to be away from home. He was officially employed for about two weeks but hung around a lot longer, helping out wherever he could.

It turned out that "second unit" was something of a misnomer on the *Convoy* shoot. All the usual elements of latter-day Peckinpah were present—drug- and alcohol-fueled paranoia, an incoherent script, a grandiose vision, an often-absent and often-raging director, and insufficient resources. Another challenge was the genuine logistical complexity of working with an actual convoy of big-rig trucks. Coburn enlisted help from his daughter Lisa's fiancé, Robert Levy, who had just successfully produced the hit road film *Smokey and the Bandit* (1977).

Then there was Peckinpah's new love affair with helicopters. There were helicopters that housed cameras for long shots of the convoy itself and others that were picture-vehicles (that is, appearing on film) doubling as police and news choppers. It seemed that whenever Peckinpah had the opportunity to fly off, he did, often leaving those on the ground to improvise the rest of the setups. The two second unit teams were often folded into first unit to allow many cameras to capture the action. Coburn sometimes used a handheld Arriflex camera himself and often found himself directing actors.

On one memorable day, the entire company was set up and ready by 10:00 a.m. for a big driving sequence. There were two helicopters with cameras, four more cameras set up on the ground, and Coburn with his Arriflex atop a water tower. Peckinpah finally came to set at 5:00 p.m., having kept everyone waiting. Coburn had stayed on the water tower for most of the day.

Peckinpah's obdurate refusals to come to set in anything remotely resembling a timely manner strained his relationships with everyone. It is a testament to Coburn's affection for the man, along with his intense desire to avoid going home, that he stayed with the project, even returning after the company had a short hiatus while Peckinpah reworked the script's ending. By this time even long-suffering Katy Haber had had enough abuse and walked off the project and out of Sam's life.[12]

Convoy was Peckinpah's most commercially successful film.

Coburn continued to work around the country while describing the status of his marriage as "coasting."[13] He was reluctant to say much, but when he did, he continued to assert that the couple was still "trying to save what has been a good marriage."[14] He took the blame on himself for being away too much. However, his remarks that Beverly was a nonprofessional and was unconnected to his career were inaccurate, vilipending her contribution over the years, and must have stung.

In the fall of 1977, Coburn looked forward to what would be his first real directing gig, a single episode of the series *The Rockford Files* starring his old buddy James Garner. It was an entertaining episode with a certain pathos, and it gained him his Directors Guild of America (DGA) membership. Garner had offered him the job as a favor after they appeared together (by chance) on a talk show and Coburn mentioned his long-held aspiration. He accepted the job with gratitude and appreciated the little bump in publicity the episode gained, but stepping into an existing company of many seasons, a well-oiled machine with established characterizations, was disappointing. He shrugged about it. "You walk up behind the cinematographer and he sets it up."[15] It was not the kind of creative directing that Coburn had been dreaming about for years. He still hoped for more.

Next he segued straight into the lead in *The Dain Curse*. This was a private-eye caper, a Dashiell Hammett book adaptation that had been first pitched back in 1973. Several of the screenplays had been declined by the powers that be until the idea to make it into CBS's first-ever miniseries suddenly sounded attractive. Coburn was still a hot property. It was quite a coup to get a movie star for the lead role for this television production. That the shoot would be twelve weeks long at locations in Pennsylvania and in New York, on Shelter Island and in Manhattan, undoubtedly added to the attraction for Coburn.

By the end of the shoot, he was sorry that he had agreed to the project. The series was planned as three two-hour segments, which amounts to the equivalent of three feature films, yet the schedule would have been enough time to shoot only one. He was frustrated because the production seemed to squander the possibilities of the literature, telling reporters he was naive to accept it. "The desire to be in a project—this sometimes overwhelms your better judgment."[16]

With his characteristic candor when speaking of the industry, he made no bones about his ongoing disdain for television as a medium, calling the CBS executives "amateurs" and "mechanics," and grumbling about the production values and compressed shooting schedule.

"The material has great depth, subtleties that are unusual for television. But a point comes when you have to say, 'Okay, this isn't going to be a really high-quality film, but it can be as high-quality a film as you can get within this form. . . .' [It all comes] down to not wanting to offend anyone. The network is willing to sacrifice integrity for greed. . . . We're expected to sacrifice—time, attention, energy, even a good performance—in the interest of something that will be mediocre. It always seems that we're working at cross purposes, making the film in spite of the people paying for it. . . . The highest they see is a filmed radio show—people, faces, talking. If you're not talking on screen, it's dead air."

This situation of starting a project keenly, only to have the enthusiasm wane once the reality of the project became apparent, was a new pattern for Coburn that would manifest more visibly over the next few years. He didn't know it, but he was about to enter a time in his life that was characterized by both increasing professional frustration and increasing physical pain and debilitation. Luckily he was still hugely popular, with U.S. television audiences who saw his past movies broadcast regularly; with audiences in Asia, especially Japan; and with viewers in Europe, especially in France and in Germany, where *Cross of Iron* was a hit.

Despite Coburn's dismissive evaluation, as a miniseries *The Dain Curse* was very well received and reviewed, called a "first class production . . . as handsome as the best theatrical movies . . . beautifully presented" by one UPI journalist, Joan Hanauer.[17] Another critic, Christopher Cobb, wrote in the *Ottawa Journal* that it was "a television blessing . . . solidly built around a host of powerful characters."[18] It also went on to be rerun in full numerous times over the next six or seven years, before being cut down into a much less coherent feature-length movie for release on video some years later. It all brought in residual income.

It may have been the continuing size of Coburn's fees for the ongoing Schlitz Light campaign that had inspired Beverly to hire a new accountant to help her take care of the family's increasingly complex finances. In December 1977 CPA Rob Harabedian was relatively young, having graduated only five years earlier. He was startled by Beverly's unorthodox domestic arrangements. "My initial meeting was with Beverly in her bedroom. It wasn't actually the bed part, but she had a sitting room off the bedroom where she held court. I met her there, and she, for the most part, was running the financial affairs for the family, and she made the decision. I did not meet Jim then and there. He was out of town making a movie. But shortly thereafter, I met Jim. He came home, and I met him again in the 'court room' of their home. Both meetings went very well."[19]

Beverly was doing some long-term planning. Soon she confided to Harabedian that she and Coburn intended to divorce. She told him that she wanted him to stay with her soon-to-be ex, because she said, "He's gonna need you." Later Harabedian confessed to feeling relieved. "Beverly was a very imposing person. She was very intimidating, especially for a young accountant out of school to be dealing with her. I think Beverly and I always got along well with each other because I think she respected me—because on certain things she wanted me to do, I wouldn't compromise. And I respected her for what she had accomplished on behalf of their family."

Her prophecy turned out to be true once the divorce proceedings got under way. Their finances were made more complex by the numerous investments and the production entities that they jointly owned—Panpiper, Scarab Productions (not to be confused with the current company of that name), and their half of Pyx Quartation.

In his personal life, Coburn was about to get another bump toward the divorce. Not long after *The Dain Curse* wrapped, he met the petite British singer-songwriter Lynsey de Paul at a party given by former Beatles manager and music producer Ron Kass and his wife, actress Joan Collins, at their home in Los Angeles. After representing the UK in the Eurovision Song

Contest, de Paul had been romantically linked to some of the most famous figures in British entertainment, including Dudley Moore and Ringo Starr. However, as a musician she was not well known in the United States. She was in the country hoping to extend her audience, who until then were mostly British and European.

The gossip columnists were quick to notice that it looked like the Coburns would not be working out their marital problems after all, and by the summer of 1978, Coburn and Lynsey de Paul were involved in a serious romance. She joined him in Antigua, West Indies, on the set of the actioner *Firepower*, which also starred Sophia Loren, old friend Eli Wallach, and a newcomer to acting, O. J. Simpson. With a light story and silly stunts, it looks like this film was conceived largely as an opportunity for the cast and crew to enjoy some tropical Caribbean sunshine.

During filming de Paul was called away from the set by her then-manager Justin de Villeneuve for an opportunity to record her next album with Rupert Holmes, who was Barbra Streisand's producer. Streisand is a meticulous perfectionist. De Villeneuve booked his friend's recording studio, Long View Farm in North Brookfield in central Massachusetts, for the sessions. North Brookfield, noted as the lifelong summer home of playwright George M. Cohan, is a small town. De Paul arrived in the tiny airport and was greeted by a local journalist, who gave her a small write-up.

"So far, her only exposure here has been reference to her under-wraps romance with actor James Coburn in a recent issue of 'People' magazine.... She explains haltingly her attraction to James Coburn. 'I know it sounds corny, but we're soul-mates. We touch the essence of each other. We met at a party in Los Angeles given by mutual friends. But, if you don't mind, I'd prefer not to publicize it. We've kept our relationship very quiet for a year.'"[20]

It seems either remarkably naive or utterly calculating to ask a reporter *not* to publicize a story about a celebrity's illicit relationship, especially after telling her all about it. This article did appear immediately in the local newspaper, the *Worcester Sunday Telegram*.

Apparently de Paul was somewhat notorious as a difficult artist. On the first day of recording, she so derided the musical ability of one of the session musicians (who was from Bob Dylan's band, Rolling Thunder Review) that he simply shrugged, packed his bass, and split. Later de Villeneuve found Rupert Holmes himself weeping on the balcony, saying, "She makes Streisand look like a pussy cat."[21] Shortly after, Coburn arrived in Massachusetts to join the party, as de Villeneuve describes in his autobiography:

"I could never work out how Coburn put up with Lynsey, talented and successful as she was and continued to be. One evening we were all together at dinner in Long View—Lynsey, Rupert, Gil [the owner], Justin and James, who had just flown up from South America. Lynsey starts to berate James. He stands up. We all hope he is going to hit her. No such luck. 'Lynsey,' he says, 'you're not talking to Rupert, you know.' Silence. I thought Rupert was going to cry.

"Eventually, the record was finished. It never saw the light of day. Lynsey said that Rupert didn't know his business. All I know is that six months later Rupert had a colossal hit personally with the *Pina Colada* song and Lynsey subsequently had other successes of her own."

After *Firepower* Coburn and de Paul were living out of suitcases, traveling back and forth between the UK and the United States. In London they lived in her tiny house. The same gossip columns pointed out the Coburns' unusual accommodations when de Paul visited Los Angeles late in the year. According to these sources, she and Coburn both stayed at the Tower Road house as guests of Beverly. He continued filming commercials for Schlitz until the fall and collaborated on lyrics for two of the songs for de Paul's next album, *Tigers and Fireflies*, which was to be released the following year.[22]

Having Lynsey de Paul stay at Tower Road can't have been comfortable for anyone concerned. There was no choice but to find an affordable new home. Initially Coburn rented a little house on Hutton Drive high in the Hollywood Hills, then another on Dixie Canyon Avenue in Sherman Oaks. Finally in 1979 he bought a smaller, but still very comfortable, house on Hollyline Avenue in Sherman Oaks, about halfway up the hill. Well hidden behind a high hedge, many trees, and a hairpin-turn driveway, it was a California ranch–style bungalow with French doors opening onto a reasonably spacious yard with a pool.

Harabedian recalled it as feeling very empty. "He acquired this house and didn't have a lot to furnish it with. My impression is that when I walked into the house that evening, everything was empty. The living room had no furniture, the dining room had no furniture, and I think the only furniture in the bedroom was his bed and a chair—maybe two chairs because I remember I was in one chair and he was in the other, and we were sitting talking."[23]

Coburn hoped to rebuild a new art collection. His friend Nik Douglas, who collected and wrote about Tibetan and Southeast Asian sacred art, sent Polaroids of a few likely pieces. But Coburn was not in a huge hurry to fill his house and would need time to rebuild his finances after the settlement. He would live there until 1994.

By the end of 1978, it was announced that he would star in *The Baltimore Bullet*, a comedy about two pool hustlers, which would take him back to New Orleans. First he would shoot a cameo, with one of the best jokes in the picture, for *The Muppet Movie*, and over January he would shoot the Olympic Games–based sci-fi *Goldengirl*, conceived as a star-making turn for newcomer Susan Anton in the titular role as a genetically enhanced superathlete. In an odd coincidence, Anton was about to enter a long-term relationship with Lynsey de Paul's ex, Dudley Moore. Both of these last two films shot locally.

Coburn described *Goldengirl* as a travesty. Unfortunately, the film became an instant anachronism when the United States boycotted the 1980 Olympic Summer Games in Moscow, where the film was set, over the USSR's invasion of Afghanistan. Instead it had a limited run in theaters over the summer. Nonetheless Anton was nominated for a Golden Globe as New Star of the Year, proving once again that astute marketing can overcome many hurdles.

Coburn was still dating de Paul when it was finally, officially announced in February 1979 that he and Beverly would divorce. The announcement brought a brief flurry of speculation about whether the new couple would themselves marry. Beverly filed the petition on April 4, 1979, defining their separation as being from March 30, 1978. The couple had still filed their 1977 and 1978 tax returns jointly, and it was negotiated as part of the divorce that they would file the 1979 return jointly also.

With his unpleasant divorce proceedings rumbling along in the background, Coburn continued to escape into his usual busy work schedule over 1979. He had long been an enthusiast of pool and snooker games. For this reason he looked forward to *The Baltimore Bullet* shoot, even though the production company was FilmFair, whose main claim to fame was as a TV commercials production house. This was their first feature film production. Like *Sky Riders*, this film is especially appreciated by aficionados of the particular sport.

Ten champion professional players were hired to play themselves as losing contestants and to act as advisers for the project. Ongoing games of pool continued between takes, while Coburn enjoyed the company and coaching. Pool expert Robert Byrne wrote about the film in his book *Byrne's Advanced Technique in Pool and Billiards*. The pros, who all knew each other, were full of anecdotes and nostalgia. They were largely unanimous in their belief that this film was going to be better than that other famous pool movie, *The Hustler* (1961), at least in portraying the game. After shooting interior scenes for a while, they filmed the final big tournament with the pros in a soundstage on the MGM lot in Culver City.

Coburn was delighted. "After twenty-seven days of filming it was becoming awfully hard work. Then the players arrived and turned everything into a party. It was fun all day long! They are fascinating characters, full of personality, confidence, and style, not sallow, pool hall stereotypes. I could hardly wait to get to work in the morning."[24]

Next the company went to New Orleans to do all the action exteriors. It seemed like Coburn never could avoid Louisiana in the summer. It was hard to leave the pool players behind. There were many uncharacteristic hugs at the final wrap, with the star "embarrassing Jim Rempe by kissing him on both cheeks."

Coburn was still in Los Angeles when Jimmy graduated from Beverly Hills High School, Class of 1979. Jimmy had no clear vision of his own future, so Coburn gave him a round-the-world airline ticket to allow him to escape what was shaping up to be a nasty fight between the parents. Jimmy set off, getting as far as Africa, where he stayed for the next several years with James Logan in what was now Zimbabwe. Jimmy worked for a canoe safari company and as an actor in some local English-language films (most under the name of Harrison Coburn). In South Africa he did commercial voice-overs and was a radio producer.

Rob Harabedian recalls, "Jim was touting on how proud he was of Jimmy, when he was with Logan in Africa, and then making money on his own and doing these things and making movies. When I saw some of the mug shots and things of him when he was doing the movies, he looked like a young James Coburn."[25] The emotional baggage of Jimmy's childhood still cast a shadow over the relationship between father and son. The saddest legacy is that while he lived, Coburn never expressed his pride to his son directly, re-creating his own father's distant reticence.

With Jimmy safely away and *The Baltimore Bullet* completed, Coburn shot his next film over the bright, warm late summer in Southern California—a light, sex-romp-style comedy, *Loving Couples* with Shirley MacLaine and Susan Sarandon. Publicity for the movie shows Coburn spoofing his cowboy persona, riding a horse down a Los Angeles freeway, wearing a cowboy hat. The movie doubled San Diego for Mexico and also shot at the beautiful art deco–style Ambassador Hotel in Los Angeles. The hotel was famous for the Cocoanut Grove nightclub, where the Rat Pack played when they were in town, and infamous for the assassination of Robert F. Kennedy in the main kitchen.

Coburn's mother, Mylet, visited the set, bringing along Coburn's aunt Pauline Coburn (Harrison's brother Darrell's widow). They were invited to spend the day working as extras. In a humorous moment noted by the *San Bernardino County Sun*, when Coburn "blew a bit of dialogue, his mother took him aside to ask, 'Why don't you know your lines?'"[26]

Loving Couples had elements of art imitating, or at least flipping around, life. Coburn's character discovers his wife is having an affair, which he comes to realize stems mostly from his own neglect of her emotional needs. In the publicity package for the film, he remarked that to have a good relationship, a couple "should be aware of their goals as a unit" and make "a commitment to the union itself."[27] He described himself as not domesticated. "I need the freedom to express myself as an individual." Like Coburn himself, his character in the film "has to ask himself whether he wants to be left alone in the world or to face life with a woman at his side. It's a question of balancing his values and finding out what really matters to him."

Coburn decided that his freedom was what mattered most at this moment. It was during this shoot that the divorce really started to turn ugly. Beverly's demands had been extreme, his reaction rather petty. According to a show cause petition filed by Beverly on November 1, 1979, he had been refusing to pay her living expenses, mortgage, or insurance since October 1 and had declared his intention to not pay any of her bills during the ongoing divorce proceedings. She claimed that he was engaging in diversion and deferment to make his income look "considerably lower than his true economic earning ability."[28] Beverly also asserted that he had excluded her from the day-to-day operations of their companies, Panpiper and Pyx, leaving her unable to pay her regular bills or keep track of his earnings.

But perhaps the greatest insult (from her point of view) was that, in what sounds like a Hail Mary of sorts, he—or his lawyers—apparently tried to contend that their marriage itself was invalid in 1959, to avoid California's community property laws. He also wanted to insist on the 1976 separation date—despite using Tower Road as his address of record on more than one subsequent movie project. Then he claimed certain gifts he had given Beverly to be community property.

Surely after more than eighteen years and ten months as her spouse, he must have known she would always vigorously defend her rights as she saw them and avenge any perceived insult. Messa said about her, "Beverly would claw you to death, without even lifting a finger."[29] The courtroom was closed to the public and the press for the proceedings, but one can imagine sparks flying in the "he said, she said" of the occasion. The judge ordered the transcripts of the proceedings at the final divorce hearing sealed.

Even after the settlement was hashed out, Beverly used Coburn's old contract with Pyx Quartation to gain even more money from him (via Scarab) for his pay-or-play contract on an unproduced film in Canada, *Midnight Matinee*. His fee from that project was supposed to be considered as his separate property. They also squabbled over whether Beverly should share in the tax liability from that income.

This was when he gave in, told his lawyers to just give Beverly what she wanted, signed away the house and art, and confirmed that he would take care of taxes. From his point of view, he had "been conned out of the house and everything in it. I knew it, but I just said, 'Take it, take it. Get out of my life.' I just wanted out. All sorts of reasons. We became incompatible on many levels, and I just did not want to be married any longer, so I just *pffft!* She wanted something else too. I could never figure out what that was, but I knew I didn't want what that was."[30]

In the eventual divorce settlement, finalized on May 13, 1980, Beverly received the house, all the contents thereof, the Rolls and the Mercedes (he kept the Ferraris), 50 percent of future residuals in perpetuity, all the interests in Pyx Quartation, sizable alimony payments for the next two years, some of their investments in oil and other stocks and holdings—real estate, a motel, a Cessna aircraft—and possible proceeds from ongoing litigation over a property development scheme in 1970 in which the Coburns and some others claimed to be the victims of fraud.

It was an entirely unequal division, which infuriated Coburn, a rage he kept bottled up. Later he believed this exacerbated his incipient arthritis. "She was greedy. And she was a nasty, selfish bitch. She hangs on to things. The arthritis started just around the time of the divorce and about two years after I moved out. It was really hard on me because I was stupid. I could not admit that I was being eaten up by this thing. The negative emotion brought on the arthritis. I did not admit I was raging inside because she got the house and all the good art, and I got nothing. I was busting my ass, and I didn't have any bread. She kept everything, and I just wanted to get out. I gave it all away. And she thought it was fair. She still owes me six Oriental rugs. But I'll never get them."[31]

For the next few years, Coburn would be working to maintain a home he didn't live in and to support an ex-wife who filled him with resentment.

It seemed a relief to escape to Canada over fall for a starring role in the low-budget Canadian film *Mr. Patman*, also known as *Crossover*, a character study about a night orderly in a mental hospital and his decline into madness. It was directed by John Guillermin, best known as the director of *The Towering Inferno* (1974), *King Kong* (1976), and *Death on the Nile* (1978), while the cinematographer was an old friend and Peckinpah favorite, John Coquillon (*Cross of Iron, Pat Garrett and Billy the Kid*).

"[John Guillermin] was a Catholic. [My character] was delivering some amphetamines to this priest, and I walk in there and look at this cross. He refused to shoot the scene, and I insisted on it. 'Shoot the fucking scene the way it's written.' And he said, 'I can't, I'm Catholic.' And I said, 'John, you haven't really been a Catholic for fifty years.' And he said, 'I know but I can't shoot it.' I said, 'Well then, step outside and I'll shoot the scene.' I had the cinematographer set up and shoot the scene.

"[Guillermin] was all over Kate Nelligan, and he wanted to fuck her so bad, he couldn't stand it. And she wouldn't have anything to do with him at all. His daughter came to town, and he had me go to lunch with them, and this lunch was two people, trying to relate to each other through me. I had no idea he was so unstable. The movie turned out to be a piece of shit, just okay."[32]

Coburn was praised for being approachable by fans seeking autographs: "He'd invariably put them at ease, grinning and personalizing the inscription"[33]—as well as for being "cool and cooperative" when additional scenes meant shooting on a Saturday.[34]

Meanwhile, at the same time, he started noticing new worsening pain in his wrists, especially whenever he played tennis. Little by little the stress and slowly accumulating fury combined with his age and, as he expressed it, his Scotch-Irish genes. Relentlessly the same rheumatoid arthritis that had crippled his father, and most likely plagued his grandfather, took over his body. "When my hands twisted, I didn't even realize it. It was like they twisted almost overnight."[35]

By the end of the three-month *Mr. Patman* shoot, Coburn was in near-constant pain. A trip to England for a few chilly months over winter didn't help. He felt like he was turning to stone.

12

The Man in the Suit

The Irish have a gene for arthritis, that when it's tripped off, can cause
disease. A deep emotional trauma or very cold weather can set it off.
Something has to set it off. Negative emotion set me off. I knew I was in
that inner rage, and I couldn't get it out. I couldn't say, "I'm feeling fine."

—JAMES COBURN, 2002

The disease attacking Coburn was debilitating as well as painful. He didn't
know what was happening, but knew he had to do something about it and
first visited a regular MD who gave him the diagnosis—rheumatoid arthritis—
and a prescription for anti-inflammatory painkillers. "You kind of blow up
when you are taking pain pills for arthritis. I hated taking them because they
didn't really do anything but mask the pain. I could always feel the pain
underneath it. It just wasn't as sharp, but it still limited my movements. The
pain was in my legs, mainly, all over my legs and in my wrists. Not so much
in my arms. Acting was next to impossible because every time I stood up, I
would break into a sweat."[1]

Without being able to move, acting would be difficult, and he still needed
an income. He questioned his doctor further. "'What do I do for it? What
causes it?' And he said, 'Well, hell, we don't know. You have to live with it,
son.' And I thought, *I'm not just going to live with it. I'm going to do something about it.*

"I was a little aware of alternative medicine. I had been taking vitamins for a long time. I called up my friend Murray Korngold, who was a clinical psychologist and started the Free Clinic, and we went to see the high colonic guy, and I went on a fifteen-day fast, water and broth, doing high colonic every other day—cleansing my unit—and it helped. I started feeling pretty good."

When it was time to break the fast, he started with watermelon as the first solid food, which was fine. Then he went to the organic food restaurant beloved by many stars, the Aware Inn, which was still open on the Sunset Strip. "I had an Aware Salad—all of those goodies—thinking it was as healthy as I could get, and immediately broke out into hives. My entire body was covered with them. I couldn't stand it. I had to get in the bathtub. Murray didn't know what to think of that. We'd been to the health food store earlier that day and saw a flyer for a cytotoxic blood test for food allergies. I went the following day, and they took some blood and tested it, and out of seventy-five foods, I was allergic to about forty-seven. And all of the other ones on the verge. So I went on his ninety-day program and didn't eat the foods I was allergic to. I lost a lot of weight."

Cytotoxic blood testing was a relatively new idea at the time. Today it is considered unreliable by most clinical allergists because of inconsistent results and false positives. Nonetheless, Coburn thought that cutting out a lot of possibly unhealthy foods might help him manage his pain and stiffness.

He was still very busy. In late April 1980 Coburn flew to Japan with Sam Peckinpah for the premiere of *Kagemusha* in the Yurakuza Theater in Tokyo, at Kurosawa's invitation. It was nice to be away, free from pressures. They went to a sushi bar, where he and Sam drank sake. "We got shrimp, sitting upside down on a little amount of rice, and their tails were still wiggling. And Sam looked at it, and I looked at it, and he said, 'I will if you will,' and I said, 'Okay, you go first.' So Sam eats one, and I said, 'How was it?' 'Great,' he answered. 'It tickles a little bit going down.'"

They went to Osaka to visit martial artist Steven Seagal in his dojo. Seagal knew a master acupuncturist whom Coburn hoped could help him. "He went over my entire body with one needle and said, 'Yes, I can cure you, but you will have to be here for about three months.' 'That would be great. I'd love to stay here for three months. But I have to go back and pay for this trip.'

"There were all these little places in downtown Osaka. We went to a little tempura place, where there was a master of tempura, and he had this cigarette hanging out of his mouth with the longest ash I had ever seen. This was one of those really special things. It was incredible. It was really fantastic stuff. So dramatic watching him make this stuff, he smoked about three cigarettes making it, and the ash never fell. I never saw him do anything with the cigarette. It was a really good, great experience. Then we got on the bullet train back to Tokyo."

Back in Los Angeles, it can't have been enjoyable to spend time in Beverly's company. But with one movie in the theater and another two about to open, Coburn put on a good show of civil behavior in public. He joined Beverly at a function at the Los Angeles County Museum of Art, LACMA, honoring them for donating rare eighteenth-century Sri Lankan painted panels to the museum for its reconstruction of a Ceylonese shrine. According to the museum, at the time these panels were "the only example of Buddhist architecture to be seen in an American museum, and the only Sri Lankan painted temple panels to be found outside that country."[2] It must have felt like yet another dig from Beverly, who continued periodically to donate art objects to LACMA over the next few years.

Once the divorce was settled, it was time for Coburn to mend his relationship with his best friend. He finally contacted Frank Messa, who was glad to be back in his life. "When Jim called me to Hollyline, I was so happy to see him again, after not seeing him for a couple of years. He told me the history of what happened. He had nothing. Beverly took all the art. The only thing he got left with was some of his financial interests."[3]

Messa immediately took charge of Coburn's house renovations, building a glass solarium and fixing up the kitchen. "That house was like a tract home when we started. We did it slowly because the money wasn't really coming in."

Coburn continued his diet. He was noticeably thinner in the summer of 1980, when he shot the straightforward actioner *High Risk* starring James Brolin and Lindsay Wagner. The director and writer, Stewart Raffill, was a former lion trainer and child actor. He was known as a B-movie director and had put together the Colombian caper story with independent financing in only a few weeks. The film shot on location in Mexico, with Coburn well cast as the suave and menacing drug kingpin that the gang of friends robs. Anthony Quinn portrayed the voluble leader of a wandering bandito gang, reuniting the two actors for the first time since *A High Wind in Jamaica*, although they had no scenes together.

In an interview Raffill notes, "James Coburn was more of an intellectual actor, the opposite of Anthony who was visceral and emotional. He was a wonderful character as well, but he was a more contained actor, he wasn't somebody who'd throw himself into a part and lose control like Anthony Quinn. Few actors will. James was also not particularly well when we did the film. He had terrible arthritis and it slowed him down."[4]

Still, Coburn knew he had to go bravely on. He was hoisted onto his horse for a bullfighting scene. Intercut long shots of the action with the bull use an obvious double, as does the shot from behind of his character dismounting—it's the wig that gives it away. With only a few scenes, he was probably in Mexico for a week or so before returning home to continue his treatments. The film had a brief run in theaters the following May 1981, and garnered fair reviews, especially for the action set pieces and the finale. Unfortunately, its small indie distribution company went out of business at the same time, and the picture found itself almost immediately overshadowed by the next weekend's big release, the blockbuster *Raiders of the Lost Ark*.

Soon after he returned from the *High Risk* shoot, Coburn traveled to the Toronto International Film Festival in September to help promote two of his movies, which opened there, *Loving Couples* and *Mr. Patman*. While there, he talked about his arthritis treatment program. It was essential that he maintain the impression that he was well enough to work. He referenced the feeling of "turning to stone" but stressed that his treatments were working. He joked about the thing he was *not* willing to give up—tobacco in the form of his favorite cigars—and reiterated his desire to direct.[5]

Loving Couples was finally released to theaters in late October 1980 to middling reviews. He was still smarting over his last two flops at the box office, which he considered entirely the fault of the production company, Avco Embassy. "They're foolish little amateur people who should be selling shoes instead of movies."[6] He mentioned that he had acquired the rights to Derek Flint and was developing a third installment, possibly centering on the son of Flint. But now Coburn was frustrated to see the studio turn away from *Loving Couples* and devote all their energy to promoting a different Shirley MacLaine movie, *A Change of Seasons* (1980), which also starred Anthony Hopkins and new star of the moment, Bo Derek.

A trip to London to see Lynsey turned out to be a setback. The cold, damp London weather and their increasingly volatile relationship only made him feel worse. Then he suffered another emotional blow with the passing of his friend Steve McQueen at the far too young age of fifty. Coburn did what he had always done and buried himself in his work. He was shooting *Looker* at the time, another prescient sci-fi picture written and directed by Michael Crichton.

In *Looker* a villainous corporation was scanning women who had been made perfect by micro-surgery, using these resultant CG images instead of actors, then murdering the women, apparently rather than paying them royalties, or to keep them silent, or . . . It was a bit confusing. The movie was technologically extraordinary because they actually did scan and re-create digital renditions of some of the actors and used the CGI alongside live action in the visual effects of the film. This was about eight months before *Tron* (1982) was released and claimed the title of the first film that mixed live action with computer-generated visuals.

At first everyone had high hopes for *Looker*. It was Coburn's first major outing in the pedestrian role that he would later come to call the man in the suit. He made the best of it in the publicity, saying, "The character's obsessed with power, although he doesn't view it that way. He feels that everything he does, up to and including murder, is justified because it's done in a righteous cause."[7]

Unfortunately, *Looker* was another box office disaster. One review called it "a confused, illogical movie . . . an illegitimate tenth cousin of both *Body Snatchers*."[8] Crichton unloaded his frustration about the process of making

Looker in a *Starlog* magazine interview, calling the whole experience "very unhappy," beginning in preproduction with the Ladd Company. "It was the most miserable movie I was ever on in my life. Day-after-day, it was *horrible*! It was difficult while I was shooting and it was difficult before I began. . . . 'Looker' was bought as a sexy comedy and somehow it became clear that the studio really wanted a suspense picture. . . . The movie turned out to be what nobody wanted."[9]

Crichton and Coburn shared equal disdain for many of the powers that be in the film industry. They could commiserate together about the stupidity around them. Crichton said, "The reality of the movie business is that it generates enormous amounts of money. . . . Because it is so lucrative, real idiots, *real* idiots, people-who-can't-park-their-car idiots, *idiots*, can survive and even *thrive*. Moviemaking is an industry which has more than its share of profoundly stupid people."

Coburn spoke derisively in the press as well, saying that viewers felt confused by the story because the editing "eliminated the entire justification for the film. . . . I thought a reel was missing."[10] Oddly he was convinced that it was intentional sabotage because the "villains' motivation for their dirty work . . . was their desire to manipulate the media, and thus manipulate the presidency."[11] He suspected that somebody had ordered the filmmakers to eliminate the scenes that might have reflected badly on the real presidency.

He and Lynsey de Paul had ended their relationship just after the *Looker* shoot and before the *High Risk* publicity tour commenced in May of 1981, and she returned to London permanently. Rob Harabedian was sorry to see her go, saying, "Lynsey was another one of the people that I really liked. She wanted things that Jim couldn't give her, namely, a family and marriage. I was sad when she left, and so was Jim."[12]

Coburn lived a bachelor life for a few years, fending off the arthritis as best he could. He still suffered from pain caused by the joint damage. "So I went through every possible kind of healing, from hands-on healing, to acupuncture, herbal treatments, hot oils, you name it, I did it. Some of it worked for a while, but you have to do it five times a week. Murray Korngold was an acupuncturist and took me through this time."[13]

The problem with combining many treatments and modalities is that if one or two help, then it can appear that they are all working equally well. Coburn had a searching attitude and, having felt let down by contemporary medicine, a predisposition to alternative philosophies. He was willing to try just about anything.

He and Messa would drive out to a clinic in Monrovia four times a week, where an electrical engineer named Evans Rapsomanikis had invented an electromagnetic machine, which he claimed combined the pain relief effects of a TENS (Transcutaneous Electrical Nerve Stimulation) unit, which causes a tingling sensation in the skin, with alleged curative properties of magnetic fields. He charged between $150 and $200 per session of sitting in the chair. Coburn believed something was happening and felt more optimistic. The Food and Drug Administration (FDA) eventually confiscated Rapsomanikis's machines, and he fled to London to avoid lawsuits, where he set up another clinic. Coburn would visit Rapsomanikis there and take these treatments, believing they revitalized him. He continued to consider Rapsomanikis a friend and to believe that he was being wrongfully persecuted by the FDA and big pharma until the practitioner's death in 2001.

Meanwhile at home he also used cannabis, as usual, and snorted cocaine for pain relief, two substances that do have documented physiological effects, for good or ill. "I knew cocaine was probably terrible, but it made me feel good while I was doing it. I stopped when it stopped making me feel good." One of the known side effects of cocaine is an increase in paranoia, which may have explained some of his beliefs about the fate of *Looker*.

Coburn's past and recent films were still very visible and finding an audience on television. He was still a name brand, still popular. His Schlitz Light commercials showed a mature yet hip guy in his prime. Outside of commercials work, it was frustrating to be offered roles simply for his name recognition, often as the best thing in a middling product.

In early 1981 he felt well enough to accept some more TV work, despite considering it "no fun." He was still skeptical about the quality of television in general but had "come to the conclusion that it's foolish to limit activities to any one desire."[14] He was to be the narrator of a new documentary series, *Escape*, that would retell real-life stories of various escapes. The pilot (and only) episode was "Midnight Express," a story that had already been made famous by the gritty 1978 movie of the same name. At the same time, Coburn joined the cast of another high-profile miniseries, a new adaptation of *Valley of the Dolls*, updated and moved from the world of New York theater to Hollywood.[15]

Today's audiences might find the miniseries slow paced. Coburn's character spent a good deal of his screen time in his office, which suffered from remarkably lousy, uneven lighting. He was quite thin, but his hands were not yet visibly deformed, and his delivery was natural and unforced. Perhaps that was partly because he wrote much of his own dialogue.

In one interview he related that he liked his character because "it gave me a chance to play a studio head, the way a studio head should be."[16] He claimed that he based his characterization on Darryl F. Zanuck, "a filmmaker, not just a money maker." Zanuck's philosophy was that you make money in order to make more movies to transport the audience, "giving them the impressions they are starved for. And getting rid of that television crap that puts them in a hypnotic state." Coburn also spoke about the straightforward nature of his process, which combined his greatest influences—George Gurdjieff, P. D. Ouspensky, and Stella Adler.

"I take in all the impressions and information [about the character]. And when the time comes for action, I just let it go. It's jazz acting. It's like when Sarah Vaughn sings a song. She sings the lyrics, but she doesn't sing it exactly the way it was written. It bears her style. That's the way it is with roles. Each character has a style. Once you find out the character's style it becomes really simple.... You don't think about it. You just let it flow."

Valley of the Dolls aired on CBS in October, to mixed reviews. Then Coburn played himself in a cameo for his buddy Lee Majors's new series about a Hollywood stuntman, *The Fall Guy*. He was also cast as a host for the unfortunately short-lived sci-fi anthology series *Darkroom*.

Initially he had high hopes for the show, saying, "It's in my contract that if I want to act in some of them and direct some of them I can do that too. I may direct."[17] He enjoyed that he could do all his work for a full season in one week and, he says, "they'll come to wherever I'm working to do them too." But he soon returned to his dismissive attitude toward television when the show was axed, as usual calling the producers amateurs "selling junk," and saying the show "has been the victim of executive diddling" in several interviews. It had a bad time slot opposite the number one rated *Dallas*, and ABC often revealed spoilers in the advertising trailers, which undoubtedly contributed to the lack of viewers for the series.

With this string of flops and disappointments, this time period was Coburn's first low point both professionally and physically. His physical pain and debilitation certainly sidelined him from many roles. Furthermore, in some projects, he was already playing the elder man character, or cameo roles that belied his age—but he was only in his early fifties, prematurely completely silver haired. On top of that, his continual public complaints about the people running the studios surely contributed to the film work drying up. Despite his spiritual studies, he could not yet see that his attention to negative impressions could be reinforcing the negativity in his life at the time.

He was still in denial about the extent of his hurt and internalized anger at Beverly, still refusing to acknowledge her past contributions to his rise to stardom. There had been a time when he chose his projects based on the whole package, especially the character he would play, the whole script beyond his own scenes, and the director. He had always enjoyed being part of the process of honing the screenplay to his strengths, relishing dialogue, offering ideas for casting, and being the leader of the ensemble. Beverly had been a trusted adviser and part of the behind-the-scenes schmoozing, net-working, and deal making that helped create Coburn's opportunities. Beverly had always sat in on meetings with directors and producers, contributing ideas and astute opinions.

Now rather than take stock of his own choices, in terms of the scripts he was accepting, he turned his disappointment outward to blame the studios, the publicists, the moneymen, or the editors for the flops. Then as soon as he started working somewhat regularly in television, he switched his criticism to the network executives. His absolute professionalism, preparedness, and work ethic on the set were never in question. But the press loved that he was outspoken, and that coverage may have lengthened his professional sojourn in the TV doldrums. It was not until later that he accepted the connection between his negative emotions and his physical health. Gurdjieff and Ouspensky would have called that the process of awakening.

Coburn was always grateful to his friends in this low time of his life—to Murray Korngold and to Frank Messa, for being supportive. He had the ability to turn professional colleagues into friends, time and time again. He credited Rob Harabedian with "saving [his] ass" and his finances, and his commercials agent, Elizabeth Dalling, for keeping him working in voice-overs for "cakes and ales."[18] Dalling was the first agent to have the audacious idea of using established U.S. stars in overseas advertising campaigns. "James was not my first famous client, but he and I had a unique relationship over twenty-five years. We became close friends and confidants. He was a mentor, and we both respected each other. He was an extraordinary man, a true star. He was a teacher."[19]

Coburn often said he owed his life to his actor friend R. G. Armstrong, who came to the house almost daily for a period of many months to give him vigorous full-body massages. "He gave me this deep-tissue treatment and kept me from turning totally to stone. He called it the 'sciatic treatment' that he learned from some lady in Minnesota. He worked on my limbs. He was the only guy I know of that did that. He used aloe vera on the skin—the towels were messed up from the aloe vera. When they went into the dryer, they blew it up. Well, we won't use those towels anymore! Part of it was done on a table, part on the chair, up and down the back. He worked on all the organs, the kidneys, liver, spleen, colon, stomach. He kept things flowing."[20]

The whole time Armstrong was doing the massages, he and Coburn also worked together on a couple of scripts. One was "Machipu," an adventure story about diving into a seemingly extinct volcano to find a whole civilization there. The other was written with a third writer, character actor Rockne Tarkington; it was a biographical tale about Tarkington's youth in Junction City, Kansas, called "Springtime in Junk Town." Coburn considered Tarkington "a real badass." They had first met on *Major Dundee* and worked together more recently on *The Baltimore Bullet*. Tarkington would go on to act in one of Stewart Raffill's more successful films, *The Ice Pirates* (1984).

In addition Messa came up with another way to keep Coburn moving. He installed a pool table in the glass solarium. "Every day he played pool with the guys that were there. And we'd bet on nine ball. You can't be screwing around. You can't make believe you're holding your stick. You've got to hold your stick. You can't be saying, 'Oh, my back hurts, my fingers are sore—which he would never do because of his pride. Anyone who's got arthritis, I say, play pool because it's got all exercises in your hand, stroking, your arm, everything. There was always guys there. It was like a pool hall, only it never got that raunchy. We'd smoke a couple of doobies, everybody got loose, drank a little bit, nobody got drunk. We drank reasonably, but most of it was very serious. The main game we were very serious about was nine ball.

"You have to put all the balls in the pockets in rotation, and when you're all done, you sink the nine ball. And then we made up our own games that were variations of snooker where you had to call the shot and call how many times you were going to bounce it off the rail. Not just slam it and watch it go around and then in there. . . . And if you don't do that shot, then you scratched.

"It was a kind of mental thing, but most of it was for him to play. He liked it to such a degree that oftentimes after everybody left, it would just be the two of us, and we would play up to nine thirty, ten o'clock. Hitting the balls around, having a grand old time, listening to jazz, not even thinking about his arthritis. He had to keep practicing, because every time he held that cue, stroked that thing back, it was all exercise for his muscles. And he got better and better. So that was the strategy."[21]

When he could, Coburn liked to spend winters somewhere warm, like the French Riviera. In the fall of 1981, he had several weddings to attend before his trip that year. Lisa married successful producer Robert Levy on September 27, beside the giant Buddha head at the Tower Road house. There was the holiday wedding of Coburn's actor friend Robert Culp in Beverly Hills. And fellow actress Josette Banzet, who had become a close friend, married pop star Tommy Roe, on December 13, 1981. "We went on our honeymoon to Paris and the South of France. We decided to go to this restaurant that I used to go to with my family when I was little. We walked in—they knew me since I was a child. We had a great table inside. I went out to the bathroom.

"On my way back, I see James at the bar. He sees me and I said, 'What are you doing here?' and he said, 'What are you doing here?' and I said, 'I'm on my honeymoon.' He said, 'Where's Tommy?' and I said, 'In the dining room,' and then he said, 'Well, come on. Let's go, baby.' We walked in—the room was very bright.

"And everybody stopped to stare. The whole room became completely mute. It was amazing, the people. They stopped talking; they stopped eating. Some of them had their fork in their hand."[22]

Despite this proof of his continuing ability to turn heads, Coburn's dramatic efforts were few for a couple years after *Looker*. He was reunited with the director of *The Dain Curse* for the potboiler miniseries *Malibu*, which gave him a minor publicity boost.[23]

He still looked virile and charismatic hosting *Saturday Night Live* in February 1982, joking about his Schlitz Light commercials with the young Eddie Murphy and spoofing his own persona in a slightly uncomfortable skit with a chimpanzee. His *Muppet Show* episode, where he taught the character Animal how to meditate, was so popular that it was rerun several times over the course of the eighties. But most of his public appearances were guest star gigs like Bob Hope's *All-Star Birthday Party at Annapolis*, where everyone, including the public audience, soldiered on through two days of outdoor taping drenched by intermittent rainstorms. He also participated in the Los Angeles portion of a children's charity telethon for Marie Osmond and staffed the phones for the DGA when a strike was being debated. Coburn still hit up Merv Griffin and similar talk shows when he had a TV movie to promote, even encouraging Merv to get the same allergy test he had. Merv apparently did so and subsequently trimmed about fifty pounds.

Coburn went to the UK and worked on a strange and rarely seen autobiographical digital art piece called *Digital Dreams* with former Rolling Stone Bill Wyman. He was enough of a heartthrob to be on the cover of the British women's magazine *Woman's Own* in September 1982, looking relaxed, "finding joy in every day," and claiming to enjoy not being in a serious relationship: "It's great not having a woman around." At the time he said, "Making anything permanent, rigid, is nonsense. The best way to kill a good relationship is marriage."[24]

However, he *did* have a woman around. Sometime in the fall of 1982, he met a young dancer from New York named Lisa Alexander. He took her to glamorous Hollywood events, around the country when he was working, to Europe for film festivals, and to Australia. She was pretty and lively, and he found her sweet and "kind of naive too.... Lisa Alexander was my girlfriend for about six years. She was well educated and a writer. She wrote—she wanted to write screenplays."[25]

It was she who, a few years later, encouraged Coburn to option the recent Marion Zimmer Bradley best-selling fantasy book *The Mists of Avalon*. For the next decade, this project was a constant underlying rumble, as he, Alexander, later his wife Paula, and a succession of writers tried to wrestle the lengthy and detailed book into a screenplay format. He often spoke of the project as in development, with the idea that he would take on the part of Merlin while Alexander was set to produce the film for Panpiper.

Messa saw that his friend enjoyed being a mentor to "this cute little thing."[26] He says, "They had already talked about how so many years in the future, they were going to part company because he was so much older than her." Coburn had already made up his mind that he would never father more children and made that clear to his new girlfriend. For the time being, they were happy together. Eventually the relationship got more serious, and she moved into the Hollyline house.

Messa noticed that Alexander did not appreciate the pool-playing therapy. "When Lisa finally got in there, she didn't like that. She was intimidated by what she called the boys club. And slowly, slowly forced the pool table back into storage, and that's where it went. So there was no more pool. There was just Lisa, with her ambitions and whatever she wanted to do."

At this point, for insurance purposes if nothing else, Coburn had to keep up the appearance that his arthritis was under control, if not absolutely cured, by the regimen of dietary restrictions, acupuncture, massage, and other alternative medical treatments he was combining. It was around this time that he was referred to Dr. Ronald Lawrence, who was an MD interested in holistic medicine.

"We sat down and talked for an hour in his little room in Agoura, getting to know each other. Just jiving, talking about things, what I wanted. He was taking notes. He was truly a Renaissance man. He knows how to do everything, from acupuncture, chiropractic, homeopath, hypnotist, a lay minister—he graduated from law school, then went into medicine. He was the doctor on two Everest climbs, has run more marathons than any man in the world. A pretty extraordinary guy. He has many people who just love him who are herbologists, and so on. He has written all of these books on pain. We have dinner and carry on. We have a lot to share and get together frequently as friends. Dr. Lawrence got me to the point where I could work because I couldn't do it. I had to turn work down."[27]

Together they fine-tuned Coburn's regimen of pain meds and vitamin supplements and moderated his diet. He was especially encouraged to steer clear of nightshade foods, which include tomatoes and eggplant. He started feeling and looking better.

In 1983 he began a highly lucrative long-term commercial print and TV campaign in Japan. The commercials were shot both in Japan and in California and began broadcasting in October. The Speak Lark ads played on his image. The first few had him speaking a few sentences in Japanese, which he had to learn phonetically, and displayed his playboy/movie star persona. Soon the ads morphed into a series of mini-narratives with Coburn as a suave spy character, mirroring the immense popularity of James Bond types in Japan. His only dialogue became the words "Speak Lark," usually uttered as a password or code for entry.[28]

He was chosen after market research showed him to have a very high recognition factor as masculine, strong, and smooth among the key demographic of young Japanese men, a whopping 63 percent of whom were smokers in the early 1980s. It was a highly successful campaign, which was nice for Coburn but perhaps not for the health of young Japanese men. The series was immensely popular, intentionally giving the impression to the Japanese that Lark, a Philip Morris brand, was a top-selling brand in the United States. (It wasn't.)

"Coburn was considered appropriate for Lark by about four out of five respondents because he 'fits the image,' 'projects a sober/adult air' and 'is foreign and goes with foreign cigarettes.' Coburn also comes across as 'likable,' 'dynamic,' 'smart and elegant,' 'polished and manly'—in short 'a strong personality.'"[29]

Messa remembers how extremely respectful the Japanese businessmen were toward him when they visited the Hollyline house to discuss the promotions: "They had a cigarette lighter that they wanted Jim to put his signature on, which he did. There's a few of those still around. I don't know where they all are. They were collector's items. These guys came over, and they had such respect for James Coburn. They would back into themselves acknowledging him. Every time he stood up, it was amazing to see the amount of respect that the Japanese had for him. I was there when he went to Japan. He got me a Shakuhachi flute, made by one of the living legends of Japan. There is so much respect for Jim in Japan that he just had to make the statement, 'I'm looking for Shakuhachi, the flute,' and they immediately took him right down to the best flute maker in Japan. He got three of them, one for me and two for himself, a bigger one and a smaller one."[30]

Meanwhile Coburn's past theatrical movies continued to be seen on both the subscriber services like HBO and on network television, but now mostly very late at night, and mostly on the weekends. New shows he did, such as *Draw!*, filmed in Canada for HBO, and *Faerie Tale Theatre*, were for made for television. It was like his worst nightmare come true—trapped back in the "inferior" medium of his youth and given no chances to direct either. However, he at least made a reasonable living from numerous residuals and the plethora of voice-over work—both narrations and commercials for everything from motorcycles and cars to a steakhouse and a cinema chain—that Elizabeth Dalling assiduously procured for him. He was the elegant face of International Master Charge, as MasterCard was then called, in a long-running series of ads.

Despite being made for cable, the comic western *Draw!* was well received and enjoyed by many. Kirk Douglas portrays an aging but still vital gunfighter who begins the movie by saving a runaway stagecoach, in classic fashion. Then in the supposedly law-abiding town of the movie setting, he wins a large pot in a poker game, drawing the ire of the local spoiled rich boy. After complications involving a gunfight (self-defense), he holes up in a hotel room with a woman hostage, who soon becomes more than a friend. Coburn plays a retired sheriff, still a dead shot, who is unwillingly drawn into the issue as the only person able to outgun "Handsome Harry." He describes his character as a lawman who "has traded his badge for a bottle."[31]

The sweet little film played on many conventions of the genre, with lighthearted homage to tropes like the saloon piano (a player piano) and the standoff in the main street. However, it also turned some on their head, particularly in the refreshing portrayal of strong female characters. There was a nice air of gentle nostalgia about seeing two grand old men of cinema westerns illuminating the screen together. The film shot in Canada with Coburn doing his supporting role in early December 1983. He was well enough to actually dismount his horse on camera.

Even while he was working through his pain, he had the additional distress of his mother's declining health. Mylet had been diagnosed with breast cancer. "My mother found a lump in her breast, and this doctor naturally wanted to remove it. I wanted her to please forget about it. 'Don't do it, Mom.' But she said, 'No, I have to have something done about it.' So she went and had it cut, and the cancer spread immediately, and got into her lymph glands, then into her bones, and she was sore and achy, and God, she just went through misery the last three years of her life."[32]

In between his travels and work, he had tried to be an attentive son. He and Messa periodically drove to Garden Grove, where she lived in the last home Coburn had bought for his parents. "Frank and I would go down and take her out to Denny's or one of those places. He's talkative, and he never had a problem getting her into conversation. She loved him. My mother always loved that I was an actor. We'd walk in there, and the first thing she would say is, 'Do you know who he is? Well, he's my son, and he's a famous movie actor, James Coburn,' loud enough for everybody in the fucking restaurant to hear. I'd say, 'Mom, shut up. Don't ever say that.' And she would say, 'Why not? You're my son and I love you, and I want everyone to know.' Mom was a Scorpio.

"She was getting angry and nasty toward the end. That wasn't her personality—she doesn't just get nasty. We had a home help nurse turn up who didn't do her job—we had to change her out. Then we put Mom in the hospital. The doctor called me and told me she was in a kind of coma. 'We can take her off the machine.' Why suffer? I went up there, and she was in her death rattle. And I told her to just let go. I said, 'Mom, just let go. Everything's okay. It's going to be better, wherever you are going to be. Just let go. I love you.' I kissed her, and by the time I got home, I got the call from the doctor that she had died. I'm glad I did that. I didn't think she knew I was there, but something knew, and I could see that she was struggling. We had that last moment together. We shared the first day of my life and the last of hers."

That last day was February 20, 1984. By chance, Rob Harabedian was with Coburn that evening. "First and I think the only time I had ever seen Jim cry. It was a very sad chapter in his life because he was alone, living in Sherman Oaks. I met Mylet several times when I was with Jim. She was a sweet lady. She absolutely was proud of him."[33]

Despite mourning, Coburn continued to work. The TV movie *Sins of the Father* was a locally shot production, a snappily paced romantic drama. It was a starring role, portraying a charismatic corporation lawyer of questionable ethics, ruthless, with a yen for his young protégé. The story line feels dated today, but he gave a believable performance. He seemed to be moving smoothly and with greater ease, despite some visible changes in his hands. One source in the production noted that it had been tough to get him for the part, and his fee was a substantial $250,000. The reviewers, like Judy Flander, considered the production reasonably enjoyable escapist stuff, saying, "The movie really doesn't have a lot to say about anything, but it is awfully well-done."[34]

Coburn spent time in Canada in November, reunited with Richard Harris and Lindsay Wagner for the low-budget TV movie *Martin's Day*. In this movie Harris portrays a disturbed criminal who escapes from prison by setting himself on fire. He kidnaps and then develops a sweet relationship with a little boy. Wagner plays the prison psychiatrist who spends most of the film trying to prevent Coburn's very straight-down-the-line police chief character from having Harris shot. Coburn spends most of his screen time in his office and the crowded police station, although he does get a little location action in near the end, swooping down in a helicopter and then clambering over some rocky ground. In one incongruous moment, he has Wagner help him to don a cardigan. The star turn is for Harris, who was fresh from playing King Arthur in the Broadway revival and world tour of the musical *Camelot*.[35] It seems likely that Coburn agreed to the gig to support his old friend, Harris, rather than for the part itself.

Then on December 28, 1984, he was saddened again by another death, that of Sam Peckinpah, at the age of fifty-nine. Hard living had finally caught up with Sam, but he had been working, prepping his next film, at the time of his passing. At the memorial Coburn spoke of the adventure of working with Sam, but he pulled out one of his favorite metaphorical phrases: "Sam took me by the hand to the cliff, pushed me over the abyss and then jumped in after me."[36]

But Coburn was more eloquent when interviewed for the Peckinpah documentary *Man of Iron*, expressing their shared philosophy about their true reality: "Those demons that existed in his personal life—they didn't seem to be real; they seemed to be more of a fantasy. His reality seemed to be making movies. The rest of it was fantasy. I feel the same way—I mean the reality is why you're working when you're making movies. Because that's the new reality. Something's being created all the time. Every day there is something new, seeing, bang—it never existed before. Life becomes a fantasy, living in the house, in Beverly Hills or Hollywood or Sherman Oaks or wherever it is, Malibu."[37]

Within a few days, he was off to Australia with Alexander, to shoot a feature film—the courtroom drama *Death of a Soldier* in Melbourne. It was based on the true story of an American soldier accused of murdering three local women in 1942. The director, Philippe Mora, became another friend. "James was a dear friend of ours for many years. We had the same great agent, Bobby Littman. He was simply brilliant in *Death of a Soldier* and wrote a key speech in it. Halfway through the shoot the real man he played showed up in Melbourne, Ira Rothgerber, and they became fast friends immediately. I got into the Academy as a young director on the strength of it. James got some great reviews."[38] The film received two Australian Film Institute nominations—Australia's equivalent of the Oscars. It was the last feature film Coburn would do for close to five years.

Now even the TV dramas dried up for Coburn. Professionally this was his lowest point. With little to do, other than Speak Lark and MasterCard commercials, a few voice-overs and narrations, and rare TV appearances as himself, Coburn spent most of the next four years traveling, including showing Alexander Kathmandu and India, the temples and art that he loved, as well as going to premieres, film festivals, and charity events. He was in London for the grand opening of his buddy Herbie Kretzmer's West End triumph, *Les Misérables*.

Then in February 1986, Coburn and Alexander were in Monaco for the Television Festival. In September they were guests at the American Film Festival in Deauville, France. He did bits on a few odd productions, such as acting in a Swedish language art film that shot in Ecuador and contributing a story to a documentary about people's experiences with reincarnation. Around this time, he also started a yearly tradition of cruising a yacht around different areas of the Mediterranean for a week or so with his new friend John Paul DeJoria, the cofounder of the Paul Mitchell hair products company. They had met when JP had visited the Hollyline house to consider buying a table carved in the form of an elephant that Coburn was selling. They hit it off, discussing spirituality, philosophy, and art. They continued taking this annual trip, without fail, for the rest of his life.

Coburn was honored by the City of Paris in November 1988, presented his award by the famous French singer and founder of disco as we know it, Regine. He returned the favor the following summer, presenting the Regine/ Veuve Clicquot Cup to the winning polo team in Bagatelle, France.

Still, it was very frustrating, not to have real work. Being a celebrity for its own sake had never been Coburn's bag. "It's so weird. I've become a celebrity not because of my sophistication but because of my body of work, so if it comes through that, it's okay. I can deal with it. But if people think I'm there just because it's a chic thing to do, to parade around and be a celebrity, I don't fancy that."[39]

In April 1989 he was interviewed by Tom Snyder for his radio show, *Sundays with Snyder*. He discussed the ongoing challenge to get *The Mists of Avalon* made, through his newest production company, Tango. But his great newfound enthusiasm was for Showscan, a new high-definition film process.[40] He was keen to promote the sci-fi short *Call from Space*, which was filmed and would be projected in the Showscan process—70-mm film at 65 frames per second. He notes that "it was a hard process to work in because it is twelve-minute reels. It requires a different technique, almost a stage technique. . . . It's like you are watching a hologram." The project was shot at MGM, but the only way anyone could see it would be to travel to Metz, France, where the film was part of a new theme park.

Tom Snyder asked Coburn about the last feature film he had made, erroneously thinking that he had retired by choice. Coburn recalled *Death of a Soldier* as his last feature, about four years earlier, and reiterated his availability for the right project.

Maybe it was just the right moment for visibility. He was cast, mostly for sentimental value, in the revisionist western actioner *Young Guns II* (1990) about Pat Garrett and Billy the Kid. He played the western equivalent of a man in a suit but did have some lines that the cognoscenti would recognize as homage to his own Pat Garrett.

By now Coburn was single again. He had been shocked to discover that Alexander was having an affair, and with one of his friends. It hurt him deeply, as Messa recalls: "They discussed [eventually separating] before anything happened. The only thing they didn't discuss was 'I'm going to betray you after a little while.' That really hurt him. I went up there and spent a couple of days with him because he was in emotionally bad straits. It was the betrayal that did it. It wasn't funny. It was a hurtful thing because he did so much for her. He took her all over the world. He educated her."[41]

Coburn's friend and manager, Hilly Elkins, noticed how distraught he was. "We watched that develop, and we watched it come apart. And we watched Jim come apart. He did not take that well. He instigated the relationship—he did not instigate the disintegration of the relationship. When that occurred, he was a very unhappy guy. He'd spend much more time at our place. He'd sleep over."[42]

Eventually he did get over his hurt, and they continued to work together on a couple of projects. He laughed, only a little wryly, about it. "She did actually fuck a friend. That was one of the reasons we declared the end of the romance. She just did it for fun. When I asked her why she did that, she responded, 'Well, it was fun.' She was young when we met. I thought I was doing great. Evidently not."[43]

Hilly and various friends occasionally tried to set Coburn up with different dates, but no one took. Josette Banzet-Roe noticed how often he was alone when he came to her charity parties or dinners. He always supported her events, either by attending or by sending over some item to be auctioned, a pair of cowboy boots from a film or a hat he had kept. Josette remembers that he'd say, "I don't want to give it away, but it's a good cause. Take it." She would always ask him if he was bringing someone, and he would always say, "No, I don't have anybody."[44]

Josette was thrilled when at last she asked the same old question, "Are you bringing someone?" and Coburn replied, "Yeah, yeah, yeah. I got somebody, and she's really something. You'll like her."

"So I'm standing there with Mayor Tom Bradley and my photographer, the film people, and all of a sudden this tall, tall James—he always stood above people because he was so tall—and he's got this little dark-haired girl next to him. And he looked at me, and he says, 'Hi, baby.' And he picks me up in the air, then puts me down like he always did, and goes back to this little girl, beautiful girl next to him, and he puts his arm around her, and he says with great pride, 'This is Paula.'

"I went to her, I put my arms around her. There was something in me that said, 'This is the right thing.' I put my arms around her, and we held it. We didn't speak. And I looked up, and I said, 'That's it, Jim. Don't look anymore.'"

13

The Mosaic That You're Putting Together

When you're dealing with it on a second-to-second basis, it's not a project. It's coming to terms with it second by second by second. In a moment there's no ticktock, ticktock. There's just whoosh. You gotta have technique. The trick and also the secret of acting is not to give it away. You see them playing the ending before the end. You save it, and that's where the power is, otherwise you're punching the air out of the balloon and it pops. It's better when you can do it without words.

—JAMES COBURN, 2002

Paula Murad was born in 1955 in Jamaica. When she was just a toddler, her parents brought the family, including her two sisters and two brothers, to Cleveland, Ohio. Her father, Leroy Murad, was a law professor.

According to Josette, Paula's relationship with her family was strained. "Her mother died young, and she wasn't talking to her father very much. Her brothers and sisters were always asking for something, even before she met James. And then after, it was worse. So she had a problem with them."[1]

Paula yearned for something more than a suburban life. She was smart and pretty, and she started to dream of an acting career. In the mideighties she moved to Washington DC where she worked as a TV host, eventually hosting a syndicated television show called *Real Estate Digest*, produced by the Northern Virginia Association of Realtors, "a magazine style collection of features and listings, used by a number of stations nationwide."[2]

Paula had been in a serious relationship for about five years. The couple had often joined their friends Lynda Lager (now Erkiletian) and her husband on outings and vacation trips. Lynda described Paula as "always so giving, always supportive, always putting herself second in the relationship."[3] Paula had hoped to be married by now and to start a family. When it became painfully clear that the relationship was never going to move forward to the next level, she "finally chose to put herself first." She decided to do what she had always wanted, which was to try her luck as an actor in Los Angeles. She packed up everything and drove alone across the country.

In 1990 she was living in a little place in Bel Air and working as a DJ for parties.[4] During Carnaval, in mid-February, the Hollywood Palladium was holding its annual lambada contest and dance. Paula loved to dance, so when she was invited along by an acquaintance, she gladly accepted.

Meanwhile Coburn's lifelong friend Pete Kameron and Red Veniero, owner of the Nucleus Nuance jazz nightclub and organic food restaurant, persuaded him to come out that night. They had noticed that their friend had been a little down in the long months since his breakup with his last girlfriend. The danger was that if he became depressed, his arthritis was liable to flare up again. It would be good to get him out in the world.

The Hollywood Palladium was a beautiful old-fashioned ballroom with a gorgeous crystal chandelier and a large dance floor. It reminded Coburn of the old happy days dancing at the Rendezvous Ballroom on Balboa Island. Just like then, this place had also attracted a big crowd.

Coburn and his buddies were waiting for the side door to open, VIP access, when he noticed a beautiful girl on her way in with a group. He did not find out until later that she had also noticed a tall, attractive, silver-haired man dressed all in black, and wondered who he was.

Once inside he made his way into the VIP room. "We walked through and saw that the dancing was rather ordinary samba stuff. There wasn't anyone really exciting, and the music was okay but nothing great. We were standing drinking champagne, and I saw in the line this beautiful, dark-haired with flashing eyes, gorgeous dame looking at me, and I looked back with great 'come hither' not knowing who she was. In a few minutes, I noticed people dancing, and there she was on the dance floor, the only one who knew how to do the lambada."[5]

With more of the serendipity that ruled Coburn's life, it turned out that he knew the mystery woman's date for the event. "Unbeknownst to me, the guy she was with was a doctor. My ex-wife had sold him our Ferrari, a Lusso in excellent shape, for nothing, for $12,000 when it was worth $50,000, out of spite. He came over to speak to me, and he brought this beautiful woman with him. He introduced himself and said, 'I just wanted to thank you for selling that car to me. I still have it, and it's wonderful. Blah, blah, blah.' All the while I'm gamming at Paula, and she's looking back at me. Then the doctor says he's going to check out the dancing on the main floor, and Paula said, 'I think I'll stay behind,' to talk to me. We made conversation for a half hour or more. Then everything seemed to be kind of over. The group she came with was leaving, so I got her phone number.

"I called her the first thing the next morning. She was quite surprised, and we made a date for that night. She was just living a short distance from where I was, up the top of Bel Air. Our first date was for dinner at either Locanda Veneta or Sushiko. After that we went out every night from that point on. She just became the love of my life. She fit all the categories for me."

The biggest surprise was that Paula had no idea that the charismatic man she was attracted to, whose conversation was so fascinating, was a famous actor. It was not until she phoned Lynda back in Washington that she learned who he was. For Coburn it was a wonderful, warm feeling to be appreciated entirely for himself rather than for his place in the world. After a short time, Paula had fallen in love. As Lynda recalls, "It was the first time she was giddy. 'He's such a beautiful man. So gentle. So loving. I can't believe that he's in my life.' When had we ever seen her this happy?"[6]

Coburn had fallen in love too. He went into full-on suitor mode, wooing Paula with promises of a very comfortable lifestyle and genuine support of her acting aspirations. But first there was one important proviso. How well did they travel together?

Not long after they started dating, Coburn was invited to Italy to receive the 1990 Merit of Achievement Award, presented by a television organization in Italy. The presentation was to take place and be filmed on June 22, 1990, at Casinó Campione d'Italia, with proceeds of the event going to Variety Club of Italy—Children of Lifetime Fund. The main attraction was the hotel. The stars being honored and their plus-ones would be staying at the historic, super-luxury hotel Villa d'Este (originally called Villa Garrovo) on Lake Como.[7]

Who could fail to be dazzled by the level of luxury, sophistication, and comfort that this world-renowned hotel offered? There was even an episode of *Lifestyles of the Rich and Famous* being filmed at the hotel during the event. One of the highlights of the weekend was when fellow honoree Lynn Redgrave entertained everyone with a spot-on impersonation of the show's host, Robin Leach. In between the official festivities, Coburn and Paula shopped for gorgeous resort fashion in Milan. At the end of the evening after the awards show, everyone adjourned to the casino where the guests were provided with a five hundred–dollar stake to get started. The pair had a fantastic night and doubled their money. Army Archerd wrote in *Variety* that Coburn "delighted the Italians by recounting tales of working for Sergio Leone."[8]

The couple had a few weeks at home before Coburn was scheduled to return to Italy to begin shooting his part in the Bruce Willis–starrer *Hudson Hawk*. First they went to Rome, hot in the summer—locals with the means to do so, leave for more comfortable climates. Their first night in Rome, the couple walked the Via Veneto. "It was not like I had remembered it from the sixties, because nobody was there. It was like a ghost town, kind of like Hollywood Boulevard. The weather was nice. I don't really like Rome—I didn't like it then, and I don't like it now. The ruins are nice, and they're fun to walk through once. But that's about all you can get out of that."[9]

There was plenty of downtime between shooting his scenes and he had no particular reason to come home. Rather it was an excuse to extend his time in Europe with Paula. The couple visited London, where he was keen to introduce Paula to Evans Rapsomanikis, and another "friend and healer who was an aikido master, Tia Honsai."

Then-seventy-eight-year-old Honsai, actually a Welshman whose birth name was Ron Thatcher, was a shiatsu practitioner who had also worked with Richard Burton and, it was rumored, Ava Gardner and Ingrid Bergman.[10]

The following year, Honsai would gain some notoriety from the bemused sports press corps as the unlikely tennis coach for Björn Borg in the latter's ineffective comeback attempt.[11]

Coburn and Paula were at the Monte Carlo Country Club in Monaco on the morning of Borg's first match. They joined Borg, Honsai, and his companions (a pair of ballerinas) for brunch in the dining room. Their meal was interrupted by autograph seekers and fans—of Borg, who patiently signed all the items thrust at him. Later Coburn and Paula watched with the world as Björn Borg, tentative and outclassed by a low-ranking player, lost definitively in straight sets while his elderly "coach" visibly snoozed through most of the match. One of the errors Honsai allowed, if not encouraged, was the use of woefully outmoded wood tennis rackets. Meanwhile Borg referred to Honsai as "The Professor."

However, that was the following year, May 1991, on another vacation. The year before, they were still shooting *Hudson Hawk*. They were in Budapest by the winter, where the soundstages were freezing cold but the vodka and caviar were excellent and inexpensive. "Some of the best Italian food I had in Europe was at the Budapest restaurant called the Marco Polo."[12] Coburn and Paula eventually spent about six months traveling all over Italy and Hungary in the course of filming. "It took us that long to make the movie."[13]

Hudson Hawk fast became a debacle, with a ballooning budget and the feeling that it was something of a junket for the cast. The film was meant as an homage to detective mysteries, spy thrillers, and Hitchcock, and includes a humorous reference to the Flint movies: the tones made by the handcuffs as they locked. Coburn portrays the lead villain of the piece, George Kaplan, named of course for the nonexistent agent for whom Cary Grant was mistaken in Hitchcock's 1959 classic *North by Northwest*. Coburn did his best, playing it straight, a mixture of the self-aware irony of Derek Flint coupled with the single-minded, dangerous obsessiveness of Bus Cummings from *The Americanization of Emily*. The problems with the show were certainly not his fault.

He brought his usual steady demeanor to work. At one point he counseled Richard E. Grant, who played one of the nuttier villains and wrote about the project in his autobiography: "Amid this furore stands Flint himself, James

Coburn, as calm and collected as those car adverts for which he does the voice overs. With his voice, gallon deep, and the requisite cigar jammed into the corner of his mouth, he is as Movie-Icon-Cool as it's possible to get. Only, his hands are arthritic and he explains that the agony of this disease has kept him from working these past few years. But he is in love with Paula, who is his constant companion and as charming and drop-dead gorgeous as you'd expect of this cinematic gunslinger. Lassos the lot of us with his silvery haired CHARM.

"He and Paula take Sandra [Bernhardt] and me out for dinner and he talks me down from the hysteria of the day. 'This is a big budget movie, with big budget egos. Enjoy.' His smile widens a couple of toothy miles."[14]

Coburn seemed to think it was a case of too many cooks, as he told journalist Lowell Goldman. "There were so many creative voices, like Bruce's and Joel's, that the director Michael Lehmann, may have been a little overshadowed by the whole thing. Everybody had a different vision, especially Bruce. He's a good kid, having a good time, very creative. Whatever he does, he does with style, panache, and personality."[15]

Interviewed by the Hollywood Foreign Press for the movie, Coburn was asked where he had been for the last *eight* years, and he cited battling arthritis. His many appearances on TV and even his starring role in the 1986 Australian film *Death of a Soldier* had passed unnoticed.

He tried to steer the interview away from criticism, speaking of acting the dynamics of the scenes. In all his years acting, it was still the actual process of working in front of the camera that continued to fascinate and inspire him. He still wanted to attempt different things, spark off the other actors, and try various ways of approaching each scene. His beliefs about comedy acting had changed little.

"Comedy takes some time; it takes some cleverness; it takes a new look at something; it takes an oblique angle at life. . . . Reality would be very heightened. . . . Heightened characters. They are not caricatures. There's a difference. . . . You [show] the characters from different points of view, you get different kinds of results. . . . I mean you've taken in the impression of the script and everything, but you haven't related to anybody and it takes time, you know, for everybody to get settled in. . . . Tentativeness—by the second day you're working, something kind of clicks. . . . After that it's pretty simple and you're just playing the dynamic of it."[16]

He revealed that he did not watch dailies anymore, preferring to focus on the collaborative aspects of moviemaking. He trusted the team. "To the actor [watching dailies] doesn't matter. It really doesn't. . . . The dynamic is what you change—the director or producer or somebody will tell you about that. If you're wearing the wrong color makeup, the makeup man will change that, or you know the dresser will fix a little bit as necessary and as far as planning it, you have to do it yourself anyway. . . . You carry it around in the back of your head, of the kind of mosaic that you're putting together."

Given how long the shoot was, it was quite a mosaic that he had to carry around.

Coburn and Paula spent time in Portofino, in the north of Italy, and drove south to the Amalfi Coast, stopping in Capri. The beautiful trip "gave us plenty of time to get to know each other."[17]

Once they got back to the United States, Paula immediately moved into the house on Hollyline, where they would stay until the Northridge earthquake in 1994. Lynda was charmed when she visited from DC. "I walked up the long, long driveway and met Jim and Rob Harabedian in the dining room. When I would visit, Jim was always very casually dressed, laid back. He answered the door with bed head. He was really down to earth."[18]

He introduced his new lady to his kids. Lisa was relieved that at least Paula was a few months older than she was herself. She says, "I told Dad, 'Well, she brings the party with her,' and he replied, 'No, she is the party.'"[19]

Coburn adds, "Paula always chided me for never ever proposing. It just seemed it was time to hook up. I was a little skeptical because I was nearly thirty years older than she was, but that didn't seem to matter then to her. I kept saying, 'You're not thinking this through clearly, baby. What's going to happen down the line? You're going to be hooked up with an old man.' She didn't seem to mind, but then she's never thought things through clearly anyway. She doesn't have to. She's a girl of the moment."[20]

He was wrong. Paula Murad had thought it through, carefully. The greatest sticking point in her mind was Coburn's absolute insistence that there be no children. Despite her troubled relationships with her siblings, she believed in putting family first and had always thought that children would be a part of her future. In the end she chose love ahead of children and directed her maternal instincts toward her niece and toward ensuring that her husband reconnected with his grown children.

Her intentions were good, but the results were not always positive. Coburn was growing increasingly curmudgeonly when the topic was children. Just as when he had been a young man, he didn't really appreciate having youngsters around, neither his grandchildren nor Paula's baby niece. "Having a baby in the house is really a drag. I can't stand having babies around mewling and puking and crying and all that crap. I only started relating to my children when they got about fourteen."

He was pleased to support Paula in her acting aspirations though. He encouraged her to take classes if she wished and to work with Josette. "She knew she wanted to be an actress," Josette says.[21] "Jim warned her that this town is very rough and the only one you can trust is Josette. She would come here, and we would work on scenes. Because Jim said to her, 'I can't help you. If I tell you things, you won't listen. The one you should go to is Josette. You should listen to her. She had plenty of hours with Stella Adler.'

"So she would come here, like a sweet little girl. We started to do scenes together. Then we went to a studio in Hollywood. We did a scene for this woman four or five times. I said to Paula, 'This is weird. This woman finds something wrong each time.' I found out later that the teacher had a thing against me because I was a Stella Adler person." By now Paula and Josette had become friends and had a standing weekly appointment to see a movie and have lunch in Beverly Hills, whenever both were in town.

Most of the time life settled into the same routine that had been established from the very beginning. The couple spent a good part of their time traveling both in the United States and abroad between Coburn's work commitments. He had made the last of his lucrative Japanese Speak Lark commercials in 1990 and continued to do numerous voice-over and narration jobs, including being the "Like a rock" voice of Chevy trucks and voicing an ongoing featured villain in the award-winning children's animated TV series for TBS *Captain Planet and the Planeteers*, Looten Plunder.

Frank Messa would often accompany Coburn to the tapings. "I went to some voice-overs, which was always fascinating. He'd sit there, and he was so good. He'd say the line. Then he'd say the line again. Then he'd say the line again, like five different times, and each one was different—had a different emphasis, had a different connotation, had a different voice, had a different tempo in his voice. I swear to God, I'll hear some of those little advertisements—not anymore, but I used to—and I'll go, 'Whoa, that was Jim's second take of the first one.' They just used it in a different position, but it wasn't a new person."[22]

Most of the films he was offered around this time were more of the same hurried, formulaic, made-for-TV fare, or what used to be called direct-to-video. At that time the ubiquity of cable was relatively new, satellite was in its infancy, and online streaming was the stuff of science fiction. Content-hungry consumers, especially in the international market, were keen to rent VHS videos and then an eyeblink later, DVDs for their viewing at home. There was a relatively thriving low-budget indie filmmaking community working around Los Angeles, producing what was in effect the equivalent of the old studio B pictures. At this point Coburn was still primarily shooting and recording locally.

It felt like his career had gone full circle and he had returned to playing the kind of standard supporting role that had started his career, rather than the lead. It got to the point that when asked who he was playing in a movie, he would answer, with a shrug, "The usual character—the man in the suit."

In the meantime he and Paula continued to soldier on reworking *The Mists of Avalon*. Eventually the whole project was sold to a German company and shot as a miniseries in Europe. Coburn retained executive producer credit but had no further creative input. The series went on to be a ratings success and to be nominated for a Golden Globe and several Emmys, winning a Primetime Emmy for Outstanding Makeup.

Coburn also filmed the pilot for what would have been a private detective procedural series with the rather appropriate name of *Silverfox*, which wasn't picked up but was released as a TV movie.

More memorable was the production of *Crash Landing: The Rescue of Flight 232*, aka *A Thousand Heroes*, the true story about the crash of a

DC-10 and the subsequent quick actions of the local rescue personnel, whose preparedness saved many lives. The story was told in a naturalistic, straightforward style, which made it remarkably suspenseful. The rescue activity was shown in forty-six minutes, close to real time, and the aftermath was genuinely moving. Coburn was happy to be reunited yet again with his ofttimes costar Charlton Heston, who played the pilot. The movie was filmed in and around Sioux City, Iowa, near the actual location of the crash, very close to Laurel, Nebraska.

Coburn and Paula flew into the Sioux City airport, where he was surprised to find a crowd awaiting them. "When we arrived, a big contingent of people from Laurel showed up at the airport to shake my hand. I was the only celebrity that ever came out of Laurel, Nebraska."[23]

One of the people in the crowd was Marian Mallat, formerly Beebee, Coburn's childhood friend, who made the trek from Omaha where she now lived. It was an emotional meeting. "He was so respectful to me that night. I remember he kind of reprimanded that reporter who tried to talk to him. He said, 'I'm visiting with my friend Marian. Step back.' I was kind of impressed by that because I hadn't seen him in a long, long time. But when I mentioned where we played ball on Winnie Burn's lot, he said, 'Oh yes. We played softball all the time.'"[24]

The folks from Laurel had been disappointed that their most famous son didn't come to the city for its seventy-fifth anniversary celebration in 1968, and again hoped that he would visit this trip as part of the centenary celebrations. Since the location was only forty-two miles from Laurel, Coburn and Paula decided to drive down there on the company rest day. "We set out specially to go there." Coburn was interested to see "what was left of my five- and twelve-year-old impressions."[25] Fate intervened.

The couple set off after breakfast in a rented car, driving along country roads through the farmland of gentle rolling hills, largely fields of alfalfa and pasture. "There's not many roads that go there." After a while the rural roads all started looking very much the same. They passed a sign that read "Laurel 12 miles." They knew they were close.

"But we couldn't find it. It was like it disappeared. It was the strangest thing. We drove all around the area. I never got to it. Very strange. We asked everybody, and they would point us in a direction; we'd go in that direction. We drove through it or around it, but we couldn't find it."

They were even pulled over by a highway patrol officer. "He had a nice, starched khaki uniform on, with a big badge." Coburn didn't think he had been driving particularly fast. "The officer who stopped us asked me, 'Do you know how fast you were going?' I answered, 'Well, I think I was doing around 45 miles per hour, that's all.' 'That's all? You're in a twenty-five-mile-per-hour zone.' 'This is the country, for Chrissakes. What do you mean twenty-five miles per hour?' After a while he finally recognized me and asked me where I was from. 'I'm from California where, if we had a road like this, we'd be driving ninety miles per hour and be very safe.'"

This was a world and another era away from the Côte d'Azur. Despite recognizing the actor, the officer still gave him the ticket.

Coburn told him that they were looking for Laurel. It turned out it was back about forty miles the way they had come. They were almost back to Sioux City, and it was getting late. They decided they had to give up and return for the sake of the early call the next morning. He never did have another chance to visit Laurel during that short, intense shoot. But it was not for lack of trying.

Apart from the strange day driving the rural back roads, he had a good experience working on *Crash Landing*. It was well received. In an interview promoting the work, he described it as cathartic, "kind of a purging for the ones who were there."[26] His driver on the film was the actual person Coburn was portraying, former fire chief Jim Hathaway.

"He was invaluable, a really wonderful, sharp guy. Knowing his reactions to the incidents and [having] him explain to me exactly what did take place, was enormously helpful. We didn't portray the actuality involved, since it's a dramatic piece but [as an actor], you still key in on certain truths. I've learned a long time ago that when you play a rodeo rider, you don't play 'a rodeo rider'—you play a person who rides in the rodeo."

Crash Landing was also nominated for three Emmys, winning one for Outstanding Sound Editing.

Straight after this, Coburn was cast as a series regular on the short-lived drama *The Fifth Corner*. Conceived in the Jason Bourne mold, it was about an amnesiac agent trying to discover his history. Coburn played the mysterious and sinister billionaire who seemed to have the answers—that is to say, the man in the suit. The series folded after only a few episodes, freeing Coburn to costar in another standout from this period, the "tongue twisting, brain teasing satire" *Mastergate*, made for rising cable network Showtime.[27]

The premium cable giants were relatively new but would soon gain reputations for making high-quality, higher-budget, audacious productions. They featured provocative stories, spectacular action, daring visuals, and stronger language than the free broadcast networks are permitted by the Federal Communications Commission (FCC) and their sponsors.

This production was a timely political satire depicting the hearings around a fictional scandal similar to the Iran-Contra affair. *Mastergate* lives squarely in the same bailiwick as *The President's Analyst* and *The Americanization of Emily*. It shot in downtown Los Angeles in the Emerald ballroom at the Biltmore Hotel, which was transformed into a Washington DC courtroom, making it an easy commute for Coburn.

The dialogue was not easy. As reviewer Harvey Solomon writes, "Echoing the playwright's emphasis on language, Coburn has nearly 20 pages of doublespeak dialogue. In full military uniform with his chest dripping with ribbons and medals, he struts erectly through the adjoining waiting room while puffing on a long cigar. During a break he said, 'If you miss an "and" or a "but" or a "which" or a "who" it throws it off just a little bit. Then pretty soon it wobbles like a top and you get all off and you have to start all over again.'"[28]

It got many great reviews including from Tom Shales at the *Washington Post*. "It seems those rascals at the CIA have been diverting funds to central American insurgents via a phony movie studio known as Monster Pictures Inc. MPI pretended to be making an $80 million war epic but when the budget swelled to $13 billion even a tax-and-spend Congress got suspicious. . . . A festival of doubletalk and triplespeak, gobbledygook and rigmarole, mixed metaphors and malaprops, stonewalling and buckpassing. . . . You'll roar."[29]

During this time Coburn's movies from the sixties, seventies, and early eighties still regularly appeared on TV schedules. Some of his TV work appeared in syndication and as reruns. Fans were still curious about him.

The publicity for various movies focused on the idea of a comeback, with the estimates of the time that he had been "gone" ranging from a few years to ten. Actually, while his main income still came from his voice and commercial work, other than those few months in 1982 to 1983 when he was frozen, and the drought of 1986 to 1989, he had continued to work. But they were small projects, low-budget independent movies, and guest parts in TV episodes, so they lacked the high profile of something like *Hudson Hawk*, and people didn't notice him. He shrugged it off and went along with the myth of his retirement caused by rheumatoid arthritis.

He explained to journalists how he coped. "Although he has resumed his career, Coburn's arthritis hasn't gone away. 'But I've gotten pretty good at dealing with it,' he notes proudly. 'I can walk again, I can run again, I can even act again.' He still takes aspirin regularly and works out three times a week. 'The doctor was right about one thing. You've got to learn to live with it.'"[30]

This was a few years before Dr. Lawrence had discovered the miracle pain-killer, MSM (methylsulfonylmethane). The truth was that Coburn sometimes needed something stronger than aspirin for his pain, including Percodan, a combination of aspirin and oxycodone. He also continued to use cannabis regularly, usually smoking it. It is a shame that he never saw the rise of decriminalized medical marijuana and the wide range of edibles and infused topicals eventually available to patients. It is a movement of which he would thoroughly approve.

Every now and then, something excellent would pop up. In the early fall of 1993, he shot a small but vital supporting role with his old friend James Garner on the big-budget comedy western *Maverick*, which would go on to be a hit the following summer. He was only needed for a few scenes, in a movie chockablock with cameos from old-time western actors and, interestingly, country singers, but it was familiar territory and he had one of the funniest lines. Messa was with him on the shoot. "That was fun too, that set. We used to eat real well on those sets."[31]

Coburn also shot in San Francisco with *Sister Act 2: Back in the Habit*, about a disadvantaged parochial high school's choir whose success in competition may save the school from closure. That movie premiered in December of 1993. He played "the usual character," the villain of the piece who wants the property. Enjoyed by the public who made it a reasonable hit, many critics thought Coburn had been wasted by the clichéd writing.

The last thing he was worrying about then was mediocre reviews. Instead he was on his extended honeymoon trip in Morocco. He and Paula were married on October 22, 1993, at Versailles outside of Paris. Barely noted in the United States, the event created a media frenzy in Paris and other parts of Europe. Hundreds of paparazzi jammed the steps of the town hall. The wedding was attended by his kids and close friends, including Frank Messa and Herbie Kretzmer and his wife, Sybil.

Kretzmer recalled his unusual friendship with Coburn at that time. "We actually went with them on their honeymoon, and you can hardly carry friendship farther than that. Coburn, you see, had acquired for his honeymoon a suite in the Mamounia hotel in Marrakech. It was so unbelievably vast that it seemed to dwarf even this magnificent soundstage. So he called me in London, and he said would Sybil and I care to join them for their honeymoon? It seemed a pity to waste so much space. And within days like Webster's dictionary, we were 'Morocco-bound.'"[32]

La Mamounia was built in 1923 adjoining a spectacular seventeen-acre garden filled with mature olive trees, which dates from the eighteenth century. The garden was a wedding gift given by the sultan of Morocco to one of his sons, Prince Moulay Mamoun. When the Coburns stayed there, the hotel was still suffering from what has been described as a "ghastly" art deco renovation in the 1980s.[33] Still, the grand suites, the famed restaurant—Le Marocain—and the gorgeous views that had once captivated Winston Churchill combined to make the experience magical, exotic, and wildly romantic.

According to Kretzmer, "In the small, crowded souks of Morocco, Jim Coburn stood out a mile and was unfailingly courteous to all who approached him, responding with characteristic modesty and friendliness, even to those who were convinced that he was Lee Marvin."[34]

Coburn enjoyed traveling with the Kretzmers. "A couple of years ago, we were driving through the South of France, Paula and Sybil sitting in the backseat, and driving through all these fields of corn. I said, 'What do you suppose the French do with all this corn?' And without breaking breath,

Herbie says, 'Write songs with it.' That broke me up. I laughed all the way to the coast."[35]

The couple had barely returned home to Los Angeles when disaster struck. On January 17, 1994, moments after 4:30 a.m. local time, they were awoken by the terrifying cracks and rumbles and the wild shaking of the 6.7-magnitude Northridge earthquake. The epicenter was only a few miles away from their Hollyline Avenue house. For twenty endless seconds, Paula and Jim clung to each other, listening to the screams of glass smashing through the pitch darkness.

"The earthquake was the most violent experience I've ever been in, that both of us had ever been through. It shook so hard. We had counted out sixteen big windows all around the house, and all of them came crashing down. On the backside of the house, the dirt came right on through. We had to clean all of the shit out. The bar was knee-deep in booze and broken bottles and glass of all kinds that we'd put together. We were in bed, surrounded by mirror everywhere. In the bedroom it was just one little crack above the doorway, going into the bathroom that broke. But in the living room, we had mirrored walls. Some of it broke, and there were big hunks of mirror stabbed deep in the floor. Really, it was awful. When I finally found the flashlight, we just walked through the house shaking, amazed by all the destruction."

One of the first people they called was Messa, down in Long Beach, about thirty-five miles to the south. "First of all to find out if I was okay down here. I said I was, and I asked him how he was. And he said, 'The house fell down.' That's all he said. I went, 'Oh my God,' and he said it was all dark there. I said, 'Hang in there. I'm on my way up.'"[36]

Messa immediately set off for the house. "I had equipped lanterns and stoves—earthquake preparedness stuff was all up at the house. Sure enough, the whole thing was worse than I thought. It was appalling. Jim took me around and showed me the damage—it was extensive. Windows were down. The only thing not down was the little television sanctuary right off the kitchen. So that's where we made the house.

"We made camp in that room. Lights and the little old stove. We sat out there like we were on a camping trip and told stories, in the dark. And when morning came, that's when the devastation took hold. Because they were both in denial about it. I mean, it happened to their house, but they didn't realize the magnitude, the extent of it.

"Paula wanted to go out and get some breakfast. 'Where is that going to be? Do you want to go all the way down to Long Beach, because that is where the first restaurant is going to be open?' Well, they didn't quite believe that. Paula had a recording device. We got in the back of the Mercedes, and it was devastating. Apartment-building garages were down, and all the way down the main thoroughfare down there in Sherman Oaks, the stores were down, the glass was broken, the thing was just like a bomb hit. Paula was sitting there recording, saying, 'Oh my God.' We went for miles to see if we could find anybody open. There wasn't anybody open.

"It finally hit Jim that it was nasty. He felt really fortunate that his house was still standing. We had checked it out when we were rebuilding, and it was solid. The parts that moved were the garage and the parts made out of brick—the fireplace—and the glass windows. The glass solarium that I had built remained intact—it just rocked and rolled but nothing fell. . . . They lost a lot of dishes and stuff.

"I found these guys on the street—construction guys with their truck. They brought up a bunch of four-by-eights—to cover the windows. It was up to Paula and Jim to clean up the bar, all the whiskey bottles that were now on the ground, unfortunately.

"Then a strange thing happened within the next couple of days—they made a tape. It was a simulation of the earthquake with them reacting. Paula made some copies and mailed it out to people—'We lived through this.'"

Messa took charge of the reconstruction of the home, all covered by insurance. Nonetheless, "Jim decided he did not want to move back into Hollyline, even though I had started the repairs."

Instead they put all their belongings in storage, living in a hotel while house hunting between trips to Europe. After a while they found a house Paula loved instantly, on Schuyler Road in Beverly Hills. Coburn was dubious. "The first time I saw it, I laughed my ass off. 'You've got to be kidding! You want to put us in a house like this? You've got to be kidding.' She said, 'Wait until you see the inside.' My little lady Paula. She came into the library and said, 'I love this room.' She loved the house from the very beginning. She's put so much into it."[37]

Messa worked with her on the renovations, keeping the vendors honest. "The contractors aren't really going to gouge you. The worst of that bunch are the so-called decorators—Hollyline was the house that I did the work on, but I wouldn't use decorators. On Schuyler we used decorators, but I would keep them in line because I know how much things cost. Why are you selling him these drapes for top dollar and then you're keeping 40 percent on top of that? What's the reason? How come this is happening? You deserve a design fee but put that up front—be honest about it. I would hold them to task. I would be the overrider—make sure things were done the way they said they would do. There would be the foreman and the head designer. If they got a phone call from me, that would make them hesitate. It was that kind of clout. I was just watching his back."[38]

Paula loved to garden, and the house had spectacular views from the pool deck and hillside garden above. Messa worked with her to create an Italian villa–style herb-and-citrus garden on the library level and to plant and build paths in the steep hillside above the main house. "It was weird how it was built—it was dictated by the lot. The elevator was there in the house. I predicted to myself that they were going to be living on the top floor. I put the garden in there, cutting up the stones, and I built the entire backyard up there for him. You could go up and sit and look out. I put the glass mirrors in the hall because it was too claustrophobic. We took that bedroom and cut the wall to make a nice arch. Everything in front of that turned into Jim's workout space."

In a sense, it was upside down, with the master suite, kitchen, dining room, and expansive living room, which would be used to great effect as a small ballroom, all on the topmost level. Friend Susan Blakely attended the weekly belly-dancing sessions that Paula organized. "We never got to the actual lesson until late—after a lot of champagne."[39]

Just like the house on Tower Road, the Schuyler house was filled with art and custom furnishings. The artwork included Asian prints and textiles, Buddhas, *thangkas*, and calligraphy. A collection of erotic Indian miniature paintings based on the *Kama Sutra* startled first-time visitors to the guest powder room. Many of the art pieces were found on their travels to Europe and India.

The home was featured in *Architectural Digest* in April 2000. Designer Craig Wright consulted with the pair on decorating and describes the home as "a stage set. It's all about their friends and the things they found on their travels. It's the theater of their life."[40] The article also notes the "draperies of Fortuny fabric, with under curtains made of gold lamé," and, perhaps inevitably, draws comparisons between this home and the work of Tony Duquette. Ironically, Beverly had yards of that very same hand-screened silk fabric in storage at the time of her death.

The article goes on, discussing Coburn's and Paula's tastes: "Their fantasies sometimes collide. 'I like subtlety,' says James Coburn. 'She likes the Wham! Bang! I keep saying, "too much, too much." She keeps saying, "not enough, not enough." We're Yin and Yang.'"

However much bravura Paula's style displayed—she joined Duquette in loving animal prints—she did not embrace the quirky found-object sculptures that Duquette had favored. Instead she commissioned works from contemporary artists like the late Tom Seghi, who specialized in photorealistic, overscale fruit still-life paintings.

Despite the coverage of the eclectic Chinese room, as they called one of their rarely used guest bedrooms, the place where Coburn spent most of his free time at home was the small sitting room off the kitchen. Here a splendid David Hockney architectural landscape filled the wall above a cushy, leather loveseat. He would sit with his feet up on a vintage leather-topped coffee table and watch football, or peruse scripts, in perfect comfort, often accompanied by Freddie, his favorite cat.

He was happy, enjoying his home, his life, and his wife. He spoke of her with great affection. "Paula has three really different personalities. And she has names for them now. Paula O'Hara is her acting self—her stage name, after her mother who was an O'Hara. She is still quite young in that personality, not quite sure of herself. One is called Paulina Murani, who's very sexy. And then she has Paula Coburn, who's really practical, always cleaning things up, always doing things. That's the one she stays in most of the time. So I ask her, 'Who am I going out with tonight?' I like Paulina Murani the best."[41]

He was full of pride that such a gorgeous creature was his wife. Katy Haber recalls the last time she saw the couple out: It was "at some kind of a party, and she was dancing. He looked at me and he said, 'Isn't she amazing?' He was just thrilled to be in her presence."[42]

Slowly, like a truck revving up a hill, Coburn's career was gaining new momentum. There was a possible series, *Greyhounds*, and voice-over work—narrations, a video game, commercials. Most of his films shot locally, but he continued to travel with Paula, often the guest of honor at film festivals and retrospectives of his career in Europe. Between times he had strong guest roles in some of the most popular TV series of the midnineties, including notably a major two-parter on the series *Profiler* and portraying Tom Skerritt's character's dad in *Picket Fences*.

If the movie parts remained supporting roles, the films themselves were getting bigger. He worked on two of the blockbusters of 1996, *The Nutty Professor* with Eddie Murphy, and *Eraser* with Arnold Schwarzenegger. On *Eraser* he shot for five days, in the early fall of 1995, playing WitSec Chief Beller. It was nice to play a good guy for a change. Heavy on stunts and visual effects, the film was scheduled for 95 days but ended up being 104. It makes the 74 days of work typical on Sam Peckinpah's films sound moderate.

Not long after that, Coburn was cast in the HBO comedy western *The Cherokee Kid*. He played the villain of the piece. Paula was unenthused by the red dye job they gave his hair for flashback sequences. "I have to sleep next to that," she remarked ruefully.[43] His following TV work included supporting roles in a made-for-cable mystery thriller, *Skeletons*, where he joined Christopher Plummer.

He also costarred in an extraordinarily prescient political satire directed by Joe Dante. *The Second Civil War* (1997) was about a corrupt governor closing his state's borders to refugees, in this case Pakistani war orphans, because of anti-immigrant prejudice, and the ensuing media circus. The film was an ensemble piece. Coburn played the president's cynical image consultant, whose devotion to his task and his client was as sincere as he was amoral. It was as if Bus Cummings from *The Americanization of Emily*, having retired from the navy, had gone into the business of politics. He looked like he was having a great time. Beau Bridges, as the governor of Idaho, won an Outstanding Supporting Actor Emmy. Time has caught up with this movie. These days it no longer feels like an absurd proposition filled with outlandish characters, but rather grimly plausible.

In January 1997 Coburn was on a cold, wet, miserable, windy set. He was playing the villainous father of a more villainous son. He was on location in Texas for the minor role in a convoluted made-for-cable thriller. The movie was ultimately released with the incongruously western-sounding title of *Keys to Tulsa*. In one of those unfortunate coincidences, the original title, *Tornado*, became untenable when the recent blockbuster *Twister* (1996) stole its thunder the summer before.

Fellow actor Marco Perella reminisces about the movie in his memoir. He portrayed the son and secondary villain of the piece and noticed that the production team was a good deal more careful of Coburn's safety than his own when stunts were involved. The shoot contained some dangerous stunts, including a car crashing through a bay window into the father's study. The car zoomed in at higher speed than expected and missed Coburn's stunt double—and Perella himself—by inches.

Huge blowing fans, reminiscent of *A High Wind in Jamaica* all those years ago, created the illusion of the climactic storm, with muddy leaves flying in the actors' faces. "It turned out to be cold, especially at one in the morning when we were shooting the scene. A week of cold, tired, special-effects movie glamour hell. All night, every night, until the subsidiary characters have been killed. The constant cry for 'more leaves!' has already become a catch phrase of the shoot."[44]

Despite the fact that Coburn had been given some of the best lines, Perella felt that his costar's performance largely relied on "that remarkably sonorous voice that sells stuff all the time on TV."

Keys to Tulsa was a quick commitment on Coburn's way to another shoot in Canada, one where he would certainly not be allowed to rely on the strength of his voice.

25. Coburn, film historian Bill Everson (*left*), and Sam Peckinpah (*center*) hanging out together in 1981 at the Santa Fe Film Festival when the theme was "The Western Film." Also in attendance that year was Charlton Heston. Courtesy of Lisa Law Productions.

26. *Left to right:* Lee Marvin, Coburn, Katy Jurado, and Sam Peckinpah at the Santa Fe Film Festival in 1981. Coburn often joked that fans mistook him for Marvin. This is a rare instance of them being photographed together. They did resemble each other when they were both young and played many similar cowboy roles. Courtesy of Lisa Law Productions.

27. Coburn with his friend Josette Banzet-Roe at a birthday party in 1992. Courtesy of the James Coburn Archives.

28. Jim and Paula at James and Robyn's wedding, 1997. Courtesy of the author.

29. Coburn and Tom Berenger share a laugh at wrap on *The Avenging Angel* TV movie (1995). Coburn wore a bushy beard and wig that helped disguise the stunt double. Photograph by Erik Heinila. Courtesy of Turner Entertainment Networks, Inc (1995).

30. Coburn, JP DeJoria, and Justin Bell with a Ferrari at the start of the Orient Express Challenge in 1991. The race was road versus train, London to Venice, to raise funds for the Royal Marsden Cancer Hospital. The ultimate winning car—Simon Le Bon and Paul Stewart. Courtesy of Terry R. Duffell Photography.

31. Coburn visiting the Kokotu-in Buddhist Temple in Kamakura, ca. 1987. Courtesy of the James Coburn Archives.

32. Coburn, Paula, and JP DeJoria on their annual Mediterranean cruise docked in Portofino, Italy, ca. 1992. JP recalls that they went shopping locally because he needed some clothes. Courtesy of the James Coburn Archives.

33. Coburn and Paula at the Hollyline house in 1991. Photograph by Paul Harris. Courtesy of Getty Images.

34. Coburn clowning around with production sound mixer Bill Reinhardt (*seated left*) while another crew member looks on during the shoot for *Skeletons* (1997). Ironically James H. Coburn IV was set to operate boom on this movie for his old friend Bill but had the chance to mix his first feature film out-of-town, so he missed the opportunity to work with his father. Photograph by James Brewer. Courtesy of William Reinhardt.

35. Coburn agreed to take part in a benefit shoot with Louis Vuitton to celebrate the World Cup 1998 to benefit UNICEF. Here he is on a Paris rooftop. Photograph by Xavier Lambours. Courtesy of Signatures, Maison de Photographes.

36. Coburn with his favorite cat, Freddie, ca. 2001. Photograph by James Coburn IV.

37. Coburn celebrates winning the 1998 Academy Award for Best Supporting Actor for *Affliction*. Photograph by Hector Mata, 1999. Courtesy of Getty Images, AFP Collection.

14

It Was a Gas

I thought it was a great role. A lot of other actors had turned it down because the character was such a nasty fuck. I thought he was an interesting character to play. He was only nasty if you were seeing him from the outside. He wasn't nasty on the inside. My hit on him was that he was trying to have his sons be real men. He wanted them to be *men*. He didn't want them to be namby-pamby—what did he call 'em? "Candy asses and Jesus freaks." That's what he had for a family, and that's what pissed him off. He told the truth, from his point of view, and people don't like the truth.

—JAMES COBURN, 2002

In around 1991 Paul Schrader sent a script he had written to Nick Nolte. It was based on a book by Russell Banks dealing with deep intergenerational dysfunction caused by rage, fueled by alcohol. It took about six years to finally get the script into production and then almost two years for it to reach distribution. But for James Coburn, *Affliction* would prove to be the pinnacle of his career.

Schrader had spent some time considering the right actor to portray the pivotal character of Glen "Pop" Whitehouse, father to Nick Nolte's character. "I wanted a man's man of that generation for the role. There weren't that many around. There were three on the list. Paul Newman—doubted he would do it. James Garner—he was getting long in the tooth. James

Coburn. He was the best of the choices, I was sure. I went through Hilly to get him. It was obviously going to be a low-budget film, but Hilly was keen on Coburn doing it. Coburn hadn't been able to work, was he even able to get around? But Hilly assured me."[1]

Coburn knew that this was a wonderful character to play, in an interesting story. "It was very straight on. There was no ambiguity about the characters and it's really fun and enriching when that happens. Villains are really fun to play, because they're usually meatier characters, because they've made decisions that haven't all been very good ones and are paying the price, with a little karma attached."[2]

Schrader met with Coburn over dinner at the Polo Lounge in Beverly Hills. "I admit I had some resistance inside me. I feared that he had reached that point that stars do, where they do the minimum amount. In his case, the voice was propelling his acting. I told him, 'Nick will not tolerate someone just showing up. If Nick feels you're not giving it your all, he's going to let you know. There will be trouble, and I am not going to be on your side.'

"There was a long pause. Coburn then said to me, 'You mean like real acting? I can do that. They don't ask me much to do that anymore, but I know how to do that.'"[3]

Nick Nolte is an actor who prepares extremely thoroughly. Schrader warned Coburn, "Nick is the most prepared of actors. He will not only do a book on his character—he'll do a book on your character, all the characters." He felt a connection to the character of Sheriff Wade Whitehouse, or at least he understood his background, what Stella Adler would have called "blood memory."[4] Like Coburn, Nolte was also born in Nebraska. As he told the *Los Angeles Times*, "I came from a small town, and I remember when we didn't have anything to do. Out of boredom we will always be in the lounge [drinking]."[5]

The company met in Montreal for a week of rehearsals prior to shooting. At first Schrader was worried about Coburn. "It was exactly what I was afraid of. The voice did all the work."[6] So he directed him to use a falsetto voice, "a Walter Brennan kind of old-man voice" to rehearse the lines. "It was the right idea." When he felt Coburn slipping back into his voice, Schrader would say, "Let's do a falsetto take. He became crotchety unpleasant in that voice. A lot of those falsetto readings are in the film, particularly in the graveyard scene. And Coburn was dealing with how I could un-man him of his voice. . . . He absolutely came through. He was an actor. He was not just a guy who had the look or the luck to make it in Hollywood films. He could act."

The experience reminded Coburn of working with Sam Peckinpah, who would have his actors repeat a line over and over, having to find a different emphasis each time, even when the actor felt he had it right. Peckinpah was often in his mind, as he considered Pop Whitehouse's alcoholism. "The constant state of his alcohol consumption—I learned about that from Peckinpah. He was never 'drunk,' but he was rather touched by the alcohol, to the degree that it caused him to have an ego kind of thing that came out, made him nasty."[7]

The shoot was a wonderful experience, despite the February freeze. Coburn had not felt this cold since working on *Charade*. Then the filmmakers ignored the extreme weather, trying to give a timeless impression of Paris. On this film the cold was almost another character. It mirrored the bleakness of the interminable, hopeless future.

"Was it ever winter! The snow was a foot and a half deep everywhere. It was freezing cold, but we were dressed for it. We shot mostly inside, but when we were outside, we were dressed for it. When we needed snow to happen, it happened. It was a magical shoot—it truly was. When we wanted a blizzard, a blizzard happened. I did my work in three weeks."

He appreciated Schrader's directing technique: "He knew what he wanted and when he had gotten it. He shaded it"—perhaps without even realizing how much guidance the director was giving him through his voice notes. "We just played the dynamic we felt at the time. We just let it go. It was all there in Schrader's writing. He's a genius. He writes for actors, and he writes brilliantly for actors. The dynamic of the character was to let everyone have it. It was a lot of fun. I enjoyed working on that movie a lot because of that. We had something to work with. We had the literature to work with; we had a great screenplay; we had great actors; we had the whole dynamic thing."

He also appreciated his coworkers, saying, "Working with great actors is the biggest joy of all." He called Sissy Spacek "one of our great actresses. Man, she was good." Of Nick Nolte he says, "An elegant performance, so restrained. He was constantly holding back, holding back, holding back for the explosion. It was fun too. Acting has to be fun, to work with people who are fun to work with and who are givers."

Coburn felt that the experience was "like purging—you felt free every day after you finished work. It was great. Like you got something out of your system." He left it all behind on the set.

"A lot of people feel it's necessary to put on forty pounds to play a fat man. I don't work that way. I don't have to do that. I act it. I work from another source, and as long as you get it out during the day, you don't have to carry it around. People who saw that film thought I was really a badass. That's what acting is. You don't have to be that to act it. You just have to understand what it is and bring it out. In *Affliction*, the way Schrader wrote it was brilliant, because everything was right on the nose. It was just so clear. It was like rolling off a log. You just had to open up, turn it on, and let it come out."

Paul Schrader took the film to the 1997 Venice Film Festival as well as Telluride and Sundance. Coburn was pleased to attend festivals with something to promote for a change, instead of merely to be honored as a celebrity. Some of his most gratifying feedback on the film came from members of the public, who would surprise him by coming up and thanking him for the reality of his performance. He told *Entertainment Weekly*, "I had no idea it was so pronounced in our society. It was amazing: people came up to me and said, 'That's my father, you played my father.'"[8]

The Oscar buzz started almost immediately, for Nolte and even more for Coburn. Reviewers were especially surprised by his performance, saying things like "a revelation" and remarking that he had "virtually come out of retirement," which was inaccurate, but it made a nice hook for the press.[9] Instead of only querying him about his relationship with Steve McQueen or Bruce Lee and about his early successes, journalists started asking him serious questions about acting and characterization.

Coburn had always believed that it made no sense to give advice, that people wouldn't take it and that he had little to teach anyone about acting or characterization. "Nothing you can say will make any difference. I can't tell anybody how to act. You find out from a teacher like Stella Adler who inspires you through impressions she would leave you with. But to give a lecture about acting just doesn't make any sense. You can't talk about it. It's hard to talk about acting. It really is."[10]

Yet when he was interviewed for *Backstage*, the actors trade journal, he distilled wonderful, useful ideas and expressed timeless advice. "You can't act with an ego. If you have an ego you've got to leave that at home when you go off to the set. Leave it back in the shower, because if you act with an ego then you're not really working. You're either denying something or you're not allowing something to happen. You've got to be open. . . . I learned a lot of technique. What technique does is allow you to free yourself from all the fears and all of that jazz. If you know what you're doing, then you can play. Then you can actually explore with your imagination. Acting is not just accident. It has to become a conscious artistic effort that you're in control of. You've got to have a point of view.

"First you have to be serious about the work, instead of wanting to be rich and famous. Then maybe you can attain some level of wealth and a little fame. But you can't count on it, unless you have the depth of understanding the process. The process comes with learning a technique. . . . That's the whole joy of acting—finding out how to do it. . . . That's what I would say to young people: if you're not interested in the work and don't submit to the work, be a model."[11]

Coburn and Paula were seen all around Los Angeles as much as possible, and they entertained at home as well. His dancing bear was out in force, as he dearly wanted this film to be successful. He noted that each of the people involved in the film had their own following, which would hopefully translate into viewers: "If it has a decent release and they spend enough on publicity to whet the appetite for something unique, dark and disturbing, then it's possible that it will gain a little bit. It has a unique kind of appeal."[12]

Nolte was not under any illusions that the film would be a popular hit, as he says in the *Los Angeles Times* piece about it: "My personal opinion is that you don't make a film for an audience. I know that's not conventional thinking. You make a story because you want to tell that story and you want to find the truth out about it. . . . The value of this film is its shelf life. This is a film you'll be pulling down five, six, ten years from now. . . . The other thing is you don't put it in a category with these films that have to generate huge chunks of money. We've only got to make back a $6 million nut." It has indeed made back that cost over the years since its release.

Copresident of Lionsgate Films, Mark Urman, was delighted to bring the talked-about movie to his distribution company. He had been a Coburn fan from way back, as he reveals to the *Hollywood Reporter*: "Coburn has really gotten the reviews of his career. There have been quotes that have said it's the role of a lifetime. It's such a change for him. I, as somebody in my 40s, grew up seeing James Coburn on the screen every decade of my life—and I've never seen him do this. It was frightening to see 'Our Man Flint' turn into this terrifying, mean old drunk."[13]

Lionsgate at the time was starting to be known as a company that would invest in these small "labors of love." Urman adds, "We know precisely what to do with them to maximize their potential." The film had a limited release in late December 1998, making it Academy Award eligible. Both Nolte and Coburn received numerous nominations, including for Golden Globes, Independent Spirit Awards, and SAG Awards. Nolte won Best Actor awards from both the National Society of Film Critics and the New York Film Critics Circle, while the film received second-place honors from both groups. In a sweet extra, twelve-year-old Brigid Tierney, who played Nolte's daughter, won a Young Artist Award for Best Supporting Young Actress.

But even before the publicity snowball for *Affliction* got rolling, Coburn received a huge boost to his happiness when Dr. Lawrence introduced him to the sulfur-based supplement MSM. It felt like a miracle. "Within three days I was pain-free. There was a smile on my face from my ass to elbow. All of a sudden it was groovy. Wow. I could sleep at night. It was really great. Dietary sulfur."[14] He started telling his friends, like Robert Vaughn, about it whenever anyone complained of joint or muscle pain, and they found they had the same positive results. Eventually Coburn appeared on *Larry King Live* with Dr. Lawrence, enthusiastically relating his personal experience.

Soon he was newly revitalized and back at work doing guest spots on a few TV series and made-for-cable miniseries, and continuing his voice-over commercial work between interviews and flying visits to film festivals. He was still waiting for something that he considered good literature to come along. As often happens, he began receiving plenty of angry-old-man scripts, none on a par with Schrader's.

In the midst of this campaign, he was pleased to get a call from Mel Gibson, inviting him to do a cameo role, uncredited but fun, on Gibson's latest big-budget actioner, *Payback*. It was exactly the opposite kind of movie from *Affliction*. Coburn went in for his half day of shooting, had fun, and thought no more about it. But then he was invited back for more scenes. Then he got yet another call to come back for reshoots after the director, Brian Helgeland, was fired just two days after winning an Academy Award for *L.A. Confidential* in 1998. The part expanded to several nice scenes, and Coburn was still having fun, especially when he found out his old friend Kris Kristofferson was now in the cast. He also reunited with one of his *Keys to Tulsa* costars, Deborah Kara Unger. His character, Justin Fairfax, remains uncredited. The theatrical version was released a few weeks before the 1999 Academy Awards to a strong opening. Years later a director's cut, put together by Helgeland, was released on DVD. The two versions are quite different, especially in the character development. In one version Justin Fairfax survives; in the other he dies.

Suddenly in 1998 Coburn was as busy as he had been during the early sixties. Between interviews and days on *Payback*, he made a quick trip to Australia to participate in the miniseries *Noah's Ark*. The flood exteriors were shot in the horizon tank at Point Cook RAAF Base outside of Melbourne. Coburn portrays "The Peddler"—good luck finding him in the book of Genesis. That project left both Bible scholars and film critics scratching their heads. Then Coburn zoomed out to the Carolinas to do a role in *Shake, Rattle & Roll: An American Love Story*, and then in early spring of 1999, he took the lead in a Hallmark film that was shooting over several weeks in Santa Barbara, with the working title *Atticus*.

Later called *Missing Pieces*, this was the film shoot that Coburn referenced that wonderful evening of March 21, 1999, when from the Academy Awards stage, he thanked the production for giving him Monday off. He was going to need that time to recuperate from an evening—a whole weekend—of parties. He and Paula had already attended the Independent Spirit Awards, held the night before in a marquee tent by the beach in Santa Monica. A month earlier they had also been at the party that is the Golden Globe Awards. He had worked with or was friends with most of the people in the room.

But the Oscars were the big one. Paula had spent an afternoon at home with a couple of her friends, including Lisa and this author, trying on a selection of dresses to determine the perfect one for the big night. She even practiced walking in her gown. Paula recalls in an interview that before the ceremony, "Jim didn't prepare a speech on purpose. What if he prepared and didn't get it? He doesn't remember how he got on stage."[15] He didn't remember shaking Nick Nolte's hand or fellow nominee Geoffrey Rush's hand as he passed in front of them from his seat in the front row. He made his way up the wide, gently curved steps to meet Kim Basinger and stood, a little breathless, genuinely astonished, looking at his statue. His speech was heartfelt and a little halting as he, unprepared, recalled the names of the producers and others to thank. He mentioned his friends Hilly Elkins and Bobby Lipton, and then he dedicated the award to Paula, gazing down and blowing her a kiss. After the ceremony, he told reporters that he hadn't had time to thank his kids and named Jimmy and Lisa.

During the commercial breaks, his friends and well-wishers mobbed the couple in their seats. According to Paula, they spent the rest of the evening "just floating. My head was just exploding."

They were in for a long night of partying and celebrating. Frank Langella was sitting nearby and spoke to Coburn once he returned to his seat after questions in the press room. He interpreted Coburn's "I just want to go home" as a panoptic "fatigue of the spirit,"[16] rather than merely the rueful expectation of what would be a *very* long night. Paula even had a second gown waiting, one that was easier to walk in—and dance in—of sparkling rainbow lace. She says, "When we arrived at the Beverly Hills Hotel, everyone stood and gave him a standing ovation. It broke my heart, it was so wonderful. It was a glorious moment in time. Just glorious."[17]

Several weeks later the Coburns hosted a celebration aboard a small, chartered boat. Family, old friends like John Paul DeJoria, and newer colleagues, including David Caruso (who had worked on *Hudson Hawk*), mingled to cruise around the southern bay in the gorgeous late-spring Southern California weather. Paula had decorated the large round tables with gauzy fabrics in floral prints, with centerpieces of clustered spring blooms.

"I got a telegram from Schrader afterward that said, 'Congratulations, you were wonderful, but always remember, the work is really the thing.' And he was right," Coburn agreed.[18] "That's what it's really about, the work. It's not about winning anything. The recognition was nice, yeah sure, because I've been doing this for a long time. But you need the vehicle."

Later in the year, they hosted their whole family at what was expected to be an annual getaway for Thanksgiving. In 1999 everyone, including his new four-week-old grandchild, drove to Sedona, Arizona, to stay in a beautiful five-bedroom chalet for the long weekend. Coburn didn't join in the hikes up the red dirt paths, but he did keep up his exercises, using a broomstick as a tool, twisting and turning, quite vigorously, out on the deck in the afternoon. Then he stopped to hydrate, taking a long swig from a glass of clear liquid before continuing. Turned out, it was not water in his glass, but vodka. Later he said, "You have to keep moving or you freeze."[19]

Despite his efforts, in 2000 Coburn was not as energetic as he would have liked. While his arthritis pain was under control, he had a slowly worsening heart condition. His own father had died from heart problems, almost certainly connected with his rheumatoid arthritis. For a brief time, Coburn's cardiologist had him trying steroids. These made him cranky and hard to live with. He became nasty to the people around him. Rob Harabedian recalled comforting Paula, who was so distraught, she considered leaving. "I would say, 'You can't do that. He really needs you. This is not the real Jim. You know this is not the real Jim.' And I remember that as soon as they changed the medication, life was good again."[20]

Coburn had started suffering unpredictable bouts of arrhythmia, which the steroidal meds did little to help. Doctors implanted a cardiac stimulation device, similar to a pacemaker, in his chest. This made him feel better, although if it went off, the result was like being hit by a Taser. He was forbidden from driving, which was a source of disappointment so acute that he sometimes ignored doctor's orders and made short journeys anyway.

His heart condition meant a new regimen of diuretics. Having to go to the bathroom so often was a real drag. He worried that taking frequent breaks might impinge on his work and become noticeable. It is the kiss of death for an actor to be considered "uninsurable." For this reason actors, especially older ones, tend to keep any health problems secret for as long as they can. He had recuperated from the implant surgery discreetly out of town, in a rented beach house in Laguna Beach, south of Los Angeles.

But he was still very busy working, doing his car and truck commercials, narrating a documentary, and working both locally and out of town. His part in *Intrepid* (aka *Deep Water*) shot on the *Queen Mary* in Long Beach. He presented at the Academy Awards in March, laughing his way up the red carpet, and again enjoying the delight of being a respected presenter without stress. He claimed the "enviable job of getting close to one of the five gorgeous, talented, sexy women" who turned out to be Angelina Jolie.[21]

Over June and July 2000, he went to Cleveland to join Rob Lowe in a low-budget made-for-TV action thriller, *Proximity*, about an implausible prison murder conspiracy. The film was universally dismissed. In August he was back in Los Angeles and started recording the voice of Henry Waternoose III for the Pixar production *Monsters, Inc.*, which would go on to be an Oscar winner. Coburn would continue to go in for recording sessions over the next year and a half as Pixar honed and developed the story, until it came out just before Thanksgiving 2001.

Then he had a role in another Hallmark/Showtime production—a gently uplifting family melodrama called *Walter & Henry* directed by Daniel Petrie, the veteran director best known for *A Raisin in the Sun* (1961) and many television directing credits over his fifty-plus-year career. This picture earned Petrie a Directors Guild Award nomination. Incidentally, his wife, Dorothea G. Petrie, had been an associate producer on *Crash Landing* back in 1992.

Of actors, Daniel Petrie once said, "You have to create an atmosphere for them to work without imposing on them. All the actor has to do is think the thoughts of the character."[22] This dovetailed nicely into Coburn's primary approach to acting: "You don't just say the lines, ever! If you're just saying lines, you're not acting—you're just saying lines. But you're playing a character, and the character is saying those lines. They're playing actions. Playing ways of going about getting the other actor to do something, getting what you want."[23]

Walter & Henry shot in Toronto over early fall, and it reunited Coburn with Kate Nelligan from *Mr. Patman*. He played a somewhat stern grandfather, softened through bonding with his preteen grandson over music, when the boy's father, his son, is admitted to the psych ward. The three generations of men share musical talent. Coburn was noticeably limping, and the arthritis in his hands was written into the script as the reason he could no longer play his beloved piano.

Another highlight from this period was a digital short, *The Yellow Bird*, written and directed by friend Faye Dunaway. Coburn played a fire-and-brimstone preacher with a rebellious daughter. The film showed at Cannes and on the WE network, and although he had time to attend the Los Angeles premiere, he didn't travel to Cannes.

At the time, he had just returned from playing the estranged father to Cuba Gooding Jr.'s character in a film to be called *Winterdance*, after the Gary Paulsen book that inspired the script. Perhaps that title made it feel too serious—this was a lightly humorous story about discovering one's background and finding family set against the backdrop of the Iditarod. For the release, the title was changed to the more Disney-esque *Snow Dogs*.

Coburn's character, Thunder Jack, was another crotchety man, mourning the loss of his paramour, very set in his mountain man ways, and fearing the old age that would take his lifestyle from him. Despite the slapstick elements to the comedy, he took the role seriously.

"To move from tragedy to humor, you play it all the same. You never lose touch with that reality—you keep that basis of grounding in that humor—and you can take it any place as long as you can resolve it. As they say, the art is in the resolution. But you have to take it out as far as you can go, as long as you can resolve it. He was in love with this woman and didn't want to admit it because she was dead and gone. That was his cover-up. But finally he admits it—he says it. It had some nice parts—it was a broad enough spectrum to attract a lot of people—made a lot of people cry. It was great. Made a lot of people laugh too."

Gooding played Thunder Jack's long-lost son, Ted Brooks, who was given up for adoption in infancy and now is discovering a startling inheritance. As a city boy from Miami, an intellectual, a dentist, his lifestyle is as far away from his old dad's as it could possibly be. Much of the story's comedy, such as it was, came from the fish-out-of-water aspect. Eventually after various obstacles, including making friends with the dog team that is now his, and entering the big race, Ted reconciles with Jack.

The Canadian shoot was another uncomfortable situation, due again to the weather. However, Coburn was in very good spirits and particularly enjoyed the opportunity to learn how to work with sled dogs. One of the dog team trainers who worked with him, Laurie Niedermayer, wrote a memoir describing her experiences working on movies that feature sled dogs. On one particular day in late January 2001, she had a knee injury, so another driver, Stuart, took Coburn out to train for what was supposed to be about a fifteen-minute run.

"After about 25 minutes, I started to get concerned and asked one of the production assistants why the ambulance had followed the team out. I was told it was because Mr. Coburn had an external pace maker and supposedly, if it got too cold it could stop working. . . . All I could think was that I'd go forever down in history as the mushing consultant that killed Mr. James Coburn.

"Finally, after forty-five minutes the team came barreling over a slight rise with Mr. Coburn on the runners and Stuart in the basket. I could hear Stuart saying 'You could start to apply the brake now sir. . . .' To which Mr.

Coburn laughed and said in his inimitable style, 'No way—let's see what these puppies can do!'

"Then they blew past me as if I wasn't even there and Stuart's eyes were huge with a mixture of surprise and fear before we managed to get them stopped, just before they ended up on a nearby road. Mr. Coburn was laughing and joking while we turned them around and headed back to their truck."[24]

Frank Messa went up to Calgary for a while to keep Coburn company. "I had a good time up there too. Part of my deal with him on the set was to keep him centered, so to speak. He needed conversation most of the time, and if you could keep up a good conversation with him, then that just bided the time. Because I can tell you from my own experience, they were boring, the sets. Because he gets all dressed up, then he sits around, waiting to be called, and waiting to be called. He knew that—he's been in eighty movies."[25]

Jimmy also went up and spent about a week with his father. As it happened, he was there in the days before the pivotal reconciliation scene, set when the father and son characters are trapped in a snow cave. Coburn rehearsed the scene, running lines with Jimmy, adding a rather beautiful piquancy to the situation.

The marketing for *Snow Dogs* gave the impression that it was going to be a talking dog movie, which would fit with Disney, but they only talk in a dream sequence. It seemed that it was intended as a family film, but many adults found the humor childish. Some reviews were not kind, citing clichéd writing and an excess of pratfalls—a corny script not saved by two Oscar winners. One kinder reviewer asserts, "Aware he deserves better, [Coburn] chews the scenery with gusto."[26] However, as often happens the public felt differently and the film did respectable business at home and abroad.

Coburn was still hoping for something pithy, what he could call good literature. He was therefore very pleased when in mid-2001 he was offered a key part in the ensemble of *The Man from Elysian Fields*, a complex morality tale. It was a good role for him, subtle and elegant. He had a sort of connection with one of the stars, Anjelica Huston, who also starred in the upcoming *Mists of Avalon* miniseries.

But the person most excited to be working with him was Andy García, who claimed that he had become an actor because of James Coburn. "I wanted to be James Coburn when I grew up.... I went to see *The Magnificent Seven* like probably everybody, and to this day I remember how that entrance affected me. It was a really quintessential moment in American cinema."²⁷ Some years later when he was in *The Untouchables* (1987), García took the opportunity to draw inspiration from that moment and make "a little bit of private homage on my part to him." It is the first time you see his character, in the gun range, practicing his fast draw.

During the *Elysian* shoot, Coburn and García spent time together at the end of the day, sharing a drink, Bacardi 8, and conversation. García was impressed by his "extraordinary appetite for jazz, for the unknown, and for the spontaneous moment." Whenever García expressed how much he had enjoyed the day, Coburn would always reply, "It was a gas."

Olivia Williams starred as Coburn's wife and talked to *Venice Magazine* about the experience of working with him. "It was wonderful. You'd never know that he wasn't long for this world. He was full of energy and was funny and charming and stubborn and brilliant. What an honor. I remember my dad waking me up and bringing me downstairs to watch *The Magnificent Seven* on the telly when I was little. I couldn't believe it, here I was playing his wife, it was so surreal. It was one of those jobs that came at the last minute. They asked me with about three days left in pre-production. I flew out into this wonderful pre-existing situation. The script appealed to me. And then married to James Coburn and shagging Andy Garcia—how bad can life be? [laughs] I'll take it!"²⁸

One day there was a time when the discussion about a scene stretched on and on. Finally Coburn, who could probably see it going in circles, declared, "Aww, come on. Let's just shoot this fucker!" It made a strong impression on García, who wrote it down, perhaps without realizing that Coburn was once again referencing his old friend Sam Peckinpah.

Roger Ebert, who had not always appreciated Coburn's acting in years past, reviewed the film, saying, "This is a rare comedy of manners, witty, wicked and worldly, and one of the best movies of the year," and added kudos for his performance, "a pitch-perfect balance between sadness and sardonic wit. Listen to his timing and his word choices in the scene where he opens his wife's bedroom door and finds [García's character], not without his permission, in his wife's bed. You can believe he is a great novelist."[29]

The film first premiered in Canada in September 2001 at the Toronto International Film Festival. Between festivals, Coburn had time that year to spend a few days in a luxurious hotel in Laguna Beach with all the kids and grandkids for the family Thanksgiving celebration. Then he was refreshed and ready to work.

He went along when director George Hickenlooper took the film to the Seattle International Film Festival and Sundance Film Festival in January 2002, incidentally at the same time that *Snow Dogs* premiered in the theaters. It was grand to have another good work to promote. An attendee at the Sundance screening, cinematographer Alan J. Sutovsky, wrote a letter to *Variety* speaking of Coburn's warmth and charm on the movie's Q&A panel: "Strong yet humble, he expressed himself in the manner of the intelligent and thoughtful artist that he was," then met up with him again, by chance, the next day.[30] "His openness and willingness to engage me in conversation was more than enough to make the entire Sundance trip worthwhile. . . . He reached out and shook my hand. Warmth, fortitude and conviction radiated from this man; it was all there in his hands, his voice, his smile."

Immediately following the *Elysian Fields* shoot, Coburn embarked on the film that no one knew would be his last. It was the low-budget gentle mystery *American Gun* that took him all over the country. He shot in winter in Vermont, then warmed up in Florida and Las Vegas. At the time, he was actively promoting MSM for Gero Vita, along with Dr. Lawrence. But a slow-healing inflammation in his foot was also giving him some trouble.

Despite this, writer-director Alan Jacobs told the *Los Angeles Times* he found the actor professional and "straightforward," completely aware of the budget constraints of this little project, and willing to work through his pain.[31] He embodied his motto, Go Bravely On. "He was so good about it. He was in four states for the better part of 40 days, making this low-budget film. You needed him to walk, he walked."

The gentle and nuanced performance, and the other fine performances by the rest of the cast, including Paula, made Coburn appreciate the movie. He did all he could to promote it. Jacobs says, "He came out for two of the screenings we did here in LA. He also made calls to a couple of the film festival directors, and he put in a call to some prospective buyers. Whenever we needed him to make a call, he was there."

The film showed on the festival circuit over the summer and fall of 2002. It garnered strong attention, excellent reviews ("propelled by a career-highlight performance from Oscar winner James Coburn") and a prize at the Seattle International Film Festival in June.[32] The Hamptons International Film Festival in October gave him a career achievement award, but he was too ill to attend either event so far from home. Nor could he attend the showing at the New Orleans Film Festival in October.

Unfortunately, Coburn's feet were still causing more pain than anything else. It was very frustrating. Because he couldn't walk, he couldn't work, and it preyed on his mind. He was uncomfortable. But he used his time productively to record his memoirs, the recordings that form the backbone of this book.

He finally admitted that his old resentments hurt only himself during his low years. "Inside I was fucking pissed off—I was really rattled. I felt I'd been cheated, you know, and probably was a bit. But it was my own fault. It wasn't anybody's fault but my own. I don't blame anybody for it, but I did for years. That was the rage I couldn't let go. It took me a long time to get over that.

"But that's what negative emotion does. You have to work against negative emotion. People don't even realize there is such a thing as negative emotion. They'll say, 'Oh, don't be so emotional!' What do you mean 'emotional'? Positive emotion is great. Positive emotion can lead to a great many joyous things—loving and so on. Well, there's the other side of the coin called negative emotion. When there is something eating at you, unless you get it out right away, it's going to continue to grow and eat like a cancer. Broken hearts lead to a lot of ailments.

"My life seems to be totally fatalistic. I just have to go along with it. Even all this has something to do with a phase, I guess. I sit here with my edema-filled leg and foot, suffering like hell through all of that—through weeks and weeks of suffering. You've got to give up your suffering. Unnecessary suffering is something that kills you. Gurdjieff said to give up your unnecessary suffering. I guess there is some necessary suffering. You have to deal with pain in a conscious way. I've been so emotional. I don't know what it is.

"Now in this strange package of pain and anxiety I've developed into, it's about moving away from this pain and anxiety. Pain and anxiety is something that takes my attention, and it's the hardest thing in the world to do, just absolutely, especially having the hiccups, being reminded with every breath."[33]

He shot an episode of *Arli$$* for HBO and arrived with a cane on June 1, 2002, to receive a lifetime achievement award from the Stella Adler Academy of Acting. There was a dinner catered by Wolfgang Puck and an enjoyable jazz band providing music. Director Arthur Hiller bought a page in the program that says, "Jim in my book you did a lifetime achievement in 1964. One terrific actor! One terrific guy!"

As summer progressed, Coburn became quieter. The house he shared with Paula started to feel too big, too expensive, and they considered listing it for sale. Meanwhile he planned his estate, coming up with the idea of creating a charitable foundation. He became increasingly anxious, worried about being alone, "in case some foolish thing happened." He needed the reassurance of Paula's near-constant presence.

In August Paula had the opportunity to join actress friend Susie Blakely and her husband, publicist Steve Jaffe, at the annual Valley of the Moon Vineyard grape crush. She wanted to go and stomp some grapes. In hindsight some of their friends thought that Paula had dragged Coburn up there against his will, or at least against better judgment. But he had been adamant. He did not want to be left behind, especially on his birthday.

Josette Banzet-Roe was convinced that it was his own idea to attend. "She didn't push him to go. He wanted to go. And she drove the car. And they arrived in Napa Valley. I came with a girlfriend, and she drove. If I had known they were driving, I would have gone with them. But it was the last moment that he said he wanted to go. He was happy when he got there because I saw him. He said, 'I wanted to drive, but she wouldn't let me.' He was all smiles, happy."[34]

The owners of the vineyard were Steve Jaffe's clients, and they agreed to create a wonderful surprise birthday celebration for Jim in the evening. After the grape crush in the afternoon—"none of the men stomped the grapes"[35]—and a rest back in their cabins, everyone came down to dinner in the wine warehouse. "There must have been over a hundred people."[36]

Susie described the scene of "massive wine barrels, twinkly little lights strung across the ceilings, and a sumptuous meal accompanied by more than a few bottles of their top-of-the-line wines. One after another of the many assembled guests rose to toast James on his special day. He had such a good time.

"After we had all gone to bed in our little cabins on the grounds of the winery, our phone rang. It was Paula. She said James was sick and had experienced some kind of heart event. Steve called a client who was a cardiologist, and he told us to rush James to the hospital in Marin County. Paula took him ahead by ambulance."[37]

Susie and Steve followed to the hospital, where the cardiac team was ready and had whisked Coburn away for treatment. Steve recalled they were waiting near the elevator, pacing, anxious for news. The elevator doors opened, and attendants wheeled out a gurney on which reclined a relaxed and smiling Jim Coburn. He said cheerily, "Oh hi, guys. How you doing?"[38]

After a few days, Paula moved him to a San Francisco hospital. They stayed in San Francisco for about four weeks, consulting with a cardiologist there. Messa went up for a while, as did Jimmy, before Coburn took yet another ambulance for the long drive home to Los Angeles.

His recovery was slow and frustrating. He needed physical assistance at home. He was still strong willed, refusing to be pushed into more physical therapy, refusing even to swim in his pool. It was a very bad sign that he was unwilling to move. Susie Blakely noticed the change. "It was tough to see that house that had been so full of life and fun, so full of sickness."[39] For the next several months, Paula was in near-constant attendance, as indeed he demanded from her, only getting a short respite when someone else came over.

He continued recording his memoirs and expressed his deeply felt philosophical ideas. "What kind of world is this? It's hard enough to have peace in the house. I mean to have peace on earth, good will toward men—if you can do it, do it! But we have a code of revenge. We have to fight in order to justify our existence somehow—for some reason, that I can't figure out. It has to do with international and national egos, that we have to kill anything that stands in the way of our way of thinking.

"So what if somebody thinks differently than we do? Peace starts inside. You can be peaceful without any kind of regret. Be willing to forgive, forget all the junk that's been heaped upon you, and say, 'So what? Let me help you out.' Then maybe there's a chance, but it starts at home. It starts in your heart. It starts in you. You don't have to say, 'I don't like it.' You can say, 'Hmmm, interesting.' That's enough."[40]

He had at last developed the serene ability to accept contrary views that he sought so intensely back in 1966.

On Saturday morning, November 16, 2002, Coburn entered Cedars-Sinai Medical Center in Los Angeles for an investigative procedure. He had been having worsening heartburn, and he needed an endoscopy to examine a hiatal hernia. Surgery went well. He spent Sunday in his hospital bed watching television, kept company by Jimmy for most of the day. He grumbled some that Paula wasn't there sitting with him and had instead taken the rare opportunity to go for a hike. Messa stopped by for a while too. All seemed well. Coburn went home the next morning, with every expectation of a full recovery.

Jimmy had only just arrived home from work on Monday when he got the call that his father had collapsed and been taken to the hospital by paramedics. He dashed out of the house and raced the ten miles back to Cedars from his home in Playa del Rey. His father had suffered a massive heart attack. He had been listening to music, working out the playlist for the upcoming family Thanksgiving dinner. Paramedics came and transported him to Cedars, but it was too late.

The announcement of his passing was made, and the obituaries started. Fans put bouquets on his star on Hollywood Boulevard. Some days later the house was full of people again, this time for a private memorial service. The family was part of it, in the living room upstairs, with the featured photo on the piano being the one Jimmy had taken of his father nose to nose with Freddie, his cat. His ashes are interred below a black granite stone bench, beside a water feature, in Westwood Village Memorial Park Cemetery.[41]

Then two months later, a more public memorial service at Paramount Studios was held, with speakers coming from New York and even London to honor his life. The man who had seen the untimely deaths of three of his closest friends—Bruce Lee, Steve McQueen, and Sam Peckinpah—was gone.

Epilogue

Naturally Paula was deeply affected by Jim Coburn's passing. At first she found it very hard to let go, even of items that had been promised to people. Celebrations, like the annual Christmas Eve party at his daughter Lisa's home, were too loud, too happy, for her grief. She showed up, wearing a beautiful silver leather dress, but just couldn't stay. The house, the sale of which was put on hold for the time being, felt cold and strange. Josette came over to visit as often as she could. "Paula used to cry and say, 'I can't live without him. I don't want to stay in the house without him.'"[1]

Slowly Paula started appearing in the world again. She arranged a trip to Venice with Jimmy, Lisa, and a few others to sprinkle some of Jim's ashes in the city he loved. They stayed at the Hotel La Fenice and ate at Harry's Bar in his honor.

Eventually she started feeling better. Rob Harabedian recalls that "Paula had a real lust for life. There was a period where she was really sad. There was a mourning period. But I think then she kind of got past that."[2] She still loved dancing and would again hold belly-dancing parties with her friends. She seemed happy. One day she invited Jimmy and Lisa to come to the house and choose books from the library for their own homes. These included beautiful picture books on film, art, and photography.

She and Josette still had their standing appointment to see a movie and have a meal at Kate Mantilini's in Beverly Hills once a week. It was on these outings that Josette noticed a small cough—"*hem, hem*"—persisting week after week. Paula claimed that her doctor had told her the cough was from drinking too much red wine. But that was not true. Paula was suffering from stage IV lung and brain cancer.

For a while she disappeared, giving out the story of a jet-setting vacation. However, Paula had really gone to an alternative clinic in Mexico. She had sought care in Los Angeles and been given such a hopeless prognosis that the alternatives sounded like her best chance.

She kept her illness a secret from almost everyone, except for her friend Lynda Erkiletian, later Josette, and her assistant, who would become her caregiver. She continued to insist that they maintain the happy fiction of her travels, preferring to be remembered as vibrant and vital, not wanting to have to deal with people's pity and sorrow. Paula spent her final days in hospice care at her home. It was close to the end when she finally allowed her friends and family to visit her and say goodbye. She passed away on July 30, 2004.

Since Jim's death, her primary concern had been her husband's legacy. Together they had created the James and Paula Coburn Foundation (JPCF), with the aim of supporting several arts and medical charities of interest to them both.

Today JPCF has given smiles to children in the developing world born with cleft lips and palates, created a beautiful meditation garden at the Motion Picture & Television Country House and Hospital (formerly called the Motion Picture Actors' Home), provided medical care for indigent cancer patients, and supported the Los Angeles Philharmonic and the Los Angeles County Museum of Art, where much of the Coburn art collection now resides. New projects include this biography and the development of a graphic novel using Coburn's likeness for the main character. For many years, JPCF sponsored the KCET Cinema Series, where every summer fans got to see one of Coburn's vintage movies projected on a big screen, where they are meant to be.

Many of his classic films have recently generated renewed interest among filmmakers, film historians, and academics who are rediscovering the work of Sam Peckinpah and Sergio Leone. Quentin Tarantino cited Coburn's early supporting actor television roles as an influence in creating his recent film *The Hateful Eight* (2015). A reimagined version of *The Magnificent Seven* (2016) has been made with a diverse cast, and there has also been a remake of the historical war film *Midway* (2019).

In the end Jim Coburn had one simple message: "Love is the answer. And it truly is. But when you get right down to it, what is it? What is love? Where does it come from, and where does it go, and how do you direct it? And if you've got it, what do you do with it? It's an emotion; it's not an emotion. It's something. But it's got to be real. It's not mother love. It's not love of country. It's pure love and how to do it. There are some people who can really do it, and you've met them. I've met them too. They sit in that seat of love, in the glory of it, and can be whatever the fuck they want to be.

"Love is an action. It's not something you get. It's something you do. You do things with love. And it manifests into something greater than you are. Which is perfect."[3]

Afterword

In 1994, when I first met my future husband, he was working as a boom operator (the person who moves the microphone on a long pole over the actors' heads to record dialogue) and I was in the art department on a small direct-to-video movie. He had the same name as the famous actor James Coburn, who was popular in my home country, Australia. It didn't seem possible that the son of someone renowned in the business would be eking out a living in the scattershot world of low-budget filmmaking. I assumed the name was a coincidence.

I was wrong, and my new friend James, whom his family still calls by the diminutive "Jimmy," *was* the son of the famous actor, and he is in fact James Harrison Coburn *IV*. We didn't start dating until eighteen months later, at which time I learned from his mom, Beverly, that Jim Sr. had never chosen to help his son professionally, never "said a word for him," even in an industry where nepotism is the norm. And that irritated her to no end. She was being a little unfair, as his dad did help him, and later us, in other ways, including paying for our baby daughter's health insurance when our resources were lean.

One day early in our relationship, I was doing a big cleaning project. James invited me to take a break and get a quick bite to eat. I got into his car, dressed in my grungy work clothes, hair unwashed, no makeup at all, and I don't think I'd even brushed my teeth. I was dismayed when I realized that he was driving up, up, up into Beverly Hills. He was taking me to meet his father and stepmother, Paula. I protested, but he, with charming obliviousness, assured me it would be fine. So much for making a good first impression.

When we got there, all I could do was make the best of it, smile, and hope I got the chance to explain that this was spur of the moment and I meant no disrespect. James Coburn came to greet us. I held out my hand and said, "It's very nice to meet you, Mr. Coburn," and he immediately took my hand and replied, "Call me Jim."

And there it was. That voice, that big smile, and the simple good manners.

Over the years, what with Jim's schedule of work and travel, and our busy lives, we did not meet very often. There were rare big parties at the house and birthday dinners for various family members, usually at local, fancy-to-me restaurants. Jim's presence usually caused not so much a big stir but more of a rippling sense of deference in the staff and interested looks from the other patrons. It wasn't intrusive. This was Beverly Hills, after all, and stars are commonplace. Every now and then, someone would approach him, usually a middle-aged lady, and thank him for the pleasure he and his movies had given them over the years. He was always gracious, grateful, and kind, but after all those years, never surprised.

Jim and Paula came to James's and my wedding in Las Vegas in February 1997. I think they were expecting that it would be a bit silly, married by an Elvis, standing in a line. But it was a very proper scheduled ceremony, with Cupid's Wedding Chapel full of our friends and a real reception that my mom had arranged, including a cake made by one of Beverly's nieces. The manager of the chapel got those familiar big, round, oh-my-goodness eyes when she saw who walked in as father of the groom.

One time, before our daughter was born, we decided it would be nice to treat James's family for a change, so we invited Jim, Paula, Lisa, and her partner to join us at one of our favorite restaurants, the Border Grill in Santa Monica. It was popular and always busy, so we made a reservation for our evening. James and I arrived first and were informed that their policy was to seat people once the entire party had arrived. We were invited to sit at the bar to wait, which was fine. I must admit, I was smiling to myself, as I rather expected that they would be surprised when they saw who was in our party.

A few minutes later, Jim and Paula arrived, and there was that sudden frisson of energy that he always created when he entered a place. We greeted them, and I explained the policy that we couldn't be seated until the others had arrived too, but that we could wait in the bar. Jim was perfectly amenable to following the rules and was moving with happy purpose toward the bar (I think he liked the idea), while a hasty conference seemed to be happening between the hostess and a person I assume must have been the front-of-house manager. A moment later, the latter stepped forward and said, "Oh, I think we can seat *this* party at once."

We paraded to our table. As usual, heads turned and people whispered. The usually excellent service was even better. Someone told the kitchen who was out there, and there was a constant show of faces peeking around the corners or over counters. The Border Grill was owned and operated by two celebrity chefs, Susan Feniger and Mary Sue Milliken. After a while Chef Feniger visited our table during the meal, which had never happened before, when it was just James and me.

Jim didn't demand to be treated differently. He didn't need to. He was completely willing to just be a regular guy and wait at the bar, knowing it was very unlikely that he would be expected to sit there for long. He was happy to accept whatever deference or preference was offered. He reminded me of a venerable old lion, looking out over his piece of the savanna, accepting all offerings as his due, but not needing to roar for them. He knew all he had to do was show up, and all the rest would follow.

I knew Jim didn't care for kids and babies much, although he didn't broadcast the extent of his dislike or complain about them in my presence when I brought his granddaughter to the house or to those family dinners. That would have been rude, and he was never rude.

There is only one photograph of Jim holding his grandbaby Jayn. It is the only time he ever held her. I had plopped her suddenly onto his lap—I think I said, "Here, hold this"—and dashed upstairs for the camera. He had never asked to hold her, and I suspect he didn't trust his arthritic hands to do it safely. Neither did I, to be honest, but he was sitting on a sofa at the time. Paula later thanked me, saying, "I'm glad you did that."

She was fighting a losing battle to sway the feelings of a lifetime. Jim Coburn may be one of the least paternally inclined men who ever lived, and he certainly wasn't the kind of grandpa who would have wanted to play with the baby. Whether he would have come to enjoy his granddaughter's company as a young adult is a futile conjecture.

He and I talked about education once, when I let him know that we intended to homeschool. He seemed neither for nor against, but he did explain, with enthusiasm, his philosophy about education in general. If only schools taught history, social studies, and other subjects in relation to the fine arts of any culture, it would be a much better way to engage the students. He had come upon this idea in the early 1960s from his sculptor friend Edmund Kara, whose own school education had been under this model. Yet it was not something Jim ever sought to implement with his own kids.

Part of the reason Jim didn't seek to promote his son's film career was that he unfortunately dismissed the value of the work that James did as a boom operator. Certainly he was very pleased once James became a full-time production sound mixer. Jim told me, "It was better than . . ." and made a gesture of lifting both fists over his head. I often wonder if he would have changed his mind had he ever seen his son at work and witnessed the elegance and efficiency James brought to booming. I guess he forgot his own lowly start cleaning the bathrooms at the movie theater in Compton.

I've spent the last three years getting to know Jim Coburn better by listening to his recorded words and opinions on many subjects and discovering the genuinely high esteem in which he was held by the people who worked with him and knew him personally. I've tried to reconcile the divergent stories of the hardworking actor, spiritual seeker, and good friend with the absent, oblivious father and opinionated old grump. I've learned more about him since his passing, and about Paula for that matter, than I ever managed to learn while they lived. I'm sorry for that. I wish I had known how much he enjoyed a nice debate. I wish I had gotten to know Paula better. You always think you will have more time, don't you?

ACKNOWLEDGMENTS

This book would not have been possible without the work of Nancy Mehagian, whose recorded conversations with Jim over 2002 were intended to form the foundation of his memoirs, had he lived. I also heartily thank the kind folks who shared their personal memories of him in interviews or at the memorial. These include Josette Banzet-Roe, Richard Benjamin, Susan Blakely, Seymour Cassel, Jerry Chapman, Karen Chapman, Elizabeth Dalling, John Paul DeJoria, Hilly Elkins, Lynda Erkiletian, Andy García, Katy Haber, Rob Harabedian, Arthur Hiller, Herbert Kretzmer, Stephen Lodge, Marian Mallat, Frank Messa, Philippe Mora, Johnathan Rand, Mark Rydell, and Paul Schrader. Nor would the work have been possible without the posthumous contributions of Beverly Coburn and James Logan, whose correspondence added extra insight and richness.

I cited many books, articles, film production records, and other information sources, and read even more. I am grateful to all those authors, historians, and journalists for their work. These especially include the memoirs by his friends James Garner, Linda Lee, and Robert Vaughn.

My research was aided immensely by Edward Tryon, late historian of Laurel, who scoured the archives of the Laurel, Nebraska, newspaper. I thank the staff of the Margaret Herrick Library at the Academy of Motion Picture Arts and Sciences, and the Charles E. Young Research Library at UCLA Special Collections, both in Los Angeles. Paula Coburn had begun the process of collating a lifetime of material for the James Coburn Archives, now held by the James and Paula Coburn Foundation (JPCF). I also have now watched almost all of Jim's films, TV episodes, and commercials, thanks to YouTube, TCM, HBO, the KCET Cinema Series, and other sources for classic films.

I want to thank our first editor, Ali McCart Shaw of Indigo, Editing, Design and More, in Portland, Oregon, for her insightful commentary and editing. At Potomac Books, a huge thank-you to Tom Swanson, Taylor Rothgreb, and the editing team led by Elizabeth Zaleski, especially copyeditor Debbie Anderson, along with the wonderful design team.

For keeping me on track and being my accountability buddy, special thanks to Julie Fogg, of SparkiCreative.

I would also like to thank the JPCF—Lynda Erkiletian, Aaron Lager, Rob Harabedian, and Cynthia Webb—for this opportunity to offer something tangible to Jim's legacy. And finally I wish to thank the family, Lisa Coburn and James H. Coburn IV, for their memories, notes, and immeasurable support.

APPENDIX

Poems and Letters

When Beverly Coburn passed away in 2012, among her many papers we found a small collection of love letters from Jim. She kept these even after the divorce and two moves. Unfortunately, none of them were dated. Although it has been possible to work out from the content when some were sent, such as the one referencing events during the filming of *Duck, You Sucker* (1972), for the rest it is impossible to be specific as to when they were written and sent. For this reason, I have not included them in the main text.

However, the passionate and erotic writing illuminates not only the nature of their grand love affair but also Jim's poetic soul, the glimpses of which appear in his army journals.

I.   To worship you, and
        Half that already spent.
        I vow that every moment
        (In you, near you with you without you)
        The music you play on my spine will be
        Songs of love for you
        Ringing free through life.
        Space and times, timeless
        Infinite, eternity.
        ~J.

2. My love,
The moon is half again. I've watched it rise and fall, when it rests the great electronic circus above dusts us with its sparkling cosmic glory. When full the heavens disappear and look reflected. Is the holy hotness morning bound, bright, bringing pinched spirits to my face, juicing flow to my body's skin, desire to my soul. You are my sun, my moon, my woman, my love, my naked universe moving up to greet me, pumping incandescence, sliding slowly into the infinite, rising rhythms, plunging, pounding, sounding the Universal Depths, bathing in liquid desire Dreaming of heaven my soul splits—sending streams of light into the cave of the sacred jewel, where at once irradiated sparks of joy dance in my heart.

   It is in us, when we are one
   I love You

3. In the stillness
   Of the Greyness
   The Dusk, you turn
   To Dawn.
   The Blown Dusty
   Pathway you line
   With Damp, Dark
   Trunked Trees,
   Cool and Something
   Sweet—
   The Wind, the Breeze
   The Air, the Fire, Flame
   And Ash

4. I've just finished 'The Human Zoo,' which has been filling time, since you left me without real status stimuli or super sex to tranquilize my nervous system. So here I am struggling to stimulate (artificially) my behavior being head-fucked by a book. Interesting but it's not like

penetrating a deep moment, probing writhing timelessness, feeling passion pulling, and coming full in the mouth of time.

5.   Molded clouds of time
Bring memories of fused
Images.
Molding clouds on wine
Bring desires with envisioned
Fission.
Awake, alone, floating
In the sand less space of
The timeless.
Then together flesh, force, friction
Fire, fission, blue sails, flame forth.
Smoldering coals heat the space
Between the two a kiss apart.

Nerves strain with desire's
Weight
Black hair finds my
Face, feels then flees
The white fingers on
The pillow playing.
Deep pools penetrate
The Darkness, seeing sprightly
Rhythmed figures damply
Drying on the shore.
Darkly is the shadow
Forested, then embraced.
In spaceless Timelessness
Asleep, alone, Dreamless.

NOTES

PROLOGUE

1. Paul Schrader, interview with James and Paula Coburn Foundation (hereafter JPCF), March 3, 2009.

2. Hilly Elkins, interview with JPCF, November 2008.

3. James Coburn, "Actor in a Supporting Role Acceptance Speech," 71st Academy Awards, Los Angeles, March 21, 1999. Transcript and YouTube video, 3:46, Academy Awards Database, http://aaspeechesdb.oscars.org/link /071-2/.

1. THE DAYS OF FUN AND FROLIC

1. James Coburn interview recorded by Nancy Mehagian, 2002, James Coburn Archives, JPCF.

2. The *Laurel NE Advocate* in Nebraska noted when Harrison's grandfather, J. H. Coburn, left each year to winter in Long Beach, California, for the sake of his wife, Jane. "Grandma Coburn," as she was known in town, suffered from bronchitis in cold weather, a susceptibility little Jim Coburn would later inherit.

3. Coburn never really knew his uncle Paul, who died of a ruptured appendix at the age of nineteen, when Jimmie was only three years old. Paul had been a popular youth, known for his beautiful singing voice. Another son, Daniel Dutton Jr., was six months old in the 1910 Census. He died later that year.

4. Coburn, Mehagian interview.

5. Elsie Steere had married another local lad at the age of sixteen. The young couple did live in Chicago, while he was in college, staying with his brother

and family. Then they moved to Sioux City, Iowa, from where her husband was drafted, and he mobilized on the very same September day as Darrell Coburn. Both were sent to Europe in the last big push of the war, when the Allies were putting one hundred thousand new men a day into the field. Darrell came back, albeit injured. Elsie's husband did not. She brought her young son to her mother's boardinghouse, which is where she was living when D.D. started courting her. Records show there was a daughter stillborn, named Jane for D.D.'s mother, in April 1926.

6. By coincidence Altha Coburn's maiden name was also Johnson, anglicized from Johannson, but this was a very common family name. However, it meant that in Coburn's youth, there were a lot of Swedish-speaking cousins in the region, all named Johnson, but from two sides of his family. Mylet's parents had both immigrated from Sweden but met and married here in the United States. Coburn's grandfather Frank Johnson had been married at least twice before and left behind quite a passel of children in Europe. Many of his descendants now live in Norway.

7. Coburn, Mehagian interview.

8. Lois Love to Mylet Coburn, September 16, 1977, Oskaloosa, Iowa, James Coburn Archives, JPCF.

9. Marian Mallat (formerly Beebee), interview by Edward Tryon, ca. 2005, on behalf of JPCF.

10. Coburn, Mehagian interview.

11. Mallat, Tryon interview.

12. Coburn, Mehagian interview.

13. Coburn also remembered staying at a tepee-themed motel, but since the Wigwam Motels were not built on Route 66 until 1936 and later, it seems likely that he is conflating one of his later childhood trips to Laurel with the initial journey.

14. Mallat, Tryon interview.

15. Johnson, *Compton*, 51–64.

16. Coburn, Mehagian interview.

17. U.S. Census Bureau (1940), Federal Census, https://1940census.archives .gov/.

18. Coburn, Mehagian interview.

2. OH, THIS ARMY

1. Coburn, Mehagian interview.

2. James Coburn, handwritten Army Journals, July–August 1951, James Coburn Archives, JPCF.

3. Coburn, Mehagian interview.

4. Coburn, Army Journals.

5. Coburn, Mehagian interview.

6. Coburn, Army Journals.

7. Coburn, Mehagian interview.

3. A BEAUTIFUL TRIP

1. Coburn's roommate at the time was Zev Buffman, who would go on to be a highly successful Broadway producer and entertainment entrepreneur.

2. Vaughn, *Fortunate Life*, 44.

3. Coburn, Mehagian interview.

4. "Open Wilder Play in Little Theater," *Los Angeles Collegian* 49, no. 1750 (November 10, 1953).

5. Jim Butler and Bill Wilson, "Two on the Aisle," *Los Angeles Collegian* 50, no. 1775 (March 16, 1954).

6. Jim Butler, Warren Obluck, and Bill Wilson, "If You Asp Us," *Los Angeles Collegian* 50, no. 1793 (June 4, 1954).

7. Jim Butler, Warren Obluck, and Bill Wilson, "Scoring the Circle," *Los Angeles Collegian* 50, no. 1794 (June 8, 1954).

8. Coburn, Mehagian interview.

9. Warren Obluck, "Dying Embers," *Los Angeles Collegian* 51, no. 1794 (January 18, 1955).

10. Bob Jackson, "An Urbanized Rustic," *Los Angeles Collegian* 52, no. 1814 (April 26, 1955).

11. "Country Girl Cast Lines Up for Test," *Los Angeles Collegian* 52, no. 1815 (April 29, 1955).

12. La Jolla Playhouse was founded in 1947 by Gregory Peck, Dorothy McGuire, and Mel Ferrer, financed by David O. Selznick, with the idea of bringing film stars to work in excellent theater in Peck's hometown. From 1947 to 1964, the playhouse company occupied the La Jolla High School auditorium, and in 1955 it was at its height as a place where celebrity actors not only performed but also attended performances. See "The La Jolla Playhouse," accessed May 19, 2017, http://www.lifeofanactor.com/lajolla.htm.

13. Bob Jackson, "Art Whirl," *Los Angeles Collegian* 52, no. 1825 (June 7, 1955).

14. Coburn, Mehagian interview.

15. Shaw's song was recorded by Eddie "Rochester" Anderson (https://web
    .archive.org/web/20160331134544/http://parsec-santa.com/music/sydshaw
    .htm, captured March 31, 2016). An early use of the phrase is in the Jacobean
    comedy of manners by John Fletcher, *The Wild Goose Chase*, in 1621. The
    phrase features in a few hymns, including, rather ironically, one from the
    temperance movement of the 1910s. Bruce Lee also adopted the phrase, being
    quoted as saying, "Go bravely on, my friend, because each experience teaches
    us a lesson." See John Little, *The Warrior Within: The Philosophies of Bruce Lee*
    (New York: Chartwell, 2016), 184.

16. Coburn, Mehagian interview.

17. Joanne Linville, interview by the author, July 2015.

18. Coburn, Mehagian interview.

19. Witcover, *My Road, Less Traveled*, 272.

20. Coburn, Mehagian interview.

21. Mark Rydell, speaking at the James Coburn memorial service, Paramount
    Studios, Los Angeles, December 18, 2002, JPCF.

22. From 1955 to 1957 actress-director-writer Julie Bovasso directed the avant-
    garde Tempo Theatre at that venue. See Wally Gobetz, *Hamilton–Holly
    House* photo, with commentary, https://www.flickr.com/photos/wallyg
    /501652979.

23. Coburn, Mehagian interview.

4. THAT'S THE PART I WANT TO PLAY

1. Beverly Coburn, in conversation with the author, December 2012.

2. LeFevre, "James and Paula Coburn."

3. Coburn, Mehagian interview.

4. John Whalen, "The Trip," *LA Weekly*, July 1, 1998.

5. Coburn, Mehagian interview.

6. Nicholas Chennault, "Great Directors: Budd Boetticher," *Great Western
   Movies* (blog), March 6, 2014, http://thegreatwesternmovies.com/tag/budd
   -boetticher/.

7. Coburn, Mehagian interview.

8. Mirisch, *I Thought We Were Making Movies*, 94.

9. Coburn, Mehagian interview.

10. G. Lovell, *Escape Artist*, 201.

11. Coburn, Mehagian interview.

12. Wallach, *My Anecdotage*, 205.

13. G. Lovell, *Escape Artist*, 206–7.

14. Coburn, Mehagian interview.

15. Vaughn, *Fortunate Life*, 112.

16. Coburn, Mehagian interview.

17. Sam Peckinpah script for *Klondike*, episode no. 1, December 15, 1959, Sam Peckinpah Papers, Special Collections, Margaret Herrick Library, Academy of Motion Picture Arts and Sciences, Los Angeles (hereafter SPP).

18. This is the address noted as the Usual Residence of Mother on James's birth certificate. Extensive renovations occurred in the 1990s, so the original appearance of the 1948 structure is unknown.

19. Coburn, Mehagian interview.

20. After Tirella's death, Coburn agreed with the police report and came down on the side of driver Doris Duke, at least in hindsight. "He'd been working with her for about nine years. It was total accident. He was opening the gate, and the car started to roll forward, and Doris went to step on the brake and accidentally hit the gas" (Coburn, Mehagian interview). But according to Lisa Coburn, Beverly spoke with Tirella by phone as a close friend often—he had reported Duke's hostility at the time, and his own increasing wariness. Beverly believed that Duke murdered Tirella in a fit of anger. The Tirella family also believed it was the intentional act of a woman scorned, and they sued Duke. Eventually she settled the case out of court. Beverly deeply missed her close friend and interior design mentor.

21. David Jay Brown, "Interview with Edmund Kara by David Jay Brown," March 29, 1996, http://www.edmundkara.com/interview/.

22. Coburn, Mehagian interview.

23. Newhart, *I Shouldn't Even Be*, chapter 9.

24. A. Lovell, *Don Siegel*, 56.

25. In his biography Bob Newhart mentions that another actor was a source of leaks about on-set tensions, for which one of the publicists was blamed erroneously and fired from the movie (Newhart, *I Shouldn't Even Be*, 147–48).

26. David Bongard, "'Conversation' in Glossy Production," *Los Angeles Herald-Express*, November 5, 1961.

27. Coburn, Mehagian interview.

28. G. Lovell, *Escape Artist*, 228–29.

29. Coburn, Mehagian interview.

30. Beverly Coburn to James Logan, ca. August 1962, Beverly Coburn private papers.

31. Coburn, Mehagian interview.
32. Garner and Winokur, *The Garner Files*, 79.
33. Coburn, Mehagian interview.
34. G. Lovell, *Escape Artist*, 231.
35. G. Lovell, *Escape Artist*, 237.

5. GLADLY AND WILLINGLY

1. Coburn, Mehagian interview.
2. Beverly Coburn to James Logan, November 15, 1962, Beverly Coburn private papers.
3. Beverly Coburn to James Logan, November 26, 1962, Beverly Coburn private papers.
4. Coburn, Mehagian interview.
5. Beverly Coburn to James Logan, November 15, 1962, Beverly Coburn private papers.
6. Coburn, Mehagian interview.
7. Clark, *Dream Repairman*, chapter 4.
8. Coburn, Mehagian interview.
9. Paris, *Audrey Hepburn*, 84.
10. Coburn, Mehagian interview.
11. Beverly Coburn to James Logan, November 26, 1962, Beverly Coburn private papers.
12. Coburn, Mehagian interview.
13. Beverly Coburn to James Logan, November 26, 1962, Beverly Coburn private papers.
14. Coburn, Mehagian interview.
15. Clark, *Dream Repairman*, chapter 4.
16. Coburn, Mehagian interview.
17. Garner and Winokur, *The Garner Files*, 85.
18. Garner and Winokur, *The Garner Files*, 88.
19. Coburn, Mehagian interview.
20. Garner and Winokur, *The Garner Files*, 84.
21. Coburn, Mehagian interview.
22. This was produced by Norman Lloyd, who had been the director of *Billy Budd* at La Jolla Playhouse in 1955.
23. Arthur Hiller, interview with JPCF, September 6, 2008.
24. Coburn, Mehagian interview.

25. Sinclair, *London: City of Disappearances*, chap. 1.

26. *Throne of Blood* had been filmed in 1957 but didn't open in the United States until the end of 1961.

27. Coburn, Mehagian interview.

28. Herbert Kretzmer, speaking at the James Coburn memorial service, Paramount Studios, Los Angeles, December18, 2002.

29. Coburn, Mehagian interview.

30. Strait, *James Garner*, 212.

31. Coburn, Mehagian interview.

32. David Zeitlin, letter to the editors of *LIFE Magazine* (October 21, 1964), David I. Zeitlin Papers, Margaret Herrick Library, Academy of Motion Picture Arts and Sciences, Los Angeles.

33. Bosley Crowther, "'The Americanization of Emily' Arrives," *New York Times*, October 28, 1964.

34. Jerry Bresler memo, January 6, 1964, SPP.

35. Coburn, Mehagian interview.

36. Buick, *Tiger in the Rain*, 235–39.

37. Coburn, Mehagian interview.

38. Callan, *Richard Harris*, 141–42.

39. Coburn, Mehagian interview.

40. Hilly Elkins, speaking at the James Coburn memorial service, Paramount Studios, Los Angeles, December 18, 2002.

41. Weddle, *If They Move*, chapter 5.

42. "Mackendrick: The Man Who Walked Away 1/6," YouTube video, 9:58, from a 1986 Scottish Television documentary, posted by robinofgray, June 3, 2010, https://www.youtube.com/watch?v=qfeLZYVIGsY.

43. Beverly Coburn to James Logan, January 17, 1963, Beverly Coburn private papers.

44. Amis, *Experience*. Quoted in *A Thousand Words* (blog), "Deborah Baxter Smiles, Martin Amis Falls, and Rebecca Cries," posted by Alex Waterhouse-Howard, February 8, 2008.

45. Deborah Baxter, *My Blog*, July 1–3, 2008, http://deborahbaxter.com/Deborah_Baxter_Website/Blog/Blog.html.

46. "Chilling Changeling," *Newsweek*, July 12, 1969.

47. "Mackendrick," YouTube video.

48. Joseph Finnigan, "From Television Fare into Film Career," UPI, *Albuquerque Journal*, November 27, 1964.

6. THE BRASS RING

1. Goodman and Wilkinson, *Tony Duquette*, 157.
2. Coburn, Mehagian interview.
3. Knight, *Hollywood Style*, 208–10.
4. There is arguably no better commentary on the genre conventions of spy movies than the good-humored spoof *Austin Powers: International Man of Mystery* (1997) starring Mike Myers.
5. Daniel Mann, director, *Our Man Flint* (1966), Twentieth Century Fox, written by Hal Fimberg and Ben Starr.
6. Beverly Coburn to James Logan, January 17, 1963, Beverly Coburn private papers.
7. Coburn, Mehagian interview.
8. Hal Fimberg, "Show Beat," *Danville Register*, August 31, 1966.
9. Coburn, Mehagian interview.
10. "'Our Man Flint' hits Broadmoor," *Colorado Springs Gazette-Telegraph*, March 20, 1966.
11. Goldman, "Our Man Coburn." Coburn repeated this idea many times in various interviews over the years.
12. Mann, *Our Man Flint*.
13. Mann, *Our Man Flint*.
14. Saul David memo to Darryl Zanuck, May 14, 1965, Saul David Papers, Special Collections, Margaret Herrick Library, Academy of Motion Picture Arts and Sciences, Los Angeles (hereafter SDP).
15. Coburn, Mehagian interview.
16. Patricia Davis, "James Coburn Finally Gets to Play Hero Role," UPI, *Lebanon Daily News*, February 19, 1966.
17. Geoffrey Shurlock, memo to Walter Mirisch, August 30, 1965, Motion Picture Association of America, Production Code Administration Records, Margaret Herrick Library, Academy of Motion Picture Arts and Sciences, Los Angeles (hereafter MPAA).
18. Geoffrey Shurlock, memo to M. J. Frankovich, November 1965, MPAA.
19. Geoffrey Shurlock, letter to M. J. Frankovich, December 28, 1965, MPAA.
20. Geoffrey Shurlock, letter to M. J. Frankovich, January 5, 1966, MPAA.
21. Gile, "Rich Harvest."
22. Schickel, "Happy Crime without Punishment."
23. "Cinema: The Bank Bit," *Time*.
24. Mel Heimer, "My New York," *Kane Republican*, July 11, 1966.

25. Coburn, Mehagian interview.

26. Jerry Chapman, interview by the author, May 27, 2014.

27. James H. Coburn IV, interview by the author, May 2014.

28. Coburn, Mehagian interview.

29. Clifford Terry, "Girls Plot to Rule World in 'Flint' Film," *Chicago Tribune*, April 10, 1967.

30. Harry Haun, "A Heavy Dose of 'Why Spy,'" *The Tennessean*, March 31, 1967.

31. Saul David, Hal Fimberg, and Gordon Douglas letter to *Hollywood Reporter* and *Variety*, May 14, 1965, SDP.

32. Lisanti, *Fantasy Femmes*, 153.

33. Hal Fimberg, shooting script of *In Like Flint*, MPAA.

34. Fimberg, "Show Beat."

35. Richmond, *Hollywood Dish*, 280.

36. Lisanti, *Fantasy Femmes*, 153.

37. The producers had some resentment that Coburn refused to continue with the franchise and made certain that the public knew it was his "fault." Over the years other Flint scripts came his way, including an idea for a TV series and a concept called "Son of Flint." None were good enough to tempt him. At one time in the early eighties, Coburn attempted to buy the rights from Fox to develop more Flint stories himself, but that never came to any conclusion.

38. Unsigned memo, *Waterhole #3* script notes, July 15–19, 1966, Paramount Pictures Production Records, Special Collections, Margaret Herrick Library, Academy of Motion Picture Arts and Sciences, Los Angeles.

39. Geoffrey Shurlock to Erwin S. Gelsey regarding *Waterhole #3*, June 1966, MPAA.

40. Coburn himself wrote, and was credited for, the lyrics for the little doggerel ditty "Durango" that he croons in *Waterhole #3* while trying to persuade the sheriff to abscond with him to Mexico.

41. Margaret Blye, who played O'Connor's daughter in this film, went on to play his girlfriend years later in the TV series *In the Heat of the Night* (1988).

42. Review of *Waterhole #3*, *New York Times*, October 11, 1967.

43. Roger Ebert, review of *Waterhole #3*, Roger Ebert.com, November 3, 1967, http://www.rogerebert.com/reviews/waterhole-no-3-1967.

44. Coburn, Mehagian interview.

45. Needleman, "G. I. Gurdjieff."

46. John Kent, "The Man Behind 'Our Man Flint,'" *South Bay Daily Breeze*, October 23, 1966.

7. THE HORSE'S MOUTH

1. Coburn, Mehagian interview.
2. Amory, "James Coburn."
3. Coburn, Mehagian interview.
4. Evans, *The Kid Stays*, 132.
5. Coburn, Mehagian interview.
6. Flicker was one of the founding members of this group in Chicago and later ran the offshoot Compass Players in St. Louis. It was the precursor to Second City Improv. The games and their rules of comedy improv, which still apply today, were formed and honed by Compass between 1954 and 1959.
7. Coburn, Mehagian interview.
8. McNally, *Long Strange Trip*. The Grateful Dead were initially approached about portraying the band but rejected the offer as Paramount would not give them full creative control.
9. Film dialogue quoted in Evans, *The Kid Stays*, 132.
10. Geoffrey Shurlock to E. G. Dougherty, memos June–September 1967, MPAA.
11. The joke that all the FBR agents were under 5'4" was actually a parody of a certain short-statured Hollywood agent, who was known for having surrounded himself with even shorter staffers, something that Bluhdorn and Evans had discussed (as noted in Evans, *The Kid Stays*).
12. Evans, *The Kid Stays*, 133.
13. "Larry Karaszewski on *The President's Analyst*," YouTube video, 3:47, posted by Trailers from Hell, January 10, 2014, https://youtu.be/PzMB3k45fLo.
14. Howard Thompson, "'The President's Analyst' Opens Here," *New York Times*, December 22, 1967.
15. Dave Ewing, producer/director, "Ted Flicker Trailer," Video, 4:30, posted on FilmStew.com, March 26, 2015. *Ted Flicker: A Life in Three Acts* (in production), Bayside Productions, Inc. and IFP.org, Trailer from 2008 on FilmStew.com, http://filmstewdotcom.blogspot.com/2015/03/theodore-flicker-jedgar-hoover-presidents-analyst.html.
16. Gross, *Last Word*.
17. Amory, "James Coburn."
18. Robert Parrish had directed a movie in that familiar locale, Durango, Mexico—*The Wonderful Country* (1959) starring Robert Mitchum—just as that region was becoming popular for filmmakers.
19. The movies were *The Bobo* and *Casino Royale*, both released in 1967.

20. In another of those strange connections that seem to be a big part of Coburn's life, Mick Jagger would shortly star in a movie directed by one of the writers of *Duffy*, Don Cammell, along with James Fox who was one of the dissatisfied sons in *Duffy*. Like *Duffy*, that movie, *Performance*, would also have a strong counterculture element, featuring hippies and drug use.

21. Coburn, Mehagian interview.

22. Gerard Garret, "James Coburn Leads New Mystic Fad," *El Paso Herald-Post*, November 4, 1967.

23. Coburn, Mehagian interview.

24. James, "This Man They Call Flint."

25. James Coburn to Beverly Coburn, undated, Beverly Coburn private papers.

26. Hirschhorn, *Films of James Mason*, 190.

27. Robert Parrish, director, *Duffy* (1968), Columbia Pictures, dialogue.

28. As it turned out *The President's Analyst* was the only film project completed by Panpiper. However, Coburn used his company to option and develop various projects over time, including many years later for what would become an Emmy-winning miniseries, Marion Zimmer Bradley's *The Mists of Avalon* (2001).

29. Coburn, Mehagian interview.

30. N. Southern, *The Candy Men*, chapter 35.

31. Coburn, Mehagian interview.

32. Sleep therapy was a controversial practice starting in the 1920s and 1930s. It meant drugging patients into *deep* sleep for extended periods (even months) in order to administer electroconvulsive therapy and other treatments painlessly. After a relatively high proportion of deaths, the treatment regimen fell out of favor. The sleep cure of the sixties popular culture (also mentioned in *Valley of the Dolls* [1967]) was a lighter version, where exhausted people, primarily "hysterical" women, would be kept somnolent through the use of barbiturates—"sleeping it off." However, there is little evidence that this sleep cure was actually a widespread practice by the 1960s in Europe.

33. Coburn, Mehagian interview.

34. Coyote, *Sleeping Where I Fall*, 149.

35. Kripal, *Esalen*, 208–9. The party was held July 29, 1966. Guests included Rock Hudson, Glenn Ford, Dennis Hopper, and Tuesday Weld, along with Wood escorted by Roddy McDowall. She was deeply offended by Perls's words and behavior and would later satirize this type of confrontational therapy in the comedy *Bob & Carol & Ted & Alice* (1969).

36. James, "This Man They Call Flint."

37. Kimmis Hendrick, "The Coburns Learned to Listen," *Christian Science Monitor*, May 28, 1968.

38. When last heard from, the people of the tribe had moved to the city of Ensenada where there was work. Today the manner of Beverly's intervention might be considered problematic, but in the second half of the 1960s, this was considered a worthy cause. Many of their friends donated items and cash, and as she says in the Kimmis Hendrick interview, "wildflower seeds to scatter along the highway."

39. Spooky Stevens, press release for *Hard Contract*, 1968, Spooky Stevens Papers, Special Collections, Margaret Herrick Library, Academy of Motion Picture Arts and Sciences, Los Angeles.

40. Coburn, Mehagian interview.

41. L. Lee, *Bruce Lee*, 104.

42. Uyehara, *Bruce Lee*, 114.

43. L. Lee, *Bruce Lee*, 21–22.

44. Coburn, Mehagian interview.

45. L. Lee, *Bruce Lee*, 103–4.

46. The plantation was originally built in 1808. In the early 1970s Rosebank was purchased by a family who restored it, and it is now listed on the National Register of Historic Places.

47. "Cinema: Ménagerie à Trois?" *Time*.

48. Vincent Canby, "'Last of the Mobile Hot-Shots' Opens," *New York Times*, January 15, 1970.

49. L. Lee, *Bruce Lee*, 124.

50. Coburn, Mehagian interview. Oddly, this sounds remarkably like *Kung Fu Panda* (2008).

8. A DIFFERENT KIND OF MAN

1. Coburn, Mehagian interview.

2. Karen and Jerry Chapman, interview by the author, May 2014.

3. Coburn, Mehagian interview.

4. This was most likely the sanctuary run by the late Pat Derby and her then husband, Ted, who were animal trainers for film and TV, and who pioneered affection methods. Pat Derby wrote the first book exposing the inhumane treatment of film animals, jump-starting the animal rights movement in 1976. She passed away in 2013, still running an exotic animal sanctuary for retired

and rescued circus elephants. See PAWS Wildlife Sanctuaries, http://www
.pawsweb.org/paws_wildlife_sanctuaries_home_page.html.

5. Coburn, Mehagian interview.

6. Burroughs and Anslinger, "Playboy Panel," 53–74, 200–201.

7. Coburn, Mehagian interview.

8. Weisser, *Spaghetti Westerns*, 100.

9. Coburn, Mehagian interview.

10. See the appendix for Coburn's poems and letters to Beverly.

11. James Coburn to Beverly Coburn, Beverly Coburn private papers—undated,
but the text clarifies the time period as ca. late June to July 1970.

12. Coburn, Mehagian interview.

13. Frayling, *Spaghetti Westerns*, 145.

14. Bondanella, *History of Italian Cinema*, 364.

15. James Coburn quoted in United Artists Corporation, *Duck, You Sucker* press
release, ca. October 1971, James Coburn Archives (JCPF).

16. United Artists Corporation, *Duck, You Sucker* press release.

17. Crist, "Grounds for Complaint."

18. Seydor, *Authentic Death*, chapter 6.

19. James H. Coburn IV, author interview.

20. Coburn, Mehagian interview.

21. Singleton, *Learning in Likely Places*, 305.

22. Coburn, Mehagian interview.

23. Dr. Prince had also been involved in Dr. Janiger's LSD research and was an
uncredited extra in *The President's Analyst* and a few other fairly esoteric films,
evidently just for fun. More information about the World Conference on
Scientific Yoga may be found here: Dhirendra Brahmachari, Facebook post,
May19, 2014, https://www.facebook.com/dhirendrabrahmachari/photos/a
.480079995456458.1073741827.472410496223408/480079998789791/.

24. Coburn, Mehagian interview.

25. Camilla Snyder, "Mrs. Reagan At Bat for State Mansion during 'Best-Dressed'
Home Awards," *Los Angeles Herald Examiner*, January 19, 1971.

26. Coburn, Mehagian interview.

27. Frank Messa, interview by the author, January 19, 2015.

28. Ann Henken, "Best Dressed: Young, Adventurous Included Among 50 Chosen in World," *San Bernardino County Sun*, January 12, 1970. Coburn was one
of the fifty named on the International Best Dressed List.

29. Coburn, Mehagian interview.

30. Messa, author interview.
31. Coburn, Mehagian interview.
32. Messa, author interview.
33. James Logan to Beverly Coburn, undated, Beverly Coburn private papers. The three films he mentions were from 1968 and 1969, suggesting that this was from 1969 to 1970.
34. Roger Ebert, review of *Junior Bonner*, Roger Ebert.com, September 20, 1972, http://www.rogerebert.com/reviews/junior-bonner-1972.
35. Stephen Lodge, interview by the author, September 2, 2015.
36. United Artists Corporation, *The Honkers* press release, ca. May 1972.
37. *The Honkers* was only recently released on DVD. There was a mass-market paperback tie-in book, written by Thomas Chastain, primarily a mystery-detective novelist who also wrote several Perry Mason tie-in books. See Thomas Chastain, *The Honkers* (N.p.: Award Books, 1971).
38. L. Lee, *Bruce Lee*, 125.
39. Multiple letters, Stirling Silliphant Papers, UCLA Special Collections, Charles E. Young Research Library, University of California, Los Angeles.
40. Coburn, Mehagian interview.

9. BOOM, BOOM, BOOM

1. Cook, *Lost Illusions*, 303.
2. "Dorothy's Ruby Slippers," Fact Sheet, *National Museum of American History*, accessed August 22, 2018, https://americanhistory.si.edu/press/fact-sheets /ruby-slippers.
3. Bingen, Sylvester, and Troyan, *MGM: Hollywood's Greatest Backlot*, 275.
4. Cook, *Lost Illusions*, 304.
5. Wasson, *Splurch in the Kisser*, 163.
6. Vincent Canby, "The Screen: Breezy James Coburn in *Carey Treatment*," *New York Times*, March 30, 1972.
7. Wasson, *Splurch in the Kisser*, 165.
8. Leydon, "James Coburn."
9. Wasson, *Splurch in the Kisser*, 164.
10. Leydon, "James Coburn."
11. Wasson, *Splurch in the Kisser*, 166–67.
12. Leydon, "James Coburn."
13. Coburn, Mehagian interview.
14. Marilyn Beck, "Angry James Coburn Charges 'Greedy Studios Wreck Films,'" *Daily Times-News*, December 16, 1971.

15. Kent Donovan, "Despite Photography Flick Is Disjointed," *Manhattan Mercury*, May 21, 1972.

16. Kit Bauman, "James Coburn as Star: Only Salvation of Film," *Corsicana Daily Sun*, April 24, 1972.

17. Canby, "The Screen: Breezy James Coburn."

18. Giles M. Fowler, "Star's Project a Mind(er) Bender," *Kansas City Times*, March 1, 1972.

19. Minder Bender Pulp Comic Book, produced by James Coburn, Christopher Pearce, and Paul-Michel Mielche, 1971, SPP.

20. Fowler, "Star's Project."

21. Elkins, interview with JPCF.

22. "Jim Coburn Says Title Is Important," *Colorado Springs Gazette-Telegraph*, June 24, 1972.

23. "Security or Danger: Which Does a Man Need?" *Robesonian*, April 9, 1972, 11.

24. Coburn, Mehagian interview.

25. Mark Jones, "Pickpocket Says Easiest Theft inside Jacket Pocket," *Redlands Daily Facts*, August 24, 1972.

26. *Harry in Your Pocket* turned out to be the only feature film directed by Bruce Geller, a successful TV director whose greatest claims to fame were creating the monumentally popular series *Mission: Impossible* and later the private-eye procedural *Mannix*. He was killed in a plane crash in 1978.

27. Alden Schwimmer to Edwin Appel, October 1971, Bruce Geller Papers, UCLA Special Collections, Charles E. Young Research Library, University of California, Los Angeles (hereafter BGP). Unlike MBP, they were not a self-funded organization, still dependent on studio and distribution funding. Robbins left the company when Warner Bros. declined to finance an adaptation of his novel *The Betsy*.

28. James H. Coburn IV, interview by the author, February 2016.

29. Susan Sward, "Stars Skimp on 'Grass' Funds," *Independent*, September 20, 1972.

30. James Coburn's contract regarding *Harry Never Holds*, BGP.

31. "Producer-Director Uses Luxury Yacht," *Statesville Record and Landmark*, January 6, 1973.

32. Messa, author interview.

33. Allan Carr, "Carr Report," *Colorado Springs Gazette-Telegraph*, November 10, 1972.

34. Richard Benjamin, speaking at the James Coburn memorial service, Paramount Studios, Los Angeles, December 18, 2002.

35. The Carlton is the headquarters of the Cannes Film Festival and was the hotel featured in *To Catch a Thief* (1955) starring Cary Grant and Grace Kelly. Reportedly Grant visited Cannes during the shoot for *The Last of Sheila* to see his daughter when she was visiting her mother, Dyan Cannon.

36. Benjamin, speaking at the James Coburn memorial service.

37. Braverman, "*The Last of Sheila*," 85.

38. Braverman, "*The Last of Sheila*," 87.

39. de Rosso, *James Mason*, 232.

40. Monaco, *Encyclopedia of Film*, 507.

41. Simmons, *Peckinpah*, 171.

42. Katy Haber, interview by the author, September 28, 2015.

43. Weddle, *If They Move*, 463.

44. Weddle, *If They Move*, 468–69.

45. Kasindorf, "World of the Executive."

46. Weddle, *If They Move*, 469.

47. Coburn, Mehagian interview.

48. Haber, author interview.

49. "Peckinpah Back to Old West for Pat Garrett," *Colorado Springs Gazette-Telegraph*, May 26, 1973.

50. Haber, author interview.

51. Leydon, "James Coburn."

52. Weddle, *If They Move*, 479.

53. Seydor, *Authentic Death*, chapter 7.

54. Simmons, *Peckinpah*, 183.

55. Coburn, Mehagian interview.

56. Cocks, "Outlaw Blues."

57. Coburn, Mehagian interview.

58. Eventually Coburn and Silliphant sold the script, and it was produced in 1977, as *Circle of Iron*, starring David Carradine. Coburn was disappointed with the result, which he called "embarrassing."

59. Coburn, Mehagian interview.

60. L. Lee, *Bruce Lee*, 205.

61. Coburn, Mehagian interview.

10. THE ONLY REALITY

1. Dorothy Manners, "Coburn Doesn't Sidestep Touchy Questions," *Los Angeles Herald Examiner*, October 14, 1973.

2. Lemmon, *Twist of Lemmon*, 82–84.

3. Manners, "Coburn Doesn't Sidestep."

4. Clive Arrowsmith interviewed in Mark Murray, director, *Paul McCartney and Wings: Band on the Run* (2010), iTV, posted by Beatle Archive HQ, January 26, 2013, https://youtu.be/IfQaqJn7dC8.

5. Richard Brooks to Stephen Murphy, May 28, 1975, Special Collections, Margaret Herrick Library, Academy of Motion Picture Arts and Sciences, Los Angeles.

6. Dorothy Manners, "Richard Brooks: The T-Shirted Wonder," *Evening Herald*, June 21, 1975.

7. Bridget Byrne, "Coburn: Making Movies Is the Only Reality," *Los Angeles Herald Examiner*, April 28, 1974.

8. Philip Judge, "Enter the Gentle Dragon," *National Star*, November 1974.

9. Byrne, "Coburn."

10. Dorothy Manners, "James Coburn to Pursue Goal of 'Possible Dream,'" *Anderson Herald Bulletin*, September 4, 1974.

11. Haber, author interview.

12. Messa, author interview.

13. James H. Coburn IV, interview by the author, November 2015.

14. Johnathan Rand, interview by the author, May 21, 2014.

15. Elkins, speaking at the James Coburn memorial service.

16. Messa, author interview.

17. Seymour Cassel, speaking at the James Coburn memorial service, Paramount Studios, Los Angeles, December 18, 2002.

18. Messa, author interview.

19. Coburn, Mehagian interview.

20. Messa, author interview.

21. Coburn, Mehagian interview.

22. Guy Webster in "James Coburn—Guy Webster Photography," YouTube video, 1:50, from Jim Whitney documentary on Guy Webster, posted by Guy Webster Photography, September 12, 2014, https://www.youtube.com/watch?v=YYdf1yOzg6g. Coburn's daughter, Lisa, disputes that this naked yoga practice occurred.

23. Coburn, Mehagian interview.

24. Haber, author interview.

25. Coburn, Mehagian interview.

26. Josette Banzet-Roe, interview by the author, January 7, 2015.

27. Rex Reed, "'Omen' Gives the Devil Bite," *Manchester Journal Inquiry*, July 3, 1976.
28. Coburn, Mehagian interview.
29. Quoted in Peggy Blizzard, "Local Hang Glider Team Stuntmen for 'Skyriders,'" *Tustin News*, May 8, 1976.
30. Dean Tanji, "*Skyriders* Memories," December 1, 2013, http://www.ozreport.com/data/SkyRiderMemories.pdf.
31. Coburn, Mehagian interview.
32. Lisa Coburn, interview by the author, October 16, 2015.
33. Juanita Rodriguez, "'Hard Men' Borrows from Other Westerns," *Idaho State Journal*, May 14, 1976.
34. Coburn, Mehagian interview.
35. Roberts and Gaydos, *Movie Talk*, chapter 6.
36. Coburn, Mehagian interview.
37. Ted Haworth to Sam Peckinpah, April 14, 1976, SPP. Haworth was a multiple Oscar nominee himself and had worked on several Oscar-winning films. It seems only deep affection for Peckinpah kept him working on this film, up to eighty hours a week.
38. Coburn, Mehagian interview.
39. Haber, author interview.
40. Coburn, Mehagian interview.
41. Haber, author interview.
42. Coburn, Mehagian interview.
43. Raskin, Lichtig & Ellis attorneys for the petitioner, Property Settlement Agreement, November 1976, Beverly Coburn private papers.
44. Coburn, Mehagian interview.

11. SHOE SALESMEN

1. "Presentation of His Holiness the XVI Gyalwa Karmapa," The History of The Werner Erhard Foundation, accessed June 30, 2017, http://www.wernererhardfoundation.org/karmapa.html.
2. Joe Segura, "Buddhist Leader from Tibet meets Mickey Mouse," *Independent, Long Beach*, February 4, 1977.
3. Coburn, Mehagian interview.
4. Messa, author interview.
5. Coburn, Mehagian interview. This event is also mentioned in Levine, *Miraculous 16th Karmapa*, 154. In that book another story is told about an

invitation-only blessing ritual that could describe the Tower Road house (pp. 232–33).

6. Messa, author interview.

7. Coburn, Mehagian interview.

8. Messa, author interview.

9. Ken Williams, "Coburn Defends Peckinpah Violence," *Journal News*, May 19, 1977.

10. Sandra Pesmen, "Actor James Coburn's Arm Was Giving Him Trouble," *Chicago Daily News*, May 7, 1977.

11. *Convoy* script notes, 1977, SPP.

12. Haber, author interview. Haber found a bugging device that Peckinpah had planted in her room. This was the last straw. She went on to work as one of the producers for the classic Ridley Scott film *Blade Runner* (1982).

13. Dorothy Manners, "No Lawyers for Them," *Grand Prairie Daily News*, May 31, 1977.

14. Dorothy Manners, "No Super Secrecy Here," *Grand Prairie Daily News*, June 10, 1977.

15. Jerry Buck, "'Valley of the Dolls' Made into Miniseries," Associated Press, October 19, 1981.

16. Clarke Taylor, "CBS to Air Hammett's 'Dain Curse,'" *Los Angeles Times*, December 29, 1977.

17. Joan Hanauer, "Dashiell Hammett Mystery Outclasses Regular TV Mayhem," *Salina Journal*, May 22, 1978.

18. Christopher Cobb, "'The Dain Curse' a Television Blessing," *Ottawa Journal*, May 27, 1978.

19. Robert Harabedian, interview by the author, July 17, 2015. Coburn had been shooting *The Dain Curse* in New York and Pennsylvania at the time.

20. Sybil Farson, "A Ton of Talent in 89-Pound Rock Star: Tiny Mite Seeks U.S. Stardom," *Worcester Sunday Telegram*, June 25, 1978.

21. de Villeneuve, *An Affectionate Punch*. Excerpt on *Diary of a Studio Owner* (blog), uploaded by Gilbert Scott Markle (undated), accessed February 12, 2020, http://www.studiowner.com/essays/essay.asp?books=0&pagnum=123.

22. The songs are called "Melancholy Melon" and "Losin' the Blues for You."

23. Harabedian, author interview.

24. Byrne, *Byrne's Advanced Technique*, 174–77.

25. Harabedian, author interview.

26. "Mylet Coburn," *San Bernardino County Sun*, October 24, 1979.

27. 20th Century Fox media/theater publicity package for *Loving Couples* by an anonymous staff writer, *Cinefantastique* Magazine Records, Special Collections, Margaret Herrick Library, Academy of Motion Picture Arts and Sciences, Los Angeles.

28. Raskin, Lichtig & Ellis attorneys for the petitioner, Order to Show Cause, November 1, 1979, Beverly Coburn private papers.

29. Messa, author interview.

30. Coburn, Mehagian interview.

31. He also was allocated a number of debts, including for the Cessna.

32. Coburn, Mehagian interview.

33. "Gentleman Jim," *San Bernardino County Sun*, April 20, 1980.

34. "Roll 'Em," *San Bernardino County Sun*, May 4, 1980.

35. Coburn, Mehagian interview.

12. THE MAN IN THE SUIT

1. Coburn, Mehagian interview.

2. "Shrine Panels," *Index-Journal*, Greenwood SC, May 8, 1980.

3. Messa, author interview.

4. Taylor, *Masters of the Shoot-'Em-Up*, 38–39.

5. Arthur Bell, "Bell Tells," *Village Voice*, September 17, 1980.

6. Stacy Smith, "Coburn Smarts over Film Flops," *San Bernardino County Sun*, October 26, 1980.

7. Noah Fents, "James Coburn: Of Heroes and Heavies," *Oui*, September 1981.

8. Drew Bernard, "'Andromeda's' Crichton Strains Belief in 'Looker,'" *San Bernardino County Sun*, October 31, 1981.

9. Goldberg, "Michael Crichton."

10. Marilyn Beck, "James Coburn Film an Undeniable Flop," *San Bernardino County Sun*, December 4, 1981.

11. Dick Kleiner, "Coburn Claims Editors Sabotaged 'Looker,'" *Paris News*, January 3, 1982.

12. Harabedian, author interview.

13. Coburn, Mehagian interview.

14. Marilyn Beck, "Louise Lasser Is Back, and She's in Living Color," *San Bernardino County Sun*, March 3, 1981.

15. A full recap of the plot, including spoilers and amusing commentary, can be read at Bj Kirschner, "Jacqueline Susann's Valley of the Dolls (1981)," Miniseries Marathon, May 15, 2001, http://miniseriesmarathon.com/jacqueline-susanns-valley-of-dolls-1981/.

16. Luaine Lee, "Coburn Loves Films, Hates Film 'Deals,'" *Santa Ana Orange County Register*, November 15, 1981.

17. Dick Kleiner, "Coburn Says Film Sabotaged," *Index-Journal*, Greenwood SC, January 4, 1982.

18. Coburn, Mehagian interview.

19. Liz Dalling, interview by the author, March 27, 2016.

20. Coburn, Mehagian interview.

21. Messa, author interview.

22. Banzet-Roe, author interview.

23. A summary that may be more entertaining than the series itself may be read at Bj Kirschner, "*Malibu* (1983)," November 20, 2011, http://miniseriesmarathon .com/malibu-1983/.

24. Weedon, "James Coburn."

25. Coburn, Mehagian interview.

26. Messa, author interview.

27. Coburn, Mehagian interview.

28. At one point Coburn's spy character was so popular with Lark customers that a comic book using Coburn's likeness was prepared by Philip Morris in July 1989. The story of *Speak Lark: The Third Game* involved "Mr. Coburn" traveling to a fictional small African country to protect the leader from assassination attempts. The idea of the comic book was that it would be given away free as part of a promotional campaign. However, eventually it was determined that the comic itself was outside the guidelines for advertising to adult smokers, and very few were printed.

29. Ed Finch to Alice Liu, Philip Morris International inter-office memo regarding Lark Image Summary, May 15, 1987, Philip Morris USA Public Document Site, http://www.pmdocs.com.

30. Messa, author interview.

31. Ian Harmer, "Hollywood," *Index-Journal*, Greenwood SC, July 15, 1984.

32. Coburn, Mehagian interview.

33. Harabedian, author interview.

34. Judy Flander, "'Sins of the Father' Stars Smooth Coburn," *Ocala Star-Banner*, January 12, 1985.

35. The author worked in the wardrobe department of this production during its stay in Sydney, Australia, at Her Majesty's Theatre.

36. "Celebrities Pay Final Tribute to Cinema Director," *Santa Cruz Sentinel*, January 14, 1985.

37. James Coburn quoted in Paul Joyce, director, *Sam Peckinpah: Man of Iron* (1993), Lucida Films/A&E/BBC.

38. Philippe Mora, correspondence with author, November 23, 2015.

39. Coburn, Mehagian interview.

40. *Sundays With Snyder*, No. 31, posted by Don Brockway to *Isn't Life Terrible* (blog), June 6, 2010, http://030726d.netsolhost.com/WordPress/?p=4275. Showscan was developed by Douglas Trumbull, the FX wiz on Kubrick's *2001: A Space Odyssey*, who had also done the title animations on *Candy*.

41. Messa, author interview.

42. Hilly Elkins, interview by the author, September 6, 2008.

43. Coburn, Mehagian interview.

44. Banzet-Roe, author interview.

13. THE MOSAIC

1. Banzet-Roe, author interview.

2. Elsa Brenner, "Real Estate Agents on the Air," *New York Times*, April 16, 2006.

3. Lynda Erkiletian, interview by the author, January 2016.

4. She was taught to spin discs by Roberto Alvarez, owner of the DC eatery and music spot Café Atlántico, and Dominican Republic ambassador to the United States since January 2007.

5. Coburn, Mehagian interview.

6. Erkiletian, author interview.

7. Lake Como has attracted the wealthy, famous, and royal since ancient Roman times. Villa d'Este has been called Hollywood on Lake Como.

8. Archerd, "Good Morning from Italy."

9. Coburn, Mehagian interview.

10. In her memoir, *A Charmed Life: Growing Up in Macbeth's Castle*, artist Liza Campbell writes of the influence Honsai had over her father, Hugh, the 25th Thane of Cawdor, in the late 1960s. Honsai and his wife lived with the family for three years.

11. Kirkpatrick, "Curious Case of Bjorn Borg."

12. Goldman, "James Coburn Wings It," 32–33.

13. Coburn, Mehagian interview.

14. Grant, *With Nails*, 156.

15. Goldman, "James Coburn Wings It," 32–33.

16. Transcript of Hollywood Foreign Press group interview for *Hudson Hawk*, 1991, Argentina Brunetti Papers, Special Collections, Margaret Herrick Library, Academy of Motion Picture Arts and Sciences, Los Angeles.

17. Coburn, Mehagian interview.
18. Erkiletian, author interview.
19. Lisa Coburn, as told in *James Coburn: Bang the Gong*, the 2003 film biography written by Steven Smith.
20. Coburn, Mehagian interview.
21. Banzet-Roe, author interview.
22. Messa, author interview.
23. Coburn, Mehagian interview.
24. Marian Mallat, interview by Edward Tryon, 2003, Omaha NE.
25. Coburn, Mehagian interview.
26. Frank Lovece, "Tough Guy: James Coburn Hasn't Lost His Touch," *Index-Journal*, Greenwood SC, March 8, 1992.
27. Tom Shales, "'Mastergate' Offers Bureaucratic Satire," *Washington Post*, October 30, 1992.
28. Harvey Solomon, "Washington's Language Gridlock: Larry Gelbart's 'Mastergate' on PBS Dissects the Art of Doublespeak," *Los Angeles Times*, November 1, 1992.
29. Shales, "'Mastergate' Offers Bureaucratic Satire."
30. George Robinson, "'You Can't Get Rid of the Rheumatoid Arthritis,' the Doctor Told Me," *Kokomo Tribune*, February 21, 1992.
31. Messa, author interview.
32. Herbie Kretzmer, speaking at the James Coburn memorial service, Paramount Studios, Los Angeles, December 18, 2002. The joke references the Hope/Crosby comedy, *Road to Morocco* (1942).
33. Ed Victor, "Magical Morocco: A Return to La Mamounia, the Grand Dame of Marrakech Hotels, Newly Restored to Her (Fabulous) Former Glory," *Daily Mail*, London, May 2, 2010.
34. Kretzmer, speaking at the James Coburn memorial service.
35. Coburn, Mehagian interview.
36. Messa, author interview.
37. Coburn, Mehagian interview.
38. Messa, author interview.
39. Susan Blakely, interview by the author, March 27, 2016.
40. Cheever, "James Coburn."
41. Coburn, Mehagian interview.
42. Haber, author interview.
43. Paula Coburn, conversation with author, ca. November 1996.

44. Perella, *Adventures*, 85.

14. IT WAS A GAS

1. Schrader, interview with JPCF.
2. Simon, "James Coburn: Cool Daddy."
3. Schrader, interview with JPCF.
4. Moss, *Intent to Live*, 215.
5. John Burlingame, "In Touch with Their Inner Cavemen," *Los Angeles Times*, January 1, 1999.
6. Schrader, interview with JPCF.
7. Coburn, Mehagian interview.
8. Ty Burr, "James Coburn Looks Back on 'The Magnificent Seven,'" *Entertainment Weekly*, May 11, 2001, http://ew.com/article/2001/05/11/james-coburn -looks-back-magnificent-seven/.
9. *Siskel and Ebert*, show no. 1316, aired December 19, 1998, https://siskelebert .org/?p=3238.
10. Coburn, Mehagian interview.
11. Painter, "Grit and Glory."
12. Burlingame, "In Touch."
13. Grove, "Hollywood Report."
14. Coburn, Mehagian interview.
15. LeFevre, "James and Paula Coburn."
16. Langella, *Dropped Names*, 44.
17. LeFevre, "James and Paula Coburn."
18. Coburn, Mehagian interview.
19. James Coburn, conversation with author, November 1999.
20. Harabedian, author interview.
21. "Angelina Jolie Wins Supporting Actress: 2000 Oscars," 72nd Oscars Highlights video, 2:43, March 26, 2000, https://www.oscars.org/videos-photos /72nd-oscars-highlights.
22. Eagan, *America's Film Legacy*, 571.
23. Coburn, Mehagian interview.
24. Niedermayer, *Confessions*, 22–23.
25. Messa, author interview.
26. Neva Chonin, "Avalanche Should Bury 'Snow Dogs'/Cuba Gooding Jr. Can't Rescue Plot," *San Francisco Chronicle*, January 18, 2002.

27. Andy García, speaking at the James Coburn memorial service, Paramount Studios, Los Angeles, December 18, 2002.

28. Keefe, "Olivia Williams."

29. Roger Ebert, review of *The Man from Elysian Fields*, Roger Ebert.com, November 1, 2002, http://rogerebert.com/reviews/the-man-from-elysian-fields-2002.

30. Alan J. Sutovsky, *Variety*, letters column, December 10, 2002.

31. Ellen Baskin, "Personal Politics: Coburn's Last Film," *Los Angeles Times*, November 24, 2002.

32. David Hunter, review of *American Gun*, *Hollywood Reporter*, June 20, 2002.

33. Coburn, Mehagian interview.

34. Banzet-Roe, author interview.

35. Susan Blakely, interview by the author, March 27, 2016.

36. Banzet-Roe, author interview.

37. Blakely, author interview.

38. Stephen Jaffe, interview with author, October 2020.

39. Blakely, author interview.

40. Coburn, Mehagian interview.

41. This is the cemetery of the stars, being the final resting place of Marilyn Monroe, Burt Lancaster, Farrah Fawcett, and others. Of more interest to Coburn fans are the plots of Coburn's friends and colleagues, Alexander Mackendrick, Natalie Wood, Eva Gabor, and Walter Matthau. His once-neighbor Jack Lemmon is also buried here, along with a number of musicians Coburn knew and admired, most particularly jazz artist Stan Kenton.

EPILOGUE

1. Banzet-Roe, author interview.

2. Harabedian, author interview.

3. Coburn, Mehagian interview.

BIBLIOGRAPHY

ARCHIVES/MANUSCRIPT MATERIALS

Ancestry.com. Subscription includes access to U.S. census records up to 1940; birth, death, and marriage records; immigration and customs records; military enlistment and demobilization records; and county and city directories/ phone books. https://www.ancestry.com/.

Brooks, Richard. Papers. Special Collections, Margaret Herrick Library, Academy of Motion Picture Arts and Sciences, Los Angeles.

Brunetti, Argentina. Papers. Special Collections, Margaret Herrick Library, Academy of Motion Picture Arts and Sciences, Los Angeles.

Cinefantastique Magazine Records. Special Collections, Margaret Herrick Library, Academy of Motion Picture Arts and Sciences, Los Angeles.

Coburn, Beverly. Papers and letters. Los Angeles.

Coburn, James. Army Journals. July–August 1951. James Coburn Archives. Used with permission of the James and Paula Coburn Foundation (JPCF), Los Angeles.

David, Saul. Papers. Special Collections, Margaret Herrick Library, Academy of Motion Picture Arts and Sciences, Los Angeles. (SDP)

Geller, Bruce. Papers. UCLA Special Collections, Charles E. Young Research Library, University of California, Los Angeles. (BGP)

Lark commercials archive. https://archive.org/details/tobacco_szp47c00.

Laurel NE Advocate. Archives. Articles from 1895 to 1935 collated by historian Edward Tryon. Laurel, Nebraska.

Los Angeles Collegian. Archives. https://cdm16302.contentdm.oclc.org/digital /collection/LACCNP02.

Mann, Daniel. Papers. Special Collections, Margaret Herrick Library, Academy of Motion Picture Arts and Sciences, Los Angeles.

Motion Picture Association of America. Production Code Administration Records. Special Collections, Margaret Herrick Library, Academy of Motion Picture Arts and Sciences, Los Angeles. (MPAA)

Paramount Pictures Production Records. Special Collections, Margaret Herrick Library, Academy of Motion Picture Arts and Sciences, Los Angeles.

Peckinpah, Sam. Papers. Special Collections, Margaret Herrick Library, Academy of Motion Picture Arts and Sciences, Los Angeles. (SPP).

Silliphant, Stirling. Papers. UCLA Special Collections, Charles E. Young Research Library, University of California, Los Angeles.

Stevens, Spooky. Papers. Special Collections, Margaret Herrick Library, Academy of Motion Picture Arts and Sciences, Los Angeles.

Zeitlin, David I. Papers. Special Collections, Margaret Herrick Library, Academy of Motion Picture Arts and Sciences, Los Angeles.

PUBLISHED WORKS

Amis, Martin. *Experience*. New York: Vintage International, 2014.

Amory, Cleveland. "James Coburn." Headliners, This Week magazine, *Pomona Progress-Bulletin*, March 12, 1967.

Archerd, Army. Just for Variety. "Good Morning from Italy." *Variety*, June 26, 1990.

Bingen, Steven, Stephen X. Sylvester, and Michael Troyan. *MGM: Hollywood's Greatest Backlot*. Solana Beach CA: Santa Monica Press, 2011.

Bondanella, Peter. *A History of Italian Cinema*. London: A&C Black, 2009.

Braverman, Douglas. "*The Last of Sheila*: Sondheim as Master Games-Player." In *Stephen Sondheim: A Casebook*, edited by Joanne Gordon, 85–92. New York: Routledge, 2014.

Buick, Robert Clayton. *Tiger in the Rain*. Bloomington IN: Xlibris, 2010.

Burroughs, William S., and H. J. Anslinger. "Playboy Panel: The Drug Revolution: The Pleasures, Penalties and Hazards of Chemicals with Kicks Are Debated by Nine Authorities." *Playboy*, February 1970.

Byrne, Robert. *Byrne's Advanced Technique in Pool and Billiards*. San Diego: Harcourt Brace, 1990.

———. "Here Comes 'The Baltimore Bullet.'" *Billiards Digest*, July/August 1979.

Callan, Michael Feeney. *Richard Harris: Sex, Death, and the Movies*. London: Robson, 2003.

Campbell, Liza. *A Charmed Life: Growing Up in Macbeth's Castle.* New York: Thomas Dunne, 2007.

Cheever, Susan. "James Coburn: Beverly Hills Vistas for the Academy Award– Winning Star of 'Affliction.'" *Architectural Digest,* April 2000.

Clark, Jim. With John H. Myers. *Dream Repairman: Adventures in Film Editing.* New York: LandMarc, 2010.

Cocks, Jay. "Outlaw Blues." *Time,* June 11, 1973.

Cook, David A. *Lost Illusions: American Cinema in the Shadow of Watergate and Vietnam, 1970–1979.* Berkeley: University of California Press, 2002.

Coyote, Peter. *Sleeping Where I Fall: A Chronicle.* Berkeley CA: Counterpoint, 2015.

Crist, Judith, "Grounds for Complaint," *New York Magazine,* July 3, 1972.

David, Saul. Producer. *Our Man Flint* (1966). 20th Century Fox. Directed by Daniel Mann.

de Rosso, Diana. *James Mason: A Personal Biography.* Oxford: Lennard, 1989.

de Villeneuve, Justin. *An Affectionate Punch.* London: Sidgwick & Jackson, 1986.

Dougherty, Kevin "Wiesbaden to Re-create Eagle Club." *Stars and Stripes,* June 12, 2008. https://www.stripes.com/news/wiesbaden-to-re-create-eagle-club-1 .79974.

Eagan, Daniel. *America's Film Legacy: The Authoritative Guide to the Landmark Movies in the National Film Registry.* London: Bloomsbury Academic, 2009.

Eder, Bruce. "Pete Kameron." *All Music.* Accessed May 18, 2017. http://www .allmusic.com/artist/pete-kameron-mn0001192618/biography.

Elliot, Mark. Director. *The Lion's Roar: The Classic Portrait of the 16th Gyalwa Karmapa* (1985). Centre Productions. Produced by Kenneth H. Green. Narrated by James Coburn.

Evans, Robert. *The Kid Stays in the Picture.* New York: Hyperion, 1994.

Fletcher, John. *The Wild Goose Chase.* Oxford: Benediction, 2009.

Frayling, Christopher. *Spaghetti Westerns: Cowboys and Europeans from Karl May to Sergio Leone.* New York: I. B. Taurus, 2006.

Garner, James, and Jon Winokur. *The Garner Files: A Memoir.* New York: Simon & Schuster, 2012.

Gile, Brendan. "Rich Harvest." The Current Cinema. *New Yorker,* October 22, 1966.

Goldberg, Lee. "Michael Crichton: The Business of Moviemaking Is Science Fiction." *Starlog,* no. 91, February 1985.

Goldman, Lowell. "James Coburn Wings It on His Career, Bruce Willis, and the Flap about Hudson Hawk." *Prevue* 2, no. 44 (May 1991): 32–33.

——. "Our Man Coburn." *Starlog*, no. 151, February 1990.

Goodman, Wendy, and Hutton Wilkinson. *Tony Duquette*. New York: Abrams, 2007.

Grant, Richard E. *With Nails: The Film Diaries of Richard E. Grant*. Woodstock NY: Overlook, 1998.

Gross, Josh. *Last Word: Final Scenes from Your Favorite Motion Pictures*. New York: Knopf Doubleday, 2012.

Grove, Martin A. "Hollywood Report." *Hollywood Reporter*, January 13, 1999.

Hirschhorn, Clive. *The Films of James Mason*. London: LSP, 1975.

Hunter, David. Review of *American Gun. Hollywood Reporter*, June 20, 2002.

James, Janice. "This Man They Call Flint." *Woman's Own*, UK, issue date unavailable. Magazine pages of article in JPCF Archive.

Johnson, Robert Lee. *Compton*. Images of America. Charleston SC: Arcadia, 2012.

Joyce, Paul. Director. *Sam Peckinpah: Man of Iron* (1993). Lucida Films/A&E/BBC. Aired June 29, 1993.

Kasindorf, Martin. "The World of the Executive Production Manager." *Action: The DGA Journal* 10, no. 5 (September–October 1975).

Keefe, Terry. "Olivia Williams Opens her Heart." *Venice Magazine*, April 2003.

Kirkpatrick, Curry. "The Curious Case of Bjorn Borg: Why He Came Back After a Scandal-Ridden Retirement." *Sports Illustrated* 74, no. 17 (May 6, 1991): 32–39.

Knight, Arthur. *The Hollywood Style*. Photos by Eliot Elisofon. New York: Macmillan, 1969.

Kripal, Jeffrey J. *Esalen: America and the Religion of No Religion*. Chicago: University of Chicago Press, 2007.

Langella, Frank. *Dropped Names: Famous Men and Women as I Knew Them*. New York: HarperCollins, 2012.

Laurel History Committee. *Laurel Nebraska Diamond Jubilee, 1893–1968*. Self-published commemorative illustrated paperback (1968).

Lee, Bruce. *Bruce Lee: Letters of the Dragon: An Anthology of Bruce Lee's Correspondence with Family, Friends, and Fans 1958–1973*. Edited by John Little. North Clarendon VT: Tuttle, 2015.

Lee, Linda. *Bruce Lee: The Man Only I Knew*. New York: Warner, 1975.

LeFevre, Peter. "James and Paula Coburn: And Oscar Makes Three." *Beverly Hills [213]*, ca. 1999. Photocopy of article pages in JPCF archive.

Lemmon, Chris. *A Twist of Lemmon: A Tribute to My Father.* Milwaukee WI: Hal Leonard, 2008.

Levine, Norma, ed. *The Miraculous 16th Karmapa: Incredible Encounters with the Black Crown Buddha.* Tuscany: Shang Shung, 2013.

Leydon, Joseph. "James Coburn: His Life and Hard Times." *Take One 4*, no. 12, Montreal, Unicorn Publications, December 1975.

Lightman, Herb A. "Behind the Camera on Major Dundee." February 1965. Captured March 7, 2012. https://web.archive.org/web/20120307060259/http://majordundee.blogspot.com/2011/06/american-cinematographer-artcle-by-herb.html.

Lisanti, Tom. *Fantasy Femmes of Sixties Cinema: Interviews with 20 Actresses from Biker, Beach, and Elvis Movies.* Jefferson NC: McFarland, 2001.

Lodge, Stephen. "The Honkers." Behind the Scenes: Movies and Television from the Stephen Lodge Collection and Others. Last updated October 23, 2006. http://www.movielocationsplus.com/bts/hon.htm.

Lovell, Alan. *Don Siegel: American Cinema.* London: British Film Institute, 1975.

Lovell, Glenn. *Escape Artist: The Life and Films of John Sturges.* Madison: University of Wisconsin Press, 2008.

MacDonald, J. Fred. "TV News and the Korean War." Television and the Red Menace: The Video Road to Vietnam. Captured July 18, 2016. https://web.archive.org/web/20160718194006/http://jfredmacdonald.com/trm/11tvkorea.htm.

McNally, Dennis. *A Long Strange Trip: The Inside History of the Grateful Dead.* New York: Broadway /Crown, 2002.

McQueen, Niele Adams. *My Husband, My Friend: A Memoir.* Bloomington IN: AuthorHouse, 2006.

Mirisch, Walter. *I Thought We Were Making Movies, Not History.* Madison: University of Wisconsin Press, 2008.

Monaco, James. *The Encyclopedia of Film.* New York: Perigee, 1991.

Moss, Larry. *The Intent to Live: Achieving Your True Potential as an Actor.* New York: Bantam, 2005.

Murray, Mark. Producer and Director. *Paul McCartney and Wings: Band on the Run* (2010). iTV. Documentary special, presented by Dermot O'Leary. Posted by Beatle Archive HQ, January 26, 2013. https://youtu.be/IfQaqJn7dC8.

National Jazz Archives presents The Story of British Jazz, http://archive.nationaljazzarchive.co.uk/.

Needleman, Jacob. "G. I. Gurdjieff and His School." *Gurdjieff International Review* 3, no. 1 (1999). Last updated May 24, 2002. http://www.gurdjieff.org /needleman2.htm.

Nelson, Susan. "Villa d'Este, Hollywood on Lake Como." *Timeless Italy* (blog), July 13, 2013. https://timelessitaly.me/2013/07/13/villa-deste-hollywood-on -lake-como/.

Newhart, Bob. *I Shouldn't Even Be Doing This!: And Other Things That Strike Me as Funny.* New York: Hyperion, 2006.

Newsweek. "Chilling Changeling." Review of *A High Wind in Jamaica.* July 12, 1965.

Niedermayer, Laurie. *Confessions of a Sled Dog Addict: Tales from the Back of the Sled.* Victoria BC: Friesen, 2015.

Online Archive of California. http://www.oac.cdlib.org/.

Painter, Jamie. "Grit and Glory." Profile. *Backstage,* January 7, 1999.

Paris, Barry. *Audrey Hepburn.* New York: Berkley, 1996.

Parrish, Robert. Director. *Duffy* (1968), Columbia Pictures. Produced by Martin Manulis.

Perella, Marco. *Adventures of a No Name Actor.* New York: Bloomsbury, 2001.

Privitera, James. "James Coburn: Cinema's Tough Guy Takes on Arthritis." *Journal of Longevity* 5, no. 2 (1999).

Public Interest Advocacy Centre. "Deep Sleep Tragedy." https://www.piac.asn.au /legal-help/public-interest-cases/deep-sleep-tragedy/.

Richmond, Akasha. *Hollywood Dish: More Than 150 Delicious, Healthy Recipes from Hollywood's Chef to the Stars.* New York: Avery, 2006.

Roberts, Jerry, and Steven Gaydos, eds. *Movie Talk from the Front Lines: Filmmakers Discuss Their Works with the Los Angeles Film Critics Association.* Jefferson NC: McFarland, 1995.

Schickel, Richard. "Happy Crime without Punishment." Review of *Dead Heat on a Merry-Go-Round. LIFE Magazine* 61, no. 16, October 14, 1966.

Seydor, Paul. *The Authentic Death & Contentious Afterlife of Pat Garrett and Billy the Kid.* Evanston IL: Northwestern University Press, 2015.

Simmons, Garner. *Peckinpah: A Portrait in Montage.* Austin: University of Texas Press, 1982.

Simon, Alex. "James Coburn: Cool Daddy." *Venice Magazine,* January 1999.

Sinclair, Iain. *London: City of Disappearances.* London: Penguin, 2007. Kindle.

Singleton, John, ed. *Learning in Likely Places: Varieties of Apprenticeship in Japan.* Cambridge: Cambridge University Press, 1998.

Smith, Steven. Producer. *Biography*, "James Coburn: Bang the Gong." A&E Television Network. Aired June 12, 2003.

Southern, Nile. *The Candy Men: The Rollicking Life and Times of the Notorious Novel "Candy."* New York: Arcade, 2004.

Strait, Raymond. *James Garner.* New York: St. Martin's, 1985.

Tate, James M. "High Wind and the Lion: An Interview with Deborah Baxter." Cult Film Freak. Captured July 31, 2016. https://web.archive.org/web/20160731190741/http://www.cultfilmfreak.com/deborahbaxter/.

Time. "Cinema: The Bank Bit." Review of *Dead Heat on a Merry-go-Round*, October 14, 1966.

———. "Cinema: Ménagerie à Trois?" Review of *Last of the Mobile Hot Shots*, January 19, 1970.

Snyder, Tom. Host. "Sundays with Snyder #31," posted by Don Brockway to *Isn't Life Terrible* (blog), June 6, 2010. http://030726d.netsolhost.com/WordPress/?p=4275.

Southern, Terry, and Mason Hoffenberg. *Candy.* New York: Putnam, 1964.

Taylor, Tadhg. *Masters of the Shoot-'Em-Up: Conversations with Directors, Actors and Writers of Vintage Action Movies and Television Shows.* Jefferson NC: McFarland, 2015.

Thomson, David. *New Biographical Dictionary of Film.* 6th ed. New York: Alfred A. Knopf, 2014.

Uyehara, M. *Bruce Lee: The Incomparable Fighter.* Burbank CA: Ohara, 1988.

Vaughn, Robert. *A Fortunate Life.* New York: Thomas Dunne, 2008.

Wallach, Eli, *The Good, The Bad, and Me: In My Anecdotage.* New York: Houghton Mifflin Harcourt, 2006.

Wasson, Sam. *A Splurch in the Kisser: The Movies of Blake Edwards.* Middletown CT: Wesleyan University Press, 2010.

Weddle, David. *If They Move . . . Kill 'Em!: The Life and Times of Sam Peckinpah.* New York, Grove, 1994.

Weedon, Jo. "James Coburn: 'It's Great Not Having a Woman Around.'" *Woman's Own*, September 25, 1982.

Weisser, Thomas. *Spaghetti Westerns: The Good, the Bad and the Violent.* Jefferson NC: McFarland, 2000.

Witcover, Walt. *My Road, Less Traveled: Becoming an Actor, a Director, a Teacher.* Bloomington IN: Xlibris, 2011.

Zadan, Craig. *Sondheim & Co.* 2nd ed. New York: Harper & Row, 1986.

INDEX

Index

Baba Muktananda, 156–57
Backstage (magazine), 283
Bad Kissingen, Germany, 32
Bad Kreuznach, Germany, 29–30
Bagatelle, France, 255
Baker, Jim, 110
Balboa Island CA, 15, 260
The Baltimore Bullet (film), 231–32
Band on the Run (album), 198
Bangkok, Thailand, 137
Banks, Russell, 279
Banzet-Roe, Josette, 206, 247–48, 257, 259, 266, 295, 299–300
Barcelona, Spain, 153, 180
Barrymore, John, 202–3
Bart, Peter, 124
Basinger, Kim, xxii
Baton Rouge LA, 145
Baxter, Deborah, 97–98
Beatty, Warren, 48
Beck, Marilyn, 176
Beebee, Marian. *See* Mallat, Marian
Bella Vista, 203
Bellemont Hotel, 145
Benjamin, Richard, 184–86
Berger, Senta, 216
Bernardino County Sun (newspaper), 233
Bernstein, Elmer, 67
Bevan, Donald, 36
Beverly Hills CA, 100, 139–40, 274–75
The Beverly Hills Woman (film), 40
Billy Budd (Coxe and Chapman), 40
Biltmore Hotel, 270
Birdland (jazz club), 42–43, 47
Bite the Bullet (film), 7, 199–200
Black Bear Ranch, 138–39
Black Crown Ceremonies, 220
Blakely, Susan, 275, 295–96
Blondell, Joan, 117–18
Bluhdorn, Charles, 124, 126–27
Blunt, Jerry, 36

Blye, Margaret, 118, 321n41
Bob Bondurant School of High Performance Driving, 180
Boetticher, Budd, 60
Bogdanovich, Peter, 152–53
Bondurant, Bob, 180, 184
Bongard, David, 72
Borg, Björn, 263
Boston MA, 107–9, 174–75
Bovasso, Julie, 316n22
Bradley, Marion Zimmer, 249, 323n28
Brando, Marlon, 49, 134–35
Braverman, Douglas, 185
Bremerhaven, Germany, 26–28
Bresler, Jerry, 90, 95
Bridges, Beau, 278
Briskin, Sam, 60
British Columbia, Canada, 182
Brolin, James, 239–40
Bronson, Charles, xx, 74–77, 204
Brooks, Richard, 199
Bruce Lee (Lee), 142–44, 146, 169, 196
Brynner, Yul, 62–65, 135
Budapest, Hungary, 263
Buellton CA, 149
Buffman, Zev, 315n1
bullfighting, 40, 93–94
Bungalow (performance space), 36
Burlington House Awards, 160
Burton, Richard, 204
Butler, Jim, 41
Byrne, Bridget, 200
Byrne, Robert, 232
Byrne's Advanced Technique in Pool and Billiard (Byrne), 232

Cairo, Egypt, 136–37
California Suite (film), 186
Callan, Michael, 94
Calley, John, 85, 88–89
Call from Space (film), 256
Cambodia, 137–38

348